MASS INSANITY

MASS INSANITY

Theo Alistair

The face of terror is not the true faith of Islam...
Islam is peace.[1]

George Bush

I will cast terror into the hearts of disbelievers. Therefore, strike off their heads and strike off every fingertip.[2]

Allah

No religion is responsible for terrorism; people are
responsible for violence and terrorism.[3]

Barack Obama

I have been commanded to fight the people until they
attest that there is no god but Allah and that Mohammad is the Messenger of Allah, pray and pay the zakat.[4]

Mohammad

I wish we taught more in our schools about
the Islamic faith.[5]

Jo Biden

Islam is the heaviest chain humanity ever borne.[6]

Ernest Renan

According to Islam I am allowed to rape infidels.[7]

ISIS fighter

We are at war with Islamic terrorism.[8]

Gerald Darmanin

Islam is a religion in deep crisis worldwide today.[9]

Emmanuel Macron

Based on research we conducted in 2016, half of the second and third generations Muslims in Europe support ISIS.[10]

The Grand Mufti of Egypt

Who controls the past, controls the future.[11]

George Orwell

Those that fail to learn from history are doomed to repeat it.[12]

Winston Churchill

1 Remarks by President George Bush at the Islamic Center of Washington, DC on 17 September 2001. Available from the White House Archives.
2 Allah in the Quran 8:12.
3 Barack Obama in a speech before delegates at the White House Summit on Countering Violent Extremism, 2015.
4 Mohammad in Sahih Muslim (22) and in Sahih al-Bukhari (1399).
5 Jo Biden addressing Million Muslim Votes Summit, 2020.
6 Ernest Renan, 1883, as quoted in: Caldwell, C. (2009). Reflections on the Revolution in Europe: Immigration, Islam, and the West. Allen Lane.
7 ISIS fighter as quoted by his 12-year-old victim in an interview published in the New York Times: Callimachi, R. (2015, Aug 13). ISIS Enshrines a Theology of Rape.
8 Gerald Darmanin, who was serving as France's Minister of Interior, in an interview with RTL radio, 2020.
9 The French President Emmanuel Macron in a speech addressing separatism in France, 2020.
10 Egypt's Grand Mufti Shawki Allam in a TV interview, 2020.
11 George Orwell, through the lips of the main character in his novel "1984".
12 Winston Churchill in a 1948 speech to the House of Commons.

The faces of victims don't leave my mind
and I find it hard to contain my anger.
I cannot erase the faces of the innocent children
who were killed while celebrating the Bastille Day in Nice,
the girls who were kidnapped and enslaved in Iraq,
and the Speicher cadets from my thoughts.

To all the victims of Islamic terrorism, suppression,
and to every person who stood up and fought back,
I dedicate this book.

Published by Liberty In Print

First edition

ISBN 9788396544643

Contents

Prohibited Questions

Is Islam what motivates Muslims to attack civilians, suppress females and reject democracy? Are the terrorists devoted followers of Islam? or are they criminals who use the religion as a means to satisfy their personal desires? Could they be victims of the ancient discourse and the religious establishment? Are the founders and leaders of ISIS, Taliban, Al-Qaida, Hamas, Houthis and Hezbollah power seekers who want to attain influence through religion or are they devoted followers?

Why are Muslim countries among the poorest and the least free societies despite their vast natural resources? Why are they among the most corrupt[1], misogynistic, and dysfunctional countries[2] on Earth? Why have they been plagued with civil wars for decades? Why have the Muslim sects been at conflict with each other for centuries? What are the psychological basis and effects of these intergenerational conflicts? Why is there not one fully democratic Muslim-majority country to be found among the fifty Muslim states? Why are Muslims underrepresented in science, art, innovation and literature? Why are Muslim-majority societies plagued with chronic psychological and social diseases? What is the impact of believing in Islam and living by its teachings on the psyche? Do Islam or specific interpretations attract specific people who tend to become terrorist? What is the relationship between believing in the teachings of Islam and mental disorders?

Why do millions of Muslims desert their homelands and the whole of the Muslim world to become refugees in non-Muslim countries? Why does the majority of asylum seekers, refugees and displaced individuals worldwide come from the Muslim world?[3] Why are Muslim

---

1 Transparency International. Corruption Perceptions Index 2020.
2 Arab Human Development Report. (2020). See research papers available on their website; see also Human Rights Watch reports for the Middle East/North Africa.

communities in the West plagued with acute psychological, social and economic problems? Why are they overrepresented in crimes and underrepresented in science and literature? What motivates Muslim refugees to strive relentlessly to re-establish their previous societies' rules and culture in the non-Muslim secular, advanced and prosperous countries they immigrated to? Why do they reject the culture and values of the societies they have chosen to settle in?[4] What motivates some of the non-Muslims who label themselves as progressive and liberal to ally with fundamental Islamic organizations and radicals and support their efforts to turn secular countries into Islamic theological states?

Is the concentration of Muslim communities in the non-Muslim countries a prelude to civil conflict?

---

3 UNHCR, the UN Refugee Agency. Global Report 2019.
4 Gallup & the Coexist Foundation. (2009). The Gallup Coexist Index 2009: A Global Study of Interfaith Relations (with an in-depth analysis of Muslim integration in France, Germany, and the United Kingdom).; A Pew Research Center report (2013) showed that most Muslims believe that all laws must be sharia: Pew Research Center, (2013, Apr 30). The World's Muslims: Religion, Politics and Society. [Report]. Washington, D.C., p 46.

Moral Insanity

Can a society that includes millions of people lose its mind and how?

Can we diagnose all the people who accept slavery, paedophilia, systematic rape, looting, and mass-killing of innocent people with anti-social personality disorder?

Do the practices of the Taliban, Boko Haram, Al-Qaida, Hezbollah, Hamas, the Iranian regime, the Pakistani regime, the Islamic State of Iraq and the Levant (ISIS) represent the teachings of Islam as the millions of fighters and supporters across the world affirm or are they a proof of a mass mental disorder?

Did the Ottoman and the Abbasid caliphates that ruled the Muslim world for over a thousand years represent Islam? Which one of the current Muslim countries is a perfect Islamic state? Is Islam a remedy to or a cause of Muslims' chronic social, economic and psychological troubles? Are there various understandings and interpretations of Islam and how different are they? Do the terrorists, the imams and the sympathizers of the fifty-two Islamic factions designated as Islamic terrorist organizations by the United Nations understand Islam and follow its teachings precisely? Is terrorism the result of misinterpretation of Islam or literal application of its teachings?

Is there a common motive behind the terrorist attacks that targeted all kinds of people all over the world and were carried out by different groups of Muslims? Why have these attacks been condoned and celebrated by Muslim masses? When and how did Islamic terrorism start? When and how is it going to end? Why have Muslim countries been in a constant state of war against their neighbours? How can we understand jihad and slavery from Islamic point of view?

Are Islam and Muslims in conflict with the values of the modern civilization? Are faithful Muslims at war against the rest of humanity? Had Islam enabled science and philosophy in the past? How and why?

3

1 Jihad, Duplicity, Injustice

KILLING NON-MUSLIMS:
TERRORISING THE WORLD WITH IMPUNITY

Jihad is ordained upon you though you hate it.[5]

Allah

Fight in the way of Allah, and know that Allah is hearer, knower.[6]

Allah

In the past forty years, Muslims of different ethnicities, nationalities and backgrounds killed and wounded millions of non-Muslims in countless terrorist attacks across the world. The targeted victims were mostly civilians unaware that they were considered enemies of Allah and of his soldiers. They had never met the attackers and did not know much about Islam, in most cases. In contrast, the assailants attacked these people because they perceived them as enemies of Islam and Muslims. The killers, their ideology and the states and organizations that supported them and promoted their ideas have evaded justice so far. Neither the main culprits nor the rationale behind terrorism have been held accountable. The main criminals who prompted the killing of innocent people based on their identity and created and financed religious and political organizations that spread hatred all over the world were not held accountable for what they have done. All over the world, ignorant, cowardly and dishonest politicians, journalists and academics are assaulting the victims time and again by refusing to address the real problem and hold the powerful wealthy aggressive Islamic states, individuals and organizations accountable. They shy away from discussing the rationale responsible for terrorism.

---

5 Quran 2:216.
6 Quran 2:244.

Whenever Islamic terrorism is discussed, people introduced as moderate Muslims, human rights activists or experts join the self-serving politicians and businessmen in arguing passionately that Islam must not be examined. "They do not represent the true Islam," many experts rush to assure us after every terrorist attack. Some argue that the number of Muslims participating in jihad is small in comparison to the total number of Muslims worldwide and many of the victims of jihad are Muslims themselves, thus we must not discuss Islam, let alone examine its teachings.

This argument ignores the obvious fact that the fighters for any ideology are usually a small percentage of its followers. The individuals who orchestrated and executed the Holocaust are nothing but a small fraction of all members of the Nazi party, let alone the German nation and the nations of the Axis and the worldwide sympathisers. Hence, would it be reasonable to say that the practices of the SS (Schutzstaffel) do not represent the Nazi ideology as most Nazis were not members of the SS units and they did not take part in their crimes? Is it fair to say that the Japanese as a nation were not responsible for the Imperial Army's acts during the Second World War because the vast majority of them did not take part in these events?

When the American police brutality against Blacks in the USA or any other similar issue is discussed, it is done through highlighting racism, cultural norms or economic disparity as the core roots of the collective problem. The Holocaust is discussed as a practice carried out by groups of people in accordance with a malicious ideology, not an individualistic act carried by a limited number of extreme perpetrators who gave the orders or the specific obedient soldiers who carried out these orders. This logical approach is never applied to terrorism or other harmful practices supported and sanctioned by the teachings of Islam. Every time Muslim terrorists attack innocent people, Muslims or non-Muslims, commentators rush to argue zealously that terrorism has no religion.

The Pew Research Center conducted a major survey in 2013 to examine Muslims' perception of suicide bombings and their views of Al Qaeda, Taliban, Hamas, and Hezbollah, in twenty Muslim countries. The results indicate that more than 195 million Muslims support terrorist attacks against civilians to defend Islam.[7] Around 13 percent of the surveyed had a positive view of Al Qaeda and 23 percent said that they did not view the terrorist organization, which killed tens of thousands of innocent people all over the world, neither negatively nor positively. When asked if they thought that suicide bombings against civilians to defend Islam were justified, 37 percent of the Palestinian sample said "often", 25 percent said "sometimes", 12 percent said "rarely", 10 percent said that they didn't know, and just 10 percent said "never". Fifty-eight percent of the Lebanese, 59 percent of the Egyptians, 57 percent of the Jordanians, 39 percent of the Malaysians, and 18 percent of the Indonesians affirmed that targeting civilians with suicide bombing to defend Islam was often, sometimes, or rarely justified. Eighteen percent of the Senegalese, 14 percent of the Turks, and 6 percent of the Tunisians said that they didn't know if killing civilians for Islam was acceptable or not.[8]

In another survey conducted in 2015 to measure the support of ISIS among Muslims in different countries after it took responsibility for the recent major terrorist attacks that devastated Paris, Beirut, and Baghdad, the results show that only 28 percent of the Pakistanis viewed ISIS unfavourably. In Nigeria 14 percent of the Muslims viewed ISIS favourably. Sixty-two percent in Pakistan, 29 percent in Senegal, 25 percent in Malaysia, 19 percent in Turkey and 18 percent in Indonesia did not know if they like ISIS or not.[9]

Muslims have waged genocidal attacks against unsuspecting civilians across the world. They attacked New York City in 1993, 1994, 1997, Luxor – 1997, Tanzania and Kenya – 1998, New York City and Washington DC on 11 September 2001, Bali – in 2002, Beslan – 2004, Madrid – 2004, the Netherlands – 2004, London – 2005, Mumbai – 2008, Frankfurt – 2011, Toulouse – 2012, Montauban – 2012, Boston – 2013, Copenhagen – 2015, Brussels – 2016, Lahore – 2016, Nice – 2016, Paris – on 7 January 2015, 9 January 2015, 26 June 2015, 13 November 2015, in 2017, 2018 and in 2020, Orlando – 2016, Manchester – 2017, Westminster – 2017, Strasbourg – 2018,

---

7 Mohanty, N. (2018). Jihadism: Past and Present. Lexington Books.
8 Pew Research Center. (2013, Sep 10). Muslim Publics Share Concerns about Extremist Groups. Survey Report.
9 Poushter, J. (2015, Nov 17). In nations with significant Muslim populations, much disdain for ISIS. Pew Research Center.

Sri Lanka – 2019, Nairobi – 1975, 1980, 1998, 2002, 2012, 2013, 2014, 2015, 2019, Chad – 2020, Romans-Sur-Isère – 2020, Reading – 2020, NYC – 2020, Vienna – 2020, Palma, Mozambique – 2021, Rambouillet – 2021, Würzburg – 2021, Texas – 2022.

These attacks as well as the countless mass-shootings, vehicle-rammings, random stabbings, beheadings and suicide-bombings carried out by Muslims against non-Muslims are an indisputable proof that the whole world is a stage of an armed conflict. A war is being waged by Muslims who believe that it is their duty to spread Islam through all means including death and terror. It is oddly incongruous when the victims' societies refuse to believe what terrorists assure over and over again is their motive: to defend and spread Islam and rid the world of non-believers.

The Pakistani Muslim Malik Faisal Akram, a father of six, who stormed Congregation Beth Israel synagogue in Texas and held Jewish people hostages for ten hours on 17 January 2022, was described as "British" by almost all the major American as well as other Western media outlets. President Joe Biden said during the attack: "I don't… we don't have I don't think there is sufficient information to know about why he targeted that synagogue, why he insisted on the release of someone who's been in prison for over 10 years, why he was engaged, why he was using an anti-Semitic and anti-Israeli comments."[10] Journalists refrained from identifying him as a devoted Muslim fighting to release another devoted Muslim, Aafia Siddiqui, from the American jail, which is how he identified himself. In a recorded conversation with his brother during the standoff he stated that:

> I promised my brother when I watched him on that death bed that I will go down as a martyr… I told them bring her [Siddiqui] here she's got 84 years, they're talking to her because I'm near the prison FMC Carswell… I have prayed to Allah for two years for this… I have asked Allah for this death and Allah's with me… we'll give them war.[11]

---

10 President Joe Biden as quoted in CNN's report: Elassar, A., Watson, M. & Orjoux, A. (2022, Jan 16). FBI identifies hostage-taker at Texas synagogue.

11 A recording of the conversation was published by The Jewish Chronicle and is available online: JC Investigations Team. (2022, Jan 19). EXCLUSIVE: Texas synagogue terrorist ranted about f-ing Jews….

This Muslim was not the first one to attempt to free Siddiquie; in 2012, the chief of Al Qaeda, Ayman al-Zawahri, offered to free the American hostage Warren Weinstein in exchange for her release. In 2014, the Islamic State (ISIS) offered to free James Foley, which they beheaded later, if the Americans released the terrorist.[12]

In addition to terrorist groups, American Muslim organizations have also been campaigning to release this Pakistani woman known as the Lady of Al Qaeda. The Council on American Islamic Relations (CAIR), which describes itself as "the nation's largest Muslims rights and advocacy organization", and the Elbially Law practice held a press conference on Capitol Hill in Washington, DC, on 12 November 2021, 37 days before the terrorist attack, to call for the release of Siddiqui.[13] The executive director of CAIR-Dallas stated that "Aafia Siddiqui is serving an unjust 86-year prison sentence for a crime that she did not commit." Several other senior members of CAIR have been demanding the release of the convicted terrorist claiming that she was "innocent" and that she was "kidnapped". They accused the American army and the American justice system of targeting her unfairly because she is a Muslim. They have been campaigning, collecting money, and organizing press conferences to support her and to elevate her to an idol.[14] They even created "I am Aafia" campaign.

This Pakistani terrorist lived in the United States from 1990 to 2003 as a student. She was put on the FBI Most Wanted Terrorist list in 2004: Khalid Sheikh Mohammed, the mastermind of 9/11 terrorist attack, mentioned her name as one of the Al Qaeda operatives in the USA. She was married to his nephew and "was carrying notes detailing a mass casualty attack on New York City sites, including the Empire State Building, the Statue of Liberty, Wall Street, and the Brooklyn Bridge" when she was arrested in Afghanistan in 2008. While she was entering the interrogation room, she grabbed a weapon from one of the guards and opened fire at American soldiers. One of the soldiers returned fire and wounded her. She was arrested, treated,

12 Romero, D. & Dilanian, K. (2022, Jan 16). Who is Aafia Siddiqui, the federal prisoner at the center of the Texas hostage incident? NBC News.
13 The news about the conference as well as statements made by senior CAIR members are available on the official website of the organization: Allison, I. (2021, Nov 12). DC: Coalition to Hold News Conference to Call for the Release of Pakistani National Dr Aafia Siddiqui…. CAIR.
14 See the Free Aafia campaign website: www.freedraafia.org.

and flown to the United States to face justice. In 2010, a federal jury found her guilty on all counts related to the attack and sentenced her to 86 years in prison.[15] During her trial, she demanded that no Jews be allowed on the jury. She requested a DNA test to be carried out to exclude any Jews from her trial. She wrote a letter to President Obama to warn him of them.

Before the attack on the synagogue had ended and while the hostages were still held at gun point, several American Muslims expressed their concerns that this Islamic terrorist attack could potentially be used by Islamophobes to harm Muslims. Hence, instead of condemning the terrorist attack, sympathising with the victims and asking themselves why their religion produces such criminals, they were concerned about what might happen to the members of their group.

The Bosnian Muslim illegal immigrant Dzenan Camovic who attacked unsuspecting policemen in Brooklyn, NY with a gun and a knife on 3 June 2020 said: "I killed two police officers and my religion made me do it."[16] Three days earlier a 21-year-old Egyptian American Heba Alazhari attempted to kill an American police officer with a butcher knife outside Temple Terrace City Hall, Florida. She arrived at the City Hall at 1 p.m. and told an officer who was there that she needed help, and she wanted him to go outside with her. Once they left the building, she pulled out her concealed knife and tried to kill him.

In Notre Dame Cathedral, Nice, a Muslim from Tunisia attacked Christian worshippers killing three people and wounding several others, screaming "Allah Akbar." He beheaded two of his victims, a 60-year-old woman and a 55-year-old sexton, after he stabbed them several times. The third victim was a 44-year-old Brazilian mother of three young children, whom he stabbed several times before she managed to flee and alerted people outside the church to the ongoing massacre inside. Before succumbing to her wounds, she asked the paramedics to tell her children that she loved them.[17]

15 Romero, D. & Dilanian, K. (2022, Jan 16). Who is Aafia Siddiqui, the federal prisoner at the center of the Texas hostage incident? NBC News.
16 Italiano, L. (2020, Sep 12). Feds say man who stabbed NYPD cop confessed: I'm a worthless piece of s-t. New York Post.
17 BBC News. (2020, Oct 29). France attack: Three killed in 'Islamist terrorist' stabbings.

Like Faisal Akram and many other terrorists, the murderer Brahim Aouissaoui had been a drug addict and a petty criminal before he repented and became a devoted Muslim. This uneducated person coming from a destitute Tunisian family entered Italy illegally on a boat in September 2020, a month before he carried out his religious attack. He took a train from Italy to Nice the night before the attack despite the fact that he had no documents and did not speak the language. He chose a time when few people were inside the cathedral so he would not face substantial resistance. He wanted to kill Christians as a collective punishment in retaliation for publishing cartoons that mocked Mohammad in France. Through killing people inside a place of worship, he and his accomplices sent a message that no one is sheltered from the Islamic violence.

Six months later, another Tunisian murdered an unarmed French woman while shouting Allah Akbar. The attack took place in the entrance to the Rambouillet Police Station, and the victim was a 49-year-old civilian mother of two who worked as an administrative assistant at the station. Stephanie Monferme was returning to work from her lunch break when she was stabbed in the throat several times inside the entrance of the station. The murderer, Jamal Gorchene, intruded into France in 2009 and remained in the country illegally for more than ten years. In 2020, the French authorities rewarded him for breaching the French laws and for violating the country's sovereignty by granting him a legal residency. On 23 April 2021, he went to Rambouillet Police Station armed with a concealed knife, searching for a victim. He was walking outside the station pretending to be using his mobile phone, monitoring the entrance. Once he spotted Stephanie going in, he followed her and stabbed her several times from behind while screaming "Allah Akbar."[18] This attack took place in the holy month of Ramadan, in which Muslims strive to please Allah.

On Wednesday, 24 March 2021, an Islamic militia affiliated with ISIS stormed into the town of Palma in Mozambique, targeting various sites. They were firing randomly at people to kill as many as they could.

---

18 France 24. (2021, Apr 30). France honours woman killed in terror attack against police.

Among the victims were many African civilians as well as foreigners who worked in the oil industry. The religious fighters robbed two banks, ransacked businesses and governmental offices, and pillaged food storages. Many of the local Muslims have been suspected of aiding the terrorists.[19] Three days after this attack, another group of mujahedeen carried out a suicide bombing against worshippers in a Catholic church in Makassar, Indonesia, thousands of miles away from Africa.[20] Although both groups may have never met each other, they were sharing the same motive and goal according to their statements.

In 2017, a devoted Muslim drove a rented truck into cyclists and runners in Manhattan, killing eight people and injuring further eleven. The murderer was a Muslim from Uzbekistan, who had immigrated to the United States a few years earlier. Like all the other mujahedeen, he wanted to spread Islam through killing as many non-Muslims as possible and terrorising their society.

On 14 July 2016, the Tunisian Mohammad Lahouiej-Bouhlel drove a 19-tonne cargo truck into people celebrating Bastille Day in Nice. He killed 86 people and injured 458 others. He was driving the heavy truck at a fast speed on the pedestrian pavement in zigzag style to harm as many people as he could. Many of the victims this man ran over were children – he targeted them intentionally.

Similarly to every Islamic attack, it was an organized crime motivated by well-established religious ideas and supported by a community who had a specific collective identity. A group of Muslims living in France took part in coordinating this attack and financing it. They assisted Lahouiej-Bouhlel in acquiring the firearm and the truck and encouraged him to assault unsuspecting civilians. Two of these accomplices were naturalised French citizens. Their way of repaying the people who accepted them and gave them a country and a citizenship was by killing their children. Moreover, the attacker, who was an unemployed, uneducated convicted criminal, sent his family in Tunisia 100,000 euro in cash days

---

19 Byaruhanga, C. (2021, May 27). Mozambique Palma attack: 'I had to pay a bribe to flee'. BBC News.
20 BBC News. (2021, Mar 28). Indonesia bombing: Worshippers wounded in Makassar church attack.

before the attack.[21] To this day, the French authorities did not disclose the source of the money. The Islamic State took responsibility for this attack in a statement read by the Muslim French citizen Adrien Guihal.[22]

In 2015, Parisians were attacked by heavily armed and well-organized Muslims, most of whom were citizens of France and Belgium.[23] They killed 130 people and wounded another 413 innocent humans with bullets and explosions. The murderers were seeking Allah's satisfaction through annihilating non-Muslim French people, as they stated. Many of the victims were teenage students, going about their normal activities near the National Stadium, cafés, bars, and Bataclan theatre, but the devoted Muslims decided to kill them and traumatise the French society and every human with a conscience, to satisfy Allah.

In Northern Mozambique jihadists justified killing or wounding thousands of individuals and displacing more than 800,000 others in a war they waged in 2017 and which is still ongoing, by stating that they were following Islamic teachings that call for exterminating non-Muslims.[24] Destroying whole villages, killing people randomly, kidnapping young girls and raping and enslaving them was implementation of Allah's orders, they affirmed. These devoted believers claimed that they were following in the footsteps of Mohammad, the founder of Islam and their role model. They claimed that he had led many attacks against peaceful villages, most often massacring the men and enslaving the women and children.

21 Chazan, D. (2016, Jul 16). Bastille terrorist was radicalised within months and sent £8400 to his Tunisian family days before the attack. The Telegraph.
22 France 24. (2018, May 24). Syrian Kurds announce capture of French jihadist known for Nice attack claim.; See also BBC News. (2016, Aug 19). Nice attack: What we know about the Bastille Day killings.
23 BBC News. (2016, Apr 27). Paris attacks: Who were the attackers?
24 Baloch, B. (2021, Jun 11). Insecurity in northern Mozambique continues to forcibly displace thousands. UNHCR [Press release].; Warner, J., O'Farrell, R., Nsaibia, H. & Cummings, R. (2020). Outlasting the caliphate: The evolution of the Islamic State threat in Africa. CTC Sentinel, 13(11), 18-33.; Estelle, E. (2021, Jun 16). The Islamic State Resurges in Mozambique. Foreign Policy.; BBC News. (2022, Apr 10). Mozambique Palma terror attack: 'I can't go back'.

KILLING AMERICANS WITH THEIR MONEY: THE BETRAYAL OF THE ALLIES

The ex-head of the Pakistani intelligence agency ISI Hamid Gul affirmed that "When History is written it will be stated that the I.S.I. defeated the Soviet Union in Afghanistan with the help of America. Then there will be another sentence: The I.S.I., with the help of America, defeated America."[25]

The Pakistani president, who lived for many years in the West and whose country is dependent on the foreign aid, was among the first Muslim leaders to congratulate his brothers in Taliban on their defeat of the infidels who for decades have been supporting his country with hundreds of billions of dollars. Imran Khan stated that "What is happening in Afghanistan now, they have broken the shackles of slavery."[26] The same president went to Moscow on 23 February 2022 to meet Putin and signed deals with him while the Russian forces were attacking Kiev. This man, who presents himself as a devoted Muslim and who led boycotting campaigns against France and Denmark for publishing cartoons of Mohammad, did not utter a word that could be seen as condemnation of the Russian invasion of Ukraine. He did not show any support to the European countries which have been sending billions of euros in financial aid to Pakistan over the past 60 years.

Pakistan was not the only ally that betrayed the Americans and the Europeans in the war on terror in general or in Afghanistan in particular; several other Muslim allies supported the Taliban as well as other Islamic terrorist organizations while being supported by the

---

25 Mashal, M., Masood. S., & Rehman. Z. (2021, Apr 15). Biden's Afghan Pullout is a Victory for Pakistan. But at What Cost? New York Times.; Ramani, S. (2018, Oct 25). Why Pakistan Isn't Changing Its Taliban Policy. The Diplomat.
26 Muzaffar, M. (2021, Aug 17). Taliban have broken 'the shackles of slavery,' says Pakistan PM Imran Khan. The Independent.

Americans. This deception and duplicity of Muslim regimes when dealing with the non-Muslim countries is as old as the relations between the two parties.[27]

In a public speech aired by Al Jazeera on 2 February 2009, and available on YouTube, the Kuwaiti Abdullah Nafisi discussed a potential biological attack against the Americans. The wealthy Islamic ex-MP was talking about the killing of hundreds of thousands of innocent people:

> Four pounds of anthrax in a suitcase. Carried by fedayee [a Muslim fighter willing to sacrifice his life] through the tunnels from Mexico to the US, is sufficient to kill 330,000 Americans within a single hour, if it is properly spread in the metropolises there, what a horrifying idea [with a smile]. 9/11 will be a salad in comparison [the audience laughing, and he is laughing], am I right or not? And there is no need for airplanes, conspiracies, timings and so on. One person who has the courage to carry four pounds of anthrax and get to the White House lawn and spread these confetti all over them and then will do cries of joy [the audience can be heard cheering]. It will turn into a real celebration there... Terrorists are the most pious, the most honourable, the best people in this world.[28]

The audience's loud applause and laughter attest to their support for this call. This took place in Qatar, a hereditary sheikhdom protected by American soldiers at the expense of the American taxpayer. The Kuwaiti speaker seemed to have forgotten that his country was liberated by the Americans at the expense of the American treasury and that it is an American ally.[29] Most importantly, the ruler of Qatar allowed the event to happen and to be aired by his TV channel. Neither the Qatari Sheikh nor the Kuwaiti regime took any action afterward. This was despite the fact that both countries are dependent on the American and British

---

27 See Byman, D. (2005). Deadly connections: States that sponsor terrorism. New York: Cambridge University Press.

28 This talk is available on YouTube with English subtitles: lookhearseee. (2009, Jun 5). Abdallah Nafisi Threatens an Anthrax Attack on America. [Video].

29 Jacobson, L. (2011, Apr 27). Donald Trump says Kuwait never paid U.S. back for ousting Saddam Hussein. PolitiFact.

protection, especially against Saudi Arabia, Iran and Iraq. Moreover, both countries harshly stifle expressions of free speech inside their borders and punish criticising Islam or the rulers with long jail sentences. Also, the wealth of both countries comes from the oil that was discovered by the Americans and the British.

This is not an aberration in the way Muslim countries in general and the Gulf States in particular have been dealing with Western powers. In the past twenty years, many individuals and organizations were allowed to sponsor terrorism against non-Muslims with the protection of these states. Some of these regimes have been openly providing financial and political support to terrorists, while others look the other way when their citizens are involved in terrorism and their money is used for the purpose.

Radical Islamic organizations and individuals based in the Gulf States have amassed huge fortunes and influence through governmental protection, contracts and handouts, that allowed them to extend their influence to the Muslim communities in the West. Although many of these organizations have been indicted for supporting terrorism, they remain protected by the ruling families.

In contrast, journalists, professors, bloggers, and activists who defend human rights, tolerance and justice, have been suppressed and jailed for expressing their peaceful opinions in these sheikhdoms. This shows the double standards and hypocrisy on the side of the Gulf's ruling families on the one hand and the culpability of many Western decision makers when dealing with the petrol-rich regimes on the other hand. It also reveals the complexity of the problem and the fact that terrorism is by no means an individualistic act.

In a cable from the Secretary of State to the Department of Treasury regarding "Terrorist Finance" dated 30 December 2009, which was posted on WikiLeaks, we see a different face of the so-called American allies. The report states that "While the Kingdom of Saudi Arabia (KSA) takes seriously the threat of terrorism within Saudi Arabia, it has been an ongoing challenge to persuade Saudi officials to treat terrorist financing emanating from Saudi Arabia as a strategic priority... Still, donors in Saudi Arabia constitute the most significant source of funding to Sunni terrorist groups worldwide."[30] Needless to say, many of these groups have killed nationals of countries which maintain strong relationships with the Saudis. In the same report, Hillary Clinton complains bitterly about Kuwait's double standards:

> The US Government has consistently engaged the Government of Kuwait (GOK) about the specific activities of terrorist financiers in country, Kuwaiti charities financing terrorism abroad, and Kuwait's lack of a comprehensive anti-money laundering and counter-terrorist financing regime. While the GOK has demonstrated a willingness to take action when attacks target Kuwait, it has been less inclined to take action against Kuwait-based financiers and facilitators plotting attacks outside of Kuwait. Al-Qaida and other groups continue to exploit Kuwait both as a source of funds and as a key transit point... A particular point of difference between the U.S. and Kuwait concerns Revival of Islamic Heritage Society (RIHS). In June 2008 the USG domestically designated all RIHS offices RIHS under Executive Order 13224 for providing financial and material support to al-Qaida and UN 1267-listed al-Qaida affiliates, including Lashkar e-Tayyiba, Jemaah Islamiyah, and Al-Itihaad al-Islamiya. The United States nominated RIHS for listing under UNSCR 1267 but Indonesia placed a technical hold on the RIHS listing due concerns regarding RIHS's presence in Indonesia. Libya also placed a hold – probably at Kuwait's behest – citing insufficient information on RIHS's activities... In Kuwait, RIHS enjoys broad public support as a charitable entity. The GOK to date has not taken significant action to address or shut down RIHS's headquarters or its branches, which is consistent with GOK tolerance of similar behavior by Kuwaiti citizens and organizations as long as the behavior occurs or is directed outside of Kuwait.

Countless other reports by the United States Department of State and by different governmental and international non-governmental organisations showed that huge fortunes from Kuwait, Qatar, and Saudi Arabia have been financing radical Islam as well as terrorism all over the world.

---

30 Secretary of State. (2009, Dec 30). Terrorist Finance: Action Request for Senior Level Engagement on Terrorism Finance. WikiLeaks.

Al-Qaeda, the Taliban, ISIS and all the other terrorist organizations received billions of dollars from these countries, without which they could never have been as powerful as they were. Although many reports indicate that most of the money comes from private donors, they document that the absolute rulers of these countries do nothing or very little to stop the funding of terrorism, let alone to curb the effort aimed at radicalising Muslims. These reports usually shy from stating that the funding of terrorism would not have happened without the approval of the Gulf's ruling families or some of their members. In these countries, where citizens are monitored by several security apparatuses and are thrown in jails for an improper tweet or private talk, organizations cannot exist, and money cannot be transferred in such a magnitude without the approval of the families at the very top.[31]

It is an irony that the money which kills people all over the world comes mainly from the Western oil-consumers and ends up in the pockets of few clans whose members acts as the masters of the universe. To add salt to the injury, oil itself was discovered by American and British people, who provided expertise and worked hard in the Arabian desert to create the oil industry. To this day Western companies and non-Muslim expatriate labourers are the ones that work these oil fields, while the six ruling families' members reap the benefits.

---

31 See Conesa, P. (2018). The Saudi terror machine: The truth about radical Islam and Saudi Arabia revealed. Skyhorse; Chesnot, C., Malbrunot, G. (2020). Qatar Papers: How Doha finances the Muslim Brotherhood in Europe. Averroes & Cie.

1400-YEAR-OLD MENTALITY

So what is going on?

In every major terrorist attack, organized group of Muslims assail people they consider non-Muslims to please Allah, other Muslims provide the money, imams issue edicts that justify the attack, commentators defend Islam, and Muslim masses show their support. The immediate aim of terrorism is to murder and harm as many non-Muslims as possible and terrorise the victims' societies. The final end is to destroy all non-Muslim communities and cultures psychologically, to force them to capitulate to Islam, give up their identities and hence become slaves, not only of Allah but also of his soldiers.

The rhetoric of leaders of the contemporary Islamic terrorist organizations show that these people are psychologically living in the past. In many of the Islamic attacks, the perpetrators legitimized their aggressions by invoking ancient religious themes and events, construing their actions as continuation of a "14-century-long holy war" between Islam and the non-believers.[32] They comfort their followers by affirming that they are repeating what devoted Muslims have been doing for over a thousand years. Their main aim is to impose Islamic law on all people, thus obliterating the current universal human civilization with all its flaws, inventions and advancements. In other words, they want to take humanity back to the seventh century, eliminating technology, civil justice system, human rights, contemporary medicine, educational systems, arts – really all human progress.

They present themselves as the obedient soldiers of Allah's last and only valid religion. They seek his blessing through rejecting every idea that was not part of the original Islamic discourse and practice that existed in the seventh century, the heydays of Islam, regardless of its value.

---

32 According to the Islamic calendar, we are currently in the 15th century.

Osama bin Laden summarised this belief in a speech aired by the Qatari satellite news station Al Jazeera right after the 9/11 attacks. In this speech, he expressed his responsibility for and his pride of these attacks. He saw killing innocent people as a gallant virtuous act, in accordance with Islam. He even blamed the victims because they were not Muslims. In the same breath he said that his Muslim mujahedeen have:

> experience in using guerrilla warfare and the war of attrition to fight tyrannical superpowers, as we, alongside the mujahidin, bled Russia for 10 years, until it went bankrupt and was forced to withdraw in defeat. All Praise is due to Allah. So, we are continuing this policy in bleeding America to the point of bankruptcy. Allah willing, and nothing is too great for Allah.

In another video, bin Laden is seen talking to a number of his assistants and prominent Muslim imams who came to visit him from Saudi Arabia right after the 9/11 attacks to show their support. In this video, bin Laden was more straightforward in explaining his beliefs and the reasons for carrying out terrorist attacks against civilians. He simply repeated the saying of the founder of Islam and its main character, Mohammad: "I was ordered to fight the people until they say there is no god but Allah, and his prophet is Muhammad." He adds that "some people may ask: why do you want to fight us?" and further explains that this is the nature of the relationship "between those who say: I believe in one God and Mohammad is his prophet, and those who don't." He affirmed that his attacks were successful because "In Holland, at one of the [Islamic] centres, the number of people who accepted Islam during the days that followed the operations were more than the people who accepted Islam in the last eleven years." One of the Saudi Muslim imams replied to bin Laden describing the Muslims reaction to the attacks on New York and Washington: "everyone was overjoyed... we stayed [up] until four o'clock, listening to the news... everyone was very joyous and saying Allah is great, Allah is great, we are thankful to Allah, praise Allah. And I was happy for the happiness of my brothers. That day the congratulations were coming on the phone non-stop." He finished his talk with a verse from Quran:

"Fight them [non-Muslims], Allah will torture them by your hands and will disgrace them and give you victory over them."[33]

The terrorist attacks that killed 3000 innocent human beings were presented by all the attendants in the video as implementations of Islam. The justifications and the motivations were based on original Islamic ideas known to them and to other Muslims, as their response shows clearly. This pathological desire to live in the past is a symptom of the crisis of Muslims.

Analysing the speeches of terrorist masterminds and radical rulers such as al-Zarqawi, Abubaker Shekau, Khamenei, Abu Baker al-Baghdadi or Hassan Nasrallah, we find people who see the world through an ancient prism. They are living in the seventh century, immersed in its conflicts and obsessed with its figures and norms. They talk as if they were with the early Muslims in their invasions that obliterated the old civilizations and took its subjects as slaves. They back their ideas with what they claim to be Islamic original texts taken from the Quran and the sayings of Mohammad while ignoring all the progress and the changes that took place since that discourse was produced. They long for the destruction of human civilization which they perceive as their religious duty.

---

33 Quran 9:14.

2 Putting Islam on Trial

FENCE OF TERROR

This religion must ask itself why it produces terrorists.
Why it produces criminals not just in France but also
in Morocco, Algeria, Tunisia, Iraq, Syria[34]

Zineb El Rhazoui

Islamophobia and hate, in any form, have no place in Canada[35]

Justin Trudeau

In this book, I named some of the countless known attacks motivated by Islamic ideas. All these attacks were constructed as not Islamic by paid propagandists and people who struggle not to appear racists or are afraid of being called Islamophobes, hoping to convince us that the various groups and states and the countless Muslims who carried out all these attacks, the imams that defended them as genuine Islamic practices, and the masses that considered these attacks legitimate are all irrelevant to Islam.

The ISIS leader Abu Baker al-Baghdadi, the godfather of the Afghani jihad Abdullah Azzam, and the theorist of the Egyptian terrorism Omar Abdulrahman were distinguished professors of Islamic studies, who held doctorate degrees. The Taliban fighters are students of

---

34 Zineb El Rhazoui, a Moroccan journalist of a Muslim background, worked for Charlie Hebdo and survived the Islamic terrorist attack of 2015, in a public talk at the University of Chicago. (Recorded 2015, Feb 26). Who Is Charlie? Charlie Hebdo Journalist Zineb El Rhazoui on Freedom of Expression. [Video]. YouTube.
35 The Canadian prime minister Justin Trudeau tweeted: "Islamophobia is unacceptable. Full stop. We need to put an end to this hate and make our communities safer for Muslim Canadians. To help with that, we intend to appoint a Special Representative on combatting [sic!] Islamophobia." [@Justintrudeau]. (2022, Jan 29). Twitter.

Islam and their leaders are senior jurists. The members of the Iranian regime are theologians. These individuals along with the other chiefs and followers of jihadi movements have dedicated their lives to studying Islam. They live by its teachings and are willing to die for it. Thus, claiming that they do not understand Islam is absurd especially when it comes from a person who has never read the Quran.

The system of ideas that form the salient collective identity of the attackers and their supporters and secure the backing of the masses has nothing to do with the acts, the experts judge with no evidence or logic. Some Western commentators claim that they know Islam better than the suicide bombers who gave up their lives for it, the crowds that have been supporting them and the imams endorsing their attacks.

The same principle applies to the attempts to discuss the dire situation Muslims live in across the world. We are not allowed to examine the relationship between Islam and the chronic problems of Muslim societies. It is a mere coincidence that almost all the Islamic regimes are totalitarian, intrusive and pathologically immoral. We should accept that it is a mere fluke that the more devoted to the teachings of Islam the regime, the more oppressive, corrupt and sadistic it is. Religion has nothing to do with the way Muslim rulers have been suppressing their people for centuries, the experts keep assuring us. The fact that there has not been one well-functioning Islamic country for centuries has nothing to do with the dominant ideology. The fact that Muslims have never experienced a peaceful transition of power is a negligible issue. The central system of beliefs has nothing to do with the fact that the contribution of its followers to art, music, literature, and science in the past thousand years is negligible, we must accept. Islam has nothing to do with honour killing, high illiteracy rate, abject poverty, suppression of women or female genital mutilation that are rampant among its followers. Anyone and everyone can be blamed for the problems of Muslims – except Muslims themselves and their system of belief.

It is impossible to examine Islam without being discredited as an Islamophobe, an ignorant, a racist or bigot, and hence lose your job and credibility. This, if one is lucky enough to live in a non-Muslim country that can protect its citizens from the illiterate assassins and the furious mob. In the Muslim world, free thinkers are vilified as Jewish and Christian moles attempting to sabotage the pure and moral societies. They are incarcerated or executed on courts' sentences on blasphemy charges. Many critics did not even make it to the trials as they were killed by individuals or mobs who decided to take the law into their own hands, in accordance with the teaching of their religion, as they stated. These murderers were convinced that they were obliged to kill the enemies of Allah. They knew that according to the sharia they would never be held accountable. Most importantly, they knew that they would be seen as heroes by their societies.

Currently, people worldwide live under the censorship of Islamic aggression. Devoted Muslim immigrants and refugees are turning the societies they immigrated to into copies of the ones they deserted, with or without realizing it. Some are using peaceful means while others are loyal to violence, deception, and intimidation.

The beheading of Samuel Patty in Paris, the slaying of Theo Van Gogh in Amsterdam, the decapitation and dismembering of Daniel Pearl, the assassination of Farag Foda, Salman Taseer, Shahbaz Bhatti and the fatwas calling for the assassination of Lars Vilks, Salman Rushdie, Taslima Nasreen, Jerry Falwell, Geert Wilders, Sayyid Al-Qemany are few of many examples of the ongoing systematic purge of freedom of conscience.

It is important to stress that there have been numerous attempts to study Islam in an objective way from the first day of its establishment up to this moment. Each and every one of these endeavours has been foiled prematurely. The majority of the old scholars, nowadays dishonestly celebrated as Muslim philosophers and scientists, have been killed, imprisoned, ostracised and tortured for attempting to examine Islam or rejecting it in total or in part. Throughout the history of Islam, the free thinkers suffered dearly for being loyal to preserving intellectual integrity, and most of their work has been wiped out.

Thus, for more than 1300 years no comprehensive critical reform of Islam has been established. The states and clergy institutions have been propagating the ancient teachings and practices first and foremost as the law of the land. Violence, money and censorship have been ends and means to attain further ends in propagating the last monotheistic religion.

In the 20th century, several important Western scholars conducted major scientific studies of Islam; sadly, their work has had limited effects as they remained out of the public arena. Recently, many scholars have been attempting to transfer the scientific understanding of Islam from academic circles to the general public. Most of these people are struggling to reach a significant audience because of the limited means.

Currently, many departments of Islamic, Oriental, Arabic and Middle Eastern studies in European and North American universities are financed by autocratic Islamic governments that oppose the fundamental principles of science and critical thinking. The same Middle Eastern regimes that suffocate freedom of speech, human rights and all the values of modern civilization in their own countries are influencing the academic departments dedicated to studying Islam and the Middle East abroad.[36]

These totalitarian regimes have succeeded in surrounding Islam and through it themselves with a mental fence of fear through money, propaganda, violence and the complicity of some Western decision makers and thinkers. This left many independent universities unwilling to engage in any academic studies that examine Islamic ideas and practices in depth, despite their direct effect on human lives. While they restrain the genuine academic research about Islam or Arabs, the oil rich Muslim states have established countless departments, research centres and media outlets all over the world to promote their ideology.

As a result, many non-Muslims as well as Muslims are unable to understand the second dominant monotheistic religion in the world at a deep level. Throughout its history, Islam has been deprived of a thorough systematic intellectual examination that is necessary for any rationale to evolve.

Recently, a limited but growing number of scholars as well as ordinary people have been able to push through the wall and to break the taboo. They are creating a vibrant debate, questioning issues which were treated as mere facts. In doing so, they are standing up to the intimidation of powerful, immoral states and organizations. They are

---

36 See chapter 24 of this book, section The Treachery of Great Universities: Academia for Sale.

also rejecting the lure of joining the mainstream. It is due to these honest individuals that various destructive aspects of Islam have been highlighted and exposed.

The examination of the psychological, historical and linguistic, economic and social aspects of Islam is growing into a powerful movement. The results of these studies are reaching the general public slowly but steadily.

THE SOURCE OF TERRORISM

In order to truly combat terrorism, it is essential to examine the basis of the terrorists' values, motives and norms. The parade of Islamic soldiers willing to sacrifice their lives to promote their ideology is endless and will continue unless stopped at the source. So far, the global community has refused to grasp the true nature of the problem. Take, for instance, the case of unarmed off-duty British soldier Lee Rigby, who was run over by a car then hacked to death in the broad daylight in Woolwich, London on 22 May 2013. The killers were two devoted Muslims who converted to Islam and studied its teachings. They stated in the English court that they were "soldiers" "obeying the command of Allah."[37]

The judge instructed the jury that "being a soldier of Allah is not a defence in law," as this was their motive to commit this crime. The question is, if the UK had recognized Islam as a source of legislation, as many Muslims and non-Muslims have been campaigning for years, would the court have been able to reject Allah's order as a valid defence in law?

In that trial, the prosecutor said that "Islam is not on trial." The question here is: is this fair? Can this crime be analysed without putting Islam on trial? Can we understand this crime or any other crime without understanding the motives behind it?

The British judge defended Islam stating that the criminals' beliefs were "a betrayal to Islam." One of the defendants shouted back that "this is a lie"; the other one shouted "Allah Akbar" (Allah is greater). Did the non-Muslim judge really know Islam better than these devoted followers? Did he believe what he had said on record?

The testimony of the only terrorist who was captured alive from the group that carried out the 2015 Paris attacks has shown that putting Islam

---

37 See the report published by the British Channel 4 News (2014, Apr 8). Woolwich Murder: Michael Adebolajo lunches appeal.; Dodd, V. (2014, Jan 30). Lee Rigby murder: Michael Adebolajo applies to appeal against conviction. The Guardian.

on trial is a must. In the court hearing that started in August of 2021, the Muslim Moroccan, who was born in Belgium and has French and Moroccan citizenships, highlighted the conflict between two different identities: "we, the Muslims" and "you, the disbelievers". Salah Abdeslam shouted in the court: "I want to testify that there is no god except Allah and that Mohammad is his messenger"; after that he told the judge that he is "a fighter of Islamic State." He further stated that his motive was not personal, he was following the teachings of his religion.[38]

Consider also the massacre committed by Mohammed Merah in Paris. This crime is another example of the nature of the ongoing war waged by the devoted followers of the last divine religion against the rest of humanity including the societies that accepted them as citizens. It also highlights the incompetence of Western institutions and laws and their inability to tackle Islamic terrorism. Mohammed Merah, a Muslim born in France to Algerian parents, was an underachiever and a petty criminal before repenting and studying Islam. This French citizen carried out a jihadi attack in March 2012, seeking Allah's forgiveness for his criminal past. He started his mission by shooting an off-duty French paratrooper. His victim was a perfect target: a defenceless man wearing a uniform which represented the infidel France. Two days later, he shot three unarmed off-duty paratroopers while they were withdrawing money from a cash machine outside a shopping mall.

On 19 March, the same man attacked a Jewish school. He started by shooting at the people in the school playground, targeting children and their parents. He shot a rabbi, who was also a teacher in the school, while he was sheltering his two sons from the bullets. Mohammad Merah killed him and killed the two boys. They were six and three years old. Next, he began chasing the students inside the school. He caught an eight-year-old girl: he grabbed her hair and shot her at point-blank range while screaming "Allah Akbar".

The mother of the first victim, who was a Moroccan Muslim, went to Merah's neighbourhood seeking closure. She reported that his neighbours, all of them being Muslims with French citizenships, had told her

---

38 Mazoue, A., & Paccalin, C. (2021, Sep 8.) Chief suspect defiant on first day of landmark 2015 Paris attacks trial. France 24.

that Merah was a "hero, he is a martyr of Islam, he showed the French what power is."[39] She might have not known that serving in the French state's army is a major crime in the eyes of Muslims, thus the killing of her son is approved as equal to the killing of non-Muslims – and hence a heroic act. Not a crime.

In 2017, three Muslims carried out another terrorist attack in London. Their victims were non-Muslims who happened to be present at the London Bridge, and the motive was, again, to spread the last divine religion. They killed 8 innocent people and injured 48 through vehicle-ramming and random stabbing.

Two years later in 2019, Usman Khan, a Muslim Pakistani with British citizenship, killed three non-Muslims and injured others. He had been indicted for terrorism in 2012 along with other eight Muslims after admitting planning to bomb the London Stock Exchange, Parliament, the US embassy and assassinate several prominent individuals as well as building a terrorist training camp on a land that belonged to Khan's family in Pakistan. He had been sentenced to an indeterminate prison term with a minimum of eight years. However, the court of appeal annulled the indeterminate sentence and handed him 16 years in jail, which meant that he would be released after serving eight years. While in jail, Khan completed the main British programme for deradicalisation of Muslim terrorists known as Healthy Identity Intervention. He was released on temporary licence in December 2018. The British taxpayers were paying for his accommodation and expenses while he was planning to kill as many of them as he could. He was then invited as a speaker and a role model to a conference on offender rehabilitation that was organized by Cambridge University to celebrate the fifth anniversary of its Learning Together programme designed to help criminals reintegrate into society. The conference was held at Fishmongers Hall, adjacent to London Bridge. At 13:58 Khan started stabbing organizers and other attendants while threatening to blow up his suicide vest. He stabbed to death two of the organizers and wounded others before being chased out of the building by some of the attendants who fought back. He fled toward the

---

39 Sayare, S. (2012, Dec 20). Neighborhood Is Torn Over a Killer's Legacy. The New York Times.

north side of London Bridge and began stabbing people. The fact that he finished a deradicalisation programme successfully and was featured as an example of rehabilitating radical Muslims shows that Islamic terrorism cannot be approached only by focusing on individuals.

The cold-blooded slaying of the elected member of the British Parliament David Amess in October 2021 by the Muslim Somali Ali Habri Ali should have ushered in an open frank debate about Islam in the UK and the laws that have been enabling terrorist to kill innocent people and to live off the taxpayer money. Amess was stabbed 21 times. He was stabbed in his face, hands, legs and torso inside the church where he was meeting his constituents. In the court the murderer stated: "I want him dead. I want every parliament minister who signed up for the bombing of Syria who agreed to the Iraqi war to die." At the same time, he denied the murder.[40]

---

40 Dodd, V. (2022, Mar 21). Man accused of murdering David Amess scouted home of Michael Gove, court hears. The Guardian.

MASS MORAL CRISIS

The Taliban's return to power in Afghanistan, Hamas's reign in Gaza, Hezbollah's control of Lebanon, the Houthis in Yemen, the Iranian Islamic regime and the emergence of Boko Haram, Al-Shabaab and the Islamic State of Iraq and the Levant are a clear proof that Islam and Muslims are in a perilous predicament. The scenes of the terrified Afghani crowds desperately attempting to leave their country after it fell without resistance to the students of Islam in August 2021 attest to the severity of Muslims' predicament. These scenes show the deep division between two groups of Muslims. The members of the first one are the ones willing to die to implement Islamic laws, while the members of the second group are willing to risk their lives and leave everything behind to avoid being ruled by their fellow Muslims. But whether the ones deserting their country are against the Islamic laws or just against these laws being enforced upon them by another group might be a different issue.

The genocide of the Yazidis and Christians in Iraq and Syria at the hands of Islamic State fighters, and the support for this religious cleansing with all its inhumane practises by millions of Muslims worldwide, is an indisputable proof that Islamic teachings and many devoted Muslims are, indeed, in a huge moral crisis. The fact that in the 21st century millions of people who belong to one religion and different ethnicities, cultures and nationalities were united in supporting and justifying the mass-killing, raiding and mass-rape of entire communities based on their religious identity is an optimum proof that this religion is indeed in a crisis.[41]

The Yazidi and Christian populations are the natives of that region of the world. They had been settled there for centuries pre-Islam and

---

41 See Powell, C. (2017, Aug 11). Rape as a Tactic of War: Holding the Islamic State Accountable. Just Security.; Stern, J., & Berger, J.M. (2015). ISIS: The State of Terror. HarperCollins.; Murad, N., & Krajeski, J. (2017). The Last Girl: My Story of Captivity and My Fight against the Islamic State. Tim Duggan Books.

pre-Arab conquest. They had never assailed Muslims nor harmed them. They were extremely submissive and peaceful people, trying to live their lives according to their ancient tradition and culture in their homeland. Throughout their history, they have made countless concessions to Muslims in order to save their lives. For centuries, they accepted to be treated as serfs by the Arab invaders. But all that has never saved them. They suffered nevertheless gruesome genocides carried out by the soldiers of Allah time after time.

Tens of thousands of their Muslim neighbours joined the many thousands of ISIS fighters who stormed the peaceful villages in 2014 to kill, loot and rape. They killed all the captured males who were above 13 years old. The mujahedeen kidnapped and enslaved thousands of girls and boys. Females as young as 9 years old were sold as sex-slaves online and at markets in Iraq and Syria. The killing and enslavement of innocent people was in accordance with Islamic laws, as many jurists and average Muslims affirmed. This was the punishment for the crime of being Yazidis, Christians, or Shias. Such an event should have been sufficient to motivate research centres worldwide to examine Islam and the Muslim psyche – but it did not. A few brave thinkers who have been studying the motives behind these attacks and how the masses perceive and warrant the crimes committed by the in-group members have been swimming against the tide, risking their careers and lives.

The horrific genocide committed by Muslims did not evoke condemnation from the Muslim societies or their governments – unlike the outrage over the Danish cartoons, when millions of angry Muslims took to the streets all over the world in violent protests; there was no outcry for the victims of Muslims. Not one single demonstration to denounce the ongoing genocide against Christians and Yazidis took place in any of the Muslim countries. None of the influential Muslim imams or institutions issued a fatwa designating the criminals as non-Muslims and calling upon the masses to kill them. When asked if the ISIS fighters are Muslims, the grand Imam of Al-Azhar, the most senior religious institution in Egypt, said that they are, indeed, Muslims. He explained that as long as they believe in Allah and Mohammad and in the Islamic principles, they are Muslims and they may go to heaven after their death, if Allah decided so.[42] This proclamation is shared by all the important Muslim religious authorities of all sects. Not one important or influential Islamic institution or scholar considered ISIS fighters non-Muslims. They are all aware that the practices of ISIS are sanctioned and supported by the same texts from which they derive their values and authority, as I will show in the coming chapters. They also know that this was not the first genocide carried out by Muslims against the Yazidis and Christians and will not be the last. They have been attacking their peaceful neighbours for more than a thousand years. The most famous recent recorded genocides took place in 1640, 1892, and 2007. In each one of these massacres, Muslims attacked Yazidi villages and towns, killed males, stole their properties, and kidnapped and raped females as a retribution for their being disbelievers.

On the other hand, in an absurd reversal of justice, the same institution declared many thinkers, including the only Arab Nobel laureate in literature, apostates and banned their books. And in accordance with Al-Azhar teachings, an Egyptian court sentenced three Christian children to five years in prison and ordered a fourth to be placed in a juvenile facility for imitating the ISIS beheading of Christians in Libya in a 32-second video filmed by their teacher in 2016. The teacher was sentenced to three years in prison. The judges said in their sentence that by imitating ISIS the students and their teachers have mocked Islamic prayer, which is a crime under the blasphemy laws.[43] So beheading non-Muslims is fine, but imitating the beheading is a crime.

The millions of European and American Muslims, known for being well organized and extremely sensitive to the least criticism, seemed oblivious to all the crimes committed by their fellow Muslims in the name of Islam, whether in Iraq, Syria, Pakistan, or Afghanistan. The same can be said about the Westerners who are always prepared to show solidarity with Muslims, with or without a reason. They were all indifferent when the victims were not Muslims but the perpetrators were. The Middle Eastern governments known for their loud voices,

---

42 Abdul Hamid, A. (2015, Dec 2). Shaykh Al-Azhar mjddaan: la astatie takfir daeish [Sheikh Al-Azhar again: ISIS are not infidels]. (Arabic). AlArabiya News Channel.
43 Human Rights Watch. (2016, Mar 13). Egypt: Reverse Blasphemy Sentences Against Christian Children: 5-Year Terms for Video Mocking ISIS.

chequebook diplomacy, powerful media outlets, and intense reactions were also dead silent when it came to condemning ISIS, the Taliban or any other Islamic terrorist organization's crimes, except for the short-lived theatrical sympathy some of them stage occasionally.

There was one substantial collective reaction from Muslims in response to the crimes of the Islamic State in Iraq and the Levant: tens of thousands of them, both males and females from different backgrounds and ethnicities, migrated to Syria and Iraq to join ISIS. Thousands of these volunteers were citizens of democratic Western countries such as the US, UK, France, Ireland, Finland, Sweden, Norway. Many came from non-Arab countries such as India, Pakistan and Indonesia. Believers came from the four corners of the world and took part in the systematic mass rape, slavery and destruction.[44] They were willing to die for the Islamic State that slaughters, loots, and enslaves non-Muslims. Many more millions supported it financially and publicly defended its genocidal policies.

In 2015, the population of the Islamic State of Iraq and the Levant was around ten million and it controlled land in Syria and Iraq equal to the size of England. Regions in Afghanistan, Somalia, Nigeria, Yemen, the Democratic Republic of Congo and Philippines were seized by fighters who declared their affiliation to this religious state. In every one of these countries, groups of the local population organized and armed themselves and pledged allegiance to the Islamic State and its leader despite being thousands of miles away from him and his state. They were convinced that their fellow Muslims succeeded in resurrecting the righteous state which had perished a hundred years before at the hands of the imperial powers. They perceived that their duty was to join their brothers, be part of the caliphate and participate in its wars to conquer the world. While this state was being erected, numerous educated people were defending it explicitly or implicitly. Some were downplaying its crimes, while others were justifying them.

Significant numbers of Western elites joined in in supporting this State: either through trivializing the crimes, justifying them one way

44 Picker, L. (2016). Where Are ISIS's Foreign Fighters Coming From? National Bureau of Economic Research.; Benmelech. E., & Klor. E., (2016). What Explains The Flow of Foreign Fighters to ISIS? Working Paper 22190. National Bureau of Economic Research.

or another, or redirecting the blame from the perpetrators and their ideology to the Western powers or the victims. They were passionately arguing that Islam was not to be blamed for these Muslims' acts. They distracted the attention from the rationale behind this war to avert putting Islam and the Islamic petrol-rich regimes on trial. It is a discourse pattern that dominates every time a jihadi organization or an individual assails non-Muslims, whether that attack was directed against people in New York City, Mumbai, Moscow, London, Paris, Ottawa, Manchester, Nairobi, or any other of the many cities of the world.

The Islamic State of Iraq and the Levant (ISIS), Boko Haram, Hezbollah, Hamas and the Taliban are contemporary Islamic militarised movements that succeed in establishing states. These organizations have defeated governmental forces and swiftly conquered huge swathes of heavily populated lands that included major cities. This happened due to the substantial support they enjoy among Muslims in general, and the Muslim communities of these lands in particular. They were admired among their fellow Muslims worldwide, including ones who were citizens of the richest countries on Earth. Tens of thousands of individuals who were living in Norway, UK, USA, Australia, New Zealand, Germany, Sweden, France, and Canada saw the rationale that justifies mass killing, enslaving, and looting as a virtuous spirituality, as many of them said in their posted videos. Terrorist organizations received huge financial support from states, organizations and individuals that enabled them to acquire advanced weapons and equipment and pay salaries to their fighters. They grew superior to the national armies of several states. They were paying their soldiers wages higher than their enemies paid their own troops.

It took a military alliance of the most powerful countries on the planet to defeat these organizations, regain some of the land they controlled and stop them from establishing the Islamic Caliphate in the 21st century. However, the Taliban succeed in taking over the whole of Afghanistan; the other terrorist organizations are still powerful and active in many countries. They represent a serious threat to the world peace, mostly due to the support they enjoy. Without the Western soldiers who have been putting their lives in danger's way, these organizations would have succeeded in becoming powerful states.

In the last fifty years, many governments and organizations participated in the production of a huge body of discourse that promotes jihad
against all non-Muslims. The Islamic State (ISIS) published more than
60 books in addition to countless films and pamphlets to promote killing
all disbelievers in Islam and taking their properties as an obligation of all
Muslims. These books are based on passages from the Quran as well as
commands by the founder of Islam, Mohammad. None of the many Islamic
terrorist organizations invented a new belief, as they have been assuring
their audience continuously, thus, they did not need to defend many of
their acts before their targeted audience. Their actions were implementations of the beliefs written in the most original Islamic texts, as they argue.
Hence, they managed to amass substantial popular support among Muslims
because they were following what is considered the authentic teachings.

Yousef al-Ayeri, the first chief of the Saudi branch of Al-Qaida,
published a book to call for jihad against all non-Muslims as well as
sinful Muslims. In this volume, al-Ayeri cited 40 Quranic verses and
sayings of Prophet Mohammad that promote jihad and sanction suicide attacks against civilians. He also quoted over 30 edicts by the most
prominent Muslim theologians over the ages that authorise the collective
targeting of non-Muslims and turning their women and children into
slaves. Through using original Islamic teachings, he argued that suicide
attacks, which are presented as martyrdom attacks, are legitimate means
of implementing Allah's order to annihilate all non-Muslims. In this
book, the author used texts taught in the public educational systems
across the Muslim world to prove his argument. He simply collected
these texts and connected them to show that indiscriminate killing
and terrorising non-Muslims are the duty of every Muslim.[45] Abdullah
Azzam, the godfather of the Afghani jihad and a university professor
with a PhD in Islamic studies from al-Azhar University, declared proudly
that "Muslims are terrorist and terrorism is part of their religion, we are
terrifying, and people must be frightened of us."[46]

---

45 The book is available for download from CIA website: al-Ayeri, Y. Alamaliaat al'istishadia
[Martyrdom operations]. (Arabic).
46 The speech is available on YouTube: tanious geagea. (2014, Aug 25). Sheikh Abdullah Azzam Islamic Terrorism. [Video].; see Hegghammer, T. (2020). The Caravan: Abdallah Azzam

3 Islam: Background and Context

THE ISLAM THAT MATTERS

Islam has 14 centuries of history and millions of followers divided among many conflicting sects. The word Islam comes from the Arabic verb aslm, which means surrender.[47] According to the Islamic dominant narrative, Islam commenced when a forty-year-old Arab man from Mecca named Mohammad declared himself "the last messenger of Allah" after he was approached by an angel who delivered to him the words of God inside a cave in Mecca, in 610 CE.

Islam is first and foremost a set of connected ideas and laws that must be accepted as a whole, according to its holy book.[48] Unlike Christianity and other religions, Muslims unanimously believe that their holy book is the literal word of God with no human interference. They also believe that the sayings of Mohammad and his deeds are eternal rules established by Allah as a comprehensive manifesto to all humans and thus, they must be followed exactly over the ages. Mohammad is the perfect human being and the eternal role model for humanity and thus every human must follow him. These three notions are accepted by Muslims worldwide, regardless of their ethnicities, languages or sect. They are the foundation of Islam.

Constitutions, legislative bodies, justice systems, schools as well as governments' rules and rulings in Muslim majority countries are based on or at least deeply influenced by what can be called the general version of Islam derived from the Quran and the sayings and acts of

---

and the Rise of Global Jihad. Cambridge, UK: University Printing House.
47 The word surrender (aslm) appears many times in Quran with the same meaning: surrender; see Nöldeke, T., Schwally, F., Bergsträßer, G., & Pretzl, O. (2013). The History of the Qur'ān. Ed. and trans. Behn, W.H. Brill. for more discussion.
48 Quran 84:2.

Mohammad. This version, enforced by all Muslim states, has specific main principles that are recognized by the regimes as well as the general public. These principles have been governing all aspects of Muslims' lives for centuries.[49] They regulate the public affairs, personal space as well as social relations. They have been enforced by different regimes over the ages regardless of the people's will. These ideas constitute the Islam that is known, accepted and practiced by millions. Although many adherents do not understand the exact details of all the principles and they may not agree with some of them, they nonetheless shape their lives as long as they are Muslims. They are also imposed upon non-Muslims living in Muslim countries. Now and again, apologists would say that they do not accept this or that practice, such as jihad or polygamy, to defend Islam or themselves against inhospitable audiences. They are well aware that their personal opinion is negligible: it has no influence on other Muslims, and in many cases their opinions are irrelevant even in relation to their own lives.

The teachings of Islam derived from the Quran and the hadith – books that contain Mohammad's sayings – and the acts of Mohammad are the only source of legislation in Afghanistan, Iran, and Saudi Arabia, and the main source of legislation in Pakistan, Bangladesh, Syria, Iraq, Indonesia, Brunei, Malaysia, Indonesia, Libya, Egypt, Kuwait, Qatar, Morocco, Oman, Yemen, Mauritania, Somalia, Algeria, and the United Arab Emirates, to mention some of around 49 countries. This means that every law in each one of these countries must be derived directly from the Quran and the other books accepted as the original Islamic texts, or at least must not be in conflict with these texts. It also means that the legitimacy of the regimes in all these states is related to following and applying the religious teachings.

In Afghanistan (pre-Taliban control), Algeria, Bangladesh, Bahrain, Egypt, Iraq, Jordan, Kuwait, Oman, Pakistan, Somalia and Yemen the second article of the constitution declares that the "religion of the state is Islam." This is also the third article of the constitutions of Brunei, Malaysia, Morocco, and the first article in the Saudi, Libyan, Djiboutian

---

49 Ibn Ishaq, M. (1998). The Life of Muhammad. Translated by Guillaume, A. Oxford University Press.

and Qatari constitutions. The second article of the Iranian constitution affirms that: "The Islamic Republic is a system based on belief in (1) The One God (as stated in the phrase "There is no god except Allah"), His exclusive sovereignty and the right to legislate, and the necessity of submission to His commands; (2) Divine revelation and its fundamental role in setting forth the laws; (3) the return to God in the Hereafter, and the constructive role of this belief in the course of the man's ascent towards God (…)." The fourth article states that "All civil, penal, financial, economic, administrative, cultural, military, political, and other laws and regulations must be based on Islamic criteria. This principle applies absolutely and generally to all articles of the Constitution as well as to all other laws and regulations, and the fuqaha' of the Guardian Council are judges in this matter." Article 12. states that "the official religion of Iran is Islam and the Twelver Ja'fari school in jurisprudence, and this principle will remain eternally immutable."

The designation of Islam as the religion-ruling ideology of the state and the source of laws made it the dominant rationale that is protected by the state and hence, cannot be challenged. This is despite the fact that there are several contradicting and vague ideas in the Quran and in the sayings of Mohammad, as I will show later. Islamic jurisprudence schools were created and developed over a thousand years ago to explain and deduce applicable laws and practices based on the Islamic texts, and approved by the authority. This made the institutions of Islamic jurisprudence and the clergymen extremely powerful as they constitute the legislation and the judicial authorities. For many long centuries they have been the ones that have the authority to draft the laws based on the original Islamic texts. They can also annul any law that, in their judgement, does not fit with Islam. What makes them even more powerful is the fact that many of the sharia principles are fluid because they are based on contradicting and imprecise texts but nonetheless must be followed blindly.

Consequently, every Muslim and non-Muslim living in a Muslim state identified as such by its constitution must abide by the laws derived from Islam (sharia). In these countries, there is only one legal way for any individual registered as being a Muslim to marry, divorce or have a child, that is in accordance with the sharia. Muslim countries do not recognize civil marriage, adoption, children born out of wedlock, nor do they accept non-Muslims as equal to Muslims before the law – because of the sharia. In all Muslim countries, the laws that regulate inheritance are derived from the Quran and Mohammad's sayings. Any person born to a Muslim father is registered as a Muslim in the official records and treated as such by law, regardless of her or his belief. If such a person decided to desert Islam, they would be prosecuted according to the apostasy and blasphemy laws, which carry death penalty in some countries and lengthy periods of incarcerations in others. Apostates are considered traitors by law, thus are stripped of their natural rights.

Muslims are superior to non-Muslims and men are superior to women by law. A Muslim man can legally have four wives at the same time, but it is a serious crime for a woman to be in a relation with anyone but her one Muslim husband. A Muslim man can marry a Christian or a Jew if he wishes so, while a Muslim woman cannot marry a non-Muslim.

In Muslim countries, birth certificates contain the religion of the person. The offspring of marriages between Muslim males and Jewish or Christian females are Muslims by law.[50] Marrying a Buddhist, Hindu, atheist or agnostic person is illegal in Islam as these are considered the worst of the "immoral enemies"[51] of Allah. To this day the Muslim-majority countries do not recognize the marriage between a Muslim man and a Hindu, atheist, Buddhist or agnostic woman. Such a relationship is considered a crime punishable by death or lengthy jail sentences in around 50 states. If a Muslim woman married a non-Muslim, her marriage is invalid, and she would be prosecuted for the crime of adultery in all Muslim countries. Thus, men convert to Islam, in many cases hypocritically, in order to marry Muslim women.

In around 49 countries, the laws that govern the issue of inheritance are derived directly from the Quran which favours males to females. Hence, daughters get half their brothers' share, and widows get one eighth of their deceased husband's wealth. People cannot change the shares of

50 If Barack Hussein Obama was living in a Muslim country, he would have been compelled to practice Islam.
51 Quran 98:6.

their heirs through writing a will or any other means and there is no possible way of challenging these laws. I have witnessed countless cases where widows were forced out of their homes after the death of their husbands either by their own children or the deceased's children from other wives, who took what they saw as theirs.

Adoption is prohibited in Quran in a clear, precise language. Thus, to this day it is impossible for anyone living in a Muslim country to legally adopt. Homosexuality is a crime punishable by death in Islam, and for more than a thousand years people have been executed by the Islamic courts for the crime of homosexuality. Currently, it is punishable by death in some of the Muslim countries while others, who bowed to international pressure, use lengthy jail sentences instead. Throughout the last century, many Arabs, Iranians, Pakistanis, and Afghanis have been sentenced to death by courts and were executed for having a homosexual relationship.[52] In 2007, the Iranian president at the time defended the death penalty his country imposes on homosexuals at a forum meeting at Colombia University. He assured that "In Iran, we don't have homosexuals like in your country."[53] In a poll conducted by Gallup to measure the differences between European Muslims and non-Muslims in regard to various matters, not one person from the British Muslim sample, which contained 500 individuals, said that homosexuality was morally acceptable.[54] Only 19 percent of the German Muslims and 35 percent of the French Muslims saw homosexual acts as morally acceptable.

In 2019, the Iranian minister of foreign affairs endorsed the laws that punish homosexuality with death in a joint press conference with his German counterpart. The minister Mohammad Zarif, who lived in the United States for many years and might hold US citizenship, indicated that gay people breached the moral principles and thus, they deserved to be executed.[55] "The law is respected, and the law is obeyed," he said.

52 Human Rights Watch. World Report 2020. Human Rights Watch Country Profiles: Sexual Orientation and Gender Identity.
53 Goldman, R. (2007, Sep 24). Ahmadinejad: No Gays, No Oppression of Women in Iran. ABC News.
54 Butt, R. (2009, May 7). Muslims in Britain have zero tolerance of homosexuality, says poll. The Guardian.
55 Walsh, A. (2019, Jun 12). Iran defends execution of gay people. DW.

The Islamic regime has been hanging people publicly on homosexuality charges right from the day it took over Iran until this day.

It is extremely difficult to amend any law that is based on a well-established Islamic teaching. Instead, many societies try to reinterpret some of the original laws, if possible, in order to make some progress. These attempts have been failing in bringing meaningful permanent change because many of the Islamic laws are well established and written in plain language in the Quran – they must not be challenged, let alone permanently altered, by people who believe in Islam. Moreover, the religious institutions, which constitute an essential part of every Islamic state, are extremely adamant in their rejection of any attempt at modernisation. They are protective of their monopoly on the right to interpret Islamic texts and, consequently, draft laws and monitor their applications. Losing these powers would equal losing their main source of income and influence.

Every aspect of a Muslim's life is controlled by the religious institutions, which derive their ideas from a limited number of original texts and the official interpretations of these texts. These discourses have been considered the unalterable word of God. They have been enforced as laws by Muslim states and masses. For more than a thousand years and up to this date, these texts along with the official institutions that interpret them have moulded the life of people throughout the world. Islam is insusceptible to permanent changes because it is based on unalterable texts.

People who tend to underestimate the power of these texts and the institutions based upon them end up victims of the Islamic states and the Muslim mobs. When a certain Kuwaiti named Hussein Ali decided to leave Islam to become a Christian after his country was liberated by the Americans in 1991, he faced the wrath of the legal system of the state of Kuwait, not his family or neighbours. Kuwaiti courts of law declared him an apostate, which is a crime according to sharia, and since the constitution recognizes sharia as a main source of legislation, this carried unlimited consequences for him and his family.[56] Hussein was divorced from his wife, banned from seeing his own children and stripped off

56 Amnesty International. (1996). Kuwait. Hussein Qambar 'Ali: Death threats.; Hussein, R. (1998). Apostate Son. Najiba Pub Co.

his civil rights by the Kuwaiti regime, in application of a court sentence. The ruling, written by senior judges, declared him unfit to be a father of his own children because he defected from the only true religion: Islam. He can no longer inherit from his own parents or remain in a marriage with a Muslim woman, regardless of what she or they think. He cannot hold a public office either. He was arrested, interrogated and harassed by the police and was forced to flee his own country. Had he dared to speak publicly about his new belief, he would have been jailed for long periods of time. This took place in Kuwait in 1996, five years after the American troops liberated that country from Iraq. Many Americans died to reinstate the state regime that derives its legitimacy from Islam and its power from the American protection.

While the man was suffering for being a Christian, the American troops were protecting the Kuwaiti regime at the expense of American taxpayers, many of whom are Christians. The same soldiers protecting the Muslim sheikhs were banned from practicing their religion in public and had to conceal their religious identity not to offend the ruling family members and their Muslim Brothers allies. These rich people who demand to be treated as masters of the universe cannot tolerate the public practice of another religion within their territories despite the fact that this specific religion was practiced in this land for centuries before they were installed as royals by the British.[57]

The Kuwaiti regime destroyed and neglected numerous ancient Christian sites in their territories. In contrast, it has built countless mosques and Islamic institutions in the USA and Europe with the aim of converting Westerners into Sunni Islam. It interfered in the internal affairs of the United States brazenly, and the American leaders have never objected or demanded equal treatment. It took advantage of the American and European engineers and workers who discovered the oil and built up the industry from scratch before it took over everything under the name of naturalization.

To this day, the laws in Kuwait criminalise homosexuality and ban naturalising non-Muslims. Individuals who convert to Islam need to

---

57 Bernard, V., & Salles, J.-F. (1991). Discovery of a Christian church at Al-Qusur, Failaka (Kuwait). Proceedings of the Seminar for Arabian Studies, 21, 7–21.

remain Muslims for five years before they can apply for naturalization if they are eligible. Naturalized citizens would automatically lose their Kuwaiti citizenship once they defected from Islam. This is despite the fact that for decades before its independence, this land was inhibited by the Jewish, Hindus and Christians. In fact, Christians lived in this land centuries before Islam according to numerous archaeological discoveries.[58,59]

In every Muslim country, there are several well-financed official institutions that employ theologists dedicated to enforcing the Islamic principles on public life, both inside the country and abroad. There is a Ministry of Religious Endowment (Awqaf) and Islamic Affairs in more than 22 Muslim countries, and in other countries there are similar institutions or governmental bureaux that oversee mosques and Islamic endowments. In addition to these ministries and institutes, there are other governmental and semi-governmental organisations dedicated to spreading Islam internally and abroad. In Iraq, the Shia Endowment Institution in charge of promoting Shia Islam receives a billion dollars every year from the oil revenue, while the Sunni Endowment Institution receives another 300 million dollars to promote Sunni Islam.

Al-Azhar is one of the most powerful and wealthy Islamic governmental institutions in the Middle East. The seventh article of the Egyptian constitution that took effect in 2014 states:

> Al-Azhar is an independent scientific Islamic institution, with exclusive competence over its own affairs. It is the main authority for religious sciences, and Islamic affairs. It is responsible for preaching Islam and disseminating the religious sciences and the Arabic language in Egypt and the world. The state shall provide enough financial allocations to achieve its purposes. Al-Azhar's Grand Sheikh is independent and cannot be dismissed. The method of appointing the Grand Sheikh from among the members of the Council of Senior Scholars is to be determined by law.

---

58 See Sharkey, H. J., & Jenkins, P. (2020). The Rowman & Littlefield Handbook of Christianity in the Middle East. Rowman & Littlefield Publishers.; Baumer, C. (2006). The Church of the East: An illustrated history of Assyrian Christianity. I.B.Tauris.
59 Almutairi, M. (2012). The archaeology of Kuwait. PhD Thesis, Cardiff University.; Lawler, A. (2013). Archaeology Island: Hidden Christian Community. Archaeology (March/April).

Successive Egyptian governments have allowed Al-Azhar to control various aspects of Egyptian lives inside Egypt and to obtain significant influence over Muslims abroad. In 2022, the Egyptian government allocated 20 billion Egyptian pounds to this institution which equals one thousand and five hundred million dollars. It has its own educational system with 9579 schools and several higher educational institutions, with two million students altogether. It monitors public and private education in Egypt as well as the judicial system. The head of Al-Azhar is considered the second or the third person in the Egyptian state by law. He has the power to ratify death sentences. Furthermore, this Islamic institution receives large donations from the Gulf States which have allowed it to extend its influence far beyond Egypt. It controls and manages thousands of Islamic institutions and schools all over the world.

The Egyptian scholar Al-Qemany described Al-Azhar as "source of regression and terrorism worldwide." He explained further that this institution is anti-civilization, anti-science and anti-modernization. It disseminates hatred and ignorance and teaches Muslims to attribute all their defects and faults to the non-Muslims. Its imams call for the destruction of humanity and they are participating in terrorism worldwide.[60]

Among the countless masterminds of terrorism who graduated from this public institute is the godfather of the Afghani jihad – the Palestinian Abdullah Azzam, the head of Boko Harm, the leaders of the Afghani jihad Burhanuddin Rabbani and Abdul Rasul Sayyaf.

Omar Abdulrahman, the godfather of the Egyptian terrorism and one of the most important jihadi masterminds had a doctorate degree in Quranic studies from Al-Azhar university and worked as professor of Islamic studies and an imam for years. This blind man has issued several edicts that sanction the killings of non-Muslims and looting their properties. He also declared the Egyptian president Mohammad el-Sadat an apostate in 1981, permitting his assassination. He defended this edict in court after the assassination of the president by his followers, stating

---

60 Alhurra. (2018, Jan 24). Sayyid Al-Qemany fe halqa nariya: ladei al-jura lekasr kul al-khatout al-hamra [Sayyid Al-Qemany: I have the courage to break all the red lines]. (Arabic). [Video]. YouTube.

that the slain Muslim president was an enemy of Allah and killing him was the duty of Muslims. He was acquitted despite his admission that he did sanction the killing of the Egyptian president. He immigrated to the USA in 1991 to establish Islamic centres and recruit more followers. He was given a tourist visa and then a green card in the same year despite being on the US State Department terrorist watch list. In the US, he instructed his followers to attack American civilians and soldiers, and to blow up the United Nations, the Lincoln and Holland tunnels, the George Washington Bridge and the FBI headquarters.[61] Each one of his verdicts was an application of Islam, as he claimed, because they were based on the Quran and Mohammad's sayings and deeds. He was arrested, tried and sentenced for life in solitary confinement without parole after being found guilty of masterminding several terrorist plots.

The Muslim Brother Egyptian President Mohammed Morsi, who was elected in 2012, vowed in a public speech to release Abdulrahman from the American jail and worked relentlessly to do so but was ousted before he succeeded. When he died, the blind sheikh was given a hero's funeral in his hometown in Egypt. Thousands of people attended the funeral, showing their respect to the man who called for killing the Egyptian Christians and looting their properties.

The regimes of Iran, Turkey, Saudi Arabia, Kuwait, Libya, Sudan and Qatar have spent hundreds of billions of dollars to establish Islam as the dominant ideology inside their countries and all over the world.[62] They have built thousands of mosques, religious schools, financial organizations in Europe, the United States, Canada, Australia, China, Japan, Russia, India and all over Africa while neglecting the needs of their citizens. Each and every one of these Islamic organizations, mosques and schools receives an annual budget from the sponsoring country, which keeps it in business. These bodies are first and foremost means of political influence. The motive behind creating these institutions is to

---

61 Preston, J. (2017, Feb 18). Omar Abdel Rahman, Blind Cleric Found Guilty of Plot to Wage 'War of Urban Terrorism,' Dies at 78. The New York Times.
62 See Byman, D. (2005). Deadly connections: States that sponsor terrorism. Cambridge University Press.; Giustozzi, A. (2018). The Islamic State in Khorasan: Afghanistan, Pakistan and the New Central Asian Jihad. Oxford University Press.

provide legitimacy for the Muslim leaders in the eyes of their subjects, as they present them as true Muslims.

In the last thirty years, several Muslim countries created official institutions dedicated to proselytizing non-Muslims in North America, Europe, China, and Japan. These institutions are part of the regimes that finance them and hence serve their political agenda both internally and externally. The institutions are designed to influence the general public's opinion in accordance with the policy of the sponsor.

It is important to stress that the rich Muslim regimes have been spending fortunes on converting Europeans and Americans to Islam while neglecting their own citizens. A significant percentage of Muslims are illiterate and live in abject poverty. Many millions of Muslims have never read the Quran and they do not practice Islamic rituals. In fact, hundreds of millions of Muslims are analphabets who cannot understand the teachings of their religion. In India, the Muslim community is the least educated, with tens of millions of them not being able to read.[63] In Afghanistan, Somalia, and Mali, half the population or more cannot read or write. Forty-one percent of Pakistanis, 75% of Nigerians, 47% of Mauritanians, 29% of Egyptians and 25% of Bangladeshis are illiterates.[64] There is not one university in the whole of the Muslim world that is within the top 100 universities, and the educational systems across the Muslim countries are among the worst in every aspect. The schools in the Muslim world focus on Islamic studies which is a mandatory subject from the first year of school right until university, while they neglect science, literature, art, and critical thinking.

---

63 India Times. (2016, Aug 31). At nearly 43%, Muslims have highest percentage of illiterates: Census.
64 UNESCO Institute for Statistics. Literacy rate, adult total (% of people ages 15 and above). Data as of September 2021. The World Bank.

MAIN SOURCES OF ISLAM

There are three main sources of Islam: Quran, the biographies of Mohammad known as sirah, and the books that contain Mohammad's sayings
– the Hadith books. The one God Allah who created the world has chosen
Mohammad to be his final messenger to all humans. He spoke to him
in Arabic in the form of revelations. These revelations were delivered
to Mohammad in secret over the course of 23 years and were composed
after his death in one book named the Quran (recitations or readings).
These revelations are the literal word of God, and they must be followed
to the letter. They are not to be taken for allegories, legends or metaphors.
Substantial volumes of the language used in Quran is still being used
today by the native inhabitants of Arabia.[65]

The deeds and sayings of Mohammad are considered divine guidelines, too, that must be followed alongside the Quran because they are
pure implantations and elucidations of Allah's rules. Every constitution,
legislative body, educational system, government, and court of law's
rule and ruling in the Muslim countries are based on or considerably
influenced by these three sources.

All the important texts of Islam are written in Arabic originally and,
despite them being translated into various languages, Arabic remains the
language of Islam. It is extremely difficult to understand the religion without understanding the Arabic language and culture because the discourse
is ingrained in them. Thus, many scholars argue that Islam cannot be fully
comprehended by people who do not have a sufficient command of its
language and culture. Many of the non-Arab jurists learn Arabic to understand what they view as the divine word and to impress their audience.

Currently, Quran is composed in a single book of around 78000
Arabic words. It contains orders, warnings, criticisms, insults, promises,

---

65 See Nasr, S.H. (2004). The Heart of Islam: Enduring Values for Humanity. HarperCollins.

tales and debates. If someone highlights a deficiency in the Quran, such as a false idea, typographical error, grammatical mistake or a myth introduced as a fact, Muslims consider that person a criminal and an enemy of Islam. The Quran is a perfect book and even if it had a clear flaw, it is not an error, Muslims believe. Humans are incapable of examining, let alone criticizing or correcting the divine ideas uttered by Allah, so they must obey them blindly. The flawlessness of the Quran is one of the core beliefs in Islam, if not the core belief.

It is written clearly and plainly in the Quran that it is the literal word of Allah, the final declaration to humanity and the miraculous revelations that contain everything people need for this life and the afterlife, repeatedly. "And indeed, the Quran is the revelation of the Lord of the worlds. The trustworthy spirit has brought it down upon your heart, you Muhammad, that you may be one of the preachers in a clear Arabic language."[66] It is also written clearly in the Quran that Allah has promised to protect and preserve this text.

Thus, Muslims must suspend all critical faculties and surrender completely and unequivocally when dealing with their creator's talk. Any Muslim who dares to question the authenticity of Quran or highlight its shortcomings is instantly considered an apostate, according to all influential Muslim scholars, Islamic institutions and the official laws in the Muslim countries. If a Muslim found a mistake of any kind in the Quran and insisted that it is a fault, she or he can no longer be a Muslim. Islam as a word means surrender and surrender indeed is Islam.

Moreover, it is written in the Quran that this book has everything people need: "we have left out nothing in this book"[67]; "we sent down the book to you which makes everything clear and serves as a guidance and mercy and glad tidings to those who have submitted to Allah."[68]

Many notable thinkers have been killed over the ages by governments or the masses for rejecting or questioning the divine nature of the Quran or its eternal validity. One of the well-known incidents is the beheading of the renowned scholar Al Jaad bin Dirham by the governor

---

66 Quran 26:192-195.
67 Quran 6:38.
68 Quran 16:89.

of Iraq in the Grand Mosque of Kufa in 724 CE. He was executed for arguing that some of the passages in the Quran are metaphorical and should not be considered as literal facts.[69] The story of the beheading has been praised and taught all over the Muslim world for centuries and to this day as the legitimate way of dealing with doubters. Muslims consider criticizing the Quran a crime (blasphemy) punishable by death.

---

69 Ibn Kathir, Abu al-Fida Ismail. (1992). Al-Bidaya wa al-Nihaya [The Beginning and the End]. Vol. 1-14. Dar Al Maaref.

WHEN WAS THE QURAN COMPOSED?

> If I read the Quran, I can't tell whether this book is the word of
> God or not... but I can hope that this was a bad day for God.[70]
>
> Christopher Hitchens

Mohammad died without transcribing a complete copy of the revelations that became the Quran. The issue of who exactly composed and
organised the complete version of the Quran has been a subject of intense
debate for centuries. Usually, Muslim historians argue that at the time of
Mohammad's death, the Quran was preserved in parts in the hearts of his
companions, in addition to various written segments scattered among
them. According to the official history, the third successor of Mohammad, Uthman, undertook the project of creating a unified, complete
copy of the holy book. This project started more than twenty years after
the death of the prophet, according to the original biographies, which
are written more than two hundred years after the events. The goal of
this project was to end conflicts between the early Muslims caused by
the existence of different versions of Quran.[71]

Hence, Uthman commissioned a small team led by one of Mohammad's junior companions, Zaid ibn Thabit, to execute this huge endeavour. This team collected written fragments and added to them what
Mohammad's companions claimed was a part of Quran that they held
in their memories. This created what is known as the Uthman Quran.
The chapters of Quran are called surahs, and sentences are called verses.
They are arranged based on their length; thus, the Quran starts by the
longest surah and ends with the short ones.[72]

Uthman ordered the destruction of all existing manuscripts, declaring his book as the one and only Quran.[73] He ordered Mohammad's

70 92nd Street Y. (2013, Feb 4). Christopher Hitchens and Tariq Ramadan Debate: Is Islam
a Religion of Peace? [Video]. (Recorded on 5 October 2010). YouTube.
71 Shoemaker, S. J. (2011). The Death of a Prophet. University of Pennsylvania Press.
72 Nöldeke, T., Schwally, F., Bergsträßer, G., & Pretzl, O. (2013). The History of the Qur'ān.

companions and wives to hand over every written revelation they had. After collecting all these original manuscripts, he burned them. Uthman sent official copies of his Quran to different countries and ordered the administration of each country to use this version as the constitution. He ordered his subordinates to search for and confiscate and burn any other manuscript. Several senior companions of Mohammad accused Uthman of manipulating the original Quran.

However, there has not been one single copy of the Uthman Quran for centuries, or any older writings. In comparison, many of the older scripts of Christianity, Judaism, and of the cultures of Egypt and Iraq still exist and their age can be confirmed with radiocarbon dating technology. There is no objective account or evidence that any copy of the Quran existed at any time within the first fifty years of the claimed date of Mohammad's death, let alone during his lifetime. The oldest available segments of Quran are written many decades after the death of the prophet. Most of them are written in calligraphic form that was invented more than 100 years after the death of Mohammad. In addition, in the old Arabic language used to inscribe the Quran, several letters were written exactly the same way – b, t, th, n and y were indistinguishable from one another until dots were introduced to distinguish them many decades after the death of Mohammad. Hence, the same passage would have been read in different ways in the older manuscripts, and thus someone made the decision about which one of the possible variation should be "official".

In their epic studies of the Quran, various authors: Sprenger[74], Nöldeke[75], Wansbrough, Crone, Cook and Donner have confirmed that Quran is a manmade text that suffers from shortcomings, plagiarism and contradictions.[76] Most importantly, these studies have shown that the process of writing the current version has taken place over many

73 Muhammad ibn Jarir Al-Tabarī. (1987-1997). The History of al-Tabarī. State University of New York Press, vol. 16.; Nöldeke, T., Schwally, F., Bergsträßer, G., & Pretzl, O. (2013). The History of the Qur'ān.
74 Sprenger, A. (2018). The life of Mohammad: from original sources. Forgotten Books.
75 Nöldeke, T., Schwally, F., Bergsträßer, G., & Pretzl, O. (2013). The History of the Qur'ān.
76 See Nöldeke, T., Schwally, F., Bergsträßer, G., & Pretzl, O. (2013). The History of the Qur'ān.; Crone, P. & Cook, M. (1977). Hagarism: the making of the Islamic world. Cambridge University Press.; Crone, P. & Hinds, M. (2003). God's Caliph: Religious Authority in the First Centuries of Islam. Cambridge University Press.

decades and was not completed within a short period, as some Muslims believe. They have also shown that this process could not have started let alone concluded twenty or even fifty years after the death of Mohammad, as most of the used fonts and the terminologies were developed more than a hundred years after his death. To this day, no one has been able to prove that there was a copy of Quran written within the first century of Islam despite the huge effort and fortunes dedicated to this cause. And above all, there are many differences among the available old manuscripts of Quran.

Although Muslims believe that the Quran has been preserved by Allah and there is just one version of it, in reality, there are several versions of Quran that have been recognized as authentic for many centuries and to this day. Muslims prefer to call these versions recitations, to trivialise the differences between them. The most famous ones are the one written according to the recitation of Hafs, the one based on the recitation of Warsh, and the Qalun recitation. The first one is the dominant version of Quran throughout most of the world, while the second is dominant in Algeria, Morocco and a few other countries, and was first printed in 1905 in Algeria. Libya and Tunisia use Qalun. There are four other important versions. The differences between the various versions are minimal but sufficient to show that the Quran is a manmade text, not the miraculous infallible perfect word of God. In addition, there are various clear grammatical and spelling mistakes in all the current versions of Quran.

The book currently recognised as the authentic literal word of Allah in the Muslim world is based on the copy published on 10 July 1924 by an Egyptian governmental committee commissioned to create a standard copy of Quran to be used in the Egyptian public educational system. This manuscript was amended twice: in 1936 and 1938, by Egyptian governmental committees.[77] This Quran has been adopted as the holy book by Muslim regimes and religious institutions except Algeria, Morocco, Libya and Tunisia, who altered a few words or letters in it to make it in accordance with their accepted recitations.[78]

---

77 As above.
78 Reynolds, G. S. (Ed.) (2008). The Quran in its historical context. Routledge.

For the purpose of this book, I use the same script recognized by Muslims worldwide, written in Arabic and printed in Medina, Saudi Arabia that is based on Hafs, as the reference.[79] Every time I use a translation, I review almost all the available English translations, comparing them to the original Arabic text before I select the most accurate one. On a few occasions, I thought it was necessary to re-translate certain words because I considered the available translations imprecise; I highlight this while discussing the passage.[80] Currently, there are several websites that offer different translations of the meanings of the Quran. Through the process of comparing the well-known ones, it is obvious how in some cases translators alter the meaning of a passage to make it seem more rational or less appalling. I show several examples of that in detail in the chapters that discuss jihad and slavery.

Over the ages, theologians have composed many interpretation books, called tafsir, which praise and provide context for the Quran. Since they all start from the view that Quran is the sacred literal word of Allah revealed in a clear Arabic language, they are designed to simply glorify every Quranic passage, and not necessarily to define its exact meaning. The main purpose of the tafsir books is to document when and why every passage of the Quran was revealed and how it was understood and implanted by Mohammad and his companions, especially if a law has been established upon it. For that, they use the sayings of Mohammad and his biography. There are a limited number of interpretation books considered original by the Islamic institutions and governments, among them Tafsir al-Tabarī and Tafsir al-Qurtubai. The tafsir in general is not of major substance as Muslims believe that the Quran is Allah's message to humanity and it is understandable on its own. No interpretation of the Quran can amend a clear passage as this would contradict the foundation of the religion. The tafsir books deal mainly with minor issues and peculiar words and are limited by the text of the Quran as well as narratives of Mohammad and the history books.

---

79 Quran. (2015). Medina, Saudi Arabia: King Fahad Complex for Printing of the Holy Quran.
80 See AlquranEnglish.com website.

MOHAMMAD'S SAYINGS

The second source of Islam is the collections that document the sayings of Mohammad, known in Arabic as Mohammad's hadith (talk). These sayings written in plain language understandable by native speakers are considered divine rules that must be followed by every human infinitely. Allah informed people that Mohammad "does not speak from his inclination. It is only revelations sent to him."[81] For centuries and to this date, Muslim court rulings, schools' curricula, and mosques' ceremonies have been based on the narratives attributed to Mohammad, in addition to the Quran and the Islamic history.

There are six main books of hadith deemed official and authentic among Sunnis, who represent the vast majority of Muslims. Al-Bukhari's and Muslim's books of hadith are revered as the most authentic, thus the most authoritative, of the six books, according to Sunni Muslim governments, scholars and religious institutions. In fact, Sunnis all over the world have for centuries been viewing al-Bukhari's book of hadith as being second only to Quran as a source of jurisprudence. To this day, in almost all the Muslim countries it is sufficient for a judge to base his verdict on a hadith written in al-Bukhari to be accepted as legitimate, especially in family courts.

The author of the collection, Mohammad al-Bukhari, lived between 194 to 256 AH, thus, he was born 184 years after the death of Mohammad. He did not meet the protagonist, his companions, nor their children or grandchildren. He was born in Bukhara, in the current Uzbekistan, thousands of miles away from Arabia. He was not an Arab and his native language was not Arabic. Muslims claim that he learned Arabic and wrote his book in 232 AH, after he had travelled to Iraq, Levant and the Arabian Peninsula. Hence, according to most of the Sunnis, who make up more

---

81 Quran 53:3-4.

54

than 85% of Muslims, the most trusted book that contains Mohammad's sayings was written 222 years after his death by a man who was foreign to the language, culture and the region. The oldest available manuscript that is used as a reference for the current version was written 540 years after the death of Mohammad and 245 years after al-Bukhari.

Muslim ibn Al-Hajaj, the author of the second most authentic collection of Mohammad's sayings, "Sahih Muslim," lived between 206 to 261 AH. Hence, he was born 196 years after the death of Mohammad in present-day Iran. He was a Persian who was born and died in his native country, thousands of miles away from Arabia. Similar to al-Bukhari and all the pioneer Islamic theologians, he was not a native speaker of Arabic. According to Muslims, the book was composed around 250 AH, more than 240 years after the death of Mohammad. The oldest available manuscripts are written hundreds of years after the death of the author.[82]

The other original books that contain Mohammad's sayings were all written by non-Arabs who were born more than 200 years after the demise of Mohammad and the oldest available manuscripts are also composed centuries after the death of their authors. According to Muslims, the writers of all the books that contain the hadith did not meet the prophet or any person who lived at his time, or even within a hundred year of his time. To boost their credibility every saying written in these collections is preceded by what is called the chain of narrators (isnad) that contains five or more names. Each one of the narrators claim that he heard it from a person who himself heard from another person who was told by another man who heard Mohammad talk: "A told us that B told him that C said that D told him that E heard Mohammad saying that...." Muslims established schools dedicated to studying the chains of narrators to examine the thousands of sayings attributed to Mohammad along with their contents. Based on these sayings written centuries after the death of the speaker, Muslim jurists

---

82 Al-Bukhari, Muhammad ibn Ismail. (2002). Collection of Selected Authentic Reports of the Prophet, His Practices and Times [Al-Jami al-Musnad al-Sahih al-Mukhtasar min Umur Rasul Allah wa Sunnanihi wa Ayamoh) known as Sahih Bukhari. Dar Ibn Kathir.; Ibn al-Hajjaj, Muslim. (2019). Authentic collection [Min al-Jami' al-Sahih] known as Sahih Muslim. Dar Al Kotob Al Ilmiyah.

have created many rules that have been governing both public and private lives of people for centuries.

An example of these rules is the one related to the consequence of breastfeeding. According to the Quran, breastfeeding establishes maternal relationship. Thus, unrelated people who have been breastfed by the same woman cannot marry each other because they are considered milk-siblings. It is forbidden (haram) for a person to marry any of the parents or the children of the woman who breastfed him. The matter is vague in the Quran, as all what is written is that Muslims must not marry the women who breastfed them because they are their mothers, or the daughters of these women, but the verse does not clarify what constitutes breastfeeding. It does not specify the duration of breastfeeding sufficient to establish kinship or even the maximum age after which the breastfeeding is irrelevant. Thus, Muslim judges have been relying on hadith to rule if A is the son of B through breastfeeding and the consequences of that.

A number of imams in Egypt recently restarted an old controversy when they declared that if a woman wanted to establish kinship with a grown-up man, she can breastfeed him or make any of her sisters do that. Hence, this man becomes a relative of her and she can interact with him as such, without the need to cover. They based this edict on a hadith in which Mohammad instructed a woman to breastfeed a grown-up man who used to work at her house. Other imams were outraged by this fatwa and said that Mohammad has said in another hadith that breastfeeding is for children only and the first hadith is forgery. They accused the narrators of the hadith of being liars. The debate about how the breastfeeding must occur is another unsettled issue as some argue it must be sucking the nipples while others disagree.

Currently, some Muslim courts, mainly in Morocco, rule that one drop of milk is sufficient to establish this kinship, while others require a minimum of forty days of continuous breastfeeding, and some declare that it must last for the minimum of six months, with each ruling ascribed to Mohammad.

These contradictions result from the fact that, akin to Quran and the history books of Islam, the hadith books were written a long time after the death of Mohammad. They are based on verbal stories transmitted from one narrator to another until they reached the writers who selected what to include and what to disregard. They were a means to legitimise the existing statutes of the time of writing. Many of the books of hadith copy each other, thus many of the sayings attributed to Mohammad exist in all the books (both Shia and Sunni), sometimes with different narratives or with minor differences. Embracing the original texts and fighting over the minor differences is a source of power and income for Islamic theologians. They battle over who can recruit a bigger audience with his interpretations and thus secure stronger relation to the authority and receive more donations, fame, and influence.

The Shia Muslims, who constitute the majority of the populations in Iran and Iraq and significant minorities in Pakistan, India, Azerbaijan, Lebanon, and the Persian Gulf, reject the Sunni books of hadith in theory but not in practice. They have their own books of Mohammad's sayings, as they claim. The oldest and most important of these books is the Al-Kafi by Muhammad al-Kulayni (864-941 CE), an Iranian born more than 230 years after the death of Mohammad. The second one is "Man La Yahdoroho Al-Faqih" (To whom do not have jurist), which was written by another Persian, Muhammad al-Qummi (923-991), around 981 CE. Similarly to the Sunni official hadith books, the authors were born centuries after the death of the protagonists, they all lived far away from where the events took place and none of them was an Arab.

MOHAMMAD'S BIOGRAPHY

The third source of Islam is the books containing the biography of Mohammad and the history of first fifty years of Islam, known as sirah. These books cover the foundations of Islam. They discuss its customs, norms, practices and the founders' characters. They provide context without which significant portion of the Quran and hadith would not be comprehensible.

The earliest one of these books is the biography of the prophet written by Ibn Hesham around 820 CE, about 200 years after the death of Mohammad. This history is a rewriting of the first known history of Islam, known as Ibn Ishaq's, which had been written around 760 CE, "Ibn Ishaq's biography" of Mohammad. This book had been written at the request of the rulers of the Muslim state. It was intended to construct a specific mythology with the purpose of legitimising the existing laws, institutions and practices of the state at the time through linking them to Mohammad, his companions and his immediate successors. It seems, however, that the mythology conveyed in this book needed to be improved radically after less than sixty years. Thus, the rulers commissioned another non-Arab, named Ibn Hesham, to rewrite the official history of Islam that was written by Ibn Ishaq. The original book disappeared and all what is available of it now is what Ibn Hesham's book included. Ibn Hesham stated in his book that he had to rewrite Ibn Ishaq's history of Islam to remove all the incidents that could be seen as degrading to Mohammad.[83]

The second book is known as Al-Waqidi's history and was dedicated to documenting the wars and invasions of Mohammad and early Muslims up until 160 years after the death of Mohammad.

Most scholars consider the third book, "The History of the Prophets and Kings" written by Muhammad ibn Jarir al-Tabarī, known as

---

83 Ibn Ishaq, M. (1995). The Life of Muhammad, translated by Guillaume, A. Oxford Press.

"The History of al-Tabarī", to document the history of Islam starting from before the birth of Mohammad until 300 years after his death, as the most central record of Islam. This book contains most of the previous written accounts in addition to various sayings of Mohammad and Quranic texts. It was written around 923 CE, 291 years after the death of Mohammad, and is considered the most comprehensive and accurate book on that era by Muslims. The writer is one of the most renowned Islamic scholars; he wrote several books, among them an explanation of the Quran. For the purpose of this book, I use both an Arabic copy and an English translation done by Michael Fishbein and others, printed by State University of New York Press from 1987 to 1997.[84]

The three books that constitute the basis of Islam's story were written by non-Arabs who were born centuries after the death of Mohammad in places far from where the events, presumably, took place. They were all commissioned by caliphs to create an official history of Islam that could be used as a constitution for the Islamic empire. Their originals have been missing for centuries and the oldest available copies were produced centuries after the death of the authors. It is important to highlight that the currently existing versions of biographies have been functioning as the official history of Islam for over a millennium. They were all written in accordance with the political authorities' doctrine, thus, they are almost identical in their report of the establishment of Islam as well as many of the important events that took place in the first hundred years of its inception. We can suspect that there might have been previously written histories of Islam or at least books that were written at the same time as Ibn Hesham's or Ibn Ishaq's but had a different narrative than them, and therefore, they did not survive due to censorship.

In this book, I also use the histories written by Ibn al-Athir and Ibn Kathir, however cautiously. Although the two books are considered authentic records by Muslims, they were written more than 500 years after the events and they usually borrow from the older manuscripts.[85]

---

84 Al-Tabarī, Muhammad. (1967). Ta'rikh al-Tabarī: Ta'rīkh al-rusl wa'l-mulūk. Vol. 1-10. Dar al-Maarf.; al-Tabarī, Muhammad. (1987-1998). The History of al-Tabarī: Ta'rīkh al-rusl wa'l-mulūk. Vol. 1-39. State University of New York Press.
85 Ibn al-Athir, Ali. (1998). Al-Kamil fi al-Tarikh (Vol. 1-12). (Arabic). Dar al Kotob al Ilmiyah;

All original manuscripts of the Shia and Sunni's books of hadith have been lost for centuries. They depend on later copies which were produced many centuries after the original ones were supposed to have been written. In this book, I rely on the sayings recorded by al-Bukhari and Muslim in their books, which have been perceived as authentic in the Muslim world. Most of these sayings can also be found in almost all the other hadith books, Shia and Sunni.

These three types of texts – Quran, Mohammad's biography and hadith – are the foundation of Islam and the main source of laws in the Muslim countries. They shape the Muslim psyche and form the Muslim collective identity. They regulate the way Muslims interact with each other and with other people. Most importantly, they set the norms for Muslims' feelings and acts. They govern their judgment of themselves and of what is right and what is wrong. They influence their emotions, memories and perception. Due to the complexity and vagueness of all these texts and, in many cases, to the enormous short-comings and contradictions within and between them, the Islamic clergy was created by monarchs to interpret them and grew into a powerful institution. For many centuries, Islamic clergy constituted the judicial, legislation and the educational systems at the same time. These Muslim imams have been the legislators, judges and teachers for more than fourteen hundred years.

Currently, in every Muslim country there are persons and institutions, funded by the states, in control of deducing the Islamic ruling from the original scripts to answer various matters. These people enjoy enormous power and are well paid, as they are the ones that justify the policies of regimes through citing a specific narrative. They are the ones that can say doing x is ok because it is halal or a crime because it is haram. For example, when Saddam invaded Kuwait, countless influential jurists supported him declaring that what he did was legitimate and denounced inviting the American forces to Saudi Arabia. They stated that the American army is an infidel power that should not be allowed into the sacred Muslim lands. In contrasts, many other

Ibn Kathir, Abu al-Fida Ismail. (1992). Al-Bidaya wa al-Nihaya [The Beginning and the End]. Vol. 1-14. Dar Al Maaref.

prominent jurists declared that it is permissible in Islam to seek the help of the Christians against the infidels. They also ruled that Saddam was an infidel because he did not implement the sharia precisely.

4 The One Religion and the Eternal Leader

NOTES ON THE HISTORY OF ISLAM AND ITS ORIGINAL TEXTS

The available history of the Arabian Peninsula before Islam and the first seven decades of Islam is based on tales that were transmitted from a narrator to another until they were written centuries after the events. These tales lack evidence and, in many parts, contradict both common sense and archaeological discoveries. There is no independent source to corroborate the discourse currently promoted as factual history by Muslim governments and institutions. There is not one single archaeological proof that Mohammad or his tribe existed in the presumed time or that the events taken as facts by Muslims occurred at any point in history. There is not one authentic record of the major events of Mohammad or even his four successors who are considered the founders of Islam as a religion and as a state.

The prominent Iraqi historian Jawad Ali, who has extensively researched the history of Arabia and is considered the authority on Arab history before Islam, stated that what Muslims take as factual historical accounts are mainly fabrications, myths and hearsay.

Mohammad's tribe, Quraish, is not mentioned in any record or on any map until many decades after the assumed date of the establishment of Islam. Mecca was not mentioned in any independent source within the first fifty years of the official history of the start of Islam. There is no archaeological evidence that supports the official story of Islam. The Kaaba itself has been demolished and rebuilt several times over the ages. The last time was in the mid-1990s when the Saudis erased it and rebuilt it with concrete. Various archaeological missions that excavated the birthplace of Islam came back empty-handed. Over the past hundred years, Muslim regimes failed to find any substantial evidence that support their religion's discourse. In contrast, significant evidence contradicts the dominant narrative and paints a different story.

The original books of Islam, including the Quran, were not written during the time of Mohammad or at a time close to his.[86] In the preface of each and every one of these books, the writer indicates that he was told the dialogue by A who was told by B who heard it from C who heard it from Mohammad. It is stated in the preface of the current copies of the Quran produced and distributed by the government of Saudi Arabia free of charge that it was written based on the recitation of Hafs who learned it from Asem who learned it from Alsalmi who learned from Ali who learned it from Mohammad. Thus, even if we were to accept this unsubstantiated tale, the authors of the current Quran were born decades if not centuries after the death of Mohammad by their own admission.

It is important to stress that there has not been one original copy of any of the books considered authentic by Muslims. There has not been one copy of the Quran that was written in Mohammad's time or during the reign of his immediate four successors. This fact is what made the French scholar Ernest Renan say that "we arrive, then, from all parts at this singular result: that the Mussulman movement was produced almost without religious faith; that, putting aside a small number of faithful disciples, Mahomet really worked with but little conviction in Arabia."[87] This conclusion had been reached by many Arab, Egyptian, and Persian researchers, centuries before Renan.[88]

In summary, what Muslims consider the sources of Islam that is supposed to be followed by every human in this vast world, are narratives created and propagated on the orders of the Arab rulers in order to gain legitimacy among their subjects, centuries after the time of alleged events. This system of ideas was designed to function mainly as a constitution for the tribal state created by desert dwellers who defeated the

---

86 See Irwin, R. (Ed.). (2010). The New Cambridge History of Islam: Volume 4, Islamic Cultures and Societies to the End of the Eighteenth Century. Cambridge University Press.; Berkey, J. P. (2002). The formation of Islam: Religion and society in the Near East, 600–1800 (Vol. 2). Cambridge University Press.
87 Donner, F. M. (2010). Muhammad and the believers at the origin of Islam. Harvard University Press.
88 Ali, J. (1993). The Detailed History of the Arabs Before Islam. Third Ed. Dar al-Alam.

major civilizations of their time and conquered their lands and took their wealth but rejected their cultures and religions. All the books considered original references were commissioned by Arab tyrants for that purpose. The main ideas and themes are all in line with a totalitarian primitive ideology based on the psyche of a tribal, militarised uneducated society. The history and the teachings of Islam were written by the descendants of the conquered people on the orders of the victorious Arabs to control and regulate every aspect of private and public life of their subjects. The main story of Islam contains numerous contradictions, myths, exaggerations, inaccurate dates and locations and stolen ancient legends.

The defeated people's perspective of what had happened were destroyed except for very limited fragments. The limited accounts that survived the inferno show that the Muslim armies were indeed savage, deceptive and ruthless in their dealing with the non-Muslims as well as with Muslim doubters. People did not convert to Islam willingly and did not accept the rationale of Islam voluntarily.

The history of the civilizations and cultures that existed before Islam has been disgraced, censored and obscured from the masses. The Arabs, Iraqis, Iranians, Egyptians and Moroccans were banned from studying about their ancestors for centuries and to this day. The history classes in the Muslim world start by introducing the old civilizations as evil, immoral, deficient, and corrupt. Students are told that people who lived before Islam were living in ignorance and agony; they were liberated by the Muslim invading armies who introduced them to the true religion and changed their lives to the best. Iraqis would be surprised to know that their ancestors had a great civilization before Islam and that they were a beacon of science and literature. To this day, many Egyptians do not know much about the old civilizations that existed in their homeland. Until recently, Egyptian imams would call for the destruction of the ancient Egyptian artefacts because they were considered symbols of infidelity. The native of Arabia's understanding of their history starts from the Islamic wars. It would be an eye opener for the vast majority of them to realise that this part of the world was connected to the civilizations of its time, and its people had a rich culture and significant states.

THE GREAT CIVILIZATIONS
AND THE ARABIAN PENINSULA PRIOR TO ISLAM

To understand Islam, it is essential to understand the milieu in which this religion emerged. The Christian Byzantine Empire and the Persian Empire were the dominant civilizations of the Old World at the time of the birth of Islam. These great empires had been in conflict for centuries before Islam was born on the Arabian Peninsula. According to Muslim historians, in the sixth century Arabs were living in three societal types: they were desert dwellers (Bedouins), the Arabs settled in cities and small towns scattered mainly on the outskirts of the Arabian Peninsula and near the centres of civilizations[89], and the third type of society was composed of individuals rejected by their tribes for committing dishonourable crimes or for being illegal children or the offspring of Arab men and slave African women. They were known as Sa'alik and they were living in the mountains and in deserts by the caravan routes, making a living from looting and fighting as mercenaries.

Like in the case of similar desert inhabitants, Arab Bedouin culture was designed to enable people to survive in their cruel ecosystem. It put the clan above the person, encouraged armed conflicts, and created ruthless deceptive warriors. Arabs had a long history of internal fighting over scarce resources as well as for hegemony. One of the known wars is Dahes, which was triggered by a horse race: the loser's tribe claimed that the winner rigged the race, and the killing between the two tribes lasted for forty years, claiming many lives. The main motive was the notion of honour that is fundamental to the social cohesion.

The second group of Arabs lived in towns within or on the outskirts of the Arabian Peninsula that had water resources, such as Petra, Mecca, Yathrib and Ta'aif. The Ghassanid Kingdom in Syria and the Lakhmid

---

89 Hoyland, R. G. (2001). Arabia and the Arabs: From the bronze age to the coming of Islam. Routledge.

Kingdom of al-Hira, Iraq, were the most important Arab states. They were both predominantly Christian and affiliated with the superpowers of the time. The Ghassanids were allies of the Byzantine Empire while the Kingdom of Hira was allied with the Persians. The two Arab states were barricades against the nomads' invasions of the civilized empires. The citizens of the two states were considered enemies by the nomads.

The birthplace of Mohammad and Islam, Mecca, was a small city surrounded by mountains and dependent on trade and religious tourism, according to Muslim historiographers. Some historians argue that the people of Mecca used to spend only a few months out of the year in it while for the remainder of the time they lived and worked in the nearby port city of Jeddah or the mountain town of Ta'aif.[90] Around the sixth century, the Arabs of Mecca had become rich due to their trade with the fighting great empires and the newly established merchant routes in the Arabian Peninsula. Patricia Crone has eloquently shown in her study "How did the Quranic Pagans Make a Living?" that the Arabs addressed in the Quran were of varying socioeconomic cultures, not nomads cut off from civilization, as some argue. The Quran, especially the Meccan Quran, has references to agricultural, maritime and pastoral communities. It uses analogies from farming, pastoral, commercial and maritime cultures to relate to its audience. There are references to palm trees, grains, figs and olives as God's gifts to people. Allah asks the people if they are the ones who sow the grain and fruits or is it Allah who does that? He affirms that it is he who is doing the sowing, not people, thus people ought to be grateful to him.

These analogies show that Islam was created by people who were part of or connected to the old civilizations. It was not a product of an isolated man living in an isolated, arid, dusty town. Importantly, all the analogies are limited to the Middle East environment in general, and the fertile crescent in particular.[91] There is no reference to anything or any culture that do not exist in the Levant, such as forest, woods, lakes, or snow. There is not a single fruit foreign to the Middle East mentioned

---

90 Margoliouth, D. (2006). Mohammed and the Rise of Islam. Cosimo, Inc.
91 See Crone, P. (2016). The Qur'anic Pagans and Related Matters: Collected Studies in Three Volumes (Vol. 1). Brill.

in the whole of Quran, while dates, grapes, olives and pomegranate are mentioned numerous times.

Not one remark about the religions or cultures of Europe, India, China or even Africa can be found. It is obvious from reading the early part of the Quran that it was designed to unite the Arabs living in the proximity of the old civilizations. It was replying to a natural need of the Arabs that came from the influx of money, a rapid growth in population and the cultural connection with the advanced civilizations; Arabs became anxious for a political entity after the decline of the Persian and Byzantine empires. They were longing for a state that would unite them and end the numerous internal wars. At the same time, they were aware that the demise of the powerful Arab states in the north of Arabia left a power vacuum in the region.

Before Islam, the attempts to unite the different Arab towns and tribes were all in vain. The most powerful institution inside Arabia was the tribe. It is extremely difficult to establish a central government and a functioning state for people who are loyal only to their blood lineage. How would any administration make sure that the rules are known, let alone respected, by armed people who are in a constant state of war with each other and are always on the move? How can people who have different religions, dialects and interests unite?

Ibn Khaldun (d. 1406) contends that Arabs are savage, aggressive, deceptive, and tribal by nature. They are loyal to their clans only, as it is the only viable institution. This, he argues, is a result of their environment as well as their lifestyle. He contends that the only way to unite and control them is through religion.[92] However, the religion that can unite the fighting Arabs has to satisfy their needs and be suited to their milieu. The Arabian Peninsula is a vast, extremely volatile and harsh desert; it is the poorest place on Earth in terms of fresh water and almost all other natural resources. Some of its parts are uninhabitable all year round; some are uninhabitable in the winter and some during the summer. There are no rivers, lakes or real boundaries that can mark the different parts of

---

92 Khaldun, I. (1858/2012). The Muqaddimah. Librairie Du Liban Publishers.; Khaldun, I. (2015). The muqaddimah: an introduction to history – abridged edition. Princeton University Press.

the vast land. Thus, Arabs had to be volatile, vicious, adaptive and tribal to be able to live in this desert and survive the shortage of water, food and safety. Among the nomads, males were considered assets for their parents and their tribes as they were the fighters that could defend and provide for their tribe while females were considered a liability.

Mecca became a commercial and spiritual centre of Arabia shortly before Islam, according to the Islamic resources. It was expanding at a rapid rate due to immigration from different areas. People from all over the Peninsula were stopping in that mountainous town to take part in the trade industry. Many Arabs were Christians, some were Jews, while the majority were polytheists, and some were atheist.[93] The Kaaba was one of several centres of paganism where numerous idols, paintings and statues of various deities stood. Mecca was a free zone: one could do whatever he or she pleased as long as they were not hurting anyone physically. It was a major market and spiritual centre open to all religions, thus Arabs considered it a sacred place inoculated against wars and raids. Attacking Mecca or hunting in its surroundings was considered a great offense. This spiritual protection provided Mecca with the prerequisites to prosper and expand. It also obliged its people to be tolerant to all religions and beliefs. The Kaaba was the place were all polytheist idols as well as scriptures and paintings of Virgin Marry and Jesus and Jewish icons were displayed.

Anything and everything could be traded in Mecca openly and freely. Poets had stands where they would recite their poems and engage each other in poetic duels. Prostitutes had tents with red flags to attract customers. The slave market was the biggest such market where kidnapped humans were displayed. (This market remained functioning until the first part of the 20th century. It was closed due to the Western powers' pressure rather than the religious teachings of Islam.) The Town Hall (Dar Al-Nadwah) was where Mecca's council members decided on all their issues: religious, social, commercial and political. There was no voting and no absolute ruler; all decisions had to be discussed and agreed upon. The population of Mecca would nominate individuals who

---

93 Ali, J. (1993). The Detailed History of the Arabs Before Islam. Third Ed. Dar al-Alam.

they considered prominent to represent them in the council. The most influential men in that council were the ones known for their generosity, bravery, wisdom and cunningness, hence they could administer the city and influence the other members of the board. This form of government made people of Mecca competitive, and at the same time peaceful and tolerant.

At the beginning of the seventh century the Old World was going through a major transformation. The great civilizations, albeit prosperous, advanced and powerful, were struggling with the chronic diseases of aging empires: corruption, inequality, mass migration, cronyism, inter-conflicts, and above all the psychological resignation and passivity of the general public. The great civilizations were dying down, leaving a gigantic power vacuum. The nomads who were living next to them were yearning to take advantage of this situation.

MOHAMMAD

And they say, you upon whom the revelation has been sent down,
indeed you are a madman[94]

Someone from the valley has killed Allah and stolen his ID[95]

Islam revolves around Mohammad, his life, personality, his sayings, his
reasoning and his culture. Mohammedans is the most accurate label of
Muslims. The Prophet dominates the psyche of his followers. His persona has been ruling masses of people from beyond the grave for over a
thousand years. Muslim identity is based on the adoration of Mohammad
as the eternal leader. They have been idealizing and studying Mohammad's life in detail as the highpoint of humanity. He is the role model
for all humans, his followers believe. They derive the meaning of their
lives from comparing their ideas, feelings and acts to Mohammad's. To
understand Islam and Muslims, we need to understand Mohammad from
a Muslim point of view as well as through a critical examination of the
available records about that historical person. It is crucial to examine
how Muslims see their leader and his effect on their lives.[96]

As someone who was born and grew up in the Arabian Peninsula,
I came to realise that it is impossible to overestimate Mohammad's influence on his followers' lives. Mohammad is an essential part of every
aspect of the daily life of millions of people. The countless mosques
praise him through their megaphones from dawn to dusk; in every call
for prayer and in every prayer Mohammad is adjacent to god. In every
Muslim country, the state TV channels are dedicated to ingraining Mohammad's sayings and acts in the people's consciousness as the paradigm

---

94 People of Mecca addressing Mohammad in the Quran 15: 6.
95 Abdul-Saboor, S. (1986). Night Traveller (in Arabic). Egyptian Book Organization.
96 See psychological studies that examine how traditional large groups view their leaders, e.g.
Volkan, V. D. (2003). Large-group identity: Border psychology and related societal processes.
Mind and Human Interaction 13:49-76.

of virtue. From the first day of school, right until finishing university, countless mandatory classes teach students how to revere, follow and praise the prophet. Students must memorise his sayings and biography as part of the curriculum. Mohammad's idealized life is embedded in every Muslim's mind through powerful well-funded official institutions. Mohammedans know more about their Prophet's life than any other figure's, including their own parents. They do not and cannot see him as a historical human limited to his social environment, era and situation. He has been constructed as the one and only role model for humanity – the perfect eternal human that delivered the valid answers to all the questions. There are animated mental schemas of Mohammad inside every Muslim's brain that influence his or her ideas, feelings, and acts.

Muslim children are taught by public and private school systems, TV channels, mosques, their families and the religious institutions that the Prophet is their grand leader. He is the last messenger, the saviour and the chosen person to deliver God's final and only valid revelations to humanity though his acts and words, revelations without which people would burn in eternal inferno after death. Without Mohammad, there would have been no life on this earth and no good in the people. He is the source of morality. The British Muslim MP Naz Shah said in her address to the House of Commons in 2021: "there is not a single thing in the world that we commemorate and honour more than our beloved prophet Mohammad… for the 2 billion Muslims he is the leader we commemorate in our hearts, honour in our lives and forms the basis of our identity and our existence." [97]

Mohammad's words and acts have been protected by the sword for centuries. Every Muslim accepts that God said: "Mohammad is the messenger of Allah. And those with him are ruthless against the disbelievers and merciful among themselves." [98] Allah ordered Muslims to obey Mohammad blindly. "It is not for a believing man or a believing woman, when Allah and His Messenger have decided a matter, that they should [thereafter] have any choice about their affair. And

---

97 Mussa, M. (2021, Jul 6). British Lawmaker takes up issue of Prophet Muhammad's sanctity in Parliament. Anadolu Agency. See also Naz Shah [@NazShahBfd] on Twitter.
98 Quran 48:29.

whoever disobeys Allah and His Messenger has certainly strayed into clear error."[99] This is the unalterable commandment from Allah to humanity, as millions of people believe.

In every prayer and in every call for prayer, Mohammad is glorified as the connection between the creator and his subjects. He is present in the Muslims' psyche on an equal footing with Allah: "Obey Allah and His Messenger if you are true believers: true believers are those whose hearts tremble with awe when Allah is mentioned."[100] Mohammad and Allah are inseparable in Islam.

Regardless of their education, language or ethnicity, Muslims are obliged to memorise Mohammad's sayings and implement them literally. Mohammad's sayings are above logic, doubt and criticism.

Everyday millions of Muslims travel to Mohammad's tomb to humble themselves in front of it, seeking his approval from beyond the grave. They shout "peace be upon him" when any of his many names or titles is mentioned. He instructed his followers to name their sons after him or risk his resentment. Thus, in every Muslim family, a person is called Ahmad, Mohammad, Taha, Mustafa or Yasin, which are but a few of the many names and titles of Mohammad. For many years now, Mohammad has been among the most popular names given to newborns in the UK, Sweden, France, Germany, and all Muslim countries.

One of the Quranic verses states that: "Allah and his angels praying (yusalloona) on the Prophet you who believe pray on him and submit full submission (wasallimoo tasleeman)."[101] The translators of the Quran replaced the Word praying (yusalloona) with "send Salat" or "send blessing" or "bless" to moderate the meaning of this verse.

---

99 Quran 33:36.
100 Quran 8:2.
101 Quran 33:56.

THE REJECTED CHILD

Did he not find you (O Muhammad) an orphan
and gave you a refuge?[102]

According to the original accounts that constitute the dominant version
of Islam, Mohammad was born around 570 CE in Mecca, after the death
of his father.[103] His paternal ancestors were from the Hashemite clan of
Quraysh tribe, the dominant inhabitants of Mecca. The vast majority
of his paternal relatives were pagans who worked in commerce. There
is very limited information about Mohammad's mother Aminah or her
family. What we know from the Muslim historians is that she was from
another clan of Quraysh and that her relationship with her son was peculiar. Mohammad's mother rejected him right after his birth. She sent
him to live with a nomad (Bedouin) family who were moving throughout
the Arabian desert . They took him in exchange for money. Mohammad
spent his infancy in a moving nomads' tent, away from his mother and
his family. Even when he was returned at the age of two, his mother rejected him again and sent the two-year-old boy back to spend another
four years with the strangers.

Muslim theologians tend to justify Mohammad's mother's rejection
of him by claiming that this was the custom or that she did not have
enough breast milk to feed her baby, or that she wanted him to learn how
to speak eloquently from the Bedouins. These justifications are absurd,
as there is not one other single story about a similar case at his time or
any other time. Not one other child that was sent away from his mother
is mentioned in any of the Muslim histories. None of his companions
or relatives had been sent to live with Bedouins for any period of time,
let alone the whole first six years of life. None of Mohammad's children
or grandchildren was sent to live in the desert. If Mohammad's mother
could not breastfeed him, there must have been women in Mecca who

---

102 Allah addressing Mohamad in the Quran 93:6. See Marmaduke Pickthall's translation.
103 Sprenger, A. (2018). The life of Mohammad: from original sources.

gave birth at a previous time, and they could have helped feed the orphan boy rather than sending him away at such a young age. Even if we accepted the lack of breast milk as the true reason, did he need to be breastfed at the age of four or five or six? Many women used to die in childbirth, hence, the newborn would be given to another woman to look after him in exchange for money – but this was not the case here.

The same theologians who state that Mohammad's mother could not breastfeed him – and this is why she abandoned him – claim that he was a blessed child who brought fortunes to the Bedouins. When reading the stories of Mohammad's birth, one is astonished by the amount of contradictions and irrationalities. The same historian who would write that a light came from his mother while she was giving birth, two pages further writes that the infant was starving. In one account we read that no one wanted him, but the holy Persian fire went out, the Persian imperial palace cracked and one of their lakes dried as a sign that he was the one who would overthrow the great empire.

A few Muslim historians and jurists implied that Mohammad was born three to four years after his father had passed away.[104] This notion, although rejected by most Muslims, might explain Mohammad's abandonment by his mother. To this day, there is a disagreement among senior jurists regarding the legal duration of the pregnancy. The majority contend that it could last for up to two years and many influential jurists declared that the maximum duration of pregnancy is five years.[105] Hence, if a widow gave birth to a child up to four years after her husband's death, the child can be considered the legitimate offspring of the deceased, according to many influential Muslim scholars. The same applies to divorcees. This was the law in several Islamic states for long centuries. The Saudi, Egyptian and Kuwaiti contemporary laws designate the maximum duration of pregnancy as one lunar year, which is 354 days.

After living his first six years with strangers in the desert, Mohammad returned to his mother. But he did not stay with her for long, as the mother died, according to many historians, or may have left him again.

---

104 Ibn Sa'd, M. (2022). Kitab al-Tabaqat Al-Kabir (Arabic Edition). Ed. K. V. Zettersten. Brill.
105 See Aldardeer, Ahmed. (2010). Alsharh alsaghir al aqrab ila masalik ila madhab al-Imam Malik [The small explanation on the path closest to Malik's doctrine]. (Arabic). Dar al-Fadelah.

The mother disappears from history books and all what is written about her is that she died when she was on her way back to Mecca from Yathrib and was buried near the desert route. There is no mention of whether Mohammad was with her on that trip or if she remarried after Mohammad's father's death. There are no detailed records of a maternal uncle or a cousin of Mohammad and there is almost no information about his relationship with his maternal family. Nevertheless, Muslim historians report that Mohammad's maternal grandfather was considered a liar and a fool by his people. They nicknamed him Father of Sheep (Abu Kabsha). They recount that after Mohammad declared himself a prophet, several poets ridiculed him through comparing him to his grandfather, suggesting that he was "a charlatan like his old man."[106]

Despite tens of thousands of recorded sayings of Mohammad which discuss everything about him, from his daily interactions to his ideas and problems, the only well-known saying about his mother is the one in which he asked Allah to allow him to pray for her, but Allah did not permit it because she did not believe in Islam.[107] In the Quran there is a verse that bans Mohammad and all Muslims from praying for their non-Muslim relatives: "It is not for the Prophet and the believers to ask forgiveness for the polytheists, even if they were their relatives, after it has become clear to them that they are companions of Hellfire."[108] This was despite the fact that she died before her son received the revelations. This abnormal relationship between Mohammad and his mother could provide a partial explanation for his peculiar relationships with women (and girls) later on.

When Mohammad was six years old, his paternal grandfather took him into his house. Two years later, the ailing grandfather died, and the orphan boy moved houses once again to live with his impoverished uncle Abed-Manaf (renamed by Muslims as Abu-Taleb). He lived in his uncle's house from the age of eight until he got married at the age of twenty-five. His uncle was a pagan like most Meccans; he did not accept Islam even though he died eight years after Mohammad declared himself Allah's messenger.

106 Among them was the notable poet Al-Aswad Al-Nahshali.
107 Sahih Muslim 976.
108 Quran 9:113.

The uncle's family made him work as a shepherd in his childhood. One of the well-known incidents in Mohammad's childhood is that he was attacked by two strangers who traumatised him. Islamic scholars explain this incident by claiming that the attackers were angels who opened his heart and cleansed it from all evil. Thus, the attack is a miracle, they claim. This story, like many other legends about Mohammad, is taught in Muslims' schools all over the world as a fact that must be admired. Accepting this nonsense as facts and forcing children to believe it as such creates a submissive distressed individual and a magical thinking deceitful society. In conclusion, details written in the official Islamic accounts show clearly that Mohammad's family were poor, that he had no father, his mother rejected him and his grandfather died after he moved in with him. In the Quran, Allah taunts Mohammad that he found him "poor, stray and orphan."[109]

Commentators and historians tend to overlook the fact that Mohammad's abnormal childhood may have affected his personality and can provide a sufficient explanation for his distress and peculiar behaviour. Mohammad was a neglected and possibly abused, lonely child in a tribal society. He grew up deprived of his mother as well as a father figure, with limited education; he experienced a disturbed and unstable childhood and youth. This suffering had a lasting effect on him.

According to Muslims, Mohammad himself initiated his idealization after he gained a number of followers, to compensate for his deficient upbringing and lack of achievement. He said that he was born circumcised and on the day of his birth jinn (invisible evil creatures made of fire) were pelted with stones of fire as a mark that he was the saviour of humanity. He also said that Allah had kept dividing people into groups and selected him from the best of the best. He repeated on several occasions that he was the most articulate human being, Allah's favourite creature and the master of mankind.[110]

---

109 Quran 93.
110 Sahih al-Bukhari 7510; Sahih Muslim 2278.

MUNDANE YOUTH

Mohammad's youth was uneventful as he did not establish himself in any noteworthy way. Muslim theologians struggle to highlight any accomplishments by Mohammad before he declared himself a prophet at the age of forty. In contrast, many of his peers succeeded in professions or literature, and many were distinguished political leaders or wealthy merchants. For instance, the people of Mecca considered Amr Ibn Hisham, a counterpart of Mohammad, one of their senior leaders when he was 25 years old and elected him to the city board. They called him Father of Wisdom (Abu Al-Hakam) due to his intelligence, integrity, generosity and honesty.

While the norm was for people to work for their relatives, this was not the case with Mohammad. Despite the fact that Mohammad's paternal family owned several businesses in Mecca and some of his uncles were wealthy, they did not hire him. Neither did his maternal relatives. When Mohammad became an adult, his uncle Abu Talib arranged for him to work for a wealthy widow named Khadijah. Fifteen years his senior and with several children from previous marriages, she was an independent merchant who owned caravans that transported goods between Yemen and Syria. Mohammad worked among other people on these caravans. This allowed him to see the Levant and the Byzantine Empire as well as Yemen and the Persian colonies. He was introduced to the cultures and religions of other nations that were much more advanced than Mecca and the rest of the Arabian Peninsula. Mohammad developed a keen interest in mythologies. He became a devoted student of Waraqah ibn-Nawfal, a priest in Mecca and Khadijah's cousin. Waraqah introduced him to meditation and monotheism, in which he sought refuge.

Although rich and noble men wanted to marry Khadijah, she was not to give up her independence. At the age of forty, she decided to marry Mohammad, her poor and young employee. It is fair to assume that through marrying an orphan with no siblings, an employee who was 15 years her junior, she wanted to maintain control over her wealth as well as the household. In contrast, Mohammad did not have much of a choice; after all, he was financially dependent on her. He was a humble man with no skill, future, parents or siblings. It is worth noting that when Mohammad married Khadijah at the age of twenty-five, this was an old age to get married for the first time for an Arab man. He did propose to several women before receiving Khadijah's proposal, one of them being his cousin - but her father Abu Talib, who raised him in his house, rejected him. He preferred to marry his daughter to another man, telling Mohammad that the man was more qualified. This may have driven Mohammed to accept Khadijah's offer. Their marriage was contested by her family. Despite Khadijah being quite old, her father refused to marry his daughter to Mohammad, calling him a poor orphan, and she had to trick him to accept the marriage.[111]

The marriage lasted for more than 25 years until Khadijah's death and it was monogamous. While married to Khadijah, Mohammad did not marry another woman and did not own a slave-girl. He freed a slave and adopted him in accordance with the Arab customs of the time. Throughout their marriage, he remained financially dependent on his wife. Some Muslim historians think that the couple did not have children of their own except one daughter, Fatima. The majority, however, believe that they had four girls and two boys, all of whom, except Fatima, died during Mohammad's life. Despite much confusion and contradictions in Islamic history regarding Mohammad's children, it has been accepted as a fact that Mohammad did not have a male heir. His daughter Fatima, whom he married to his cousin Ali, the son of Abu-Talib, is the only one of his children who survived him and gave him his grandchildren: Hassan and Hussain.

Mohammad's opponents taunted him for being childless and Allah responded to them in the Quran. In his reply, Allah did not say that he would grant Mohammad offspring but rather he told him that he had given him Kawthar. What Allah meant by Kawthar is a topic of

---

111 The History of al-Tabarī, Vol. 6.; Sprenger, A. (2018). The life of Mohammad: from original sources.

a never-ending debate: some claim that it is a river in heaven, while others argue it is another name for Mohammad's daughter Fatima. In both cases, Allah's response was not satisfactory for the people of Mecca.

Throughout his life, Mohammad knew very well that his society looked down on him. Thus, he befriended underachievers and malicious individuals. Almost all his companions were individuals with little power and of low social status. In the eyes of his clan, he was the outsider who married an old widow and lived off her money. Therefore, he took refuge from his social isolation and distress in mediation inside dark caves, away from society.

RELIGION BORN IN WAR AND PLAGUE

The Byzantine-Sasanian War of 572-591 CE is perhaps one of the most pivotal events in human history. It shaped the course of humanity for hundreds of years afterward. In that war, the two great empires destroyed each other and stalled the progress of humanity for over a thousand years. They inflicted a catastrophe from which humankind has not recovered. As a result of that war, the institutions and infrastructure of those two great countries became dysfunctional and the once magnificent empires descended into failed, corrupt, unjust societies. Consequently, civil wars erupted within them, paving the way for another world-war.

The last Byzantine-Sasanian war that took place from 602 to 628 CE was the end of the old world. The two great empires fought, again, a world war that further devastated the human civilization. The Caucasus, Anatolia, Egypt, Levant, Balkans, Aegean Sea and Mesopotamia were turned into battlefields. The richest parts of the world were destroyed, and many civilized cities and towns were ransacked and reduced to ghost towns.

Mohammad declared himself a prophet in 610 in Mecca and in 622 established his state in Yathrib, a small town in Arabia. Thus, Islam was created during the last Byzantine-Sasanian war. Moreover, before and during the war, the two major Arab states that were allies of the Persians and the Byzantines were weakened, then overthrown by the Persians. The two Arab kingdoms that were governing and controlling the Arab nomads, preventing them from invading the lands of the two empires, were completely destroyed by 613. This encouraged the surrounding tribes to wage raids into the two ailing superpowers' territories. The power void allowed Arabs to invade the two fading empires under the guise of a religion that claimed to possess the truth.

Moreover, Islam emerged in a period when the Old World was devastated by plague epidemics that started in 541 and lasted until 767. The plague of Justinian (541-549), which began in the modern-day Egypt and spread throughout the Mediterranean Basin, Europe, and the Near East, had devastated both the Sasanian and the Byzantine Empires. The plague of Sheroe, which took place between 627 to 628, afflicted Mesopotamia as well as the western parts of current Iran. Many people died in that area and towns bordering Arabia were devastated which further weakened the Sasanian Empire. These plagues in addition to the wars prepared the ground for the Arab invasions.

Muslim historians report that Mohammad told his people at the beginning of his movement that his aim was to make his tribe the masters of the Arabs and to make Arabs the masters of all other nations. Five years before his death, Mohammad assured his followers that he would conquer the palaces of the Byzantines and the Persians and would turn both these nations into slaves. These prophecies that are currently preached as miracles by Muslims are nothing but a simple realization of Mohammad that the two powers were fading, and their days were numbered.

Byzantine and Persian people were psychologically resigned due to the corruption and incompetence of their ruling class, the endless wars they had fought against each other, and the plagues which killed countless people. They were fed up with the elites' immorality, stupidity and incompetence. The two great civilizations, although still mighty and advanced, were extremely frail and vulnerable as decent people lost the will to defend their countries and consequently themselves. People were simply absorbed in the daily problems and hardships caused by the corrupt administrations. They could not foresee that they might lose everything, including their lives and the lives of their beloved ones, if they failed to defend the sovereignty of their countries. They did not expect that their children could be enslaved and massacred by an enemy that was committed to destroying the civilization rather than establishing one. They were focused on their discontent and disappointment rather than the whole picture.

A PROPHET WAS MADE

They say are we to leave our gods for a mad poet?[112]

In 610 CE, at the age of forty, Mohammad was approached by the arch-angel Gabriel while meditating at night in the Hira Cave at a mountain on the outskirts of Mecca. He was instructed to recite what the angel dictated to him. He refused in the beginning, telling the spirit that he was unable to do it but eventually he did recite. After this incident he was scared and left the cave horrified, seeking shelter in the arms of his wife. She assured him that what he had seen had not been an evil spirit nor an illusion. She told him that he might be the long-awaited prophet of Arabia. They went to see her cousin and his mentor Waraqah ibn-Nawfal in search for an explanation. The old Nestorian monk told them that what happened to Mohammad could be similar to what had happened to Moses and Jesus. He should not be fearful as this might be the long-anticipated message from Allah and he might be the prophet and the messenger of Allah to the Arabs.

It is impossible for any scholar to ignore the influential role Chris-tianity played in the course of Islam. Waraqah was the one who married Mohammad to Khadijah. Mohammad was his student for more than 20 years. The ideas about Christianity incorporated into Islam are based largely on the Nestorian doctrine. In fact, Christians are called Nasara in Quran and the hadith, a name that may have been derived from the word Nestorian. Many verses in Quran as well as many of its commands and ideas are taken from Christianity.

Khadijah encouraged Mohammad to believe that he had not been hallucinating and what had happened to him was real. She accepted Mohammad's claims and supported his endeavours financially. She did not ask him to provide a proof for his extraordinary claims and he did not volunteer any. She never met an angel or witnessed a miracle. To

---

112 People of Mecca about Mohammad as reported by Allah in the Quran 37:37.

this day, all Muslims believe without a doubt in the existence of angels who are creatures made of light, dedicated to praising Allah endlessly. Gabriel is introduced as the one in charge of delivering Allah's messages to his prophets such as Noah, Moses and Jesus, and finally Mohammad. Accordingly, he had been without work for fourteen hundred years.

Supported by Khadijah's money, Mohammad began inviting people to believe in him and follow his guidance. He was promoting his religion through demonising the other beliefs and constructing them as false and immoral. During the Meccan period, Islam was based on theories and ideas less prone to violence. Nevertheless, they were not peaceful nor tolerant. The main message was the call to reject all the other gods, religions and idols for the worship of Allah. Allah is the one and only God. The creator of everything and the omnipotent. Allah created the whole world for one purpose: to be worshipped. People, animals, stones and planets exist to constantly praise Allah. Allah cannot be seen and does not communicate with people directly. He will never provide a tangible proof of his existence but he does not tolerate doubt or criticism. All the previous religions are invalid, and Mohammad is the role model for all humans.

Most of the early chapters of Quran are based on ideas from Zoroastrianism, Judaism and Christianity put together. The main theory revolves around the existence of one and only creator who entrusted Mohammad with delivering the comprehensive rules. Allah does not have any partners or children and he demands adoration. He is the source of all good, and all evil comes from the devil or the humans, who are the creations of the flawless Allah.

ISLAM AS TOTALITARIAN IDEOLOGY FROM ITS ONSET

We have revealed to you clear communications, and none disbelieve in them except the criminals[113]

Mohammad started his movement in Mecca by inviting his close relatives to accept him as their leader. He recited passages revealed to him by the angel Gabriel, along with some of his own ideas about what is right and wrong. He warned that the current life was concluding shortly, and he was the saviour from God's imminent rage and punishment. He assured his relatives that if they followed him, they would rule the Arabs and use them to conquer non-Arabs. At the same time, he accused them of being sinful and hence deserving to burn in hell eternally for not worshipping his god and for believing in many fake gods. This was despite the fact that Mohammad's god had not been in contact with people for hundreds of years, as he claimed. To make up for their crimes of not recognizing the invisible god, people were instructed that they needed to repent through following Mohammad and reject everything and everyone else. Mohammad demanded full submission to himself as tzar and spiritual leader. He assured them that he was the greatest person that ever existed, thus, entrusted by Allah to guide humanity. He demanded the rejection of polytheism, Christianity, Judaism and all other religions and beliefs instantly.

Mohammad's family disowned him, called him a mad impostor and a crook. Subsequently, he went on to proselytize the other people of Mecca and the passers-by. He called upon them to worship Allah as the one and only God who cannot be seen, approached, tested or contacted, and to reject all other religions. Mohammad was telling the people that Allah listens and knows everything but talks only to him. Moreover, he had Allah's approval for whatever he said and did, since he was the complete human. He was preaching about judgement day and eternal

---

113 Quran 2: 99, see Shakir translation.

hellfire. He recited traumatising verses that describe gruesome torment reserved for those who dared to reject Islam. "Those who disbelieve in our revelations we will drive them into a fire. Every time their skins are roasted through, we will replace them with different skins so they may taste the torment."[114] In another verse, Allah warns people that they are monitored all the time even by their body parts:

> The day when God's enemies are gathered up for the Fire and driven onward, until when they will come to it, their ears and their eyes and their skins will testify against them about what they used to do. And they will say to their skins, why did you testify against us? The skins will say, we were made to speak by Allah... then the fire is their abode, and if they seek forgiveness, they would not be forgiven.[115]

It is important to stress that the Quran was far from complete when Mohammad started his movement, or even when he died 23 years later. It was a work in progress for 23 years during Mohammad's life and many more decades after his death.[116] Whenever there was an interaction between Mohammad and people, Gabriel would descend with a passage that dealt with that interaction specifically, but which must be taken as a general rule, Muslims believe. In the Quran, we find long passages dedicated to solving Mohammad's marital conflicts through Allah's orders. Many other long passages are describing in detail minor brawls and mundane events from Mohammad's life along with his feelings. Examining these passages demonstrates that they are the product of various modest minds consumed by trivial personal matters.

The people of Mecca rejected Mohammad and his belief. They ridiculed him and laughed at his warnings and promises. They considered him a liar, and his own uncle Abu-Lahab called him a crazy charlatan repeatedly. In reply, Allah narrated a short chapter in Quran to defame this uncle of Mohammad in a childish language. Mohammad's sixty-five-year-old wife Khadijah, his ten-year-old cousin Ali, who was living with him, and a couple of friends were the first people to surrender to Islam.

---

114 Quran 4: 56.
115 Quran 41:19-25.
116 See Crone, P. & Cook, M. (1977). Hagarism: the making of the Islamic world.

During thirteen years he spent in Mecca preaching the new religion through reciting the revelations and warning people of the impending punishment kept for disbelievers in this life and the afterlife, less than 200 persons accepted Islam.[117] Some were slaves, some were freed men, some were criminals, very few were from a decent background. The one thing in common between them was that they had been extremely dissatisfied with their lives and their society, mainly for personal reasons and failures. They were hoping to change their lives through embracing this new religion and its leader. While projecting their personal problems onto the society, they were desperate to gain new social identity. They wanted different social norms, values and status from the one they had: they desired to be leaders, not the followers. Simply put, they desired to believe Mohammad's promise that they would be prominent, and their problems would disappear if they converted. The Meccans made sure to highlight time and again the fact that the individuals who accepted Islam were few in numbers and the worst of the worst in character.[118]

The few individuals who converted to Islam in Mecca surrendered utterly and unquestionably to Mohammad. They were proud to be Allah's slaves and Mohammad's followers. The prophet became their absolute leader in every aspect. They abstained from any critical thought or question as they considered it disobedience, and hence an act of war against Allah. The more the non-Muslims highlighted the deficiencies of the basic rationale of Islam, the more the early believers would suspend their judgment, surrender to it and defend it.

---

117 The History of al-Tabarī, Vol. 6.
118 Ibn Ishaq, M. (1998). The Life of Muhammad.

IF HE SAID IT, IT IS TRUE

Muslims worldwide celebrate the miracle of Isra and Miraj on the 27th day of the seventh month of the Islamic calendar. This important event called Mohammad's Isra (night travel) and Miraj (ascension into the sky) is a public holiday in Muslim countries. Millions of Muslims all over the world show their devotion through commemorating this miracle every year. Educated individuals in North America, Europe, Asia and Africa celebrate this wonder and teach it to their children as a literal fact.

According to the Quran and the hadith, Mohammad flew from Mecca to Jerusalem, and from there he ascended to heaven up in the seventh sky, all in one night. Allah sent him a flying animal called Buraq, which looked like a hybrid of a donkey and a mule, that took him on the one-night journey.[119] Mohammad met with all the deceased prophets: Adam, Abraham, Jesus, Moses, and many more. He led these historical figures in prayer and had lengthy discussions with them and with Allah. Furthermore, he visited hell and saw how people were being tortured with fire. Women were the majority of the condemned people, he told his followers. Some of these doomed women were hanged by their breasts, others by their hair, while being burned with a blaze.

In his face-to-face meeting with Allah, he got instructions for all humans, including the nature of the prayer Allah demanded. He managed to get concessions from Allah regarding the number of daily prayers. Allah initially demanded fifty prayers, but on the advice of Moses Mohammad negotiated it vigorously and in the end the two parties agreed upon five mandatory prayers per day. When he woke up in the morning, Mohammad went to tell the people of Mecca about his fascinating journey. The Meccans were astonished and called him a mad liar in response.

---

119 Quran 17:1; Sahih al-Bukhari 3886, 3887, 3888; Ibn al-Athir, Vol. 2.

His few followers believed him, however. They did not demand to see the flying animal, nor did they see any proof that their leader had in fact travelled thousands of miles back and forth in one night. They did not ponder whether it was possible or rational for a mule to fly, let alone cover that great distance in one night. They did not question why and how all these historical figures were still alive; they did not wonder how their leader communicated with them and what language he used. They did not inquire why there were people being tortured in hell while the judgment day had not taken place yet. They simply believed Mohammad's words and abstained from any critical thought or question. This was a miracle that took place in secret: there were no witnesses and no evidence. The miracle defied all the rational norms and contradicted science and logic but has been nevertheless accepted by millions of supposedly sane people. Any person who dares to discard this miracle will most definitely face the Islamic sword after being labelled kafir.

The infamous Indian imam Zakir Naik, who has a medical degree, defended the factuality of this tale against a woman who said that it was nothing but "a blatant lie" of Mohammad in a public lecture at Oxford University attended by hundreds of people.[120] Similarly, Mahdi Hassan, who hosts a talk show on MSNBC and has been presented as a liberal intellectual, affirmed in a public debate with Richard Dawkins at Oxford University that he believed Mohammad had flown on a winged beast.

When the Egyptian journalist Ibrahim Eissa questioned the factuality of this miracle, Al-Azhar as well as the general public in Egypt and many other Muslim communities were outraged. Several people filed legal complaints against him accusing him of insulting Islam and hurting Muslims' feelings through doubting this miracle. Many people took to the social media to abuse Eissa, and some called for killing him. They all seemed incredibly convinced that it was rational for a miracle to be performed in secrecy and for a winged mule to fly out of the galaxy and come back to Earth within a few hours. They could not see anything wrong with the notion of dead people coming back to life to pray under the leadership of Mohammad or with the idea of people being tortured in

---

120 The question and the reply available on YouTube: About Islam (2021, Apr 2). A Japanese girl cursing the Prophet Muhammad, and Dr. Zakir Naik responds... [Video].

hell before the judgment day which has not come yet. Muslims have been creating twisted arguments to justify this tale rather than considering it a simple lie or a delusion of a disturbed mind. What is more puzzling than Muslims by birth believing this tale is how millions of people who convert to Islam accept such irrationalities.

The fallibility of these ideas, as well as countless others in Islam, compel Muslims to resort to violence to silence critics. Many people would never dare to look at this tale with a sceptical mind out of fear. They don't want to risk being cast as apostates and face Muslims' violence. The acceptance of this tale is one of many examples that represent the absolute surrender of the human mind required from informed Muslims.

It is worth noting that there is no way of verifying that Mohammad said what current Muslims believe he said regarding this incident or any others. More importantly, Muslims attest that no evidence existed that Mohammad's account was a fact rather than a delusion. The only proof that Mohammad is indeed the messenger of Allah and the eternal leader of humanity entrusted with delivering God's verses comes from Mohammad himself. Anyone who rejects Mohammad's claims is an infidel – an enemy of Allah.

Meccan leaders' reaction to Mohammad's movement can be described as tolerant but reckless, cowardly, and naive. They did not appreciate the seriousness of the matter. They failed to foresee the consequences of this religion. They exhibited tolerance and were content with confronting Mohammad's claims through logic and debates rather than force. On the other side, Mohammad was recruiting dissatisfied and criminal individuals, convincing them that the cause of their troubles was everything and everyone but themselves. Society was constructed as an enemy. The major religions of the region and their followers were systematically dehumanized and demonized. Successful individuals were discredited as evil and deceitful. Mohammad incited his disaffected followers and encouraged them to disturb the peace, first in secret and eventually, in public.

Mohammad was dividing society, pitting people against each other and conspiring to bring about civil conflict, without facing any substantial consequences. Despite the fact that he carried out seditious attacks against polytheism as well as other religions, Meccans kept displaying self-restraint, tolerance, wisdom, cowardice, and apathy. Mohammad asserted that Allah characterized non-Muslims in the Quran as "filth", "animals", "enemies of Allah", "criminals" and gave them many other demonizing and dehumanizing labels. These titles were psychological constructs that are ends and a means for further ends. By dehumanizing non-believers, Mohammad was preparing Muslims to harm these targeted people. The Meccans did not put Mohammad on trial or do anything significant to stop his incitement. They did not prevent him from creating a state within the state and a society within the society. Rather, he enjoyed immunity while attacking the beliefs and the ideas of the society that had never accepted him.

The influential persons of Mecca were not intimidated by tales of hell, neither were they allured by promises of heaven, but they were too timid to stand up for their identity. They demanded tangible proof of Mohammad to support his grand claims rather than putting him on trial for breaching the peace and insulting people's beliefs. They asked Mohammad to perform miracles to support his claims. They simply wanted him to present objective evidence that proved he was, indeed, the messenger of the creator of this world, as he claimed. They told him repeatedly that his ideas were stolen from ancient myths and that his followers were despicable individuals.

Mohammad met the people's adamant refusal and sound intellectual challenges with insults and threats. The Quran is full of hate talk against the people of Mecca as well as against all other religions and their followers, especially polytheism - the religion of the majority in Arabia at the time. It also includes defamations against Mohammad's contemporaries and their beliefs and culture. A whole chapter of the Quran is dedicated to insulting Mohammad's uncle Abu-Lahab and his wife: "Perish the two hands of Abu Lahab and perish he. His wealth and what he earned will not benefit him. He will burn in a fire of blazing flames. And his wife, the wood-carrier will have upon her neck a robe made of palm-fiber." [121] This surah of Quran demonstrates a psychological problem on the side

---

121 Quran 111.

of the narrator. It hints that the uncle may have assaulted Mohammad and thus, he is hoping for his hands to perish. It also shows Mohammad's jealousy of his uncle's wealth and a deep hatred toward the wealthy, reputable wife. This chapter lacks intellectual vigour by any standard in any language and is recited in the prayers and taught in educational systems. Many preachers, embarrassed by the defects of this Surah, prefer to ignore it when discussing the Quran as a miracle. It is clear evidence that this book is far from perfect.

The defamation of one of the most senior leaders of Mecca, Al-Walid, in the Quran is another sharp example of the systematic dehumanization, demonization and character assassination of the opponents. According to Islamic historians, Al-Walid was deeply respected among the Meccans; they considered him a wise, insightful and great leader. In the Quran, this man is called "worthless", "sinful" and a "bastard": "do not obey this worthless habitual swearer. Scorner who spreads gossip. Hinderer of the good, transgressor, sinful. Crude and above that a bastard. It is because he has wealth and children. When our verses are recited to him, he says tales of the ancients."[122] Hence, the almighty Allah dedicated a part of his final message to humanity to abusing a mortal. The most wicked characterisation in the tribal Arabian culture is being used by Allah against a man and his mother without any justification. It should be highlighted that Arab culture, mainly nomadic, is based on the idea of blood lineage and honour. Thus, such an insult can result in the offender being harmed, especially if the one being insulted is a prominent person. This did not happen; to the contrary, the Meccans kept underestimating the consequences of such systematic character assassinations and hate talk. They saw them as the narratives of a madman. In contrast, such discourses appealed to the dissatisfied people who were jealous of Al-Walid and the Meccan establishment. It encouraged them to join this religion that sponsored attacking the rich, successful and powerful people.

The self-restraint of the Meccans encouraged Muslims to intensify their verbal attacks. Some of Mohammad's peers responded with a critical analysis of Mohammad's personality, his followers, and Islam.

---

122 Allah in the Quran 68:10-15. Several translators have watered down the word zanem which means born out of wedlock – but others did mention it.

They contended that the Quran was nothing but badly plagiarized ancient myths. Mohammad was accused by the intellectuals of Mecca of being a madman and a crook. In the Quran, we see Allah raising this idea several times. "And they say, O you upon whom the message has been sent down, indeed you are a madman."[123] Allah also documented the non-Muslims' challenges for Mohammad: "Why do you not bring us the angels, if you are truthful?"[124] The Quran records several extensive debates between the Meccans and Mohammad - in them we see how the people were winning through using sound logic and reasonable thinking, while Mohammad resorted to threats, promises and defamations. This also demonstrates that Islam was never a peaceful nor tolerant ideology at any stage of its lifespan.

123 Quran 15:6.
124 Quran 15:7.

5 Great Debates: Allah and Mohammad versus Arab Intellectuals

And they say ancient myths he has them written down,
they are dictated to him day and night.[125]

The Quran that Muslims worldwide abide by as the unalterable literal word of God contains several fascinating debates between Allah and Mohammad on the one side and Arab intellectuals on the other side. These debates highlight the ways in which Islam encourages credulity and daunts critical thinking. They also show that Mohammad's contemporaries thought he was an insignificant, mentally ill charlatan. The Polytheists, Atheists, and Christians of Mecca proved to be superior to Mohammad and Islam in both logic and ethics. An intellectual battle between critical thinking and primitive tribal reasoning takes place within these debates. A battle where human-based morality and reasoning is challenging and defeating what is introduced as absolute decrees attributed to God. The Polytheists, Atheists, and Christians displayed a great capacity for critical thinking, sound reasoning and effective civilized debating. They questioned all the fundamental ideas of Islam and refuted them thoroughly with logic, evidence and integrity.

In one of the debates, the people of Mecca said: "We will not believe you until you break open for us from the ground a spring or you have a garden of palm trees and grapes and make rivers gush forth within them in force [and abundance] or you make the heaven fall upon us in fragments as you have claimed or you bring Allah and the angels before [us] or you have a house of gold or you ascend into the sky. And [even then], we will not believe in your ascension until you bring down to us a book we may read."[126] This straightforward challenge was a golden chance for Mohammad to prove that he was indeed the messenger of Allah. All what he needed to do was to ask Allah to grant the people any

---

125 Allah in the Quran (25:5) reporting what the Meccans thought of Islam.
126 Quran 17:90-93.

of their simple demands. It should not be impossible nor even difficult for the Omnipotent who sent angels and a flying mammal to Mohammed to create a garden to satisfy the people's need for a tangible proof. However, Mohammad failed to perform any miracle and the answer to this straightforward challenge came rather from Allah in the form of words, not deeds: "Say, Exalted is my Lord was I ever but a human messenger?"[127]

Analysing this Quranic passage, we see that the people of Mecca invited Mohammad to publicly deliver solid evidence, but he failed, according to the Quran. Instead, he recited Allah's order to him to say that he is just a human and a messenger. This reply attributed to God was seen by the addressed people as insufficient. The people did not question if Mohammad was a human, they questioned if he was indeed a messenger from God. They simply wanted him to ask Allah to present them with a sign that would make them believe in the existence of the one God who controls this universe and is capable of doing major things, as Mohammad has been claiming. They wanted Mohammad to follow the examples of previous prophets mentioned in his Quran who were performing tangible miracles to convince their people. In response, Mohammad and his God promised the ones who would suspend their critical mind and believe his sayings unscrupulously that they would be rewarded with gardens after their death. "Allah has promised to the believers gardens under which rivers flow to dwell therein forever, and beautiful mansions in Gardens of 'Adn [Eden Paradise]. But the greatest bliss is the Good Pleasure of Allah. That is the supreme success."[128] This verbal reply did not satisfy the intellectual Arabs. Thus, they accused Mohammad of being a mentally disturbed, corrupt, insignificant person trying to gain power through mobilising despicable villains by preaching lies and ancient myths.

These debates are today taught to Muslim children as a victory of Mohammad against the evil Pagans who rejected the voice of the sky. This is the perfect con – because of course no one can ultimately prove or disprove anything about the "afterlife" or life after death. And to doubt Mohammad or any of the teachings, to demand tangible evidence for

---

127 Quran 17:93.
128 Quran 9:72.

scientifically impossible miracles, or to even highlight the irrationality of some of the notions in the Quran with logic is immoral and evil. Believers must surrender completely to the fantasy and live in a state of cognitive dissonance – they must doubt what they see with their own eyes and what they experience in reality. They learn to distrust their own instincts for what is right and wrong and what is real and unreal, when it contradicts the teachings. Virtue is to surrender to irrational, baseless claims. The whole foundation of scientific thinking is undermined through glorifying fallacies.

This debate is a clear example of how totalitarian-utopian ideologies and critical thinking work on two different mental systems. Critical thinking is based on demanding objective evidence to accept any claim. In contrast, the Islamic argument and all the dictatorial, tribal, primitive dogmas are based on invoking wishful expectations of reward and the primitive fear of punishment to influence people's judgment. It also speaks to the immature part of the human brain that gets excited about uncertainty connected to a reward.[129] For example, it is similar to receiving two different offers: one promises a specific job with a reasonable salary and clear responsibilities; the other promises millions of dollars without any well-defined duties or specific conditions but demands immediate blind commitment. Some people would request clarifications before committing to any agreement; others are willing to suspend their minds and sign up, hoping that their daydreams would come true. Over time, they make more and more concessions until being a member of the group becomes who they are.

The people of Mecca asked Mohammad to explain the notion of the soul: "And they ask you, [Muhammad], about the soul. Say, the soul is of the affair of my Lord. And people have not been given of knowledge except a little."[130] In this verse, we see Mohammad's failure in providing an answer to a reasonable question. He told the people that this was none of their concern and humans could not understand much because Allah did not give them adequate capability. This notion undermines Islam as it is based on the idea that Allah has created people and installed in

---

129 See Sapolsky, R. M. (2017). Behave: The biology of humans at our best and worst. Penguin.
130 Quran 17:85.

them an adequate mind, thus they can follow his orders and distinguish right from wrong. It also undermines the basis of science and logic as it bans questioning. Moreover, Greek philosophers discussed this topic and provided convincing answers hundreds of years before Mohammad's birth. Many of the Arabs at Mohammad's time were familiar with the different philosophical schools of thought and debates regarding the nature of life and the issue of the soul.

In another contest between Mohammad and Meccans, they were willing to listen and discuss Mohammad's claims rationally. "And they say, why was there not sent down to him an angel?" – again, the people asked him simply to provide evidence that he was really being contacted by an angel. They wanted a proof that he was not delusional or an impostor. Allah replied that if he sent a proof, then he would not give the people a chance to accept Islam: "But if we had sent down an angel, the matter would have been decided; then they would not be pardoned."[131] Needless to say that this argument lacks logic, thus Allah gave a second response: "And they say, why has a sign not been sent down to him from his lord? say, indeed, Allah is able to send down a sign, but most of them do not know."[132] This argument is as deficient as the previous ones as it does not provide a sufficient justification for lack of proof, hence, Allah revealed his thought yet in another verse stating that "Nothing stops Us from sending the Ayat (proofs, evidence, signs) but that the people of old rejected them." This argument says that the Meccans would not be given proofs because the old people, which the Meccans had not known, had been given proofs and they disbelieved hence Allah stopped providing evidence.

In another passage, the Quran documents how the people of Mecca challenged Mohammad and Allah to punish them for rejecting Islam. "And they had said Allah if this (the Quran) is indeed the truth from you, then rain down upon us stones from the sky or bring on us the painful torment."[133] Instead of raining down the stones, Allah replied to this direct challenge with a verse: "But Allah would not punish them

131 Quran 6:9.
132 Quran 6:37.
133 Quran 8:32, see Mihr's and Khan's trans.

while you were among them. Allah will not punish them while yet they ask for forgiveness."[134]

In conclusion, people kept demanding evidence that would support the grand claims of Mohammad but all what they got were threats, insults, excuses, promises, and empty rhetoric. Consequently, they faced Mohammad with what they thought of him:

"The disbelievers say: this is a charlatan magician."[135]

"And they say: Why is not this Quran sent down to some significant man of the two towns?"[136]

"They say are we to leave our gods for a mad poet?"[137]

"Whenever they see you [Mohammad], they take you only as a mockery: is this the one Allah has sent as a messenger?"[138]

"And they say, you upon whom the revelation has been sent down, indeed you are a madman."[139]

These verses and many similar ones negate the picture of Mohammad that Muslims have been painting over the ages. The Quran documents the low opinion Mohammad's contemporaries had of him. Interestingly, this notion was not contested by Allah. There is not one verse that presents Mohammad as a notable person independently from Islam. Allah did not proclaim that he had chosen Mohammad for his merits or deeds. It is not written that he was the wisest, the richest or even the most knowledgeable person. The Quran does not report one incident where the non-Muslims praised Mohammad. God has mentioned all kinds of tales about the miracles of the previous messengers but none by the Seal of Prophets. To the contrary, Allah told Mohammad in Quran that he found him "an orphan and gave you shelter. And found you err, so he guided you and found you destitute and enriched you."[140] This construction of Mohammad as a deprived sinner orphan represents a fundamental

---

134 Quran 8:33.
135 Quran 38:4.
136 Quran 43:31.
137 Quran 37:37.
138 Quran 25:41.
139 Quran 15:6.
140 Quran 93:6-8.

predicament for informed Muslims, especially when coupled with the accusations that Mohammad was a mad swindler. It contradicts the notion of Mohammad being the greatest man and thereby entrusted with the final revelations and ultimately, the responsibility of guiding humanity for the one and only God.

To conceal this flaw, Muslim historians have been creating and promoting unsubstantiated stories that present Mohammad as a person respected and revered among his peers prior to Islam. Tales claiming that the Meccans trusted and respected Mohammad, which are promoted by Muslims in every language, contradict several verses of Quran as well as Mohammad's biography. His biography shows that he was dependent on Khadijah all his life. He was never considered a prominent person in Mecca and had not been nominated to participate in Mecca's Governing Board (Dar Alnadwa) – this despite being forty years old and belonging to a powerful branch of Quraish. It is also important to stress that the Meccans were extremely ethical and naïve as they allowed Mohammad to preach his ideas freely. They did not systematically persecute him or his followers. All the harassment Muslims highlight are nothing but few isolated and limited incidents that can be seen as a normal reaction to Mohammad's acts. Unlike Mohammad and his successors, who resorted to exterminating whole societies and assassinating peaceful opponents as a custom, the people of Mecca were tolerant, forgiving, and cowardly passive. Not one incident has been noted in Quran that reports a killing, enslaving, raping or even torturing of a Muslim by the hands of Meccans. On the contrary, numerous Quranic passages insult and warrant aggression against non-Muslims based solely on them being non-Muslims, which will be discussed later on.

One Quranic verse records a dialogue between Mohammad and Allah related to the people's rejection of Islam: "If their evasion is difficult for you, then if you are able to seek a tunnel into the earth or a stairway into the sky to bring them a sign, [then do so]. But if Allah had willed, He would have united them upon guidance. So never be of the ignorant."[141] Here we see that his failure to provide a convincing

---

141 Quran 6:35.

proof was distressing him. He felt that the people were shunning him for his failure. This dialogue weakens the argument that Mohammad is God's most cherished human. Allah disregarded his messenger's needs and refused to support him even though his demands were reasonable. Psychotic and bipolar patients often have these internal arguments as they try to justify, verify, and actualize their delusions.

Throughout the Quran we see the contemporaries of Mohammad highlighting that Islam is based on old myths and plagiarized legends of ancient civilizations. "And they say ancient myths which he has them written down and they are dictated to him day and night."[142] Anyone who reads Quran with an open mind and compares its tales to Jewish stories of Moses, Noah and Abraham, Mesopotamian mythology, and the Gospels would objectively come to the same conclusion. The Quran is nothing but plagiarized text compiled in an unintelligible way, as many scholars have argued over the ages.

After more than ten years in Mecca, Mohammad came to the conclusion that he would never be the supreme leader through peaceful means. His followers were few and of the lowest caste, and his ideas were repulsive in the eyes of the diverse society. It is reported that after the death of Mohammad's mentor Waraqah, the revelations discontinued for a considerable period, which augmented his distress. The failure in converting significant followers and the fierce opposition he faced made Mohammad doubt his ability and suffer psychologically. It is reported in the most trusted books of hadith that Mohammad tried to throw himself from mountain tops to put an end to his life.[143] Each time an angel would prevent him from killing himself. Eventually the revelations commenced again, although perhaps not in the same style. Mohammad told the Meccans: "I came to you with slaughter."[144]

To overcome his failure in Mecca, Mohammed begun visiting different neighbouring towns, hoping to win their residents to the new religion. The first city, beside Mecca, he attempted to win over was a rich oasis called

---

142 Quran 25:5.
143 Sahih al-Bukhari 6581; Ibn Saad, M. (1998). Al-Tabaqat al-kubra.; The History of al-Tabari, Vol. 6.; Ibn al-Athir, Vol. 2.
144 Musnad Ahmad ibn Hanbal: 6996.

Ta'if, 90 km from Mecca. He went to that town to preach Islam and seek people's allegiance to him despite them being traditional enemies of the Meccans, as the people of the two towns had fought each other several times. He called on Ta'if people to accept his religion through reciting Quran and explaining his ideas. He insulted their religion and culture with arrogance, calling them wrongdoers for believing in many gods or corrupted religions. He warned them that if they did not surrender to his god and accept him as their leader, they would suffer Allah's wrath.

The people of Ta'if were not as simple as the Meccans; they chased Mohammad out of their city by force. They pelted him with stones for insulting their religion and attempting to breach the peace in their society. They understood that this man's goal was to become the absolute ruler through recruiting and mobilising the troubled, rogue and naïve individuals against the rest of the society. They did not allow him to settle in their town to divide the society and consequently ruin the city. He did not stand up to the people, and Allah did not protect him from the children's stones. He cried and felt lonely and helpless while being chased away. His bitter complaints and pleas to Allah in the hope for a divine retribution against the people of Taif, are a famous prayer Muslims repeat while in despair: "I complain to you my god from my weakness, lack of support and the people's rejection... To whom do You leave me? To a stranger who receives me with resentment. Or to an enemy you have given authority over me? If you are not angry at me then I don't mind... to you I submit."[145]

Mohammad took his revenge on this city with an army a few years later. After this failed trip, Mohammad was afraid to enter Mecca as he had committed treason by attempting to forge an alliance with the enemies of the Meccans. Thus, he stayed in a cave on the outskirts of Mecca and sent messengers to prominent Meccans seeking their protection. Two of the approached individuals rejected his request but the third one agreed and declared that Mohammad was under his protection. He along with his sons stood guard while Mohammad entered the Kaaba and freely practiced his religion.[146]

145 Al-Tabarani, S. ibn A. (2006). Al-Mujam Al-kabir (Arabic). Dar Al Kotob Alilmiyah.
146 Ibn Saad, M. (1998). Al-Tabaqat al-kubra.; The History of al-Tabarī, Vol. 6-8.; Sahih al-Bukhari 3139.

6 Violence, Blood, and Endless War

FAILED PROPHET SEARCHING FOR ABODE

After his failure in Mecca and Ta'if, Mohammad shifted his attention toward Yathrib. He appreciated the potential of this city, the nature of its people and the deep-rooted hatred between the poor, violent peasants of Yathrib and the rich, civilised merchants of Mecca. The people of Yathrib or, to be more precise, the Arab inhabitants of Yathrib were susceptible to any new dogma that would unite them and allow them to attack their rich Jewish neighbours as well as their traditional rivals – the Meccans. This town did not have a regime – there was no ruler or governing board like in Mecca. Instead, there were several minor tribal chieftains competing for limited resources. Mohammad kept approaching people who came from Yathrib to Mecca, hoping to convince them to join him. In the twelfth year into his crusade, he succeeded in converting a dozen of individuals from Yathrib. The following year, they brought around seventy people who accepted Islam as their religion and Mohammad as their leader. The converts were hoping that Mohammad, with the help of his followers, would end the internal conflict that had devastated their town for decades. They wanted to establish a new political order that would benefit them as individuals. They all pledged allegiance to Mohammad, vowing to fight to the death for him if he moved to their country. This allegiance of the people of Yathrib was the turning point in the history of Islam and in Mohammad's life. Rather than being a self-proclaimed prophet trying to gain followers through reasoning, he became a warlord supported by the swords of his followers. Islam became a warriors' creed and Mohammad – its eternal master.

Thirteen years after he had declared himself a prophet in Mecca, Mohammad, with around a hundred followers, immigrated to this town to join seventy-two locals who had converted to Islam.[147] Yathrib was an insignificant, poor farming town, situated 200 miles away from Mecca. It was on the trade route between Syria and Yemen, with more sweet water, palm trees and better weather in comparison to Mecca but of no commercial or spiritual importance. Its people made their living from farming palm trees – the only crop that could survive the desert heat – and a few basic industries. Unlike Mecca, which had a big port nearby, Yathrib was isolated from marine routes. The town was known to Mohammad from his commercial trips.

Two main Arab tribes and three Jewish communities lived in Yathrib. The Arab tribes were in a state of constant war against each other over the limited resources and ongoing tribal feuds. The animosity between them was deep-rooted. The Jewish communities, in turn, were living in forts surrounded by orchards, insulated against the never-ending Arab vendettas. They were farmers, weapon makers and savvy traders, which allowed them to be independent from their surroundings. Upon his arrival, Mohammad declared himself a prophet and a ruler of the Muslims and signed peace treaties with the Jewish communities.

The Arabs in Yathrib were deprived in comparison to their Meccan rivals. What made Mecca rich was its tolerance: anyone could come and live there, and anyone could trade; different ideas, religions, races and cultures coexisted peacefully in that city. Mecca was surrounded by rigid mountains which along with its spiritual status provided sufficient protection from Bedouin invasions. Yathrib, in contrast, did not enjoy natural or spiritual barricades and was hence dependent on its people, who were vicious fighters, to fend off any attacks. More importantly, the Arabs of Yathrib did not have advanced political or social establishments. Each one of the two main tribes consisted of several branches, and each one of these branches had its own leader. As a consequence, most of these people were willing to accept an absolute king who could unite them.

Highlighting the failure of Mohammad in Mecca and his subsequent shift toward violence is still a crime in the Muslim world. It

147 Sahih al-Bukhari 2757, 3892, 3897; The History of al-Tabarī, Vol. 6.

always has been, and one suspects it always will be, since it negates the rationale of Islam as a religion that spread through its intellectual prowess. For example, in October 1999, Dr Ahmad Al Baghdadi, a University of Edinburgh graduate and prominent professor of political science in Kuwait University, was sentenced to one month in jail for writing in an article that Mohammad failed in converting the people of Mecca to Islam.[148] Uttering this simple factual statement was considered a crime by the criminal court and the Court of Appeal in Kuwait. The judges wrote in their sentence that Al Baghdadi was guilty of insulting the basic beliefs of Islam. The ideas of Islam must be respected and not be used as a subject of mockery or ridicule, the judges stated. They further indicated that Mohammad was the messenger of Allah and his acts and words were sacred, as they were revelations from Allah. Every human must respect and adore Mohammad and follow his guidance, the judges ruled.

Al Baghdadi went on a hunger strike to protest the injustice inflicted on him and his health deteriorated as he had a prior heart condition. He was coerced into apologising for what he had written and pleaded for a pardon from the Amir of Kuwait. He was released after serving two weeks in jail. The professor did not recover from this ordeal.

After his release from jail, the Kuwaiti government kept harassing Al Baghdadi in almost every possible way. In 2005, he was charged, prosecuted and sentenced to one year in jail with a three-year suspension for stating in an article that he wanted his children to study music rather than Quran. He wrote that music makes the person a better human; he did not criticize Quran or Islam, but the judges inferred from his writing that he meant so. In that article, he was simply opposing the new regulation enforced by the Kuwaiti government on both public and private schools in Kuwait, which increased the mandatory classes of Quran and Islamic studies, replacing other subjects, especially music, science and art. He said that he was educating his children in private, Western schools from his own wallet and he wished that the government would refrain from imposing Islamic studies on these

148 Human Rights Watch. (1999, 12 Oct). Imprisoned Kuwaiti Scholar: Academic Leaders Demand Release.

schools at the expense of the curriculum. This was a crime in the eyes of the Kuwaiti rulers and their judges. Al Baghdadi died in 2010 at the age of 59 and to this day Islamists refer to him as an enemy of Islam who sought to corrupt Muslim youth.

FROM A PROPHET TO TSAR:
EXODUS AND THE FIRST ISLAMIC STATE

From the first moment he set his foot in Yathrib, Mohammad acted as an absolute tsar who derived his authority from Allah and disregarded the people. He renamed the town Medina ("city") and changed his followers' names to cut any relation with the previous religions and identities. He established a brotherhood bond between his followers that was supposed to transcend all the existing bonds, including blood. He asked every Arab man from Yathrib to choose one of the incomers – the immigrants – as his brother in Islam.[149] It is reported that some of the people of Yathrib would give their immigrant brothers half of their property, and some offered to divorce one of their wives so the immigrant could marry her.

He instructed his followers to sever their connections with all non-Muslims whom he labelled infidels, even if they were their parents, siblings, friends, neighbours, partners or companions. He reconstructed himself and his followers versus everyone else: "Muhammad is the messenger of Allah. And those with him are ruthless against the disbelievers and merciful among themselves."[150] This idea of one supreme leader and a united nation was appealing to those desperate people who were seeking a dictator saviour to rule them.

Mohammad succeeded in creating a new type of state that revolved around him, a state where all powers were concentrated in one man's hand. He was the absolute ruler and the only representative of the one God, all at once. Islam was established as a totalitarian collective identity that binds its members together and differentiates them from everyone else, with Mohammad as its nucleus.[151] Muslims worldwide celebrate the

---

149 Sahih al-Bukhari: 3937; The History of al-Tabari, Vol. 7.; Ibn al-Athir, Vol. 2.
150 Quran 48:29.
151 In contrast to Sherif's (1958) Realistic Conflict Theory and Tajfel's Social Identity Theory (SIT), here we see collective identity being created through discourse to establish boundaries

immigration (Al-Hijra) as the most important event in the establishment of Islam and the first day in their calendar.[152] The Islamic political system established by Mohammad, as Muslims believe, lasted from January of 622 CE until August of 1923 when the last Islamic state was dissolved as a result of a humiliating military defeat the Ottoman Caliphate suffered at the hands of the Allied forces.

between the members on the one hand and the rest of the people on the other hand. For further discussion see Antaki, C., & Widdicombe, S. (Eds.). (1998). Identities in talk. Sage.
152 Dates according to this calendar are denoted AH.

JIHAD

Allah has purchased of the believers their lives and their properties; for the price that theirs shall be the paradise. They fight in Allah's cause, so they kill and are killed.[153]

Allah

O prophet, fight (Jahid) against the disbelievers and the hypocrites and be harsh upon them.[154]

Allah

Immediately after his arrival in Yathrib around 623 CE, Mohammad established an army and started what he defined as the holy war – jihad[155] – to subjugate the Arabian Peninsula to his rule. The forces created by Mohammad were different from any other known at that time in Arabia, if not the whole world. Three factors contributed to the initial military successes: the militarised nature of Yathrib's society, as every person in this town was a fighter by default; secondly, the uncompromising mentality of extreme monotheism that claimed to possess the absolute truth which had existed in Arabia as a reaction to polytheism. The last and most decisive factor was the power void created by the last two Byzantine-Sasanian wars.

Every Muslim became a soldier in this religion-driven army. Whenever Mohammad decided to attack a caravan or a town, he would form an armed corps and appoint its leader. Once the force finished the mission, it was automatically dissolved, and soldiers went back to their civilian life. There was no permanent military centre or formal hierarchy within the Muslim army. Mohammad exercised his power and delivered his orders from the mosque where all Muslim males gathered five times daily. It was

---

153 Quran 9:11. Marmaduke Pickthall's translation.
154 Quran 9:73, Sahih International trans. Most of the other translators used the word "strive" for jihad, which is not accurate.
155 This word is mentioned in Quran 26 times with the same meaning, and the word "fight" is mentioned 38 times.

obligatory for every male to attend the five prayers in the mosque, where he would listen to the instructions of the prophet that covered all aspects of life. Mohammad threatened Muslims who did not attend the dawn prayer that he would burn them inside their homes. Haj (pilgrimage), where the followers would come together from all over the world, was another occasion when Muslims could convene to unite and receive instructions.

Mohammad made sure not to appoint a deputy or allow anyone to become the second in command throughout his life. He would assign a different chief each time he formed a corps to attack a specific tribe or town, if he was not to join the force. Otherwise, he was the one and only leader by default. This strategy prevented any person from acquiring permanent power and hence becoming a threat. In fact, during his reign he made sure to appoint individuals with no prior authority or charisma as military leaders or town governors, side-lining ambitious personalities who could pose a real threat to his authority. This strategy is embraced by Muslim rulers to this day. It concentrates the power in the hands of one person and limits the opposition but at the same time creates dysfunctional states because everything and everyone is controlled by one mortal person. Consequently, almost every time a Muslim ruler falls sick or dies, a crisis ensues, there is no difference between kingdoms and republics. Most importantly, in the first Islamic state there was no distinction between the civilians and the military as all Muslims were part of the army – a tradition that persists to this day in many regions.

During their first year in the new capital, Mohammad and his followers waged numerous raids against commercial caravans and defenceless villages. These unprovoked sudden attacks were sanctioned and promoted by Allah in the Quran as a duty: "Allah has purchased of the believers their lives and their properties; for the price that theirs shall be the paradise. They fight in Allah's cause, so they kill and are killed." This verse establishes killing other people and getting killed as a must to save oneself from hell and secure a place in heaven. Mohammad decreed in several sayings that any time a Muslim kills people, he has the right to take their possessions, and if a Muslim captures a person, then he owns them.[156]

---

156 Sahih Muslim 3339, 3400, 3401.

In another verse, Allah legitimated jihad by presenting it as a sound reaction to prior injustice: "Permission is given to those who fight because they have been persecuted; and Allah is indeed able to give them victory, Allah will defend those who believe; surely Allah does not love anyone who is unfaithful, ungrateful."[157] Here, raiding vulnerable people has been justified as a reaction to prior injustice and through casting the targets as infidels. This discourse is still being used by Muslims to justify unprovoked attacks against defenceless people.

Allah instructed the believers to wage war against non-Muslims starting with those nearest to them: "O you who believe, fight those of the disbelievers who are near to you, and let them find harshness in you, and know that Allah is with those who keep their duty."[158] Mohammad and his companions raided small towns and villages starting with the weaker and gradually moving toward the stronger ones. The vast majority of the victims had never interacted with Mohammad or his followers. They were attacked because they gained the status of infidels in the eyes of Mohammad and because Muslims wanted to subjugate them to his reign, take their properties, and annex their land. This simple fact known and promoted by almost all senior Islamic jurists, is sometimes disguised with fabrications which present jihad as self-defence or a reaction to prior aggression. Some current Muslim propagandists are even portraying raiding commercial caravans and kidnapping women and children as self-defence. Meanwhile, all the original books use the words invasions and raids to describe these events.

Sahih al-Bukhari, Sahih Muslim, Tarikh al-Tabarī, and all the other hadith and history volumes describe in detail the numerous invasions and raids waged by Mohammad. They state clearly that it was Muslims who were on the offensive in most of these conflicts to spread Islam by violence.

The first Islamic raid took place six months after Mohammad's arrival to Medina. He sent a cavalry to capture a commercial caravan passing between Mecca and Medina. Mohammad appointed his uncle Hamza as the chief of this armed force. The merchants and guards of the caravan were prepared to fight, thus, the Muslims withdrew. In another

---

157 Quran 22:38-39.
158 Quran 9:123.

attack known as Nakhla Raid, Mohammad sent his followers to raid commercial caravans near Mecca during a sacred month that was considered by Arabs a period of peace in which no fighting could begin or continue. The Muslims ambushed a convoy that was en route between Mecca and Ta'if, far away from Yathrib (Medina), killing and capturing the merchants and looting their possessions. The victims were busy preparing their food when they were attacked.[159] The immediate goal of these jihadi missions was to ransack the goods and kidnap people. The main target, however, was far more ambitious: an attempt to terrorize the Arabian Peninsula and break the people's will to fight. Through attacking the backbone of the economy – trade expeditions, Muslims wanted to force all the Arabs to surrender.

The word jihad is a central, discursive concept and a mental construct in the Muslim mentality. It comes from the word effort, and it means fighting with suffering. This concept creates a mental image of Muslim fighters struggling while undertaking the hard labour of combating the many enemies of Allah.[160] This concept is designed to rebuke the opposite imagery and connotations of killing and ransacking defenceless people for personal gains. This notion eases the fighters' psychological distress resulting from perceiving themselves as murderers and robbers who are attacking their own people. The Quran acknowledged the aversion to jihad among Muslims but encouraged them to disregard their conscience. Their sceptical ideas were constructed as evil notions produced by the devil to diverge them from the right track. This is a clear example of reaction formation, which is used to refute an existing real negative characteristic through claiming and exaggerating its opposite. Muslims counter the argument that they are slavers, thieves and murderers who attack civilians for evil motives through claiming that they are simply obeying God's orders altruistically despite their personal suffering.

Instead of admitting that they earned their living through raiding caravans and kidnapping women and children, they portrayed themselves as implementing the orders of the master of the universe: it was

---

159 The History of al-Ṭabarī, Vol. 7.; Ibn al-Athir, Vol. 2.
160 See Riches, D. (1991). Aggression, war, violence: Space/time and paradigm. Man 26(2), 281-297.

not their desires that motivated them – it was Allah who ordered them to be ruthless: "Fight them so that Allah will torture them by your hands and disgrace them and give you victory over them and heal the hearts of believing people."[161] This justification is still being used today: "We attacked France, targeted its population, civilians, but there was nothing personal," stated Salah Abdeslam, the member of the ISIS group that carried out the Bataclan massacre in 2015, in court.

In early jihadi attacks, the Muslims killed and captured vulnerable people, confiscated their belongings and spread terror all over Arabia. In the name of Allah, every non-Muslim was a target. The Muslim mujahedeen' tactics were simple but extremely decisive. They would take their victims by surprise, attack a soft target with no warning and show extreme brutality to terrorise other people and defeat them psychologically. More importantly, they justified each and every attack through vilifying the victims and presenting them as evil subhuman criminals that must be cleansed. When they attacked a Jewish town, they would accuse the targeted community of conspiring against Muslims. When they attacked an Arab tribe, they would claim that this tribe was planning to attack them and have been collaborating with their enemies. The accusations they levelled against their enemies were attributed to Allah, thus were indisputable.

During the last nine years of his life, Mohammad waged over thirty raids and invasions. Muslims intercepted many caravans and confiscated their goods and captured the people. They killed whoever dared to resist and went back with their spoils to Medina, feeling virtuous.[162] Mohammad personally headed several of these invasions and killed at least one person with his hand. The attacks were growing more sophisticated with time. This type of warfare was something the world had never seen before. Although looting, destruction, and kidnapping was as old as humanity, it had always been a sin that brought disgrace and disrespect on its perpetrator. It was the first time armed Arabs justified attacking commercial caravans through religious beliefs rather than personal need or criminal motives. It was not the usual robbery or

161 Quran 9:14.
162 The History of al-Tabarī, Vol. 7.

tribal vendetta, limited to specific goals, enemies and time. It was the beginning of the eternal holy war: jihad.

Through constructing all non-Muslims as a threat and as enemies of Allah that must be eliminated, believers did not need to create an elaborate, specific war discourse against each and every group they attacked. The fact that they were not bound by any ethical code when dealing with non-Muslims gave them a clear advantage over their victims, who had several binding codes of ethics and were not aware of having been constructed as existential enemies that must be wiped out.

After every battle, Mohammad divided the spoils among his fighters as he pleased. When some of his fighters disagreed with how he distributed the spoils, he produced a Quranic passage which announced that Mohammad had the right to allocate the war spoils the way he deemed suitable after acquiring one fifth of everything for himself. This completed Mohammad's bid to be the one and only source of power, as he now controlled the wealth in addition to spirituality, legislation and armed forces. Nonparticipation in jihad or defecting during battles were major crimes punishable by death.[163]

With every successful attack, the numbers and power of the Muslims rose, and their enemies' will to fight deteriorated. Over the years, the opportunists, psychopaths, as well as the defeated, converted to Islam.[164] Many from the conquered people along with their offspring came to be fighters for Islam. They became willing to give up their lives for the religion that destroyed their ancestors. Psychologists coined the term "Stockholm syndrome" to describe the abnormal cognitive bond that can develop between captors and prisoners, which can explain this behaviour. The kidnapping of Patty Hearst, who was held hostage and later participated in a bank robbery with the Symbionese Liberation Army is a classic example.

Some victims affiliate with their captives and adopt their reasoning in an attempt to make sense of their suffering and their defeat in a way that allows them to retain some agency. Through portraying their aggressors as benevolent, they create a hope for survival. One can see through

---

163 Quran; Sahih al-Bukhari 2864, 2865; Sahih Muslim 1740.
164 Sahih al-Bukhari; The History of al-Tabarī, Vol. 7, 8, 9.

a thorough examination of the defeats of societies of Iraq, Iran, Egypt and North Africa, that Muslim invasions have succeeded in obliterating the identities, languages and collective consciousness of the peoples of these nations. The conquered people have been perceiving Arabs in general, and the descendants of Mohammad in particular, as their masters, while they look down on their own ancestors. To this day, coming from Mohammad's lineage brings a person prestige and power in those lands. Currently, several heads of states claim to be descendants of Mohammad. In Iran, the current and the previous supreme leaders both claimed to be biological offspring of Mohammad to legitimise their rule over the Persian nation. The Jordanian as well as the Moroccan ruling families both claim to be nobles because they come from Mohammad. Saddam Hussein also maintained that he was a descendant of Mohammad to boost his legitimacy among Muslims.

They take the wife away from her husband and slay him like a sheep. They throw the babe from her mother and drive her into slavery; the child calls out from the ground and the mother hears, yet what is she to do?[165]

Before Islam, there was an ethical code regulating the wars, respected in the Arabian Peninsula. This code guaranteed that the wars between Arabs would never reach the level of genocide. It declared four months as sacred months during which no fighting was allowed.[166] It also limited the killing and enslaving of Arab women and children. Most importantly, caravans and commercial routes were spared from raids as they were the vital source of goods and income for Arabs – without them life would not continue in the arid desert. Religious places as well as main markets were considered off limit, too. Since water was considered sacred, it was not permitted for fighting sides to destroy water wells. These laws were respected by all Arabs with the exception of bandits (sa'alik) who were living in the mountains and the uninhabited deserts as they were disowned by their clans for their crimes.

Muslim forces allied with the bandits and received licence from Allah to breach all these rules in their fight to spread Islam and subjugate humanity. They were not bound by any ethical code in their dealings with non-Muslims. They deceived their enemies, they broke the treaties they signed, and they attacked villages and caravans during the sacred months, killing unarmed people. They kidnapped married women and turned them into sex-slaves. They carried out genocides against peaceful towns and tribes. They assassinated civilians without a warning. They

---

165 A description of the way Muslim invaders dealt with the conquered people of Damascus in the seventh century. Pseudo-Ephraem. Sermon on the End of Times, 62., as cited in Hoyland, R.G. (1997). Seeing Islam as Others Saw It: A Survey and Evaluation of Christian, Jewish and Zoroastrian Writings on Early Islam. Darwin Press, pp 260-262.
166Ali, J. (1993). The Detailed History of the Arabs Before Islam. Third Ed. Dar al-Alam.

even attacked Mecca with a huge army, killing people who took refuge in the Kaaba. There are several sayings of Mohammad that sanction the killing of women and children – for instance, it is written in Sahih Muslim that: "The Messenger of Allah was asked about the polytheists whose land was attacked at night so some of their women and children were killed or hurt." He said: "They are from among them."[167] This hadith states clearly that the indiscriminate killing of people is legal in Islam. There is not one verse nor hadith that considers killing non-Muslim children or women a crime. At best, there are some sayings that discourage such an act but without specific consequences. Thus, it has been carried out by devoted Muslims over the ages.

Mohammad's fighters felt virtuous while committing these acts as there was a divine rationale that promoted and justified them. Many of these soldiers were criminals before turning to Islam, and so were psychologically primed to accept such a rationale. They were willing to kill and raid peaceful people but needed the justification and the impunity. The Islamic ideology provided them with the much-needed justification for continuing their criminal livelihood with less guilt.

Bandits (sa'alik) also played a significant role in Muslim battles as they were Mohammad's allies and spies. Like many of the early Muslims, they found a shelter in Islam from their distress and the society's rejection. Unlike the Bedouin invasions, Muslims did not leave towns and cities after their raids – they conquered and settled. They turned the populations of the defeated towns and cities into slaves that served them. Every time the Muslim army captured a town, they would recruit some of its people and turn them against their own society. In Arabia, invasions prior to Islam were not an aim, they were a means of settling tribal disputes or g aining resources. In Islam, annihilating non-Muslims was a virtuous goal set by Allah. It was also the only means for Islam to survive and spread. In the Quran and Mohammad's acts and words, killing other people was constructed as a vital act to spread Islam; looting the defeated people was Allah's reward, and enslaving women and children was benevolent. It was advantageous for the slaves

---

167 Sahih al-Bukhari 146; Sahih Muslim 1745.

because they would be introduced to Islam and thus, they might be saved from the eternal fire.

One of central Islamic ideas is the notion that "war is deception."[168] This idea has been recognized by Muslims as a valid belief. The most trusted Sunni books: Sahih al-Bukhari and Sahih Muslim both attribute this saying to Mohammad. Shia senior theologians (ayatollahs) also have been propagating this saying as an authentic Islamic principle that must be embraced by Muslims, as it was established by Mohammad and his successors.

---

168 Sahih al-Bukhari 2864; Sahih Muslim 3377.

BATTLE OF BADR

I will cast terror into the hearts of those who disbelieve. Therefore,
strike off their heads and strike off every fingertip of them [169]

The first major battle of Islam is called the "Badr Invasion" after the water
wells where it took place in 624, less than a year after Mohammad's
emigration to Yathrib. The story of this battle is reported in all of hadith
books, biographies and in the Quran.[170] It is part of the school curriculum in Muslim countries. Also, Islamic schools in non-Muslim countries
ingrain this story into young children's memories but many Muslim
moderates tend to suppress it when discussing Islam. The story of this
battle starts when Mohammad finds out through his spies that Mecca's
main caravan is passing near Medina on its way from Syria to Mecca.[171]
The caravan had more than a thousand camels carrying all types of goods.
It was carrying the wealth of Meccans and other people who traded with
them. There were a few armed guards accompanying the caravan.

Mohammad mobilised an army to attack the caravan and confiscate
the goods and seize the people. Muslim historians and scholars report
that all Muslims, young and old, rushed to join this army. Muslim soldiers
were barefoot and half-naked, anxious to seize the wealth of the Meccans. There were more than three hundred armed Muslims, every three
or four of them sharing a camel, and the whole army had only one or
two horses, according to Muslim historians and hadith narrators. They
set up an ambush for the caravan. The news of the ambush was leaked,
and less than a thousand man rushed from Mecca to rescue their wealth.
The Meccans travelled for over 300 miles through the hot dry desert. As
a precaution, the caravan's chief circumvented the ambush and went
through the Arabian desert away from Yathrib without an adequate
amount of water. When the armed Meccans arrived near Yathrib, they

169 Quran 8:12.
170 The History of al-Tabarī, Vol. 7.; Ibn al-Athir, Vol. 2.
171 Sahih al-Bukhari 3951.

realised that Mohammad had not succeeded in seizing their goods. They were of two minds: some did not want to engage the Muslims, while others thought that confronting them could prevent future attacks. In the end, as a compromise the Meccans decided to go to Badr to rest and celebrate their triumph.

In contrast, Mohammad wanted a war. He resented returning to his capital empty handed. He knew that his soldiers were in a better shape in comparison to the exhausted Meccans, who were far away from their hometown. He knew that they needed to pass by Badr's water to refill their water bladders. Mohammad preceded them to Badr and ordered his soldiers to destroy all the wells except a few ones he could easily protect and control. This act, which violated the ancient code of war respected by Arabs, was decisive in the Muslims' victory. The Meccans were trapped: they could not turn around and go home without water – they risked dying of thirst and exhaustion in the desert. They might have also been attacked by Mohammad's army from the rear if they decided to withdraw. They did not have any option but to fight, at least in order to reach the water.

The battle took place between less than a thousand Meccans and over three hundred Muslims, according to the Islamic resources. In the beginning, several Meccans tried to reach the water to drink but Muslim fighters killed them. Then the two forces clashed and ultimately, the Muslim army defeated the tired and thirsty Meccans, killing around seventy people and capturing another seventy. More importantly, they took the property of the defeated Meccans: horses, weapons, money and clothes. After the end of the battle, the Muslims took their spoils and went back to their capital, and the surviving Meccans went back to their homeland.

The Quran contradicts itself in explaining this victory. According to one verse, Allah sent five thousand angels to fight with the Muslims[172], but in another verse, the number of the fighting angels was just one thousand.[173] Muslims reported that some Meccans were killed by invisible creatures.[174] Throughout this battle, Mohammad stayed in

---

172 Quran 3:123-126.
173 Quran 8:9.
174 Sahih al-Bukhari; Sahih Muslim 1384.

a shaded high place, watching his soldiers (and the angels) massacring the people who had allowed him to preach his religion in their country unhampered for thirteen years.

One of the leaders of the Meccan army was Amr Ibn Hisham, who was titled the "Father of Wisdom" – Abu al Hakam – by his countrymen. In contrast, Mohammad called him the "Father of Ignorance" for rejecting Islam in Mecca. He had described him as an enemy of Allah and encouraged his followers to insult him.[175] This person had shown great tolerance in response to Mohammad's constant attacks against him, his religion and his people in Mecca. In Badr, Mohammad ordered his followers to search for this man and murder him. Several Muslims deceived the old sage and stabbed him to death. After they killed him, they mutilated his body and beheaded him. The Muslim soldiers took Amr's severed head to Mohammad, who blessed the killers and celebrated the beheading of his enemy.[176] This reaction of Mohammad toward Amr Ibn Hesham is an example of a behavioural pattern. Mohammad held deep rancour toward all the prominent people of Arabia. He hated the aristocrats and encouraged his followers to be ruthless and deceptive in their attacks against them.

Most of the Islamic principles of war were established in this battle. Muslims used water as a weapon: they killed thirsty and weak people. Many of the believers killed their relatives; the way one of the Muslims beheaded his own father and how another one killed his brother has been praised as an altruistic deed. Allah and Mohammad sanctioned the slaying of prisoners of war and the mutilation of dead bodies as necessary means to spread Islam. They also authorized the enslaving of prisoners and taking ransom for releasing them.[177] Finally, in this battle the belief in Islam transcended all other relationships. The world was divided into two fighting spheres: the land of Islam (Dar al-Islam) versus the land of war (Dar al-Harb).[178] This division has not ceased yet in the Muslim psyche.

---

175 Sahih al-Bukhari 3969.
176 Sahih al-Bukhari 396, 3962, 3963.
177 See Sahih al-Bukhari, Sahih Muslim, and The History of al-Tabarī, Vol. 7; Ibn al-Athir, Vol. 2.
178 According to this notion, every country not ruled by Muslims is in war with Islam.

THE IMPORTANCE OF BADR

In several contemporary Muslim armies, there is a unit named Badr. The oldest and most powerful Iraqi Shia militia, which has been part of the Iraqi government since 2003 and to this day, is called Badr Brigades. This armed militia was founded in Iran in 1982 by the Iranian regime to fight against Iraq. Its members were recruited from among the Iraqi Shia soldiers captured by the Iranian Army who were willing to fight alongside the Shia Iranian soldiers. The idea behind its name is that it embodies an extension of the Muslim fighters who defeated the infidels in Badr. In this case, the Iraqi Shia were justifying fighting for the Iranian regime against their country by constructing themselves as an extension of the early Muslims, who fought against their own people. The fact that the initial goal of the Muslims in Badr was to ransack a caravan is obscured from the Muslim psyche. Muslim regimes have been promoting this battle and many similar ones as heroic victories of Islam.

BEHEADING CAPTIVES

That is because they opposed Allah and His messenger and who opposes Allah and His messenger Allah is severe in punishment[179]

In many contemporary terrorist attacks, we see Muslims beheading their "enemies". For instance, in 2002, the American journalist Daniel Pearl was kidnapped in Pakistan and forced to identify himself and his parents as Jewish and beg for his life before his captors slit his throat. They recorded the entire event and it was published online. In 2020, a Muslim terrorist beheaded the teacher Samuel Patty in the middle of the street in Paris after stabbing him several times for discussing cartoons of Mohammad in his history class.

These are not deviations from sharia, in the sense that Mohammad himself sanctioned and practiced the beheading of infidels and enemies of Islam (which included anyone who was not Muslim or who was not Muslim enough or not in the right way). In the second year of his reign, according to the original Islamic books of hadith and history[180], after the Battle of Badr, Mohammad ordered his followers to behead two prominent prisoners. One of them was Auqba Ibn Moyet, a cultured man who challenged and debated Mohammad in Mecca repeatedly.[181] He was an influential thinker who had rejected Islam and accused Mohammad of being an impostor but had never harmed him. He begged Mohammad to spare his life, yet Mohammad ordered his followers to slaughter the captive immediately. The powerless man screamed:

'Why would I be killed?'
'For your animosity to Allah and his messenger,' Mohammad replied.
The prisoner asked: 'Who would look after my young children?'
'The fire,' was Mohammad's answer.[182]

179 Quran 8:13.
180 The History of al-Tabarī, Vol. 7.; Ibn al-Athir, Vol. 2.
181 Ibn Kathir, A. (1992). Al-Bidaya wa al-Nihaya [The Beginning and the End].
182 The History of al-Tabarī, Vol. 7., pp 65-66.; Ibn al-Athir, Vol. 2, p 132.

Mohammad then instructed one of his soldiers to kill the prisoner through wounding him and letting him bleed to death. After his soldier carried out the order, Mohammad thanked Allah for granting him the joy of killing that helpless person.[183]

The second prisoner was a famous Arab intellectual, Nader Ibn Al-Harith.[184] This man was a citizen of the world, who had extensively travelled and lived in the centres of civilization. Like his father, he had studied in Persia as well as Alexandria. He was a musician, poet, physician and a student of philosophy – a noble man of great knowledge and integrity.[185] Meccans considered him a role model and an intellectual authority. After Mohammad declared himself Allah's messenger, Nader debated him several times. Nader challenged Mohammad to provide tangible proofs for his claims. He also criticised the Quran and Mohammad's ideas, showing their flaws and contradictions, and he highlighted their Jewish, Greek and Christian origins.[186] He contended that what Mohammad was reciting were myths inaccurately taken from the ancient civilizations and religions.

Mohammad never forgave Nader. The fact that Nader did not harm Mohammad physically or insult him, although he could have, did not matter to the prophet. The man was captured in Badr. Nader asked his captors to help him, saying that if the situation had been the opposite and they had been captured by the Meccans, he would have helped them. One of Mohammad's companions replied: "You are honest, and I know you would have, but Islam has cut our ties with all non-Muslims."[187] Mohammad ordered his cousin Ali to execute the intellectual of Mecca. The beheading of Nader has been portrayed in many paintings as well as in Muslims' poetry over the ages as a great triumph for Islam. It was the establishment of the Islamic tradition of slaughtering both prisoners and intellectuals – a tradition that has been practiced by both rulers and masses throughout the ages.

---

183 As above.
184 As above.
185 Al-Baladhuri, A. (1996). Ansab al-Ashraf [Genealogies of nobles]. (Arabic). Dar al-Feker.
186 As above.
187 As above.

Muslims were joyful and proud of their victory over the Meccans. When one of them remarked that all what they had done was killing thirsty old men who had not been prepared to fight, he was scolded by the prophet.[188] The dead bodies were thrown into the Badr well to further humiliate their people and show the cruelty of the new religion.

Mohammad and his senior followers discussed what to do with the rest of the prisoners, after murdering the two prominent ones. Some suggested that they should be all burned to death; others – that they could be freed if their folks paid ransom. Mohammad agreed with the latter: he demanded a heavy ransom in exchange for releasing the captives. Allah disapproved of this decision after it was executed.[189] Allah declared that "it is not for a prophet to have captives until he inflicts massacres in the lands but you want the goods of this life while Allah wants you to desire the afterlife and Allah is the almighty and wise."[190] In this passage, Allah has established the killing of captives as the upright course of action. Enslaving captives is less virtuous in comparison to slaughter. Mohammad went ahead with his initial plan and took money to release his prisoners. He seemed more merciful than Allah, as he was satisfied with killing specific individuals, enslaving some of the captives and freeing the rest in exchange for money. He distributed the spoils among his soldiers according to his evaluation of their performance in the fighting but after he had taken one fifth of everything for himself.

The battle of Badr is part of the Muslim psyche. Muslim governments and institutions commemorate this battle constantly as the divine victory. It is taught in schools as a source of laws, principles and ethics. Muslims worldwide study this war and infer rules and guidance from its events. Countless films and documentaries have been financed by petrol-rich governments to promote this battle. I attended a celebration of this battle in Manchester – similar to the ones that take place in mosques and schools all over the Muslim world – in which the imam affirmed that all the acts of Muslims were honourable deeds which everyone must

---

188 The History of al-Ṭabarī, Vol. 7.
189 As above.
190 Quran 8:67.

aspire to imitate. He highlighted how in this battle many Muslims had killed their close relatives and had taken their belongings.[191]

The same theme is repeated in the 1976 movie "The Message" financed by Muammar al-Gaddafi, the Amir of Kuwait[192], and king Hassan of Morocco. The film glorifies the victory of Badr and the beheading of infidels. In that film Anthony Quinn plays the role of Mohammad's uncle Hamza, introduced as the ruthless killer hero who beheads several people. In numerous scenes, the slaying of infidels at the hands of Muslims is presented as a moral act. Jihad is portrayed as an application of God's orders. Non-Muslims are vilified, and their annihilation is endorsed. The film appears in both English and Arabic and cost millions of dollars. (Ironically, the director of the film, Mustapha Akkad, was killed with his daughter in the 2005 Amman suicide bombings that were carried out by Al-Qaeda).

The Meccans along with the rest of Arabs were appalled by Mohammad's military tactics and his cruelty. They saw what happened in Badr as a proof that Mohammad was not a holy man, let alone a messenger of Allah. The renowned knight Al-Aswad Al-Nahshali documented the Arabs' reaction to the events of Badr in a famous poem:

> Inside the water well of Badr landed honourable Arab men and youth
> Kabsha's son is promising that we will resurrect
> What would be the life of carcasses and remains?
> He is incapable of preventing my death
> But would resuscitate me after my bones had decayed!
> Tell god that I am deserting the fasting month
> Tell Allah to take away my food
> And tell Allah to take away my drink[193]

As a consequence of their victory in Badr, Muslims grew overconfident, aggressive and rich. Shortly after the battle, one of Mohammad's followers

---

191 The History of al-Tabarī, Vol. 7.
192 Kuwait's Amir withdrew his support for the film due to the Saudi government's objection to it but could not recover the funds he had contributed.
193 Al-Nahshali. A. (1970). Diwan Al-Aswad Al-Nahshali. Heritage Books. Iraqi Ministry of Culture. (Author's translation.)

sneaked into the house of the female poet Asma bint Marwan, who had criticized Mohammad, in the dark of the night. He found her breastfeeding her infant while her other children were sleeping around her. He removed the infant off the scared mother's chest and stabbed her with his sword.[194] He kept pushing the sword into her until it went through her body, taking her life and leaving her children without a mother. Then he went to Mohammad to report to him what he had done. Mohammad praised this cowardly assassin and told his companions "to look at this man if they wanted to see a true believer."[195]

194 Ibn Saad, M. (1998). Al-Tabaqat al-kubra. Dar Sader.
195 Al-Wakidy [Al-Waqidi], Mohammad. (1856). History of Muhammad's Campaigns [Kitab al-Maghazi]. (Ed. A. von Kremer), pp 173; 858. Baptist Mission Press.

ALLAH CLAIMS RESPONSIBILITY

One of the most influential chapters of Quran is Al-Anfal (the Spoils). In this chapter Allah sanctions jihad and slavery in explicit language understandable to native speakers to this day. It was conveyed after the Battle of Badr. In this revelation Allah takes responsibility for the killing of non-Muslims, stating: "You did not slay them, but it was Allah Who slew them, and you did not strike when you stroke, it was Allah Who stroke, and that he might confer upon the believers a good gift from Himself, surely Allah is hearing, knowing."[196] This discourse inoculates Muslims from responsibility and guilt. The killing is Allah's doing, not Muslims'. God is the perpetrator, not the people, and no one can criticise him unless they are willing to face the Muslims' swords in this life, and the burning fire in the afterlife. This passage shifts the agency and the culpability from individuals who can be held accountable to the Deity. It also glorifies the fighters.

In another verse, Allah dehumanised non-Muslims by describing them as the following: "The evilest of animals are the disbelievers because they would not believe [in Islam]."[197] This construction also helps alleviate responsibility and guilt for the murder, enslavement and rape of disbelievers.[198] The non-Muslims are not fully human and thus, not deserving of justice (or life). Further on, Allah orders Muslims to carry out mass-killing of their enemies: "If you confront them in battle, destroy them to disperse those behind them."[199]

In the same chapter, Allah legitimized taking ransom in exchange for the release of captives: "You Prophet say to those of the captives who

196 Quran 8:17.
197 Quran 8:55.
198 Haslam, N. (2006). Dehumanization: An integrative review. Personality and Social Psychology Review, 10(3), 252–264.
199 Quran 8:17.

are in your hands: If Allah knows anything good in your hearts, He will give to you better than that which has been taken away from you and will forgive you, and Allah is Forgiving, Merciful."[200]

In this passage, the prisoners are told that if they are moral, then Allah will compensate the ransom they were forced to pay to be freed from the Muslims' prisons and for the properties taken from them. This section is designed to protect Muslims from a negative appraisal of themselves for taking ransom. The responsibility is deflected from the individuals who are demanding money to release their prisoners to the prisoners themselves.

The spoils included men, women and children from the defeated nations, the soldiers – if the Muslims decided to enslave them rather than beheading them, the animals, the lands, and the money. Some of the Muslims wanted everything to be divided equally among the fighters, others wanted to keep what they personally seized. Allah intervened, saying that the spoils belonged to Allah and Mohammad, and Muslims should fear Allah and stop arguing. Allah also granted his prophet one fifth of the spoils. Throughout the history of the Muslim conquest, non-Muslims were treated in the same way as their seized animals and lands: property of the Muslims.

---

200 Quran 8:57.

BATTLES OF UHUD AND THE TRENCH: THE MISSING GOD

One of the battles fought by Muslims under the leadership of Mohammad that is usually dodged when discussing the divine nature of Islam is Uhud. This battle took place at 625, a year after Badr. In this conflict it was the Meccans who attacked Yathrib, for the first time, seeking their revenge. The Muslims knew about the marching force as it gave a warning. They were well prepared and came to meet the attackers near a mountain called Uhud. The two forces collided, and the Muslims led by Mohammad suffered a humiliating defeat at the hands of the Meccans. They lost 85 fighters and fled from the infidels. Mohammad was assailed and some of his teeth were broken. Several of his followers fought to protect him and they saved his life. Allah did not send any angels to confront the infidels, unlike Badr, and Mohammad did not prove himself to be an undefeatable warrior. He blamed his followers for the loss, claiming that they disobeyed him and were more concerned about looting than fighting for Allah. Mohammad's uncle was among the casualties along with several of his trusted companions. The absence of Allah, the defeat of the Muslims, Mohammad fleeing the battlefield documented in the Quran have been all used by countless critics over the ages to show that Islam started as a violent manmade cult.

The Battle of the Trench is the second and the last battle in which the Meccans initiated an attack against Muslims. It took place in the fifth year after the immigration. The Meccans and their allies mobilised and marched to Yathrib to put an end to the Muslim raids on the caravans. The Muslims dug a trench with the help of the Jewish to stop the Meccans from conquering the city. In this battle, the Muslims again did not face their prepared enemies but instead, hid behind their trench. The angels did not come to support the Muslims and Allah was absent, too. After surrounding the town for a few days, the Meccans returned to their hometown and the Muslims continued with their raids. The Muslims attacked several cities and tribes immediately after the withdrawal of the Meccans. The technique used in all these raids was to attack the people when they were the least prepared to resist, inflict the maximum damage possible to paralyse the victims, take the spoils and return to Medina.

In the sixth year, Mohammad led an army to attack an Arab tribe called Banu Lihyan. "To take the enemy by surprise, he pretended to be setting out for the north" but when he reached them, they were prepared to fight and thus he withdrew.[201]

---

201 The History of al-Ṭabarī, Vol. 7.

7 Genocide and Slavery

The example of those who were entrusted with the Torah
and then did not take it on is like a donkey carrying books
retched is the likeness of folk who disbelieve the proofs of Allah
and Allah does not guide the wrongdoing folk.[202]

Allah

You will fight the Jewish and defeat them until the stones
would say you Muslim behind me a Jew, kill him.[203]

Mohammad

The Jewish were the educated and wealthy communities in Yathrib. When
Mohammad emigrated to their homeland to establish his state, they
welcomed him but showed indifference toward his religion. In their eyes,
Mohammad was another impostor hoping to be an Arab chieftain using
religion to gain power. In fact, some of them thought that he might be
a better ally to the Jews than the polytheists. They did not appreciate the
repercussions of the new monotheistic religion.

From Mohammad's perspective, the situation was completely different. He was obsessed with turning the Jewish people into Muslims.
The Quran in Mecca was based on the Israelite narratives more than
any other discourse.[204] Moses is mentioned 64 times while Mohammad
was mentioned just four times in the Quran. Through adapting various
Jewish and Christian edicts, Mohammad attempted to establish himself
as the direct descendant and the legitimate heir of Judeo-Christian
monotheism in the eyes of the polytheistic Arabs. According to the
Quran, the Jewish scholars knew precisely that Mohammad was the messenger of Moses' God. Allah declared that the Jewish people are more

---

202 Quran 62:5.
203 Mohammad as quoted in Sahih al-Bukhari 3593.
204 See Torrey, C. C. (1967). The Jewish Foundation of Islam. Ktav Publishing House.;
Nöldeke, T., Schwally, F., Bergsträßer, G., & Pretzl, O. (2013). The History of the Qur'ān.

certain that Mohammad is the successor of Moses than they are sure about their relations to their children. Mohammad wanted to impress the Jews and convert them at any cost. He prayed toward Jerusalem, copied their texts and made an alliance with them. He aspired to be Moses, King David and Jesus in one, thus, he craved the approval of their followers. Hence, there was no possible way for him to coexist with the Jews while preaching that Islam was the last revelation that abrogated all previous monotheistic religions.

In contrast to Mohammad's initial admiration of the Jews, they saw him as a common person with limited knowledge of their literature and with almost no critical abilities.[205] They noticed that the Islamic texts contained numerous plagiarized ideas and whole passages taken from the Greek mythologies, Christian bibles, Arabic poetry. Many Islamic laws are plagiarized from Jewish theology.[206] Mohammad's obsession with Jewish doctrines appalled the Jews. The fact that the Quran as well as the hadith were filled with stories about Jewish people and their prophets had the opposite than intended effect on the Jews. It made them adamant in refusing to convert to Islam. Throughout the life of Mohammad, not one Jewish person converted to Islam willingly. They did not want to fight for him and were not interested in the spoils he obtained from raiding commercial caravans, peaceful cities, and poor Arab towns.

The Jewish people of the area assumed that if they kept out of his way, they could coexist, and he would allow them to live their lives independent from his reign. They did not understand the nature of the new religion – a religion of one man, one book, one language and one rule, in which dissent cannot be tolerated. They did not understand that Islam is a totalitarian ideology that does not allow any other ideology to exist within its reign.

Thus, from the day they rejected Mohammad as their leader, Jewish people were seen as an existential threat and were not given enough time to reconsider their position or organise to defend themselves. The Quran shifted from admiration into extreme animosity. The Jews were

---

205 Nöldeke, T., Schwally, F., Bergsträßer, G., & Pretzl, O. (2013). The History of the Qur'ān.
206 Crone, P. & Cook, M. (1977). Hagarism: the making of the Islamic world.; Ali, J. (1993). The Detailed History of the Arabs Before Islam. Third Ed. Dar al-Alam.

called "monkeys", "donkeys" and "cowards". Allah stated that Jews and polytheists are the worst enemies of Muslims.[207] Mohammad prophesised that one day the Muslims would annihilate Jews with the help of everything, including trees and stones. He said that there shall not be two religions in Arabia.

Although Mohammad signed treaties with every Jewish community in Yathrib, he did not uphold any of them. He attacked each one of the three Jewish communities, one at a time. When Muslims attacked a Jewish town, they assured the other Jews that their motive was related to a specific act done by the attacked group. They promised the other Jewish tribes that if they did not support the attacked tribe, Muslims would honour the treaty they had signed with them. The first attack against a Jewish tribe came after Mohammad defeated the people of Mecca in the battle of Badr. Hoping to capitalize on his unexpected victory, he went to the market of Bani-Qaanaaq, gathered the Jews and told them to believe in him and accept Islam before Allah defeated them in the same way he had crushed the Meccans. He said that they knew that he was the real Messenger of Allah. The Jews replied: we are warriors and if you waged a war on us, you would know that you have not been in war before. According to al-Tabarī, the most trusted Islamic historian, Mohammad recited the verse of Quran that says: "If you fear treachery from any people, throw back to them (their treaty), Allah does not love traitors."[208] Mohammad then said to his senior followers that he feared that the Jewish of Bani-Qaanaaq were planning to wage a sudden attack against Muslims, thus the peace treaty signed by him was void. Another Muslim historian reported that a Muslim killed a Jewish man for harassing a Muslim woman in the Jewish market and then one of the Jews killed that man. This incident was what made Mohammad annul the peace treaty. Mohammad rallied his followers and attacked that Jewish community without prior notice or a declaration of war. Taking the targeted people by surprise is one of the Islamic war traditions. The details of the attack, reported in almost all the Islamic sources, show that Mohammad waged an unprovoked

207 Quran 5:82.
208 Quran 8:58.

sudden attack against the Jewish community without informing them that the peace treaty he had signed with them was being annulled from his side. When they saw his army coming toward them, the Jews ran and sheltered in their forts and closed the gates. He besieged them for fifteen days. The other Jewish communities of Yathrib did not come to help Bani-Qaanaaq. They stood idly by, watching Mohammad attack. They did not think or behave as a united group; they were divided, and each tribe thought it would not be attacked by Muslims. After fifteen days of siege, the Jewish village surrendered.

Mohammad ordered his followers to gather all the Jews and tie them with ropes. He declared that they were guilty of treason and deemed them all criminals. Children, women and elderly people were all categorized as traitors by the messenger of Allah. He was ready to execute them but Ibn Salol, a noble man from Yathrib, intervened. He stood up to Mohammad and told him to release all the captured Jews. When Mohammad refused and attempted to disregard him, Ibn Salol grabbed Mohammad firmly by his collar, while shouting: "leave them, they are my allies. Do you want to kill over seven hundred humans in an hour? I will never allow you to do that." Muslims were watching this powerful old man confronting their leader but none of them intervened. Mohammad conceded saying: "take them, take them and release me." He instructed his soldiers to release all the Jews but to deport them out of their hometown immediately. He then ordered the confiscation of all their properties. On Mohammad's command, Muslims ransacked the Jewish homes and farms. The lands, houses and all the belongings of the Jews were divided among the Mujahedeen after Mohammad took one fifth of everything for himself. To this day Muslims consider Ibn Salol a symbol of evil. They call him the Head of Hypocrites.

In this battle, collective punishment against civilians has been sanctioned as righteous after it was practiced by Mohammad. The narrative of this battle is part of the school curriculum all over the Muslim world. Harming people and looting their property is legitimised by presenting the victims as conspiring against Islam. This paranoia used to justify the attack has been presented as rational thinking. It is fair to say that without this money Mohammed would never have been able to finance his state and wage wars against other Arab tribes and cities. Allah in the Quran and Mohammad in the hadith as well as the tradition have labelled Jews as evil disbelievers who must be cleansed.

Two years later Mohammad attacked the second Jewish community, Bani-Al Nazir. According to all the important Muslim historians and scholars, Mohammad went to these people seeking financial help. They lived a few miles away from Medina. They had a fort surrounded by palm plantations.[209] They agreed to help him and asked him to wait until they could collect the money and give it to him. While he was sitting with his followers waiting, he stood up suddenly, told his companions to stay and left. After his companions grew weary of waiting for their leader, they went back to Medina to find Mohammad in the mosque. He gathered his followers and told them that Allah had informed him that the Jews had been about to assassinate him by throwing a huge stone at him from a rooftop of the house near which he was sitting. Thus, Allah ordered him to escape immediately. Muslims, as expected, believed their leader with no discussion. None of them inquired why the Jews had not captured him and his companions upon their arrival to their town, or why they had not hurt the companions who had been left behind. Muslim historians tell us that Mohammad immediately assembled an army and waged a sudden attack on this Jewish tribe. When the Jewish community saw the army approaching, they ran to their fort and closed their gates, leaving behind their livestock. He besieged them for fifteen days, cutting off all supplies. He ordered his soldiers to cut and burn the trees to force the Jews to surrender.[210] Allah assured Muslims that the destruction of the trees was an implantation of his will. In the end, Bani-Al Nazir conceded and gave up their money, weapons and farms to the Muslims. They were expelled from their homeland by Mohammad on the orders of Allah. They travelled to another Jewish town, Khyber, with nothing but their clothes. The story of Mohammad's attack on this Jewish town is also taught in Muslim public schools. It is constructed as the right and virtuous course of action when dealing with all non-Muslims, not only Jews.

209 Sahih al-Bukhari 4028, 4031.
210 Sahih Muslim 4324.

KILLING PRISONERS
AND ENSLAVING WOMEN AND CHILDREN

In 627 CE, Muslims led by their prophet attacked the last Jewish town near Yathrib. The hadith and the history books report that Gabriel came down to Mohammad right after the Trench War concluded. He asked him if Muslims had indeed put down their weapons and when Mohammad said yes, the angel told him that the angels had not, and he and Muslims must take up their arms again and move to attack the Jews of Banu Qurayzah.[211] Mohammad ordered his followers to grab their weapons and march immediately. He did not provide a justification as it was the order of Allah to wage an offensive war.[212] Again, the attacked community was given no warning or explanation and there was no declaration of war. They found themselves surrounded by an army.

Mohammad besieged Banu Qurayzah's fort from all sides, cutting off water and food supplies. Muslims set the trees surrounding the Jewish fort on fire to force a surrender. After 25 days, the Jews submitted to Mohammad hoping for a fair trial, or even to be expelled from their homeland like the other tribes he evicted before. Mohammad ordered his followers to disarm the Jews and to tie every one of them. They were hungry, exhausted and terrified captives waiting to know their fate. Women, children, and the elderly waited for their non-negotiable sentence.

Mohammad ordered one of his followers to issue the verdict without a trial. The judge he appointed was known for his deep hatred of the Jewish. His ruling was such: all men shall be killed, all women and children shall be enslaved and divided among the Muslim soldiers as spoils along with all the Jewish property.[213] Mohammad celebrated this verdict, saying that "this was Allah's order" and it must be implemented immediately. Jewish

---

211 Sahih al-Bukhari 4117, 4118, 4119.
212 See Sahih al-Bukhari.
213 Sahih al-Bukhari: 3804, 4121,4122.; The History of al-Tabarī, Vol. 7.

men were taken in groups of two to three to be slaughtered in trenches that were dug in the market, without being told what was going to happen to them. While group after a group were being slaughtered, the rest were unaware of the ongoing massacre. After the Muslims killed all the men, they stripped young boys of their clothes to check for pubic hair. Based on that, Muslims decided who was a child and who was not. If a boy had pubic hair, he was considered an adult and was slain, otherwise he was deemed a child and condemned to slavery for the rest of his life. According to the Muslim historians, two hundred children were slaughtered after having been deemed adults. The original Muslim books also report that two children (who did not have pubic hair) and several women were killed on the direct orders of Mohammad, with no explanation given.

The main executioners were Mohammad's cousins: Ali ibn Abi Talib and Al-Zubayr.[214] These two individuals are cherished and respected role models among Muslims. Many devotees name their newborns after the two executioners.

According to Tabari, between 600 to 900 humans were killed in that bloodbath. After this massacre, Mohammad divided the women and children along with the seized property among his soldiers as spoils. He took one fifth of everything, including children and women. Mohammad sent some of the captives to Najd to be sold in exchange for horses and arms. He used some of the money to keep up his harem, which was filled with wives, servants and slave-girls.[215] He took a girl named Rayhana as a slave after killing her husband and the rest of her family. Some Muslim historians indicated that Mohammad deserted her later on because she sought to remain Jewish. Others say that he offered to marry her and enforce hijab on her but she preferred to remain a slave-girl.[216]

Allah celebrated this victory in the Quran: "Allah brought down from their fortresses those people of the book who had supported them and cast such terror into their hearts that some of them you kill and some of them you take captive."[217] In this verse, Allah has legitimised

---

214 The History of al-Tabarī, Vol. 8.
215 The History of al-Tabarī, Vol. 8.; Ibn al-Athir Vol. 2., p.185.
216 As above.
217 Quran 33:26.

killing and enslaving people who surrendered. It has been an everlasting authorisation for genocide.

After the massacre of Banu Qurayzah, Mohammad sent numerous cavalries to raid Arab tribes and towns. In one of these raids, a Muslim force waged a sudden attack against a small settlement of a tribe called Banu Fazara. The attackers killed and wounded many people of this clan, who were not prepared to fight. They also captured women and children. Among the captured was an old woman called Fatimah bint Rabiaa, titled Umm Qirfah. She was deeply respected among her people and was considered their leader. The Muslims "tied each of her legs with a rope and tied the ropes to two camels, made the camels run into different direction splitting her in two."[218] They had killed her sons before that; they took her daughter to Medina as a slave. There, Mohammad gifted the girl to one of his soldiers.

The story of Anna Tutundjian, one of the victims of the Armenian genocide, shows that the same mindset created by Mohammad when dealing with non-Muslims persisted over the ages. Anna recalls how in the summer of 1915, when she was 11 years old, Ottoman soldiers came to her town, Sivas. They rounded up all the Armenians and other non-Muslims. They separated the men and boys from the females and children. Anna saw her father, uncles, and cousins being executed by the Turks. After killing all the men and boys, the soldiers took male infants and toddlers from their mothers, including Anna's brother. They buried the babies in the ground up to their shoulders and crushed them with their horses before the eyes of the helpless women. Anna saw her brother killed. The Ottomans took the women and girls on a death march through the Syrian desert. Many died on the way, and the few who survived were psychologically devastated. During this journey, Anna was kidnapped by a Muslim man. She found herself one of twenty girls this man captured. They had to work in his estate and bear him children. At the age of 12, Anna gave birth to a baby girl. The following year, she gave birth again. She escaped a few months later, leaving her two daughters behind. Fifty years passed before she could speak about her suffering and reconnected with her daughters.

---

218 The History of al-Tabarī, Vol. 8., pp 95-97.; Ibn al-Athir, Vol. 2., p 208.

KHAYBAR KHAYBAR YOU JEWS,
THE ARMY OF MOHAMMAD WILL RETURN

When you meet those who disbelieve, strike their necks
until when you have inflicted slaughter upon them
then tighten their shackles.[219]

Allah

It is prohibited to you your mothers and daughters and sisters...
and married women except your hand possession.[220]

Allah

After the Banu Qurayzah genocide, Khaybar was the only remaining
Jewish town in Western Arabia. It was a big town 150 km away from
Medina composed of several forts attached to each other. Many of the
Jewish people who were expelled by Mohammad from their homes in
Yathrib took refuge in this town. Mohammad led an army to invade
Khaybar in the seventh year after immigration, less than two years after
the massacre of Banu Qurayzah.[221] To prevent the nearby Arab tribe from
aiding their Jewish allies, the Muslims camped first in a valley between
Khaybar and the houses of the Arab tribe Ghatafan. Upon learning that
Mohammad was on his way to invade the Jewish community, the Arabs
mobilised and travelled to help their allies. After they travelled a day's
journey, they came to the conclusion that the Muslims were setting an
ambush and that the main target was their properties and children, not
the Jews. Hence, they went back to protect their homes. Once the Arabs
were back in their homes, Mohammad attacked Khaybar.[222]

Before the Jews realised what was happening, the Muslim army had
managed to besiege all the forts of Khaybar, cutting the town from the

---

219 Quran 47:4.
220 Quran 4:23-24, see Sahih International trans.
221 Sahih al-Bukhari 4195, 4196, 4197.
222 The History of al-Tabarī, Vol. 8.; Ibn al-Athir, Vol. 2.

outside world and gradually advancing inside the forts. After a few days of fighting, Muslims conquered two of the four forts. They killed the men and enslaved the children and the women. The inhabitants of the remaining Jewish forts surrendered after resisting for two weeks. Witnessing the holocaust inflicted on their relatives broke their will. Mohammad deported them from their homes after he took all their belongings and seized their properties. He divided the captives, the lands and the properties among his soldiers after keeping for himself the lion's share. To this day, the victory of Mohammad over the Jews of Khaybar is present in the collective psyche of Muslims as their virtuous triumph against the evil people who rejected the correct religion. Protesters all over the world have been chanting the mantra "Khaybar, Khaybar you Jews, the army of Mohammad will return," to threaten Israel and its backers.

8 Mohammad and Girls

A significant portion of the Quran as well as the hadith is dedicated to stories related to Mohammad's interactions with women. These stories have been influencing the perception of women and girls for centuries as they are taken for what differentiates between what is right from wrong and the acceptable from the unacceptable. They have been the source of Islamic laws and norms.

WAS HE A PROPHET OR A ROBBER?

From the captives of Khaybar Mohammad took for himself a young Jewish girl called Safiyyah.[223] She was described in the history and hadith books as a stunning, newly wedded teenager from a prominent family. Her groom was tortured on the orders of Mohammad to reveal where his people had hidden their wealth. After discovering the treasure, Mohammad ordered his cousin Ali to behead the prisoner. The girl's father and brothers were also slain in front of her eyes. She was initially given to one of Mohammad's soldiers but when the prophet found out that she was exceptionally pretty, he ordered the follower to leave her for him and gave him other captives instead. To terrorise her, the soldier who brought her to Mohammad made sure to make her see her dead father and brothers' decapitated bodies. She threw herself at the dead bodies of her beloved ones.[224]

The books of hadith and history report that on the way back to his capital, the prophet ordered his followers to set up a tent for him so he could spend the night with Safiyyah. He ordered one of the women to prepare the girl for him and a soldier stood outside the tent all the night to guard the prophet from the Jewish girl. Senior Muslim jurists defend this incident through saying that she was a hand-possession of the prophet, thus, he had the right to have intercourse with her.[225] They also claim that she had had her period while in the possession of the prophet, thus, she was fit for intercourse with her master. The fact that he did not wait until he reached his home is perplexing even to the most gullible of Muslims. It seems that he wanted to demonstrate his virility. Currently this event is used as proof that Muslims who seized married

---

223 Sahih al-Bukhari: 4211, 4212, 4213.
224 The History of al-Tabarī, Vol. 8.; Ibn al-Athir, Vol. 2.
225 Al-Asqalani, Ibn Hajar. (1959). Fath Al-Bari fi Sharh Sahih al-Bukhari. (Arabic). Maktabah Salafiyah.

or widowed slave-girls have the right to establish sexual intercourse with them once they had their periods.

The story of Saffiyyah is an essential part of the rationale of Islam. It is recorded in detail in all the important original Islamic books. It is known to every educated Muslim. It is taught in the public schools across the Muslim world as well as in Islamic schools in non-Muslim countries. Students are instructed to glorify this act of Mohammad and to praise Allah for granting Muslims this victory over the peaceful.

I first came across this narrative in Islamic studies class: I was a 14-year-old, and this story was part of the curriculum in the public schools' system. I remember vividly how the students were outraged by it. We were shocked. Many of us started arguing loudly that the prophet could not have done such an immoral deed. The teacher, an Egyptian Muslim Brother, was puzzled himself; he did not seem convinced that this story was moral, but he knew that it is written in the original books and therefore, it is part of Islam. He was terrified and angry at the same time. He could not say that the original sources of Islam were wrong and risk being cast as an apostate, which meant losing his job, his family and being charged with the crime of blasphemy. He could not say that it is moral to steal, kill and enslave people because they did not want to convert, either. He was not capable of explaining why Mohammad could not pardon these people and let them live their lives the way they wanted. He was unable to explain why the prophet invaded them in the first place and why he took their wealth. Students were yelling that it was impossible for any decent man, let alone the most moral creature, to enslave a girl. Some shouted: was he a prophet or a robber?

The teacher kept repeating loudly that Saffiyyah was very lucky to have been saved from the eternal torture of afterlife and to have got to be with the master of the universe, unlike her family, who would burn in hell eternally. He also assured us that she was extremely happy as she had been released from her misery of being an infidel and saved by the prophet. The others – they rejected Allah, thus, they deserved to be killed. The booties Muslims stole were their reward from Allah for killing these infidels.

This argument did not convince any of us. We kept arguing furiously that it was impossible for a human being to fall in love with someone who had killed her dad, husband, brothers and all her relatives. One student shouted: how would she love him when she just saw her own mother and sisters being sold to slavery and her people being banished from their homes? Another said: could he not have freed her and allowed her to decide if she really wanted to be with him or not? The third asked: what is honourable about being a sex-slave? Another shouted: why did Mohammad need all these women? he was an old man, why would he want a kid? The teacher kept repeating the same clichés Muslims echo whenever faced with such questions. He even told us that Muslims killing the boys was a good thing because this would have reduced their torture in hell. Many students responded by cursing Allah, Islam, Mohammad and the ministry of education for forcing such a hideous story on us.

Unfortunately, many, if not most of these students had to convince themselves that they were wrong, and the society was right. They had to note down that Saffiyyah was blessed to have been chosen by Mohammad to be his hand-possession, to get good grades, which many did not. We were not allowed to use the word sex-slave in the exam and had to use the watered-down "hand-possession" instead. Pupils were instructed to write down the conclusion of this story as: Allah is severe in His punishment and generous in His reward. The take-home messages they attempted to ingrain in our psyche were: killing non-Muslims and taking their property is legitimate because it was ordered by Allah and implemented by Mo-hammad. Slavery is legitimate because it frees people from the chains of worshipping fake gods. Other people's suffering is good, and rape is moral.

Saffiyyah was not the only slave-girl of Mohammad. He owned at least three more girls. One of the other known sex-slaves of the prophet was the Egyptian Christian Maria. She was given to him as a gift when he was well over fifty years old and she was a teenager. He fathered a son with her named Ibrahim. Muslim historians report that the son died as an infant, in suspicious circumstances. Mohammad kept Maria in an orchard he had seized from the Jewish, away from his house.[226]

---

226 The History of al-Ṭabarī, Vol. 8.; Ibn al-Athīr, Vol. 2.

An Egyptian eunuch owned by Mohammad was in charge of keeping people away from the prophet's hand-possession. Like all the women Mohammad married or owned, Maria was not allowed to marry after his death and was not allowed to travel or directly talk to males. Thus, she lived all her life in solitude in accordance with Mohammad's orders. She is remembered by Muslims today as the hand-possession of the prophet – a great honour, they say.

In another incident reported by Muslim historians and taught in schools, Mohammad asked one of the female captives who belonged to the powerful Arab tribe Banu Tamim if she would rather stay with him or go back to her husband. She asked to go back to her husband and he allowed it.[227] Moreover, it is reported by the trusted hadith books that Mohammad asked a young captive girl from a noble Arab family Banu Jaun to give herself to him. "She said, why would a royal give herself to a plebeian (souqa)? The Prophet raised his hand to pat her so she would calm down. She said, I seek refuge with Allah from you. He said, you have sought refuge with one who gives refuge."[228] He then ordered his soldiers to release her.

Mohammad also owned a slave-girl named Juwayriya. Al-Bukhari reports that "the prophet raided the tribe of Banu al Mustaleeq while they were unsuspecting and their cattle drinking by the water. He killed the fighters, enslaved the children and women and took a girl named Juwayriya Bint al-Hateth for himself."[229] A number of Muslim historians attempt to alter the story by claiming that there was a battle between that Arab tribe and the Muslims; Mohammad defeated them, took them as slaves and divided them among his soldiers. They claim that Juwayriya was given to one of the Muslim fighters and then she went to Mohammad and asked him to free her. The prophet proposed to marry her, which she accepted, and she became one of his many wives, not a slave. This distorted story contradicts the original texts and displays to which degree some so-called scholars are willing to lie. The main event of this

227 Ibn Sa'd, M. (2022). Kitab al-Tabaqat Al-Kabir (Arabic Edition). Ed. K. V. Zettersten. Brill. Vol 8., p 154.
228 Sahih al-Bukhari 5255.
229 Sahih al-Bukhari 2541.

invasion is this: Mohammad raided an Arab tribe that was not at war with him. Its people were not prepared to defend themselves. They were oblivious to the possibility of a raid, as is shown by the fact that their cattle were left by the water, making them an easy target. Mohammad took the Arab women and children as slaves and distributed them among his soldiers after taking his share. Whether he took the 20-year-old girl as a slave or married her under duress when he was 58 years old is irrelevant – neither act can be cast as ethical.

CONSPIRACY AGAINST THE PROPHET

There is the incident in which Mohammad is caught by one of his wives with a slave-girl in the wife's bedroom. In this event, we see passages in the Quran that seem to be written for the explicit purpose of justifying what most would see as immoral and unethical behaviour. In this incident, Mohammad's wife Hafsa – the daughter of Omar, who was at least thirty years younger than him – asked his permission to visit her parents. Once back, she found him inside her bedroom with the Egyptian concubine Maria. To silence her, Mohammad took an oath not to have sex with this slave ever again in exchange for the wife keeping what she had seen a secret. Hafsa, however, did not keep her promise and told his other wife Aisha about it. Allah interfered with a Quranic passage:

> O Prophet, why do you prohibit [yourself from] what Allah has made lawful for you, seeking the approval of your wives? Allah has already ordained for you [Muslims] the dissolution of your oaths. And Allah is your protector, and he is the Knowing, the Wise. And Allah is Forgiving and Merciful. If you two [wives] repent to Allah, [it is best], for your hearts have deviated. But if you conspire against him – then indeed Allah is his protector, and Gabriel and the righteous of the believers and the angels, moreover, are [his] assistants. And when the Prophet disclosed a matter in confidence to one of his wives (Hafsah), so when she told it (to another i.e. Aishah), and Allah made it known to him, he informed part thereof and left a part. Then when he told her (Hafsah) thereof, she said: "Who told you this?" He said: "The All-Knower, the All-Aware (Allah) has told me.[230]

The above verses are excellent material for a satirical show. An old man who has been introducing himself as the supreme leader of humanity,

---

230 Quran 66:1-4.

the wisest, the most respected, and the most ethical is being humiliated by two of his wives. The old general seems helpless, confused and scared. Thus, he makes a concession after a concession to preserve his status. Allah the omnipotent intervenes to protect his troubled representative from the girls, sending a revelation to threaten the two of them.

These revelations have been considered the literal word of God that must be revered and followed, for over a thousand years. In this divine declaration, Allah warns the two girls that he and his angels and all the believers will take the side of Mohammad and protect him from their wicked conspiracy. He also permits his man to continue the relationship with the slave-girl. Paranoia, grandiosity and pettiness are the best descriptions of Allah's reaction to the wives' rebellion.

The arguments that accept and justify the notion that the creator of the universe indeed narrated such a passage are farcical. This shows that in order to believe that the Quran is a divine revelation people must reject the basis of logic and sound thinking. They must reject the simple evident explanation for baseless, irrational, contradicting, convoluted talk. The whole story can be seen as an ancient legend constrained to its era and characters. This passage could have been, indeed, irrelevant and thus harmless to current humans if not for the people who insist that the Quran is the literal word of God. From this passage they comprehend that an oath is not important and having sex-slaves is halal.

BANNING ADOPTION: BOUNDLESS CRUELTY

The story of Zaynab bint Jahsh and Mohammad is reported in the Quran and hadith books also cover it with some minor differences. To this day it is being taught in schools worldwide as an essential part of Islam and as a source of legislation. This tale sheds light on Mohammad's personality, the nature of his followers and his social environment. It shows that the Quran was created to justify Mohammad's personal desires regardless of the consequences.

It starts with a paternal aunt of Mohammad who had a son named Ubayd-Allah and a daughter named Zaynab. Ubayd converted to Islam in Mecca and emigrated to Ethiopia with a number of the early Muslims years before Mohammad's immigration to Yathrib. They were sent by Mohammad to spread Islam in Africa and to establish a stronghold there. In Ethiopia, Ubayd-Allah deserted Islam and converted to Christianity, the dominant religion of that land at the time. In retaliation, Mohamad annulled his cousin's marriage to his Muslim wife on the grounds that he became a non-Muslim, and a non-Muslim man cannot marry or remain married to a Muslim woman. Mohammad then married Ubayd's wife and added her to his harem. To this day, this woman is considered one of the revered wives of Mohammad. Courts all over the Muslim world annul marriages of Muslims who desert their religion and do not recognize a marriage between a non-Muslim male and a Muslim female. The rulings of these courts of law are based on the Quranic texts that prohibit such a relationship, the hadith, and this precedent.

Ubayd's sister Zaynab as well as her family remained Muslims in Mecca and immigrated to Yathrib. After Muslims established their state, Mohammad proposed to Zaynab that she should marry his adopted son Zaid. At that time, Mohammad followed the Arab tradition before Islam of freeing and adopting young slaves. The adopted son was called Zaid Ibn Mohammad – Zaid Son-of-Mohammad. Zaid was one of the earliest converts and a devoted follower of his father. When Zaynab refused to marry Zaid, Allah interfered declaring in the Quran that: "It is not for a believer, man or woman, when Allah and His Messenger have dictated a matter that they should have any option in their decision. And whoever disobeys Allah and His Messenger, he has indeed strayed in plain error."[231] Hence, Zaynab was forced to obey Mohammad's order to save her life. Here, Allah's threat to Zaynab in regard to such a trivial matter is one of the cognitive schemas in Muslims' psyche. Allah and the grand leader of humanity are concerned about a very private matter and compelling a female to marry someone against her will. This blurs the boundaries between private and public life and gives authority figures unlimited power. It prepares the ground for parents to control their children's decision regarding marriage. It also provides justification for the rulers to interfere in the personal issues of the people.

As the father of the groom, Mohammad went to visit the newlyweds. Zaid was absent and Mohammad saw the bride semi-naked. He lusted for her instantly, tried to conceal his feelings and was deeply distressed, according to the Islamic sources. Allah sent Quranic revelations to deal with his messenger's predicament and to establish general rules for the Muslims. Allah outlawed adoption affirming that "He has not made your adopted sons your sons. That is your saying by your mouths, but Allah says the truth, and He guides to the way."[232] Furthermore, Allah ordered Muslims to strip their adopted children of the names they gave them: "Call them by [the names of] their fathers; it is more just in the sight of Allah. But if you do not know their fathers – then they are [still] your brothers in religion and those entrusted to you."[233] After that, Allah declared that "The Prophet is more important to the believers than themselves, and his wives are their mothers."[234] Later on, in the same passage, Allah described the predicament his messenger experienced in relation to Zaynab: "And when you said to the one Allah bestowed favour and you bestowed favour: keep your wife to yourself and be

231 Quran 33:36; The History of al-Tabarī; Ibn al-Athir; Tafseer al-Tabarī.
232 Quran 33:4, Sahih International trans.
233 Quran 33:5, Sahih International trans.
234 Quran 33:6, Sahih International trans.

careful of Allah; and you concealed in your soul what Allah would bring to light, and you feared men, and Allah had a greater right that you should fear Him." After that, Allah issued a verdict: "But when Zaid had accomplished his want of her, We gave her to you as a wife, so that there should be no difficulty for the believers in respect of the wives of their adopted sons, when they have accomplished their want of them; and Allah's command shall must be fulfilled."[235] These passages are taught to students all over the world as an example of the greatness of Mohammad. This event is constructed as a sacrifice on behalf of Mohammad and an example of Allah's adoration of him at the expense of other people. Allah annulled the marriage of Zaid and Zaynab and married her to Mohammad who was much older than her. Believers have been presenting this marriage as a miracle because it was performed by Allah. Zaid was the only one mentioned by name in the Quran from all of Mohammad's companions to be told that his marriage is annulled along with the father-son connection to Mohammad.

From that day on, adoption, which had been considered an honourable tradition, became illegal and a sin and has remained so until this moment in every Muslim country because of the Quranic passages. A Muslim cannot give his name to a child and treat them equally to his biological children. Non-Muslims are not allowed to adopt in Muslim countries because Islam is the rule of the land. Allah banned adoption and prohibited people from giving their names to anyone but their biological offspring born in an Islamic marriage (nikah), and whoever defies this order would be punished according to blasphemy laws. This ban also applies to the millions of non-Muslims living in the Muslim countries. The millions of Egyptian Christians cannot practice adoption in their ancestors' land because of constitution that declares Islam as the source of legislation.

If we analyse this story rationally, we will reach a conclusion that we are looking at a distressed person attempting to satisfy his personal desires regardless of the consequences. He punished his cousin for deserting Islam by annulling his marriage and taking his wife. He humiliated

---

235 Quran 33:37.

his aunt's family by ordering their young daughter Zaynab to marry a poor freed man against her will. He changed his mind after seeing the young woman undressed, so he divorced her from her husband and took her for himself without consulting her, her husband or her family. This despite him being married to several wives and being decades older than her. He knew that people would look down on him as he was forcing his adopted son to divorce his wife, therefore, he annulled and criminalised the entire practice of adoption that has benefited humanity over the ages and was deeply rooted in the Arabian societies. The feelings of the girl, her husband, her family or anyone else did not matter to Mohammad or to his God. This Islamic law banning adoption has had millions of victims over the centuries. The orphans and children born out of wedlock who could not be adopted and have a stable family have suffered the greatest, but people who wanted to adopt these children have also suffered immensely.

SHE WAS FAITHFUL

The Quran as well as hadith report about the Ifk (false accusation) incident. The sources say that Aisha was accused of having an affair with one of Mohammad's soldiers. The story ensued during one of the invasions, when Aisha went missing from the army. She appeared the next day riding with a soldier. She claimed that she had missed a necklace and went searching for it and didn't notice that the army had left its campsite. By the time she went back, it was dark and there was no one at the site. Then Safwan (the soldier) appeared in a strange coincidence and took her on his camel, and it took them a whole night and part of the next day to catch up with the army. Mohammad did not notice that she was missing, nor did the people responsible for guiding her camel.

Several of Mohammad's companions and relatives, among them Aisha's cousin and a cousin of Mohammad, spread the rumour that Aisha had an affair with Safwan. Mohammad confronted Aisha and asked her to admit if it was true. For a month the situation was tense, and Aisha and her parents were ostracised by the community. After a month, Mohammad recited Quranic verses that presented what happened as false accusations – Ifk, without mentioning Aisha, the soldier or the accusers' names. Mohammad arrested and whipped three of the four main accusers eighty lashes each as punishment for accusing his wife of adultery. The fourth one was Ibn Salol and Mohammad would not have dared to harm him.[236] Critics claim that Mohammad waited for a month to make sure that Aisha was not pregnant before coming up with these passages and allowing her to come back to his home. Whipping people 80 lashes for accusing married women of adultery without presenting four witnesses became an Islamic law that has been enforced over the years.

---

236 Quran 24:20-26; Sahih al-Bukhari 4141, 4142, 4143.; Ibn Hisham, A. (1990). Al-Sirah al-Nabawiyyah [The Life of the Prophet]. Vol. 3, p 310-311. Dar Alkitab al-Arabi

Muslims are banned from having more than four wives at a time, but Mohammad is an exception. Allah has ordered the believers to limit the number of their wives to 4 and divorce the rest, otherwise it would be considered adultery, Mohammad, however, was exempted from that rule: he was initially instructed by Allah to keep his 11 wives as well as his slave-girls. There was one condition: he does not marry new wives or exchange the current ones; but if he wants to marry any of his cousins who emigrated with him then that is allowed: "O prophet, we have made lawful for you all your wives whom you have given their dowers and what your right hand owns of what Allah has given to you of the captives as spoils of war and the daughters of your paternal uncles and the daughters of your paternal aunts and the daughters of your maternal uncles and the daughters of your maternal aunts who emigrated with you."[237]

This passage permits slavery and states that it was Allah who gave the captive girls to Mohammad and the other Muslims. In the same verse, Allah gives another privilege to the prophet, which is that any free Muslim woman can give herself to him as a slave if he wanted to wed her: "and a believing woman if she gives herself to the Prophet if the Prophet wishes to wed her a privilege for you only, not for the (rest of)[238] the believers, we know what we have ordained for them concerning their wives and those whom their right hands possess in order that no embarrassment for you [Mohammad] and Allah is Forgiving, Merciful." Allah is permitting women to give themselves to the Prophet as slaves. This permission contradicts the general understanding that free Muslims should not become slaves. Hence, Allah declared that this exception is his command and he announced it in the form of Quran to relieve Mohammad from any embarrassment.

---

237 Quran 33:50.
238 This is Sahih explanation.

NO MARRIAGE AFTER MY DEATH

Another Islamic commandment that highlights the personality of Mohammad is the ban on remarrying his future widows. He imposed this ban to prevent his wives from remarrying after his death. It is reported that during Mohammad's life, one of his followers said that he would marry Aisha once Mohammad passed away. The enraged Allah replied instantly with a revelation: "It is not for you that you should annoy Allah's Messenger, nor that you should ever marry his wives after him truly such a thing is in Allah's sight an enormity."[239] Hence, Allah banned many women from their natural right of remarrying and having children in order to protect the feelings of his beloved messenger after his death. Almost all these women were very young when Mohammad died and none of them had children with him. Aisha for instance was 17 years old when Mohammad died. They all lived the rest of their lives in isolation. Mohammad's successors enforced this law strictly. They barred the twelve widows and the concubines from remarrying, travelling and from leaving their homes. Instead, they were honoured by being given the title "Mothers of Believers". No one is allowed to marry his mother.

---

239 Quran 33:55.

9 The Demise of the Prophet and the Killing of His Grandchildren

CONQUERING MECCA AND DESTROYING OTHER RELIGIONS' IDOLS

Mohammad invaded Mecca and conquered it with a huge army made up of Muslims and mercenaries eight years after he left it for Yathrib, in 629 CE. Few Meccans resisted but were crushed brutally. Once he controlled Mecca, Mohammad ordered the execution of several men and women, telling his soldiers to decapitate them even if they were holding to the Kaaba's curtains. He destroyed all the icons and symbols of the other religions, including Christian and Jewish religious icons. He gathered the Meccans and told them that he would free them but they must convert to Islam and fight for him like the other Muslims, which they did.

MORE INVASIONS

In the same year he conquered Mecca, Mohammad and his army along with the Meccans marched toward Ta'if. The people of Ta'if together with another powerful tribe Hawazin had gathered and camped with their women and children in a valley called Hunayn, between Mecca and Ta'if. The Muslims attacked them there and a bloody battle ensued in which many thousands were killed or wounded. The Muslims were defeated in the beginning but managed to regroup and waged a lethal attack against their opponents who fought bravely but were outnumbered.

Muslims captured 6000 women and children in addition to the livestock of the Hawazin. Mohammad divided the spoils, including the children, among his followers but only after he took one fifth of everything for himself. From among the captives, he gave his cousin Ali a girl called Raytah, gave his son in-law Uthman a girl called Zaynab and gave his friend Omar another girl as slaves.[240] Many of the enslaved girls were married and their husbands were still alive, thus, some of the Muslims were not sure if they could have them as sex-slaves or not. Allah intervened with a Quranic text that sanctions sex-slavery of the captive married women.

Some of the relatives of the captured women and children came to Mohammad and accepted Islam and pledged their allegiance to him. They begged him to free their people and give them back their livestock. Mohammad asked them if "the possessions or their wives and sons were more important to them, they said that they want their wives and sons." After they begged him repeatedly, he released some of the married women and the boys he and his family possessed, and some other Muslims did the same while the rest kept their prisoners as slaves. Al-Tabari detailed that one of Mohammad's companions took an old

240 The History of al-Tabari, Vol. 9. p 29.; Ibn al-Athir, Vol. 2.; Ibn Hisham.

woman from the captives because he thought that her children would pay high ransom to free her.[241] This practice is still ongoing; taking ransom to release kidnapped people is practiced by the Islamic Iranian regime as well as the various Islamic terrorist organizations.

241 As above.

THE SWORD VERSE THAT UNITES THEM

The last year of Mohammad's life was extremely volatile and charged with stressful events. In that year, Allah ordered him to sever all ties with non-Muslims and to wage war against everyone at once. In the verse Muslims appropriately label "the sword verse", Allah declared war on the rest of humanity: "So when the sacred months have passed away, slay the idolaters wherever you find them, and take them captive and besiege them and lie in wait for them in every ambush, if they repent and keep up prayer and pay the levy (zakat), leave their way free."[242] This verse abrogated all the previous passages that sanction peaceful relationships between Muslims and non-Muslims. The concept of idolaters mentioned in this verse applies to all non-Muslims. Thus, they were declared enemies that must be eradicated. Verse 29 of the same chapter al-Tawbah has the same idea in a more precise form: "Fight against those who don't believe in Allah, nor in the last day, nor forbid that which has been forbidden by Allah and his Messenger and those who don't acknowledge the religion of truth [i.e. Islam] among the people of the book [Jews and Christians], until they pay the ransom (jizyah) with willing submission, and feel themselves submissive."

Waging war against everyone was the natural conclusion of Mohammad's journey from a failed prophet in Mecca to a victorious ruthless fighter in Medina. He rejected polytheism and was rejected by the Jews and the Christians. Thus, the survival of the new religion was dependent on remaining in a constant state of war.

The Islamic state established by Mohammad was financially dependent on the spoils from raids and invasions as well as slavery (riqq). Mohammad said that "if a slave disobeyed, he has defected from Islam."[243] Most importantly, this religious state was psychologically dependent on

---

242 Quran 9:5.
243 Sahih Muslim 1768, 1769.

remaining in a continuous conflict that united the Muslims and gave them a purpose. The number of followers was increasing drastically and their infighting and demands grew exponentially within a very short time due to the success in defeating other people and acquiring their wealth and women. Thus, to prevent a mutiny they had to remain in a perpetual state of war against external enemies. They also needed a cruel dictatorial authority.

THE PROPHET IS HALLUCINATING

In the last year of Mohammad's life, there was a drastic change in how fellow Muslims perceived him. It seems that he lost his halo. Many of his senior soldiers publicly showed disobedience to their king. Both Mohammad and many of his followers realized that he would not have a male heir to succeed him, and his power was diminishing as he was aging.[244] He attempted to name his cousin and son-in-law Ali as his successor to protect himself but the senior Muslims foiled that attempt. A number of his prominent followers attempted to assassinate him on his way back to Medina from his last invasion. The assassination attempt on Mohammad's life is reported in detail in the most trusted Islamic books. In these passages, we see a different Mohammad to the one that was raiding cities and towns with loyal soldiers few years earlier. He was resigned and afraid of his own followers who grew bloodthirsty. He was travelling with a few of his trusted companions ahead of his army. While he was crossing a narrow straight in the mountains, a group of armed men tried to attack him. He ordered his bodyguards to engage them before they reached him. After a brief skirmish, the attackers escaped back to the army. He did not attempt to punish them. He did not even disclose their names or confront them. In the Quran, Allah states that some Muslims defected and were trying to deceive Mohammad and kill him.[245] Allah did not name the attackers, nor did he punish them.

A few months later, the old frail leader fell sick with an acute fever, less than ten years after he established his state. There has been a debate among jurists for centuries whether the man died due to an illness or was poisoned. Some historians accused an anonymous Jewish woman of poisoning their prophet. They claimed that she had given him poisoned

---

244 The History of al-Tabarī, Vol. 9.
245 Quran 9:74.

meat three years prior to his death and the poison killed him slowly.[246] In contrast, Shias implied that he had been poisoned by one of his wives, and most likely Aisha, who is the daughter of Abu Baker.

On his deathbed, Mohammad attempted one more time to pave the way for Ali to succeed him. He ordered his followers to form an army and invade Syria.[247] He instructed all the senior Muslims to join the army except Ali, who was ordered to remain in Medina. He appointed an 18-year-old boy with no experience or influence to be the general of this army. This appointed leader was Osama, the son of Mohammad's freed slave Zaid. Mohammad ordered all the senior leaders, including his fathers in law Abu Baker and Omar, to obey the newly appointed leader as a clear sign that he wanted to marginalise them. He encouraged all his followers to join the army, saying: "invade the Romans to gain blond girls."[248] Most of the prominent persons refused to comply with their prophet's orders, thus, the army remained stationed outside Medina, waiting for Mohammad's death. The appointed head of the army could not force his powerful soldiers to obey him and could not move without them. Mohammad was helpless; all his repeated pleas to Muslims to listen to him and move on with the mission were in vain.[249]

On the last Thursday before his death, his house was filled with his followers and he asked for ink and a slate.[250] He stated that he was about to write a guide for Muslims which if they followed, they would not stray. Some people wanted to get him the ink and the slate, others refused adamantly.[251] Finally, his senior assistants took control of the scene, saying that Mohammad was hallucinating, and the revelations of Allah were sufficient enough to guide them, although they were not written in a single book. Mohammad was outraged and told the attendants to leave his house, saying that they should not argue in the presence of a prophet.

During his last days, he was in pain and was losing consciousness time and again. His wives and uncle forced him to take some herbal

---

246 Sahih al-Bukhari 4428.
247 The History of al-Tabarī, Vol. 9.
248 Tafsir al-Tabarī; Tafsir ibn Kathir.
249 The History of al-Tabarī, Vol. 9. Ibn Hisham.
250 Sahih al-Bukhari 4431.
251 Sahih al-Bukhari 4432.

medication against his will. These tales show how Mohammad lost his authority. His own bodyguards were challenging him constantly, and his own followers defied his orders. Mohammad's last teaching to his followers was to evict disbelievers from Arabia.[252]

Mohammad died at the age of 63, without appointing a successor or a written will.[253] His corpse remained in his house for three days.[254] It seems as if his family hoped that he was going to resurrect from the dead, or they were in a shock and did not want to accept that he was no longer alive. His dead body started to decompose, and thus his uncle Abbas said that he was just a human and must be buried.

Omar's reaction to the death of Mohammad was hysterical: he threatened to assault anyone who dared to say that Mohammad had died. Abu Baker, on the other hand, showed an unexpected composure; he declared that whoever was worshipping Mohammad must know that Mohammad was indeed dead but whoever worshipped Allah must realise that Allah does not die.[255]

All the senior companions were absent from the burial of their supposedly beloved prophet; they were busy fighting over the succession. The ones who washed his body, prayed on him and buried him were his close family and a number of insignificant followers.[256] The main contenders to succeed Mohammad were Saad Ibin Abada, who was a powerful tribal leader from Yathrib, Ali ibn Abi Talib – Mohammad's cousin and son-in-law, Omar, and Abu Baker – the oldest confidant of Mohammad and his father-in-law. A secretive meeting organized by Saad and the people of Yathrib to nominate a successor and be united against the Meccans took place on the same day Mohammad died. Abu Baker knew about the meeting and went to attend it with Omar and several senior Meccans without an invitation. In that meeting, the people of Yathrib were divided while the Meccans were unified, which was usual. Abu Baker was chosen to be the successor of Mohammad (caliph) by Omar first and then the

---

252 Sahih al-Bukhari 4431.
253 Sahih al-Bukhari 4447.
254 The History of al-Tabarī, Vol. 9.
255 Sahih al-Bukhari 4454.; The History of al-Tabarī, Vol. 9.
256 As above.

Meccans who approved Omar's move. Once the Meccans declared their support for Abu Baker as the caliph of Mohammad, the majority of the attendants pledged their allegiance to Abu Baker, despite fierce opposition from Saad and a limited number of individuals from Yathrib.[257]

Omar played a key role in appointing Abu Baker to the throne, securing the position of the "crown prince" for himself. Ali along with Mohammad's daughter and their relatives refused to accept Abu Baker as a ruler. Mohammad's clan – the Hashemites – supported Ali in his challenge to introduce himself as the legitimate heir of his cousin and father-in-law. Fatima was a vocal supporter of her husband Ali, as Shia claim. She delivered a fierce speech attacking Abu Baker and Omar in the grand mosque, claiming that her husband must become the ruler. This mutiny is the prelude of Shia Islam and its source of legitimacy. Ali and his followers' opposition did not have a significant effect as Abu Baker had a much stronger backing, especially among the Meccans. They saw Ali as a threat to their interests because he was young and belonged to the same clan as Mohammad. In contrast, Abu Baker was in his sixties and from a different clan. They believed that all the clans that constitute Quraish should share the power rather than it being concentrated in the hands of just one. To quell the rebellion of Mohammad's family, Abu Baker confiscated their sources of income. He seized the farms that had been taken from the Jewish people and given by Mohammad as a gift to Ali and Fatima. Abu Baker justified depriving Fatima of what she considered her inheritance through claiming that Mohammad had said prophets do not pass on financial inheritance.[258] Next, Omar led an armed force that went to Ali and Fatima's house. He threatened to set the house on fire if Ali and his supporters did not come out and pledge allegiance to Abu Baker.[259] Ali and his followers refused and remained inside the house. The force stormed the house, assailed Fatima and arrested Ali along with a number of his followers. They took him to the grand mosque and forced him to declare his allegiance to Abu Baker as the legitimate successor of Mohammad and hence, the

---

257 As above.
258 Sahih al-Bukhari 4240, 4241.
259 The History of al-Tabarī, Vol. 9.

absolute ruler. Although Ali showed his compliance to the established regime in public, he continued to disclose his opposition whenever the circumstances allowed it.[260]

This struggle over the succession of Mohammad between Ali and his supporters (Shia) on the one side and the rest of Muslims who accepted what had happened as Allah's will and adhered to the tradition of Mohammad (Sunni) on the other side has not concluded yet. To this day, Muslims are divided between Shias, who believe that Abu Baker and the majority of Mohammad's companions were traitors and Ali is the legitimate caliph, versus Sunnis, who see Abu Baker as a legitimate successor of his companion and son-in-law Mohammad. Shias derived their understanding of Islam from the Quran and the tradition transmitted by Ali and his children and their supporters, while Sunni depend on the same Quran and the tradition transmitted by all the companions of Mohammad. The differences between the two sects are peripheral in many essential matters because they both believe that the Quran is the literal word of Allah. Hence, they share the vast majority of the principles. The struggle for power, money, and influence has been and is expected to remain the main motive behind the bloody conflict between the two groups and between the rest of the world and them.

---

260 As above.

THE RUTHLESS SUCCESSOR, ISLAM'S CIVIL WAR, AND THE CALIPHATES

After the death of Mohammad, his kingdom collapsed instantly. The Muslim civil war began and has not ended to this day. The vast majority of Arabs who converted to Islam during Mohammad's reign deserted the religion once they knew he had deceased. Arab towns and tribes left Islam for different reasons and in different ways. The majority went back to their previous lives and identities. Many tribes returned to Christianity, others to polytheism, and some created new religions. A number of individuals declared themselves prophets and gained support among their communities. An important figure we know about was a woman named Sajah who declared herself a prophet and won considerable support, especially from her own tribe Tamim. However, the most important religious movement in Arabia after the death of Mohammad was led by Musaylamah, who created his religion either before Mohammad or at a similar time to the establishment of Islam in Mecca. He was an influential orator and gained tens of thousands of followers. His movement was peaceful and did not engage in any conflict. Mohammad invited him to accept Islam, but he declined. The number of his followers was larger than the Muslims, thus Mohammad never attacked him.

According to Muslim historians, after Mohammad's demise, three towns remained committed to Islam: Mecca, Medina, and Ta'if. These cities were dependent on Islam. Their inhabitants knew that they would become the target of other Arabs' revenge for the invasions and raids waged under Mohammad's command, once the victims gained back their independence. The people of these three towns were also economically dependent on the invasions and could not survive without continuing that business. Yathrib (Medina) was heavily populated by warriors from all over the Arabian Peninsula, who made a living by invading non-Muslims' towns and seizing their properties, children and women. Mecca was no longer a centre of paganism, as all the idols had been destroyed. It was now the centre of Islam and its people depended on Muslim pilgrims and slave trade. Thus, the Medinans and the Meccans were extremely committed to fighting all the rebellious Arabs.[261]

The first caliph Abu Baker took power three days after Mohammad's death. This man had secured his position by being loyal to Mohammad all his life. He had given his six-year-old daughter Aisha as a wife to the then-52-year-old prophet. He started his rule by mobilising all Muslims to annihilate the defectors without a warning. He waged a genocidal war against all Arabs, starting with the weaker. He categorized every disobedience as an act of war against Allah, which was punishable by death for men, slavery for women and children, and the confiscation of money. He used the verse in Quran that says: "The penalty for those who wage war against Allah and his Messenger and strive upon earth [to cause] corruption is none but that they be killed or crucified or that their hands and feet be cut off from opposite sides or that they be exiled from the land. That is for them a disgrace in this world; and for them in the hereafter is a great punishment"[262] as his mantra.

This creed was established as the divine law employed when dealing with any person who dared to challenge the Islamic ruler. Abu Baker sent his armies to attack the towns and tribes that left Islam, refused to recognize him as the successor of Mohammad or wanted to attain some degree of autonomy. Muslim armies were raiding the targeted people in the dark of night, without a warning. They would kill as many men as they could, confiscate all the properties and enslave all females and children.[263] This tactic, originally established by Mohammad, had become an essential part of the Muslim mentality. Muslim fighters started by attacking the most vulnerable and least prepared communities. In many cases, the people were paralysed by the sudden attack, which allowed the Muslims to exterminate them ruthlessly. People were often slain at dawn while sleeping in their beds.[264] During these raids, non-Muslim

---

261 The History of al-Ṭabarī, Vol. 10.
262 Quran 5:33.
263 The History of al-Ṭabarī, Vol. 10.
264 As above.

men would sometimes run away, leaving behind their children and wives to be enslaved by the invaders.

When some of Abu Baker's advisors asked him not to attack the Muslim tribes that did not want to pay zakat to him, he replied that he would attack any tribe which was paying its zakat with one camel's leash missing. What was decisive for the downfall of the revolting tribes was the fact that they were trying to defend themselves and their property rather than uniting and waging offensive attacks against the Muslims. Each and every tribe and town fought independently against the aggressors. Thus, they were all defeated by invading armies which were better prepared and more ruthless, as they consisted of fugitives, thugs, and mercenaries in addition to the devoted Muslims. One of imam Ali's known advice to Muslims was to be on the offensive, as people attacked inside their homeland would be defeated. Many males converted or reconverted to Islam in order to participate in these battles known as Apostasy (Ridda) Wars. Joining jihad allowed the person to commit all kinds of crimes and atrocities with full immunity. The sheer animalistic fear caused by the horrific tales of Muslims' tactics made many tribes and towns capitulate unconditionally.

Abu Baker's reign lasted for two years during which tens of thousands of Arabs were killed at the hands of the Muslims. The fighters who survived this war became extremely rich due to the spoils they acquired from their victims. Moreover, each one of these fighters got many slave-girls, several wives and vast lands. They fathered many children with the wives and the slaves. The one way to earn a living in that society was invading other people to conquer more land and wealth. This made joining jihad a necessity, both for poor youth as well as for the experienced fighters and their children. The nature of the Islamic state made the population extremely obedient, aggressive, and merciless all at once. This resulted in a paranoid society, in which everyone distrusted everyone. Any person could easily be designated as an enemy of Islam. It was enough to say or do something that would merit an accusation of apostasy, a charge that has been used by Islamic regimes over the ages to warrant the killing of innocents. The caliph's position became extremely frightening – no one could hold him accountable, as he was the heir of

Mohammad and had all the power over the whole nation. Thus, many ambitious people sought to become the caliph; many lost their lives for attempting to do that while others succeeded in killing the caliph and sat on his throne.

Before he died, Abu Baker appointed Omar as the next caliph, with complete disregard for public opinion. Omar became the absolute ruler of a fully militarized, sadomasochistic religious society. Every Arab was armed, had been in battle and could not survive without new spoils. Killing other people, acquiring their property and enslaving their women and children was the only trade Muslims had. The slaves and the people of the conquered nations were the working force, while the majority of Arabs were the fighters responsible for increasing the number of the working force, and Mohammad's companions were the rulers, judges, teachers and propaganda officers. There was no written copy of the Quran or Mohammad's hadith. Thus, the companions were the ones deciding all matters based on what they were taught by Mohammad.

Omar started his reign by sending these vicious fighters to invade the centres of civilization. He created institutions based on Islamic teachings to regulate jihad, slavery and spoils. Every adult Arab male was a soldier on the payroll of the state or working for the state in another capacity. The main goal of the Islamic state was to conquer the world and subjugate it to the reign of Mohammad's caliph. Muslims invaded Iraq, Persia, Egypt, Levant and India during Omar's reign. In their invasions of the centres of civilization, Muslim fighters saw themselves as the soldiers of God entitled to everything they desired. They constructed their victims as the sinful enemies of God, thus subhuman, that must be cleansed from the earth. The mass killing, deception, enslaving, looting, destruction were the means through which Muslims conquered the old world.

Killing people after promising not to harm them was an essential practice in the Islamic invasions. It was established during Mohammad and the so-called guided caliphs' reign and continued afterward. In 630, Muslims led by Khalid ibn Al-Walid attacked an Arab tribe called Banu Jadhimah on the orders of Mohammad to convert them to Islam. They accepted the new religion under duress and confirmed that they were Muslims. Khalid, however, ordered them to put down their weapons to show that they were sincere, which they did. He handcuffed them and ordered his soldiers to behead them because they were lying, as he declared. Several of the handcuffed prisoners were executed before another Muslim cavalry which was passing by intervened and stopped the killing. When the relatives of the slain people went to Mohammad to complain, he responded that he was innocent of what Khalid had done and paid the people some blood-money as compensation. He did not punish his soldier and kept appointing him as a head of expeditions.

During the reign of Abu Baker and Omar the Muslim soldiers massacred the Persians, Iraqis, Egyptians, and North Africans after promising not to harm them if they did not resist. One of the most famous examples is the Battle of Ullais, also known as the Battle of Blood River (633 CE), in which the leader of the invading Muslim army, Khalid ibn al-Walid, vowed to Allah to create a river of the blood of the Persians and their Arab allies, if Allah gave him victory over these people – who were defending their lands and lives. At the beginning, the Muslims were met with fierce resistance by the Sasanian soldiers and their Christian Arab allies, thus, they reverted to deception, vowing that they would not harm the ones who gave up their weapons and surrendered. Group after group of the Persians and the Arabs capitulated. The Muslims handcuffed them and took them to the river's banks where they beheaded them and threw their bodies into the water that turned red from the blood.[265] Then, the Muslims cornered the rest of the soldiers who were withdrawing. They beheaded every person, creating a river of blood in the desert. Over 70000 human beings were killed by Muslims in that battle, which was and still is presented in a glorifying way in public schools, mosque speeches and media productions of Islamic countries.

Ten years into his reign, Omar was assassinated by a Persian man called Abu-Louloa (father of Louloa) while praying inside the grand mosque in Medina. The assassin had been a craftsman and a soldier before he was captured by Muslims in one of their attacks against his country – Persia. The Arabs enslaved him and took him into forced labour in Medina. He would cry when he saw the convoys of captured

---

265 The History of al-Tabarī, Vol. 13.

children and women brought into Medina as slaves.[266] He decided to avenge the injustice brought upon his people by the Arabs through killing their leader. He stabbed Omar, along with several other Arabs, during the dawn prayer. He then stabbed himself when they surrounded him and died from his wounds. Omar's son killed Abu-Louloa's child daughter and several other innocent Persians as a revenge for his father. Among the slain people was the Persian general who had betrayed his own people, converted to Islam and fought with the Arab invaders.[267] He was a loyal adviser to Omar but that did not save him from the Muslims' indiscriminate wrath.

On his deathbed, Omar named six people as his qualified successors. He ordered them to convene and elect one of them within three days of his death. He ordered fifty armed fighters to guard the meeting place and if the six failed in naming a caliph, they must all be killed. Ali was one of the contenders, but he lost to Uthman who was chosen by four out of the six to become the next caliph.

Uthman, who became caliph in 644, was Mohammad's son-in-law, as he had married two of Mohammad's daughters consecutively, though they both died without bearing children. He was from the Umayyad clan of Quraish and one of the early people who accepted Islam. During his reign, Muslims captured new countries and converted many nations through jihad. Uthman was giving his clan, the Umayyads, the lion's share of the spoils and the conquered lands. He installed his cousins into key positions in the occupied countries and allowed them to act as absolute kings. His cousin Muawiya was appointed as the absolute ruler of the richest region of all: the Levant, which includes Syria, Palestine, Jordan and Lebanon. Uthman appointed his half-brother as the governor of Egypt and another cousin as the governor of Iraq. These individuals were extremely cruel with the natives and unfair with the Arabs. They kept most of the seized lands, wealth and slaves for themselves and their relatives. Mohammad's senior companions and close relatives

266 The History of al-Tabarī, Vol 13., p 683.
267 Zarrinkub, A. (1975). The Arab conquest of Iran and its aftermath. In R. N. Frye (Ed.). The Cambridge History of Iran, Volume 4: From the Arab Invasion to the Saljuqs. Cambridge University Press, pp 1–57.

who grew wealthy and powerful due to the spoils they received began to feel marginalised by Uthman when he seemed to prepare his sons and relatives to succeed him. They began demanding more power and bigger shares in the seized wealth and slaves.

In 656, Arab soldiers in Iraq and Egypt revolted against Uthman's representatives, accusing them of corruption, nepotism and apostasy. They sent big armed delegations to Medina demanding that the caliph dismissed his relatives from the governorship of Egypt and Iraq. Many of the people of Medina joined the protesters with other demands. Uthman pretended that he accepted them all and promised to remove his corrupt relatives from power and compensate the people for past injustices. He gave the Arabs of Egypt and Iraq written letters containing the dismissal of the governors and told them to go back to their countries. While on their way to Egypt, the protesters intercepted a man that was carrying a secret letter to the governor of Egypt from Uthman. In that letter, the caliph ordered his deputy to slaughter the disobedient people once they were back. The delegation of Arabs from Egypt warned the Arabs of Iraq against trusting the caliph. The two groups went back and surrounded Uthman's house. This time, they demanded his abdication. He refused and said that Allah had installed him in this position and he would never resign. Several of Mohammad's widows as well as many of his relatives and senior companions such as Ali ibn Abi Talib took part in the rebellion against Uthman. Aisha played a key role in this revolution. She used to display Mohammad's clothes and shoes in the mosque, saying: "these things have not dissolved yet while Uthman dissolved Mohammad's religion. He must be killed, he defected from Islam." A few days after the siege, angry Muslims stormed the house of their caliph and killed him, wounded several of his supporters and cut off his wife's hand. One of the assassins said that he stabbed Uthman one time for Allah and nine times for himself.

The revolutionists brought Mohammad's cousin and son-in-law Ali ibn Abi Talib to the throne as the fourth caliph and forced everyone else to pledge allegiance to him. Aisha, Muawiya – the cousin of Uthman, who was the de facto king of the Levant – and many other influential leaders objected to Ali's rule right from the onset. The first armed disobedience movement against the new caliph was led by Aisha and her cousin Talha and Mohammad's cousin Zubayr. The three left Medina (Yathrib) accompanied by their supporters and marched to seize Basra in Iraq. Their plan was to control the rich and heavily populated city and declare it as their capital, which they did after killing the representatives of Ali and their supporters. After learning that Aisha and Zubayr controlled Basra, Ali mobilised his followers and marched to fight them. The two armies clashed in what is known as the Battle of the Camel. It was named after the camel Aisha was riding, as it became the rallying point of her army. In this battle, tens of thousands of Muslims were killed on both sides, and among the casualties – several of the founders of Islam. Although Ali won the battle, he became a weak caliph due to the loss of thousands of his soldiers.

Uthman's cousin Muawiya, who had been the governor of the Levant for decades, remained adamant in this refusal to recognize Ali as a legitimate caliph. He affirmed his control over his territory and waged a successful attack to capture Egypt. This provided him with substantial economic resources which allowed him to recruit more soldiers. Meanwhile Ali, after defeating Aisha's mutiny, moved the capital from Yathrib to the Iraqi city Kufa, which was a garrison for the Arab invading armies that had conquered Iraq and Persia. From there, he mobilised a huge army to fight Muawiya and to recapture the Levant.

Thirty-six years after Mohammad's death, the Mohammedans were divided between two fighting camps. The majority of the founders of Islam and their children were fighting for imam Ali, while the majority of the Meccans were with Muawiya, the descendant of the people who had been killed in the Battle of Badr fighting Mohammad. The two sides fought several bloody battles where tens of thousands of people were killed and wounded between Ali and Muawiya.[268]

The war ended when Ali was assassinated five years into his reign by one of his followers during the dawn prayer in the Kufa mosque in Iraq. The assassin belonged to an Islamic sect called Kharijites that considered both Ali and Muawiya apostates. Ali's son and Mohammad's grandson

268 See Crone, P. (2004). God's rule: government and Islam. Columbia University Press.

Hassan succeeded his father as a caliph and ruled a part of the Muslim world for a short time, but he could not stand up to Muawiya. Therefore, Hassan signed a conceding agreement with Muawiya, acknowledging the latter as the legitimate caliph of Mohammad. Muawiya promised Hassan a huge annual sum from the treasury and that he would succeed him. Hassan and his brother Hussein, the only male grandchildren of Mohammad, were hoping to outlive Muawiya and become caliphs after his death. However, after consolidating his grip on power, Muawiya renounced his promises to Hassan. He transformed the political system into a hereditary monarchy ruled by his clan, the Umayyad, ending the Guided Caliphate in which any person from Quraysh could become caliph. He made Damascus the capital of Islam. In 670, Muawiya poisoned Hassan with the help of one of Hassan's wives, ending the last potential threat to his reign. He stifled all other opponents, either with violence or money.

It is a great irony that Muawiya, who had rejected Islam, fought against Mohammad for more than twenty-two years and converted under duress after the fall of Mecca, ended up as Mohammad's caliph. The vast majority of Muslims worldwide consider Muawiya a legitimate Islamic caliph despite his struggle against Islam and despite the fact that his father had been the leader of the Meccan army that fought Mohammad in several battles. His father had also been the leader of the caravan which Muslims had attempted to attack but which had managed to evade them in Badr. Mohammad had killed Muawiya's brother, his maternal grandfather and maternal uncle in Badr and married his half-sister.

Muawiya was a politician who knew how to use the discourse of Islam, the money seized from the conquered nations, and the slaves to establish himself and his family as a ruling dynasty, and to whitewash their history. He established the Umayyad Caliphate as a hereditary kingdom ruled by the house of Umayyad in accordance with the teachings of Islam. Muawiya, and all his successors alike, derived the legitimacy from the fact that he was implementing Allah's orders, which he made sure to have written, explained and re-explained in a way that suited him. He appointed his son Yazid as his crown prince and forced everyone to pledge allegiance to him. In general, senior Muslims who fought with Mohammad, and the people of Yathrib in particular, were pushed to the margin of power by the Umayyad Caliphate but were given substantial wealth – which was but a small fraction of what had been stolen from the conquered nations – as a reward for their support and silence.[269]

---

269 The History of al-Ṭabarī, Vol. 18-19.; Ibn al-Athir, Vol. 3-4.

ARABS REVENGE AGAINST MOHAMMAD
AND THE FRAGMENTATION OF THE NATION

After the death of Muawiya – the fifth successor of Mohammad, his son and crown prince Yazid assumed the throne in 680, supported by the Arab generals. The grandson of Mohammad, Hussain, who was living in Yathrib, refused to accept Yazid as a legitimate caliph. He accused him of being an apostate. He secretly orchestrated an armed rebellion to topple the Umayyad Caliphate and reinstate his clan as the ruling dynasty. Forty-eight years before the day Hussain attempted to become the head of the Islamic state, his grandfather Mohammad had died, and their family had lost its reign for almost thirty years. His father Ali ibn Abi Talib had gained power through a coup and lasted as a caliph for less than five years, from 656 to 661. His short time in power had been tainted by civil conflicts and rebellions and ended with his assassination.

This time, Hussain sought to regain his dynasty's throne and to establish himself and his descendants as the caliphs of his grandfather. He started his movement in Medina, hoping that the descendants of the founders of Islam would follow him the same way their parents and grandparents followed and fought for his father and grandfather. But these people, as well as the vast majority of Muslims of Arabia, let him down. It seems that they did not want to repeat their fathers' mistake and allow one person to be Jesus and Caesar in one. Hussain said that there were not twenty men in the whole of Arabia who loved Mohammad or his relatives. Hence, he shifted his attention to Iraq, hoping that the Iraqis would fight for him the same way they fought for his father. He based his claim to power on the assertion that his grandfather had designated his father and him as the legitimate caliphs. After convincing a number of Iraqis to be his soldiers via correspondence, he sent his cousin to Kufa, his father's capital, to recruit as many fighters as possible. His cousin garnered certain support and sent him a letter telling him to relocate to Kufa and make it his capital, the same way his grandfather did with Medina. Hussain gathered his family and all the people who were willing to fight for him and moved toward Kufa. Meanwhile the new Umayyad caliph, Yazid, was not to repeat his grandfather's blunder of waiting for his enemy to gain power and establish a stronghold. He appointed a shrewd, ruthless man as the governor of Kufa and instructed him to nip any disobedience in the bud with extreme violence and cruel collective punishment. This man arrested most of the rebellious individuals and their relatives. Through promises of reward and threats of severe punishment, he managed to dissuade the people from joining Mohammad's grandson and convince them to remain loyal to the state and its legal Islamic caliph. Hussain's representative was captured and executed in public; an army was sent to intercept Hussain before he reached Kufa.

THE BATTLE OF KARBALA

On the tenth day of the first month (Muharram) of 61 AH, known as Ashura[270], which was 10 October 680 CE, two Muslim forces clashed at a place called Karbala in Iraq. One was the army of the state, loyal to Umayyad caliph Yazid. The leader of this army was Omar ibn Saad, the son of one of the early Muslims in Mecca and a relative of Mohammad. The second was a rebellious force composed of around 100 fighters, most of whom were Mohammad's descendants and relatives, led by Hussein.

The caliphate's soldiers massacred the grandson of their prophet along with his children, half-brothers, nephews, cousins, and supporters in the Battle of Karbala. The soldiers decapitated the relatives of their prophet and put their heads on spears. They captured Mohammad's granddaughters together with over a hundred women and children and treated them as slaves, in accordance with sharia. They took them, along with the severed heads, on a victory march all the way from Karbala to Damascus more than 700 kilometres away, passing through several cities and towns. Yazid was extremely jubilant to see the defeat of Hussain.[271] In a known poem, Yazid said that Mohammad's clan had played with authority and that he took revenge on Mohammad for what he had done in Badr and in other invasions. He declared that there had been no divine revelations nor godly orders and all that had happened was a game.[272]

---

270 The name Ashurah comes from the word for number ten in Arabic: asharah.
271 Sahih al-Bukhari 3538.
272 The History of al-Tabarī, Vol. 19.; Ibn al-Athir, Vol. 4.

THE BATTLE OF AL-HARRA

Less than two years after the Battle of Karbala, the people of the holiest sites in Islam, Medina and Mecca, revolted against the Umayyad rule. Yazid sent an army to subdue the two cities once and for all. His forces marched first toward Medina, the first capital of Islam and the stronghold of Mohammad's companions and their children who had been declared apostates for rejecting the legitimate caliph. In 683, a battle took place at a site called al-Harra on the outskirts of Medina and where the fort of the Jewish Banu Qurayzah once stood. The attacking army defeated the fighters of Medina, killing, wounding and capturing thousands. Among the casualties and the captives were many of Mohammad's companions, their children and grandchildren. The commander of the army ordered the execution of many of them. The Umayyad army stormed Medina, killing and looting. The soldiers were instructed to destroy the population and erase their identity as a punishment for disobeying the Muslim caliph, which equalled rejecting Allah. The army commander declared a three-day period in which his soldiers could do whatever they pleased to the city and its inhabitants. This Islamic military tradition called estepahat (permission) applies whenever Muslims conquer a city by violence.

The Umayyad soldiers raped thousands of girls and it was the Muslim historians who reported that over a thousand unmarried girl gave birth as a result of this rape. The children who resulted from the mass-rape were called the Harra's children.[273] The soldiers also looted everything they could get their hands on and destroyed the properties. When a woman who was a relative of the army commander came to him hoping that he would release her captured son, he ordered his soldiers to behead the boy and to give the severed head to the mother. After conquering

---

273 Ibn Kathir, A. (1992). Al-Bidaya wa al-Nihaya [The Beginning and the End]. Vol. 8., p 221.

Medina, the Umayyad army marched toward Mecca. They stormed it and besieged the rebels who held in the grand mosque for 64 days. During the siege, the Umayyad army shelled the mosque with stones and burning objects, setting the Kaaba on fire.[274] They withdrew only after they knew that Yazid passed away, however, less than a year later another Umayyad army conquered Mecca after killing and wounding thousands of its people. The two holy cities were reduced to an insignificant position and have never regained their status as important centres.

---

274 The History of al-Tabarī, Vol. 19., pp 210- 220.; Ibn al-Athir, Vol. 4.

THE BIRTH OF SHIA

The supporters of Ali (Shiatu Ali), led by the ones who did not participate in the Battle of Karbala, used these events, especially the murdering of Hussein, as a rallying point to create Shia Islam as a political religious movement. The main aim of this movement was to overthrow the Umayyad dynasty and install Mohammad's immediate descendants as caliphs. They used the beheading of Mohammad's grandson as the main narrative.

To this day, millions of Shias across the world commemorate the Battle of Karbala in a dramatic way during Ashura to gain supporters for their ideology. The crowds shriek while listening to their imams describe in detail how the sinful Muslim soldiers attacked and massacred imam Hussein and his supporters. They describe in detail how they beheaded Hussein along with his followers and relatives and placed the severed heads on spears. They lament that the women and girls who were Mohammad's relatives were taken as slaves to the palace of Yazid. They relentlessly emphasise the notion that Hussain was the genuine heir of Mohammad and he and his followers were the true believers while their opponents were enemies of Allah. Shia perform self-flagellation, sometimes harming themselves with sharp objects to show their sorrow and remorse for not protecting Hussein. These commemoration rituals are the cornerstone of Shia Islam. Their spiritual leaders have been using these events to distinguish Shia from other Muslims whom they portray as either supporters of the Umayyad, thus enemies of Islam, or heretics because they do not follow Mohammad's teachings transmitted via his grandchildren. They declare that the true Muslims are the Shia and the Shia alone, because they are the ones who supported Hussein in his failed coup attempt against the disbelievers' regime. They also argue that Hussein and his grandchildren are the legitimate imams based on sayings attributed to the Prophet. Shia believe that the legitimate political/religious leader of humanity after Hussein was his son Ali, and after him his son Mohammad, and then his son.

There are several combating main Shia sects, among them the Twelvers, who constitute the majority in Bahrain, Iraq, Iran, and Azerbaijan, and significant minorities in Lebanon, Syria, Kuwait, Saudi Arabia, Qatar, and Pakistan. The Zaydi Shias who live mainly in Yemen have been in power in that country for over a thousand years. The Ismaili Shia who established several states such as the Fatimid, the Nizari and the Qarmatians are currently very small minority within Muslims. Finally, Kaysanite Shia are the smallest Shia group. Each one of these groups is divided into subgroups, and each one of the subgroups has its own jurisprudence school and political/religious leadership. The main difference between the main Shia sects is related to the succession of Mohammad. Some sects believe that the legitimate succession stopped at the fifth grandson of Mohammad (Zaidi), others believe it stopped at the seventh (Ismaili), while others yet believe that it is still ongoing (Nizari, Ismaili).[275]

Currently, the vast majority of Shia are the Twelver Shia. They believe that the last legitimate Imam is the twelfth imam who is the ninth grandchild of Hussain; he is called Mohammad ibn Al Hassan and his title is Mahdi (the Guided). He was born in 869 CE in Iraq and he went into hiding when he was a child in 874 CE to avoid being captured by the soldiers of the caliph of his time. Thus, he is also called the Hidden Imam. Shia have been firmly believing that Mahdi is still alive and he will return one day to re-establish his reign over the whole world. They have been praying for his return for centuries in vain. Shia children are taught that Mahdi is their supreme leader who has been influencing the world with the permission of Allah. To this day, educated Shias argue ardently that it is logical and ethical to believe that a man has been living for over 11 hundred years in secrecy, without any evidence, and to ingrain such an absurd idea into children's psyche. The only proof for his existence is the words of the ancient imams who declared that they corresponded with the Mahdi in the first seventy years of his hiding. The Shia claim that the Mahdi told the last of his four direct deputies

---

275 Crone, P. (2014). Medieval Islamic political thought. Edinburgh University Press.

through correspondence that he would go into complete hiding and would not communicate with anyone directly until he comes back to rule the world and avenge his killed fathers. This took place over a thousand years ago and since that date Shia jurists have been acting as the Mahdi's representatives responsible for guiding the people and collecting taxes until the Mahdi comes back and takes control.

The vast majority of Muslims at Hussein's time supported the Umayyad Caliphate; they took the name Sunnis, a term which comes from following the Sunnah (practices and orders) of Mohammad, and to this date still recognize the Umayyad Caliphate as legitimate Islamic state. They understand the killing of Hussain in different ways. Some argue that his killing was wrong while others justify it. For instance, the influential Sunni jurist Ibn Taymiyyah (d. 1328) declared that Hussein was killed by his grandfather's sword as he rebelled against the legitimate caliph, a crime punishable by death in Islam.

THE NATION OF ISLAM IN PIECES: SUNNI, SHIA, AND MANY OTHERS

The reign of the Umayyad was plagued by civil wars and countless bloody struggles. Many different groups and sects staged coup attempts and armed revolutions to topple the ruling dynasty. To remain in power, the Umayyad waged countless invasions against other nations, sending Muslim youths to die in faraway battlefields. They also established mass killing of citizens based on suspicion as a legal measure to stifle any opposition. They practiced collective punishment such as burning the houses and imprisoning the children and women of their real, potential, and expected opponents and their relatives and neighbours. They burned parts of cities and killed tribes and entire families as a punishment for individuals' acts.[276]

They appointed ruthless governors to the various regions and instructed them to turn the population into obedient serfs through all sorts of indiscriminate violence, establishing the tradition of Islamic governorships. The most notable governor was Al-Hajjaj ibn Yusuf who ruled over Iraq for ten years. He killed thousands of people without trial and established the destruction of suspects' and fugitives' houses and indefinite incarceration of their families as a legal procedure. He oversaw the invasion of the Indian subcontinent and Central Asia as well as other regions and annexing them to the Muslim Caliphate. He crushed several revolutions by committing horrific genocides. He ordered every Muslim to join the army and beheaded defectors in public. He played an important role in writing and standardising the Quran. Upon his death, he had over twenty thousand starving tormented prisoners in his jails, many of whom were women and children. This man has been glorified by modern TV series and films as a distinguished Muslim statesman.[277]

---

276 Crone, P. (2014). Medieval Islamic political thought. Edinburgh University Press.; The History of al-Tabarī, Vol. 19.; Hawting, G. R. (2002). The first dynasty of Islam: the Umayyad caliphate AD 661-750. Routledge.; Ibn al-Athir, Vol. 4.
277 Al Awamleh, T. (Producer). (2003). Al Hajjaj [TV broadcast]. Arab Telemedia Productions.

After eighty years in power, the Umayyad caliphate was toppled by an armed revolution led by members of Mohammad's family named the Abbasid. They were the descendants of Mohammad's uncle Abbas. The Abbasid were brutal even in comparison to the Umayyad; they committed countless genocides against all their opponents as well as peaceful civilians who were not part of the conflicts. Tens of thousands of people were massacred, and cities and towns were wiped out, in many cases without another reason except to terrorise the rest of the population. They adopted the Sunni Islam as the religion of the state. Their reign lasted from 750 to 1258. The peak of their power came during the first hundred years of that long period, as they were absolute rulers with very autocratic ruthless traditions. After that, their power fractured, and many parts of the Muslim world seceded from under their control. Their later caliphs were for the most part hostages of the military leaders who were Persians or Turks. Several Abbasid caliphs were executed by their army commanders, some of them days into their reigns. One of the caliphs ended up blind, begging people in the streets, after his Turk generals ousted him, burned his eyes and seized his money and women.

During the reign of the Abbasid, members of the Umayyad dynasty took control over Spain and Portugal and ruled that region for hundreds of years independently.[278] Moreover, several local governors succeeded in breaking away vast regions and establishing their hereditary kingdoms while keeping a nominal allegiance to the Abbasid caliphate. Shia dynasties led secretive militarised religious movements that succeeded in seceding and then controlling important regions, creating several Islamic states; some of them lasted for hundreds of years, such as the Fatimid Caliphate which existed from 909 to 1171 and controlled North Africa and Egypt. Turk and Persian Sunnis established kingdoms and principalities within territories of the Abbasid. The struggle between competing Sunni states and the conflict between the Shia on the one side and the Sunnis on the other side have never ceased to exist. Religious wars between Muslims have claimed the lives of massive numbers of people over the ages, with every party claiming to be following the

---

278 See Fernández-Morera, D. (2016). The Myth of the Andalusian Paradise: Muslims, Christian, and Jews under Islamic Rule in Medieval Spain. Open Road Media.

correct teachings of the Quran. This caliphate ended with the destruction of Baghdad at the hands of the Mongol in 1258.

The last powerful Islamic state was the Ottoman Caliphate. It was founded by a Turkmen tribal warlord named Osman, who immigrated with his tribe, the Oguz, from Mongolia to Anatolia.[279] He started as a leader of a militia that invaded the Christian Byzantine outposts, and then established a small principality in Bithynia and declared himself as a prince around 1300. After him his descendants assumed the power, taking advantage of the power void created by the destruction of the big Muslim states by the Mongols. They managed to conquer more lands and build a powerful military force. They declared their state an Islamic caliphate ruled by the dynasty of Ottoman in accordance with Islamic teachings. The mission of this state was to subjugate the whole world to the one and only valid religion. They waged wars against all the other states and kingdoms. This religious state lasted for 700 years and controlled a huge area and millions of people. Its laws were based on the Quran, the books of hadith and Mohammad's biographies as explained by the Hanafi jurists. It adopted and re-enacted the principles of Islam established by Mohammad and his successors. Similar to its predecessors, it was loyal to the indiscriminate violence and to suffocating oppression when dealing with its subjects as well as its enemies. It was at war with the Persian Islamic states for more than 300 years as well as many other Muslim states and communities. It also faced several revolutions and over the years, many parts of the Muslim world seceded from its rule.

This state crushed the Byzantine Empire along with many other states in Europe, Asia, and Africa and annexed their lands but failed in establishing a significant civilization. It committed countless religious genocides and atrocities against non-Muslims. The damage this caliphate caused to science, philosophy, art, industry, law, human rights, music, and literature is catastrophic. It destroyed the existing cultural institutions in the countries it conquered and waged a war against science and literature. It banned printing for more than 300 years[280]

---

279 See Masters, B. A. & Agoston, G. (Eds.). (2009). Encyclopedia of the Ottoman Empire. Infobase Publishing.; Murphey, R. (2006). Ottoman Warfare, 1500-1700. 1st Ed. Routledge.
280 Pektas, N. (2015). The Beginnings of Printing in the Ottoman Capital: Book Production

and censored music, literature, and art. Its focus was on jihad against non-Muslims and against Muslims who did not want to be ruled by the House of Ottoman. Throughout its existence, the Ottoman Caliphate was in a state of war both internally and externally. Its subjects were exposed to every kind of injustice. It was one of the most savage and regressive states created by humankind. One of their rituals was the killing of the caliph's brothers once he got a son to avert any struggle over power. This murder was sanctioned by the religious authority, like all the other crimes they committed over the ages.

Many of the Ottoman's Muslim subjects fought beside the European powers against the Caliphate during the First World War. They were willing to give up their lives to end the suppression, poverty, and injustice of the Islamic rule.

and Circulation in Early Modern Istanbul. Osmanli Bilimi Arastirmalari, 16(2), 3-32.

10 The Quran – An Angry, Cruel God

Allah is an enemy to the disbelievers [281]

The dominant one of the three main sources of Islam, the Quran, was written long after the death of Mohammad. While it is considered by Muslims the "unalterable," "eternal," "sacred" and "literal word of Allah," critics have argued that it is confusing, contradicts itself, discourages critical and independent thought, and promotes what most civilized people would consider unethical and even illegal behaviour, such as genocide and slavery, including sex slavery. In fact, they claim that the confusion and contradictions exist because it was written to give permission for and to justify Mohammad's acts. There are numerous examples of Mohammad being found in compromising or objectionable situations, and it is after the event that passages would appear in order to explain and sanction the Prophet's position and threaten anyone who would dare to challenge him.

---

281 Quran 2:98.

> Those who disbelieve in our revelations we will drive them
> into a fire. Every time their skins are roasted through, we will
> replace them with different skins, so they taste the torment [282]

During their legal trials, both Saddam Hussein of Iraq in 2005 and Hosni Mubarak of Egypt in 2011 showed up to the courts clutching copies of the Quran. They were showing their commitment to the book. The two corrupt, criminal tyrants garnered considerable support by brandishing the holy book. Muslims believe that the Quran is the eternal, divine miracle and the proof that Islam is the one and only righteous religion. The author of Quran made sure to emphasize the notion that it is a discourse designated to rescue people from their suffering and ignorance. The Quran says that it contains "marvellous information," "the finest stories," "the moral values" and "superior ideas."[283] It is sufficient to guide humans in every field. It is written in Arabic, in flawless superior language that cannot be matched by humans, its author stated. The author of the Quran also challenged humans and jinn to produce similar narratives. The whole of humanity cannot produce such a fabulous text, the author pledged. These ideas are the cornerstone of Islam. They have been propagated since Muslims established their first state fourteen hundred years ago, according to all the Muslim sources.

In the second half of the 20th century, numerous well-funded institutions were created by petrol-rich Muslim countries to print and distribute free copies of the Quran all over the world. These regimes have also created thousands of schools worldwide dedicated to teaching Quran. For the past fifty years, the Quran has been taught in each and every public and private school in Muslim countries as a mandatory subject. Students, Muslims and non-Muslims, have been required to study Quran every year throughout their academic lives all over the Muslim world and

---

282 Quran 2:98, see Pickthall's translation.
283 Quran 2:2; 12:3; 6:92.

in the Islamic schools abroad. Universities in over fifty countries award PhD degrees in Quranic studies. The Quran is the only book millions of poor people in sub-Saharan Africa, Egypt, Morocco, Bangladesh, India, Pakistan, Afghanistan, and Iran have ever possessed. Mountains of books, articles and documentaries have been produced with the petrodollars to argue that the Quran contains scientific miracles. They claim that several modern scientific theories and discoveries had been revealed in the Quran centuries before they were discovered by the non-Muslims. They also maintain that the Quran motivates sound thinking, and through studying Quran people can advance accurate knowledge.

Muslims usually fail to mention that studying the Quran is utterly different from any other type of learning. It entails memorising, praising and defending each and every word and sentence written in that book in contrast to discussing, understanding and evaluating its ideas or language. Believers contend that every human must live by the instructions of the Quran as it is the eternal miracle sent by Allah to humanity through his most perfect creature: Mohammad. Many Muslims when asked how they know that Quran is indeed the literal word of Allah would reply that it is written in it. Criticising the Quran and displaying its numerous faults and contradictions is a major crime in Islam, which many have committed over the ages.

Countless people have lost their lives for what Muslims have viewed as desecration of the divine revelations. In 2021, thousands of Bengali Muslims attacked the Hindu minority, killing and wounding many of them, and vandalized dozens of their temples.[284] This collective attack by the majority against a peaceful minority was a retaliation for a picture posted on an unknown Facebook account that showed a copy of Quran placed at the feet of a Hindu idol.

Another notion usually veiled when discussing Islamic terrorism is the Quranic passages that call for terrorism. For instance, "Prepare for them all the force you can and the cavalry to terrorise (turhiboona) the enemy of Allah and your enemy."[285] The Arabic verb turhiboona (ter-

---

284 The Associated Press. (2021, Oct 17). Muslims, Hindus protest amid communal violence in Bangladesh. ABC News.
285 Quran 8:60.

rorise) and the noun irhab (terrorism) come from the same linguistic root ra-ha-ba (terror).[286] To this day Arabs use the word turhiboona as "terrorise". Nonetheless, many of the translators of Quran into English did their utmost to alter its meaning and not to use the word terrorise. With the exception of few who used the words "strike terror into (the hearts of) the enemies of Allah and your enemies", the rest inaccurately used words such as "dismay the enemy", "frighten", "overawe" or "instil awe in the hearts of the enemy of Allah and your enemy".

---

286 See Wehr, H. (1974). A Dictionary of Modern Written Arabic. (Ed. J. M. Cowan). Macdonald & Evans Ltd., pp 287, 249.

ALLAH'S DEFEAT IN HIS WORDS

They say ancient myths he [Mohammad] has had them written down and they are being dictated to him day and night.[287]

Allah

The disbelievers say: why was the Quran not sent down to him all at once?[288]

Allah

The idea that the Quran is the exact word of Deity was contested right from the onset. The people of Mecca described the revelations Mohammad recited upon them as "ancient myths dictated to Mohammad."[289] They found the notion that these passages were faultless farcical. They assured that they could create superior narratives if they wished to and that there were plentiful talks finer than the Quran. Mohammad's contemporaries told him time and again that the Quran was a compilation of plagiarised ancient tales of no value. They argued that the ideas of Quran were not original nor exceptional.[290] They assured that Mohammad and other people were the narrators, not Allah.

These arguments were documented in the Quran itself: "Those who disbelieve say this Quran is nothing but a lie that Mohammad fabricated, and others helped him with it."; "They say ancient myths he has had them written down and they are being dictated to him day and night."[291] This conception of the Quran as manmade forgeries has been propagated by almost all the important thinkers and philosophers currently called Muslims in Wikipedia and Western media programs. The majority of Middle Eastern medieval scholars have discredited the Quran and its

---

287 Quran 25:4-5.
288 Quran 25:32.
289 Quran 7:31.
290 Quran 25:5; 83:13.
291 Quran 25:4-5.

ideas vigorously. They have assured that this manuscript is incompatible with ethics, science, logic, and philosophy.[292]

Studying the Quran with an objective mind would lead to the conclusion that "The book is strikingly lacking in overall structure, frequently obscure and inconsequential in both language and content, perfunctory in its linking of disparate materials, and given to the repetition of whole passages in variant versions. On this basis it can plausibly be argued that the book is the product of the belated and imperfect editing of materials from a plurality of traditions."[293] It is a book full of irrational ideas, lies, grammatical mistakes, and immoral beliefs.

The structure of the book has no clear logic. Each sentence is named ayah (verse); they have all been categorised under the same name despite the fact that they are extremely different in style, length, and format. The chapters (surah) of the Quran are heterogeneous and chaotic, which causes the book to lack specific logic, plot, and a unifying goal. It suffers from dysfunctional repetitions: the same story can be found in several different chapters with no justification. The style of the Quran is flawed, and many passages contradict each other. It is filled with histrionic language, flights of ideas, and ambiguous concepts. Countless people over the ages have composed mountains of books to defend the shortcomings of the Quran through various interpretations and justifications. Sometimes, each sentence is explained differently by the same writer. The various translations of the Quran show how on many occasions each one of the different translators offers a significantly different meaning of the same text.

---

292 Hecht, J. M. (2004). Doubt: A History: The Great Doubters and Their Legacy of Innovation, from Socrates and Jesus to Thomas Jefferson and Emily Dickinson. HarperOne. Kindle.
293 Crone, P. & Cook, M. (1977). Hagarism: the making of the Islamic world.

IRRATIONAL IDEAS

The foundation of the Quran are irrational and immoral ideas presented as factual accounts, divine explanations of complex phenomena, answers to the existential questions, and God's direct commands to humans. As it is impossible to analyse the whole Quran in this book, I decided to focus on a few examples which illustrate some of the important ideas related to the topics at hand.

One of the most irrational, illogical and immoral concepts propagated in the Quran is the notion of jinn. Jinn are mentioned 16 times in ten different chapters. They are presented as mainly evil invisible creatures made from fire who possess superpowers. They fly and interact with humans and can harm us in various ways. Jinn is the title of a whole surah in the Quran. In it, Allah described in detail how a group of jinn overheard a recitation of the Quran. They were so fascinated by what they had heard that they converted to Islam instantly. They went back to their folks and preached the belief.[294] Muslim students worldwide are introduced to the notion of jinn as a fact that must be accepted. Rejecting the idea that there are invisible creatures made out of fire living among and interacting with humans means rejecting the factuality of the Quran and hence, insulting Islam. This is an act of apostasy/blasphemy punishable by death in 13 Muslim countries, and by heavy jail sentences in the other Muslim states.

On 22 March 2020, the dictator of Iran, the Supreme Leader Ayatollah Ali Khamenei said in a public speech broadcast live by the official Iranian TV channels that Iran is being attacked by "jinn and human enemies that help each other."[295] This was his justification for the failure

---

294 Quran 72.
295 Sinaiee, M. (2020, Mar 23). Army Of Jinn, America And Coronavirus In Khamenei's Imagination. Radio Farda.; MEMRI. (2020, Mar 26). IRGC Cyber Division Confirms Supreme Leader Khamenei's Assertion That 'Demons Are Assisting The Enemies' With Statements

of the corrupt Islamic regime in dealing with the coronavirus pandemic that claimed the lives of thousands of Iranians, as well as its failure in every other aspect. The Islamic regime has turned Iran into a country that blames its mistakes on the jinn and unspecified human enemies but not on its corrupt, dictatorial Islamic rulers and laws. Thus, it would never hold accountable the real delinquents who ruined that beautiful, ancient country. It would never put Islam on trial to examine if it is fit to be the source of law in the Persian land. This old, superstitious, semi-illiterate dictator who ruined the lives of tens of millions of humans with his illogical idea and his corruption have brought nothing but ignorance, poverty, injustice and agony to one of the oldest nations of the world. Nevertheless, he did not invent this myth – he was simply providing a justification based on the Islamic vision of the world. The notion of jinn and their effect on people's lives was asserted countless times in Mohammad's sayings, in addition to the Quranic verses. Muslims must believe that jinn are conspiring to harm people.

Thousands of imams make a lavish living and gain fame and influence by specialising in extracting jinn from people's bodies through reciting Quran over the possessed individuals. All over the Muslim world as well as in Europe and America, people who are psychotic or suffer from other psychological disorders are diagnosed as being possessed by jinn or struck by an "evil eye". Preachers make these diagnoses in accordance with the Quran and the tradition.[296,297] As a cure, they recite the Quran in a loud voice and an emotional tone, which may cause the person to experience a seizure or a panic attack. This is usually described as the jinn's reaction to the Quran. TV and radio stations invite preachers on a regular basis to speak about jinn possessions. In these interviews, the different preachers usually describe their triumphs in removing

That 'The Israeli Mossad Is... Using Demons' And 'The Jews Are Experts At Sorcery And At Creating Relationships With Demons'.

296 See al-Shimmari, M. (2021). The Physical Reality of Jinn Possession According to Commentaries on the Quran (2:275). In A. Böttcher & B. Krawietz (Eds.). Islam, Migration and Jinn: Spiritual Medicine in Muslim Health Management. Palgrave Macmillan.

297 Khan, Q., & Sanober, A. (2016). 'Jinn Possession' and Delirious Mania in a Pakistani Woman. American Journal of Psychiatry 173(3), pp 219-220.; El Kholy, H. (2004). A discourse of resistance: Spirit possession among women in low-income Cairo. In H. Sholkamy & F. Ghannam (Eds.). Health and Identity in Egypt, pp 21-4. American University in Cairo Press.

jinn from humans and hence, eliminating their psychological suffering and biological sicknesses. The famous Kuwaiti healer Jassem Bahman claimed time and again that by removing jinn from clients he healed their crippling illnesses. He repeatedly detailed in TV interviews how he imprisoned the jinn in his ring's stones. These claims by this charlatan or many others have never been publicly challenged by scientists. Psychologists and psychiatrists do not dare to publicly state that there is no such thing as jinn.

Beating people to extract the jinn while reciting the Quran is another common practice all over the Muslim world and hardly a day would pass without a report of someone losing their life due to injuries resulting from the jinn-extracting beating. In one of the countless reported incidents, a 23-year-old newlywed girl died at the hands of a notable imam in September 2021 in Cairo. She was tied with ropes and beaten to death by the imam who was removing jinn from her. The girl was suffering from psychological distress identified as a jinn possession by her family in accordance with the teachings of Islam, thus, they commissioned the man, who had a reputation as an expert in dealing with jinn through reciting Quran and beating.[298] Countless women have filed complaints of rape and sexual assault against imams who assaulted them while they were undergoing jinn removing rituals, which is usually done in private and behind closed doors.

In November 2002, the Kuwaiti Newspaper Al-Anba published an extensive reportage about the jinn. Several professors of Islamic studies who teach at Kuwait University were asked to explain the notion of jinn and whether they can harm people or not. The PhD holders stated that it was reported in the Quran and in the hadith that jinn did exist and interacted with and harmed people in various ways. Therefore, denying the existence of jinn was a defection from Islam. They explained further that jinn could take the shape of animals, humans or any other thing and that they can kill and steal food and gold from humans, according to Islam. They also confirmed that jinn could get inside humans

---

298 Al-Ahram. (2021, Sep 10). 'Bidaei iikhraj aljin': Altafasil alkamilat limaqtal earus Hulwan amam usratiha ealaa yad dajal fidyu wasuar ['For the sake of taking out the jinn': Full details of the killing of the Helwan bride in front of her family at the hands of an impostor]. (Arabic).

and control their bodies causing fits and delirium. Jinn could also have sexual relationships with humans but do not reproduce with us, the scholars indicated.[299]

It is extremely difficult for a foreigner to this religion to imagine living in the constant anxiety caused by the belief in jinn and angels and all the other invisible creatures.

---

299 Al-Shafei, L. (2021, Nov 18). Akaduu 'ana aljina yadkhul fi al'iinsan wayasraeuh wayata-sabab lah bikathir min aleilal wal'amrad [Islamic jurists assured that jinn can steal, kill and harm in other ways]. (Arabic). Al-Anba News.

ALLAH AND THE WEAPONS OF MASS DESTRUCTION

Among the narratives designed to insert fear, cruelty, credulity and blind obedience in the Muslims' psyche is the story of Saleh. In it, a man named Saleh was selected by Allah to be his messenger. He was ordered to convert his people to the worship of the one and only God. He received revelations containing divine laws that must be followed by all the people without discussion. But the people did not accept Saleh or his revelations and demanded tangible proof. Saleh and Allah accepted the challenge and they transformed a stone into a live she-camel as a sign that Allah was capable of everything and that Saleh was, indeed, his messenger.

Most people remained sceptical despite having seen the miracle with their own eyes. One night, a man killed that camel, grilled it and ate it with his friends. Allah told Saleh to leave the city immediately as he was about to avenge his camel. Allah destroyed the whole city, killing every living soul and demolishing everything. He did not spare children, women or animals. All this because some men killed a camel. Allah declared that he "destroyed them with all their people."[300] This was despite the fact that the majority of the people did not take part in the killing of that camel, thus they were not responsible for it. Interpreters of the Quran as well as notable jurists justify the mass-killing of the innocent people by claiming that as long as they did not stop the camel's killer, they were accomplices and deserved to be exterminated. They also highlight the notion that these people rejected the true religion, thus earning the severe penalty. These arguments along with the Quranic story have been used to justify the genocides inflicted on innocent people by Islamic regimes over the ages. When Saddam was annihilating hundreds of Kurdish villages with chemical weapons, senior jurists were defending his crimes through repeating Saleh's story.

---

300 Quran 27:51.

Following this logic, many jurists have ruled that American civilians are responsible for any actions taken by their administration, such as invading Iraq or supporting Israel, even if they voiced their disagreement with the administration's decision – they are still guilty of rejecting Islam, the one and only valid religion. Danish, Swedish, French, and other Europeans are all considered responsible for their governments' failures to stop the critics of Islam from expressing their thoughts, thus, they deserve to be annihilated, according to many Muslim Jurists and laypeople.

The Iraqi thinker Ahmad al-Qabanji commented on Saleh's tale, saying that Saddam and all the criminal dictators were more merciful than Allah. These humans used weapons of mass destruction because they could not target their enemies precisely, but Allah chose to exterminate innocent people intentionally. If he was fair, he should have held responsible the ones who did the killing. Al-Qabanji asked why Allah would kill children, women and elderly people who did not take part in the killing of the she-camel. He also wondered if it was fair to kill humans because they had killed an animal and ate it. Can someone describe such god as just, let alone merciful or wise?

Another tale in the Quran where Allah exterminated a whole city is the story of Lut. The people of the unnamed town were all homosexual. They would not obey Allah's orders delivered to them via their prophet Lut to abstain from their sinful sexual practice. Thus, Allah decided to punish all the inhabitants of this town. He set up a trap by sending a group of young attractive boys, who were in fact angels disguised as humans, to Lut's house. These angels pretended to be guests and Lut welcomed them with anxiety. Lut's wife betrayed her husband and told the people of the city that there were good-looking boys in her house. A crowd surrounded the house, demanding the boys be handed out. The angels told Lut to take his family, but not his wife, and leave the city immediately. He did, and Allah sent a rain of stones that exterminated the town's entire population.

It is from this tale that jurists infer that death is the appropriate punishment for homosexuality. They reason that since the Creator killed the population of a city because its people practiced or condoned homosexuality, it is the duty of every human to terminate homosexuals.

Moreover, Mohammad ordered the killing of anyone who practiced homosexuality.[301] All the senior jurists are unanimous in supporting the killing of homosexuals. They disagree on the appropriate means of doing it: some propose throwing them from high-rise buildings, while others rule that they must be stoned to death.

The notion that the Earth is flat has been conveyed in more than seven different Quranic verses in a clear language.[302] Also, according to the Quran, the sun sets in a muddy water-well every night.[303] The sky is a roof that has seven lairs. The stars are beams and an anti-devil rocket system. Allah built the world in seven days and his throne is built on water. Black magic is real and damaging, and people can harm each other with it. Envy in Islam is the act of eyeing someone's fortunes with bad intentions; this act is sufficient to cause tangible and even lethal harm. In the Quran, Allah stated that he takes away the spirit from people when they fall asleep, thus sleep is a form of death.[304] In addition to that, ants have human cognitive capacity. They can comprehend, predict and talk to each other in the same way intelligent people do. In the Ants chapter of Quran, Allah reports that as King Solomon was passing with his army by "a valley of ants, one of the ants said o you ants get into your dwellings so that Solomon with his army would not crush you unintentionally. He smiled at her words and said oh my God please help me to thank you for all your blessings."[305] In the same chapter, Allah informed us that birds also have human cognitive capacities and a language parallel to smart people, and that they used to work as spies for Solomon. The story of a spy hoopoe that travelled all the way from Jerusalem to Yemen on a clandestine reconnaissance mission to search for sinful people is written in detail in the Quran. During this trip, the hoopoe discovered that the people of Yemen were worshipping the sun rather than Allah and that they were ruled by a queen. He reported his findings to Solomon and apologised for not seeking prior permission to go on the spying mission.

---

301 Sunan Abu Dawood 4462; Sunan al-Tirmidhi 1456; Sunan ibn Majah 2561.
302 See Quran 88:20; 50:7; 15:19; 13:3; 71:19; 51:48; 79:30.
303 Quran 18:86: "Until, when he reached the setting of the sun, he found it setting in a water well of dark mud, and he found near it a people."
304 Quran 39:42.
305 Quran 27:18-19.

Solomon pardoned the hoopoe and ordered him to deliver a letter that contained an ultimatum to the Yemeni queen. She and her people must submit immediately to his will or he is going to destroy them, Solomon wrote. He also ordered a jinni to steal the throne of the queen to intimidate her. The jinni managed to go from Jerusalem to Yemen and back carrying the throne in a split of a second, according to the Quran. As a result, the queen surrendered and came with her followers to Solomon to concede, pledge her allegiance and accept him as her master. This tale is taught at public schools all over the Muslim world as a factual, historical account authored by Allah for humans to use as a guide. Students need to accept that all creatures worship Allah and that animals have languages similar to humans. They must celebrate Solomon's coercion of people and approve of the stealing of the throne because it was done by one of Allah's messengers. In order to accept this tale as factual, people must reject the foundation of science, philosophy, and morality.

Another influential story in Quran is the tale of Yunus (Jonah). This biblical story appears in four different chapters in the Quran. It is another example of delusional reasoning. In this tale, Yunus resigned his post as a messenger of Allah after he failed in his mission. He left his hometown on a ship, seeking a new beginning. Allah did not accept the resignation of his messenger; thus, he sent high waves to rock the boat. When the ship was about to sink, the passengers decided to throw a person into the sea to reduce the ship's weight. They did a draw and three times Allah made sure that the name of Yunus would come up. The passengers threw the helpless man into the sea where a whale swallowed him. Intact, he stayed inside the whale for three days, praying and crying to Allah to forgive him. After the tremendous pain and agony he experienced, Allah decided to pardon him and ordered the whale to expel him onto the shore. After Yunus recovered from his wounds, Allah sent him to a new group of people to deliver his message, which he did this time with success. Muslims all over the world are compelled to believe that a human lived unharmed inside a whale for three days. They also must praise Allah for being merciful but cannot lament the fact that he was, indeed, a childish dictator with a shallow mind, as illustrated by the fact that he subjected a human to such a trauma – unless they do not mind being accused of apostasy.

THE TALE OF THE MURDERER SAINT

One of the most destructive ideas ingrained in the Muslim psyche by the Quran and the books of hadith is the idea that the events of the past, present, and future have been predetermined by God. Every act, feeling and talk has been scripted before the creation of this world. Allah knows and has determined everything (this belief is called Al-Qada wal-Qadar).

This notion is amplified in the story of a nameless sage who met with Moses and went with him on a long journey. This man was close to Allah, thus Allah granted him the ability to know the past as well as the future. In the story, Moses accompanied the wise man to learn from him. The man told Moses that he would not be able to stay with him for a long time because Moses was not granted the ability to know the future. He ordered Moses not to ask any question unless it was him who brought the topic up. During their short journey, the sage killed an innocent child, vandalised a ship, and built a wall for free in a town that treated the guests badly. With each one of these incidents, Moses could not restrain himself and asked the sage to explain his odd behaviour. After first and second incident, the sage told him to keep quiet and follow him. After Moses objected for the third time, the wise man told Moses he could no longer remain with him and they must part but before that he would explain why he did what he did. He said he killed the innocent child because he and Allah knew that this child would grow up to be a wicked man and cause trouble for his good parents. Thus, he killed him hoping that God would give his parents a better son. The reason for vandalising the ship was that the local ruler was going to confiscate it from its good owners, however, if it was damaged, the king would lose interest in it. Finally, he fixed the crumbling wall in the evil village because underneath it was a hidden treasure that belonged to two or-phans of a good man and the sage wanted it to remain hidden until the children were old enough to dig it out.[306]

The wise man could not ask God to guide the child he predicted would do evil in the future – he killed the boy. He could not tell the sailors that the king was about to confiscate their ship and allow them to decide what to do. Could he not ask Allah who is all-knowing and almighty to stop the evil king and protect the sailors? Why would the sage order Moses to suspend his mind? What good can come from banning questions?

By propagating these stories in educational systems, the praise of ignorance, self-doubt, and blind obedience are implanted in the psyche of millions of children. By presenting this story as factual and its characters as virtuous, these systems are indoctrinating young people into accepting irrational myths as facts, rejecting critical thinking, and becoming afraid of speaking their own mind.

Each one of the preceding tales is designed to implement or reinforce a specific immoral and illogical idea within the Muslim psyche. In every Quranic tale there is a preface that contains the main characters and the setting, the plot, and the conclusion. The preface of every story is designed to direct the audience's emotions and allegiance toward one of the characters and against another. It sets up who the good people are and who the bad ones are.[307] Thus, it predetermines who the readers should identify with and support, and who they need to detest. The plots of the stories are designed to create a specific mindset by designing a struggle that has abnormal events and attractive details. At the conclusion of every story, the characters and the principle which were constructed in the preface as Islamic obtain victory. There is usually a threat for those who chose not to abide by the Islamic understanding and a promise of reward for those who submit and comply. When it is critically examined as a whole, we find that each story contains cognitive distortions, illogical ideas, and an invalid ending that makes it contradict logic and sound thinking.

Many intelligent people who analysed these stories tend to abandon Islam altogether; others find a way to reject these tales to preserve their mental stability but hold on to the religion. The average uninterested,

306 Quran 18:70-82.
307 See Quran 18.

202

uneducated Muslim tends to focus on a specific part of the tale or the rhythm, or on memorizing some lines without examining the whole text.

Over the centuries, Muslim regimes and organizations have been immensely successful in indoctrinating illiterate psychopaths and distressed individuals, turning them into bloodthirsty chameleons, anxious to harm whoever happens to be presented as a threat to the group through the application of the Quran and the other original texts. The same masses that display tremendous servility when dealing with the in-group authority, especially the religious hierarchy, are extremely violent when dealing with the out-group members. Animosity and paranoia toward other people's cultures and beliefs is entrenched in the Quranic narratives. The other side of the coin are obedience and cruel penalties designed to keep the masses in check.

The first and the longest chapter of the Quran is named the Cow. It is one of the lengthiest, most incoherent and lacking internal logic, yet influential passages ever written. It takes its name from a story about a Jewish person who was killed in a mysterious way. The Jewish people asked their prophet to solve the crime and prove that he was indeed connected to Allah. The prophet spoke with God who instructed him to order the people to sacrifice an orange cow. The people kept asking for a specific description of the designated cow and with every question God would add more details to make the task harder. Finally, the special cow was slaughtered and part of it was used to tap the dead person's body. Once they complied with this divine one-time ritual, the dead person was resurrected, named his murderer and died again. In this story, the prophet is not identified, neither are the dates or the location.

In the same chapter, there is a verse that Muslim preachers often use to deceive naïve audiences. In it, Allah says: "There is no compulsion in religion the right direction is henceforth distinct from error and he who rejects the false deities and believe in Allah has grasped a firm handhold which will never break Allah is hearer knower."[308] In this verse, Allah does not forbid coercing people into converting to Islam, as many fraudulently claim; he is stating that it is clear for all people that Islam

---

308 Quran 2:256.

is the right religion and others are false. Therefore, forcing people to accept it cannot be seen as aggression. This is the salient understanding among the Muslim theologians and masses based on other verses which sanction killing infidels, as well as Mohammad's biography, and his sayings. A few jurists argued that this passage bans Muslims from coercing Christians and Jews into converting to Islam, as long as they are paying the levy and being obedient. Others explained it through saying that the prisoners of war who are Christians and Jews and elderly should not be forced to convert to Islam, but young ones must be compelled, otherwise they would be filthy and could not be used as servants in believers' households. Moreover, even the few jurists that explained this surah as a ban on forcing people to convert to Islam ruled that the verse had been abrogated by other verses which call for fighting all non-Muslims until they convert. In summary, this passage has nothing to do with tolerance, unless labelling people who are not Muslims sinners and other religions as false equals tolerance.[309]

---

309 Tafsir al-Qurtubi.

QURANIC SCHIZOPHRENIA

The production of incoherent narratives that lack general thinking and clear direction and contain abrupt shifts between unrelated subjects is identified in clinical psychology as a symptom of mental disorder. There are several forms of this symptom, the most prevalent being referred to as the flight of ideas. Flight of ideas is common among schizophrenics and patients suffering from bipolar disorder, especially during the manic episodes.[310] Their speech disturbance is understood to reflect a disorder in the reasoning which in turn manifests a deep mental problem related to the perception and construction of the self, others, and the world.

In the Quran, there are many narratives that are, indeed, flights of ideas. One of the least coherent passages that contains abrupt shifts between unrelated topics and lacks an overall sense is the following: "And if you fear that you will not deal justly with orphans marry such women as seems good to you two and three and four but if you fear that you will not do justice then only one or what your right hands possess this is more proper that you may not deviate from the right course."[311] Many translators have added words as well as commas and semicolons to make this passage comprehensible. In doing so, they have drastically changed the meaning of the original text. They did this to transform an irrational narrative (flight of ideas) into a vague text that could be explained and defended, then glorified.

To analyse this passage, it is useful to divide it into three parts. In the beginning, the narrator opens with a conditional clause: if people are afraid not to be fair with orphans. Logically, it is expected that he would finish this introduction with something related to dealing with orphans, either advising people to be fair or cautioning them against hurting the

---

310 American Psychiatric Association (APA). (2013). Diagnostic and statistical manual of mental disorders (5th ed.).
311 Quran 4:3.

vulnerable orphans. This does not occur, instead, the narrator shifts the topic toward permitting polygamy, ordering men to marry women they like, as if men usually married women they detested. Many translators add the words "girls" or "females" after orphans (yatama) to make the first two parts seem somehow connected. This is a blatant fraud, as these words are not part of the original text. In Arabic, the sentence as a whole is ambiguous and unintelligible – however, its first part is clear as it talks about orphans (yatama) specifically. The word "yatama" denotes both male and female children who lost one or both parents and are hence incapable of managing their own affairs. This word appears in the Quran 23 times and each time it applies to orphans of both sexes. Thus, the first part of this verse is not related to the rest in any logical way.

In the second part, Allah is telling people to marry "two" and "three" and "four" women rather than saying you can marry up to four women at the same time. He uses "and" instead of "or". Some jurists argue that "and" was correct and hence Muslims may have nine wives at the same time, not just four. In the third part, the narrator says that if a Muslim thought that he would not be fair with multiple wives, then he can limit himself to just one wife or the slave-girls he owns. Hence, Allah is declaring clearly that the general rule for Muslim men is to have more than one wife, the exception being just one or just slave-girls. It also warrants sexual slavery. This was the common practice of Mohammad, his companions, and all the influential Muslim figures throughout the past 1400 years. They all had several wives and numerous sex-slaves; the ones who did not, were indeed the exception. Polygamy and sex-slavery have been practiced as legitimate norms among Muslims for more than 14 centuries because they have been legalized by Allah in Quranic texts. It is important to stress that before Islam many Arabs were Christians who did not practice polygamy.

This verse is a good example of the predicaments that informed Muslims face when dealing with Islam on the one hand and the values of modern civilization on the other. They are often torn between the Islamic teachings, which they must accept as valid, eternal rules, and their conscience, which cannot uphold such ideas or justify their consequences. If they refuse polygamy, corporal punishment and slavery, they need to reject significant parts of the Quran. Consequently, they reject the idea of the Quran being the word of God and hence, there is no unified religion. On the other hand, if they accept the idea that Quran is the literal word of God preserved by him, then they must also defend polygamy, slavery, hijab, misogyny, jihad, and all the other similarly abhorrent acts.

Another obvious example of nonsensical talk is a sentence which regulates the places where Muslims can eat: "There is no restriction on the blind nor any restriction on the lame or any restriction on the sick nor on yourselves to eat from your own houses or the houses of your fathers or the houses of your mothers or the houses of your brothers or the houses of your sisters or the houses of your father's brothers or the houses of your father's sisters or the houses of your mother's brothers or the houses of your mother's sisters or where you hold its keys or of a friend no blame on you whether you eat as group or individuals but when you enter the houses greet yourself a greeting from Allah blessed and good thus Allah makes clear the verses to you that you may understand."[312]

This sentence composed of 75 words with no punctuation is another clear example of the fallibility of some Quranic passages. The author starts by declaring that we must understand that there is no restriction on blind or lame people. This make the audience expect that Allah is about to give them specific privileges related to their disability but instead, he adds everyone to this group and informs us that people can eat from their houses. Do people need such a divine permission to eat at their homes? Does the creator of the universe need to send an angel to deliver such a message? The sentence continues in an extremely disorganised style to inform the reader that it is permissible for people to eat at their relatives' and friends' houses through highlighting each and every case separately. The translators did their utmost to make this passage comprehensible in English. They added the word "house" after "friend" and they added several commas and full stops that changed the meaning and the wording of the unalterable narrative of God. One of the bizarre orders in this passage is the instruction for Muslims to greet themselves when entering

312 Quran 24:61.

their houses. I have seen many individuals say al-salam alaikum when they get into their empty home, in compliance with this verse.

Let us look at the verse that regulates retribution: "O you who believe retaliation is prescribed for you in the matter of the murdered; the freeman for the freeman, and the slave for the slave, and the female for the female. And for him who is forgiven somewhat by his brother, prosecution according to usage and payment unto him in kindness. This is an alleviation and a mercy from your Lord. He who transgresses after this will have a painful doom."[313]

This passage has perplexed commentators for centuries. It is supposed to deal with the retribution for murder but in reality, it does not do that, and instead it classifies people into three different hierarchal groups without clarification. Some Muslims attempt to explain this idea by indicating that a Muslim man must not be killed if he killed a woman or a slave. Others indicate that this verse regulates the retaliation in war. Others say that the verse has been abrogated by another one and as such it is not relevant to sharia, however, it should not be removed from the Quran.

Another verse that negates the theoretical foundations of Islam is verse 17:16. In it, Allah declares that: "when We intended to destroy a city we would command its affluent then they sin in it consequently the word (of punishment) is justified hence We would destroy it completely."[314] In this passage Allah presents himself as aspiring to destroy innocent cities and creating excuses to achieve his premeditated evil goal. He also boasts that he practices genocides against whole populations.

In the Quran, there are two main contradicting notions regarding the nature of its discourse. The salient idea propagated throughout the book is the notion that the Quran is an unalterable, comprehensible, literal word of God containing rules that must be followed faithfully. In contrast, there are two verses admitting that the Quran has major flaws. In one of them, Allah says that there are specific coherent verses and other verses which are not: "It is he who has sent down to you the book in it are verses [that are] precise and they are the foundation of

313 Quran 2:168.
314 Quran 17:16, see Sahih International translation.

the book and others unspecific. As for those in whom hearts are sick, they will follow that of it which is unspecific, seeking discord and seeking an interpretation and no one knows its interpretation except Allah. But those firm in knowledge say we believe in it. All [of it] is from our Lord."[315] This indicates that there are vague passages within the Quran. The verse describes people who highlight the vague passages as sick at heart. It also admits that some parts of the Quran need to be explained, and this contradicts the notion that it is clear and comprehensible.

Furthermore, Allah states that some parts of the Quran were annulled or forgotten: "Whatever a verse do we abrogate or cause to be forgotten, we bring a better one or similar. Know you not that Allah is able to do all things?"[316] Here we see the writer of the Quran admit to mistakes. If the Quran has verses that were abrogated, then it cannot be the perfect text created by the all-knowing lord of the universe.

The two passages are currently used to defend the Quran's numerous contradictions and shortcomings by the same people who believe that it is the unalterable word of God. They also use the latter one to label people who dare to highlight the contradictions of the Quran as sick at heart, truth rejecters, and hence enemies.

---

315 Quran 2:106.
316 Quran 2:6.

The Repentance (Al-Tawbah) is the last surah revealed to Mohammad. It is the conclusion of Islamic ideas, and it is one of the few relatively coherent and clear chapters of the Quran. It focuses on the topic of jihad and the relationships between Muslims and non-Muslims in a comprehensive way. In this surah, Allah sets specific rules to regulate the interaction between Muslims and non-Muslims, as well as among Muslims themselves. He starts by nullifying all the agreements and pacts between Muslims and non-Muslims: "Freedom from (all) obligations (is declared) by Allah and his Messenger to those of the Mushrikeen[317] with whom you made treaty."[318] One exception was made for the non-Muslims who were loyal, did not harm Muslims and honoured their commitments with Muslims and with Mohammad. They were given a four months' truce; after that, Allah ordered his soldiers: "Then when the Sacred Months have passed, slay the infidels (Mushrikeen), wherever you find them, and capture them and besiege them, and ambush them in every way. But if they repent and perform the prayer (As-Salat), and pay levy (zakat), then leave their way free. Surely, Allah is forgiving most merciful."[319] In a subsequent verse, Allah orders Muslims to attack all non-Muslims: "Fight them Allah will punish them at your hands and will disgrace them and give you victory over them and heal the chests of the believers." Allah explained and defended these commands through presenting the non-Muslims as dangerous, deceitful, and two-faced. He warned that if the Polytheists gained the upper hand, they would exterminate his followers ruthlessly. This despite the fact that Polytheists had the upper hand and had not killed the Muslims. Afterward, Allah

---

317 This term designates polytheists, pagans, idolaters, and all disbelievers in the oneness of Allah.
318 Quran 9:1.
319 Quran 9:5.

accused Jews and Christians of being Polytheists due to the Jewish's belief that "Ezra is the son of Allah" and Christians' belief that "Messiah is the son of Allah."[320] In the 12th verse, Allah warns Muslims of the infidels who converted to Islam, stating that they need to monitor them as they might "break their commitment", thus must be fought again. Fighting people is constructed as the test through which Allah distinguishes the true believers from the hypocrites.

In the 23rd verse, Allah orders Muslims to reject their "parents and siblings" if they did not convert to Islam. The next verse states that Muslims who love their family, homes, money, and business more than Allah and Mohammad and jihad are disobedient and as such will be punished. In verse 28, Allah orders Muslims to prevent non-believers from entering the holy land. Consequently, the majority of the inhabitants of that land were barred from passing by, let alone living in it. This is despite the fact that this place was their and their ancestors' homeland and it is where their homes and places of worship existed for centuries beforehand. He justifies depriving these people of their legitimate right to their land by constructing them as najas (filth). Thus, their entry into the holy land would damage its sanctity, therefore they must be banned by force. Many of the Quran's translators tend to soften the language used in this verse by translating Arabic "najas" as impure or unclean. This translation is misleading. The notion of pure (taher) versus filth (najas) is an important theme in Islam. Purity and filth are defined both in the spiritual sense and the material sense. Muslims follow the pure guidance, therefore their souls are pure while non-Muslims follow immoral beliefs, therefore their core is filthy. On the physical aspect, Muslims are materially clean because they do the ritual wash (wudu) before every prayer. They also perform a specific ritual wash (ghusl al-janaba) after having sex (seen as a filthy interaction) and after touching a thing or a person who is filthy. From the point of view of sharia, there are specific things that are considered najas by default, thus, if a Muslim does touch them, then they must thoroughly wash with water. Human faeces and non-Muslims are considered najas and to a lesser degree blood, semen, dogs, and pigs.

---

320 Quran 9:30.

Thus, pigs and dogs must be avoided. These animals must be kept away from mosques as they can contaminate the place and make it unfit for prayer. Infidels are categorized as similar to these non-human objects and thus, they are not allowed into mosques unless to be converted. Through this construction, the Quran is psychologically paving the way to exterminating all non-Muslims: as it is logical to cleanse faeces and blood from one's clothes, it is also logical to remove these humans from the face of the earth.

This is the most important surah of Quran along with the Anfal (Spoils) as they set the way Muslims think, feel and behave toward all non-Muslims as well as other Muslims. It divided all humans into two categories: true Muslims versus infidels (Mushrikeen). True Muslims are the ones that believe in the oneness of Allah and in Mohammad and follow all their orders. They perform the Islamic prayer, pay the Islamic zakat, follow sharia and strive to spread Islam. In contrast, all non-Muslims are members of the Mushrikeen group by default, whether they are Polytheist, Christians, Jewish or Atheists. They do not believe in Allah as the one and only God or in Mohammad as his last Messenger. Thus, they are enemies who must be subjugated. This also applies to disobedient Muslims who reject Allah's orders. Over the years, many Islamic sects have been considered Mushrikeen. Prominent Sunni jurists have categorized Shias as Mushrikeen because their adoration of the family of Mohammad is a type of worship, and this contradicts the Islamic belief in the oneness of Allah. In contrast, some Shia jurists contend that the Sunnis are the Mushrikeen as they worship Mohammad's companions and caliphs. In both cases, the construction of a group as Mushrikeen is intended to sanction exterminating them.

In the Tawbah, Allah warrants the annihilation of all non-Muslims. It is the final solution par excellence. Here, the Quran has completed dehumanizing all non-believers in Mohammad's teachings. It is a clear and precise mandate to obliterate all humans except one group. Even the allies of Muslims were given an ultimatum to fully convert to Islam and attest to it through performing the five daily prayers and paying levy, or to immigrate from their homeland within four months – otherwise they faced being wiped out. Muslims are instructed clearly to deal with people based on the in-group versus out-group mentality. In-group people are obliged to exterminate the members of the out-group. It does not matter if the non-Muslim was a relative, neighbour, or philanthropist.

Take the example of Margaret Hassan. Margaret and her husband stayed in Iraq to help the Iraqi people during the Iran–Iraq war (1980-1988). After Saddam's invasion of Kuwait in 1990 and the 1991 war, she remained in Iraq. She continued to help the local population even during the American invasion of 2003 and the civil war that ensued. Margaret used her dual citizenship to bring in medication for the needy and to highlight the suffering caused by the sanctions and the siege enforced on that country. She coordinated humanitarian efforts to bring necessary medication especially for children with cancer, wheelchairs for the disabled, and prostheses for the maimed. In 2004, when armed Sunnis captured her and put her on TV, they forced her to plead for her life. Her crime was that she was a Christian. The Muslim mujahedeen declared in the video they published that they killed the 65-year-old, while assuring their supporters that she was a kafir. She rejected Islam, and this is a crime that cannot be pardoned.

The best way for non-Muslims to save their lives from the mujahedeen during Mohammad's reign was to convert, pay the tax and join the Muslim army. This tradition continued throughout the history of Islam: people kept converting in order to save their lives and the lives of their loved ones. After becoming Muslims, they had to show that they were indeed true followers through participating in jihad, praying, and paying zakat. Conquered people and their children eventually became soldiers of this religion, dying for it rather than against it. They killed and subjugated their relatives and countrymen who have chosen to preserve their identity and defend their right of self-determination.

At the end of the Tawbah, Allah reminds Muslims that he is the most merciful and forgiving. Through insisting that Allah is the most merciful and forgiving, the author of Quran makes clear that exterminating people for rejecting Islam is a legitimate, necessary and justified deed since it is the order of the most merciful. It is a pre-empted defence against any expected criticism based on categorizing such ideas as cruel and vengeful. The verses afterward explain and justify genocides of all the non-Muslims through defining them as evil, dishonourable, and an imminent danger to Muslims.[321]

In addition to this chapter, Quran as well as the tradition have many narratives that can be used as a licence for killing, raiding, enslaving both Christians and Jews as well as non-Monotheists. These narratives have been used by ambitious psychopaths to create criminal cults that flourished on looting and carnage for centuries. Some of these cults have been terminated by courageous people who fiercely fought them, while other grew into states ruled by criminals. Every now and then, a new ambitious group of psychopaths resurrects these Quranic passages and uses them to mobilise the distressed masses in order to create a religious state aimed at conquering the world.

---

321 Quran 9:6-11.

11 It is Our Duty to Kill You

The evilest animals according to Allah are the disbeliever they would not believe.[322]

Those who disbelieve among the people of the scripture (Jewish and Christians) and the idolaters will abide in the fire of hell. They are the worst of created beings.[323]

Despite their importance within social psychology, the concepts of dehumanization, demonization, and collective identity have for the most part been obscured from the general public. The three topics are extremely related to one another and relevant to the understanding of any dictatorial ideology. Dehumanization can be characterized as the process of defining a specific person or a group of people as subhuman by stripping them of essential characteristics that distinguish humans from non-humans. Dehumanizing a group of people is an end as well as a means to achieve further ends. Effective dehumanizing rhetoric is a well-designed discourse that invokes specific emotions and ideas among the targeted audience with the aim of justifying harming the members of the dehumanized group. By defining a specific group as subhuman, the individuals who are presented as part of this group are denied the natural rights of humans. Subsequently, harming them is sanctioned.

Speakers tend to present the dehumanizing rhetoric as a mere fact to make it appealing and less subjective.[324] They start by creating a group identity that diminishes individual differences between the members of the targeted group. By highlighting the group's lack of some specific collective characteristic that distinguishes humans from non-humans, they deny the targeted people their basic rights. This is usually done by

---

322 Quran 8:55.
323 Quran 98:6.
324 See Potter, J., & Wetherell, M. (1987). Discourse and social psychology: Beyond attitudes and behaviour. Sage.; Antaki, C., & Widdicombe, S. (Eds.). (1998). Identities in talk. Sage.

claiming that the targeted group lacks morality, self-discipline, and rationality, and that its members are united, evil and dangerous. The notion that this group is aggressive and greedy in a way similar to wild animals or insects is common in dehumanizing discourses. Usually, the severity of dehumanization is related to its final goal. The way Islam constructs its followers and the way it describes its enemies has never been examined from a psychological point of view – especially the discourses that contain dehumanizing concepts or rhetoric.

Islam categorizes all people based on their collective identity and allocates rights and duties accordingly. People are not conceived as individuals who have personal identities and equal rights but as members of groups, first and foremost. The individualistic feelings, ideas, abilities or achievements are irrelevant in Islam. People are parts of religious groups, and each group is constructed as either equal to one's group and hence an ally or a threat and hence an enemy. Every person is conceived as a prototype of his or her group and must be treated as such. This may be partially because Islam is a product of a desert ecosystem and its creators' personas. It is a religion that was born in an extremely poor and harsh environment that lacked water. In that environment, an individual could not survive on his own and at the same time could not trust other people. People lived by means of their clan and died for it. The groups were mainly formed either through blood lineage, tribal alliances or religious affiliation. Intergroup as well as intragroup fighting was the norm in such volatile communities. Strangers were perceived as an existential threat and potential prey. Islam in its view of people incorporated the idea of categorizing people and thus evaluating them based on their collective identity: "you are either a good member of our group or a threat to us and hence must be eliminated." If you are a good group member, then you must maintain this status constantly by following the group's rules and rulings and fighting for it. Disagreement is treachery.

Several unjust practices common in Muslim majority countries are based on the deep-rooted religious system that dehumanises and demonises all non-Muslims with the use of a pseudo-logical rationale. Non-Muslims are portrayed as below humans: "Those who oppose Allah and his messenger are among the lowest."[325] Allah declares in the

Quran: "The evillest animal according to Allah are the disbeliever they would not believe." In another passage, Allah describes non-Muslims as filth: "You who believe in Allah's oneness and in his messenger, the Mushrikeen are filth (najas). Do not allow them near the sacred mosque after this year."[326]

Jewish scholars have been described in the Quran as "donkeys carrying books". Non-Muslims are also presented as "deaf, mute, blind and unable to understand".[327] Several hadith explain that the deafness, blindness, muteness, and inability to understand are related to the right and wrong. "They are infidels because they cannot distinguish right from wrong. They cannot see, hear, say or even understand the true religion. They are similar to animals who hear Mohammad's talk but cannot understand it."[328]

Allah warned Muslims against harbouring positive feelings toward non-Muslims: "You will not find people who believe in Allah and the last day loving those who oppose Allah and his messenger, even though they be their fathers or their sons or their brothers or their clan."[329] True believers do not and cannot love their own fathers or sons unless they are Muslims. Muslims are ordered by Allah to consider their own family as enemies if they reject Islam: "O you who have believed, do not take your fathers or your brothers as allies if they have preferred disbelief over belief. And whoever does so among you – then it is those who are the wrongdoers. Say, [O Muhammad], if your fathers, your sons, your brothers, your wives, your relatives, wealth which you have obtained, commerce wherein you fear decline, and dwellings with which you are pleased are more beloved to you than Allah and His Messenger and jihad in his cause, then wait until Allah executes His command. And Allah does not guide the defiantly disobedient people."[330]

Disbelievers of Islam are presented as a lethal threat to Muslims. Allah has warned Muslims repeatedly against non-Muslims. "Fight them;

---

325 Quran 58:20.
326 Quran 9:28.
327 Quran 1:171.
328 Tafseer al-Tabarī.
329 Quran 58:22.
330 Quran 9:23-24.

Allah will punish them by your hands and will disgrace them and give you victory over them and heal the breasts the chests' of the believers."[331] In the preceding verse, Allah warrants the killing of non-Muslims indiscriminately: "Would you not fight a people who broke their oaths and determined to expel the Messenger, and they had begun you the first time? Do you fear them? But Allah has righter that you should fear him, if you are [truly] believers."[332] In another text, Allah presents attacking non-Muslims as a preventive measure that must be undertaken to protect Muslims from the potential aggression of non-Muslims: "They do not observe toward a believer any pact of kinship or covenant of protection. And it is they who are the transgressors."[333]

In verse 9:29 of the Quran, Allah designates another group of enemies that must be attacked by the Muslims. "Fight against those who don't believe in Allah, nor in the last day, nor forbid that which has been forbidden by Allah and his Messenger and those who don't acknowledge the religion of truth [Islam] among the people of the book [Jews and Christians], until they pay the ransom (jizyah) with willing submission, while humiliated."[334] Hence, any person who meets one of the stated characteristics deserves to be killed at the hands of Muslims, unless they were Jewish or Christians and chose to surrender and pay the levy with submission.

Allah dehumanised all non-Muslims through categorizing them as filth. They are subhuman and subanimal, too. Non-Muslims are impure creatures that must be banned from being near the sacred place, as the mere existence of these people damages its sanctity. Allah ordered Mohammad, and through him all Muslims, to fight the non-Muslims and to be harsh with them: "you Prophet fight against the disbelievers and the hypocrites and be harsh against them."[335]

These verses have been used to designate Muslims as enemies of Allah if they fail to forbid what is forbidden in Islam. It is important to

---

331 Quran 9:14.
332 Quran 9:13.
333 Quran 9:10.
334 Quran 9:29, see Muhammad Taqi-ud-Din Al-Hilali & Muhammad Khan trans.
335 Quran 9:73, see Sahih International trans.

stress that there has never been a clear list of things forbidden in Islam agreed upon by all Muslims. Some Muslims think it is forbidden for women to show their faces; some outlawed the temporary marriage while others think it is halal. Controversies among Muslims regarding what is haram and what is not are a never-ending saga and have been used by different Muslim groups to discredit their opponents and warrant harming them. Disbelievers and hypocrites are to be treated the same way. According to tradition, hypocrites are people who claim to be Muslims and behave as Muslims but deep at heart – they are not. This notion has been used by various Islamic groups and sects to justify attacking other Muslims after describing them as hypocrites.

The people who are not enemies of Allah are the Muslims who believe in Allah as the one and only God and forbid what is forbidden by Allah. Thus, they cannot disagree with any principle of Islam. Hence, a Muslim cannot remain a Muslim if they reject Quran as literal word of God, or women's hijab, or the ban on eating pork, or drinking alcohol. Rejecting the notion that men are superior to women can be sufficient to deem the person an enemy of Allah.

In Islam, people are divided into three main groups: Muslims, people of the book – which denotes Christians and Jews, and all other people. Muslims are instructed by Allah in the Quran to consider (all) other Muslims as their brothers, as long as they are devoted Muslims. This brotherhood entails specific benefits and duties. The prophet explains that a Muslim is a brother to every other Muslim, thus shall not desert or harm him. Muslims are responsible for supporting each other to attain the final goal, which is entering heaven in the afterlife. Muslims must compel each other to obey Allah's orders, such as fasting, praying, abstaining from prohibited food and drink, and most importantly participating in jihad. As per Mohammad's words, any person who dies without taking part in an invasion and has not considered it, dies as a hypocrite.[336] The way non-Muslims are constructed throughout Quran, the biographies, and hadith is designed to dehumanize them and normalize their collective extermination.

---

336 Sahih Muslim 1271.

Non-Muslims are dehumanized not by people but by Allah, the merciful creator of everything, through his last revelation that has been recorded in the Islamic holy texts.

In Quran, there are two main labels used to designate non-Muslims: kafirun (infidels/disbelievers) and Mushrikeen (polytheists/idolaters). These two terms have been used interchangeably by Muslims against all non-Muslims as well as other Muslims. Infidels are all the people who reject Islam as a whole or reject any of its countless essential principles. Innumerable wars have broken out between Muslim sects on the ground that every group accuses the other groups of being infidels for rejecting what they see as an essential part of Islam. For instance, Sunni and Shia Muslims have been massacring each other in Nigeria, Egypt, Lebanon, Syria, Iraq, Iran, Pakistan, Afghanistan, and India over the notion of who are the Muslims and who are infidels. Senior Sunni imams have been denouncing Shia as disbelievers and vice versa for centuries.

The other label for non-Muslims is Mushrikeen. It designates the people who do not believe in the oneness of the God – Polytheists. All Christians and Jews are included in this group. They are seen as Polytheists as they worship other gods beside Allah, according to Islam. Christians have the Holy Trinity, Virgin Mary, and saints, while the Jewish worship Ezra and their rabbis. They are sometimes considered "people of the book," thus better than the rest of disbelievers in Islam because their books, although have been spoiled and are not worth of being followed, still hold some divine basis. Thus, the people of the book have been given two options, if they want to keep their lives. The first one is to convert to Islam; then they will be treated as second-class Muslims who constantly need to prove their sincerity. The second option is to become a member of dhimmis which means a semi-slave. Dhimmis have very minimum rights in Islam. They do not have the right to practice their beliefs in public, they cannot own weapons and must show their subordination while paying annual heavy levy (jizyah). They cannot protect themselves, and if a Muslim killed a dhimmi, his punishment is light, but if a dhimmi killed a Muslim, he shall be killed. Mohammad established that a Muslim shall not be killed for a non-believer (kafir). The notion of dhimmi ended when the victorious powers of the First World War conquered and directly administered the Muslim world. The scripts that call for suppressing Christians and Jews are still taught all over the Muslim world as an essential part of Islam. Imams tend to lament that these practices have been suspended since Muslims are weak – but one day they would rule the world and re-enact them.

Atheists, Pagans, Buddhist, Hindus, Pantheists, Agnostics, and all the non-monotheistic people are considered infidels (kafirs) by Muslims in accordance with the Quran, hadith, and biographies. The way to deal with this group of people prescribed in Islam is very clear and straightforward: adult males must be massacred, children and females enslaved and forced to accept Islam, and all their property shall be distributed among the Mujahedeen after the Prophet or his caliph takes his share.

In conclusion, in his last message to humanity Allah considers worshipping any other deity beside himself as the worst crime and he describes the disbelievers as "the fuel of the inferno,"[337] "filth,"[338] and "the worst animals."[339] Hence, rejecting Islam is worse than murder and rape. If you commit a genocide, even against Muslims, while being a Muslim, you have a better chance of being salvaged in the afterlife than the most humanitarian persons who are not Muslims. This distortion is a cause of psychological distress for Muslims, especially when dealing with non-Muslims. On the one hand, they want to cooperate with the majority of humankind who are non-Muslims and lead a normal life, in which their behaviours result from their own needs and desires rather than ancient texts. On the other hand, they are obliged to hate, disrespect and harm all sort of people to save their skin. They must suspend their judgment to maintain their collective identity.

---

337 Quran 98:21.
338 Quran 28:9.
339 Quran 22:9.

THE MYTH OF THE PEOPLE OF THE BOOK:
TABOO GENOCIDES OF CHRISTIANS

Gone are my people, but I exist yet,
Lamenting them in my solitude [340]

In 2014, the Sudanese judge Abbas Khalifa asked the defendant Mariam Ibrahim if she would renounce Christianity and return to Islam – she replied: "I am a Christian." She explained that she had been a Christian all her life like her mother and that she married a Christian man, had a child with him and was currently pregnant with her second child. After this admission, the 27-year-old girl was sentenced to death for converting to Christianity and to 100 lashes for adultery by the Sudanese court of law in accordance with the beliefs of Islam. Her father, who was never part of her life, was a Muslim, thus, according to Islam, the source of legislation in Sudan, she is a Muslim, and no one can change that. The sentence was celebrated by the Muslims, who saw it as the fair punishment for deserting Islam.[341] Mariam was jailed together with her husband and a 20-month-old son. She was denied a transfer to the hospital and gave birth inside the jail. The United States, the UK and Italy intervened and saved her along with her family.

One of the myths Muslims propagate about themselves is that they have some sort of bond with Christians and Jews. They attempt to deceive Christians into believing that Islam respects Christianity through highlighting the notion of the people of the book – a notion which Mohammad used in his failed attempts to win over the Christians and Jewish when he was toothless in Mecca but rejected after he established his state, and then waged a genocidal war against both groups. Muslim imams do not inform their naïve audience that this notion has been abrogated by Allah himself in the holy Quran and in the practices of Mohammad and his successors. Considering Christians and Jewish infidels and enemies

---

340 Gibran, Khalil. (1916). Dead Are My People.
341 Reuters. (2014, May 15). Sudanese woman sentenced to death for converting to Christianity.

of Muslims is a well-established pillar of Islam. Each and every Muslim caliphate had killed and suppressed Christians and Jews as an application of the Islamic teachings.[342]

The Ottoman religious genocides of the Arab, Armenian, Assyrian, and the Greek Christians in the 20th century were the final chapter of the Islamic invasion and conquest of Asia Minor and the Levant. From 1913 to 1923, Turk Muslims completed the annihilation of the native Christian population in what is today Turkey and the Levant. They killed between 300,000 to 900,000 Greek Christians, 600,000 to 1500,000 Armenian Christians, 200,000 Arab Christians, and another 250,000 Assyrian Christians. Most of the victims were women and children exterminated for their religious identity. Hundreds of thousands of women and children were raped before being murdered. Millions were evicted from their homes. This organized holocaust, which eliminated the remaining disbelievers from their homeland, is still a taboo.

In the Great Famine of Mount Lebanon, the Ottoman forces barricaded the areas where Lebanese Christians lived since pre-Islam, cutting off the food supply. On 26 May 1916, Gibran Khalil Gibran wrote: "The famine in Mount Lebanon has been planned and instigated by the Turkish government. Already 80,000 have succumbed to starvation and thousands are dying every single day. The same process happened with the Christian Armenians and was applied to the Christians in Mount Lebanon."[343] Before these massacres, Muslim Turks had carried out countless genocides against Christians all over the territories they occupied. The Constantinople Massacre of 1821, Aleppo Massacre of 1850, Batak Massacre of 1876, and Adana Massacre of 1909 are a few examples of the systematic cleansing of the Christians at the hands of the Ottomans in accordance with the teachings of Islam.[344]

342 See Davis, R. C. (2003). Christian Slaves, Muslim Masters: White Slavery in the Mediterranean, the Barbary Coast, and Italy, 1500-1800. Palgrave Macmillan.; Hoyland, R. G. (2015). In God's path: The Arab conquests and the creation of an Islamic empire. Oxford University Press.; Fernández-Morera, D. (2016). The Myth of the Andalusian Paradise.

343 As quoted in the National: Ghazal, R. (2015, Apr 14). Lebanon's dark days of hunger: The Great Famine of 1915-18.

344 Angold, M. (Ed.). (2006). The Cambridge History of Christianity: Volume 5, Eastern Christianity, Cambridge University Press.; Shirinian, G. N. (Ed.). (2017). Genocide in the Ottoman Empire: Armenians, Assyrians, and Greeks, 1913-1923. Berghahn Books.

Recently, a Muslim posted a question to the influential imams running IslamWeb[345]: "Can we excuse Muslims who do not consider Christians infidels?"[346] In their lengthy reply, the Muslim imams cite the verses: "They surely disbelieve (kafara) who say Allah is the Messiah, son of Mary."[347] and: "They surely disbelieve (kafara) who say Allah is the third of three, there is no God but the one Allah. If they don't cease from this saying, a painful torment will afflict the disbelievers among them."[348] In another verse, Allah accuses Jews and Christians of deliberately rejecting the true religion: "say you follower of the book why do you disbelieve in Allah's verses while Allah is witnessing what you are doing."[349]

The same reply referenced several influential jurists who discussed the judgment of the Muslims who abstained from considering Jews and Christians infidels. The two most senior contemporary Saudi jurists, Ibn al-Athaymen and Ibn-Baz, have declared clearly in their published books that it is the duty of every Muslim to classify both the Jewish and Christians as infidels. They ruled that any Muslim who does not consider the adherents of the two religions infidels is an infidel himself. "He is one of them," they wrote explicitly. Ibn-Taymiyyah, one of the most important theologians and the spiritual godfather of Sunnis in general and Salafi movements in particular, has declared repeatedly in his many books, which are to this day widely distributed, that it is an essential part of Islam to consider Jews and Christians infidels and treat them as such.

A contemporary influential Muslim imam wrote an entire book entitled "Takfeer and its conditions"; in it as well as on his website he firmly declared that Muslims do not need a proof to consider the Jewish and Christians infidels; it suffices to know that they simply do not believe in Islam.[350] Nonetheless, he cited 24 verses of Quran, three of Mohammad's sayings, and several decrees issued by senior jurists as

---

345 It is a website run by influential Muslims scholars from the oil-rich Qatar and available in several languages.
346 Fatwa No. 352600. (2017, Oct 5). Aljahl bikafr alyahud walnasaraa wanahwihum.. alhakmu.. walwajib [Not knowing that Christians and Jews and similar people are infidels]. (Arab.).
347 Quran 5:72.
348 Quran 5:73.
349 Quran 3:98.
350 Mohamad Shams Alden's website. (n.d.). Takfeer wa zawabetoho [Takfeer and its conditions]. (Arabic).

further evidence that Christians and Jews must be considered infidels and it is the duty of Muslims to treat them as such. One look at Muslim genocides against Christians and the Jewish throughout the history is sufficient to prove that Islam is based on the animosity towards all non-Muslims, including the followers of these two monotheistic religions. The description of a person as a disbeliever is a licence to hurt that human in every possible way, including killing and enslaving, and it was Allah who described both groups as disbelievers.

In his book "Minhaj al-Saliheen", which is supposed to be the guide for Muslims on all matters, the Shia Grand Imam Ayatollah Al-Khoei[351] declares that Muslims are obliged to fight the People of the Book: Christians and Jews, until they convert to Islam or pay the jizyah while they are humiliated. Al-Khoei defines jihad as fighting to spread Islam. He rules that according to Islam, there are three groups of people that must be fought against:

The first group includes all the infidels who are neither Christians nor Jews. These people must be invited to submit to Islam; if they did not accept then they must be fought until they submit or are killed, and the Earth is cleansed from the filth of their existence. This is accepted by all Muslims based on the Quran verses: "who fights in the cause of Allah, and is killed or defeats, we shall give him a great reward." "And fight them until there is no fitnah (disbelieve) and the religion, all of it, is for Allah..." The second group includes the people of the book: the Christians, Jews, and with them Sabaeans and Zoroastrians. These people must be fought until either they convert to Islam or pay the jizyah while being humiliated. This is based on Allah's command: "Fight against those who don't believe in Allah, nor in the last day, nor forbid that which has been forbidden by Allah and his Messenger and those who don't acknowledge the religion of truth [Islam] among the people of the book [Jews and Christians], until they pay the ransom (jizyah) with willing submission, while humiliated."[352]

351 Al-Khoei was the main spiritual leader for over 50 million Shias from 1970 until his death in 1992. To this day, millions of people worldwide follow his edicts which have been published in this book.
352 Al-Khoei, A. (1989). Minhaj Al-Saliheen. (Arabic). Iran: Mahr. Part One, p 360. (Author's

The third group contains Muslim aggressors who disobey the legitimate ruler or attack other Muslims unjustly; they must be fought by all Muslims until they submit to sharia.

A Muslim mob assailed Deborah Samuel, a 19-year-old female student, inside her school in Sokoto, Nigeria on 12 May 2022. The angry Muslims ganged up against her, beat her with sticks and stones until she fell to the ground motionless. Her bloodied body was covered with car tires, doused with petrol and set on fire. The attackers, many of whom were students at the same school, filmed their beating and burning of the lonely defenceless girl and posted it online. In one of the videos, the girl is seen lying in the ground while many men are beating her viciously with long thick sticks; others were throwing stones and bricks at her. In another clip, a man is seen screaming in hysteria that he set her ablaze while he waves a box of matches in his hand. The one who was filming him was shouting "Allah Akbar".

The events started when Muslim students accused the Christian girl of blasphemy against Mohammad in voice notes she posted in her class WhatsApp group.[353] The voice messages did not contain any direct mention of Mohammad or Islam, but Deborah complained in them about the nature of messages posted in the group. She said that this group is supposed to be for things related to the classes, and "not for all these nonsense things." She was hinting at the Islamic messages that would usually contain praises of Mohammad and Allah posted by Muslim students. They were offended that a Christian would dare to criticise their Islamic ideas and considered her talk blasphemy. They grouped and brought other Muslims from outside to kill the girl in the most savage of ways. She was first hidden by the college's security but the mob overwhelmed the guards and dragged her to the main yard while beating her fiercely and pelting her with stones and bricks.

The crime was overlooked by the major media outlets, politicians, journalists and human rights activists. A few days after the slaughter,

---

translation.) In this edict, he cites verses of Quran: 4:74, 8:39 (see Al-Hilali & Khan trans.), 9:29.
353 Finch, W. (2022, May 14). Christian female student is stoned, beaten to death and set on fire by mob at Nigeria school for posting blasphemous statement against Prophet Muhammad. Daily Mail.

Muslims of Sokoto took to the streets demanding the release of the two suspects who were arrested by the police for their role in the killing. They vandalised public and private properties, assaulted Christians and looted their shops.[354]

The imam of the National Mosque of the Nigerian capital Abuja, Ibrahim Maqari, blamed the victim and defended the killers. Maqari, who graduated from Al-Azhar before obtaining a doctorate in Islamic studies and is considered an influential moderate imam by the state, wrote on his Twitter account that: "It should be known to everyone that we the Muslims have some red lines beyond which MUST NOT be crossed. The dignity of the Prophet (PBUH) is at the forefront of the red lines. If our grievances are not properly addressed, then we should not be criticized for addressing them ourselves."[355]

---

354 Finch, W. (2022, May 14). Muslim youths riot and demand police release two suspects arrested after Christian student was stoned to death and her body torched in Nigeria after being accused of blasphemy against Prophet Mohammad. Daily Mail.
355 Maqari, I. [@profmaqari]. (2022, May 12). Twitter.

WAS HITLER A STUDENT OF ISLAM?

Is it fair to say that the rationale used by the Nazis to bring about the holocaust was inspired by Islamic teachings? Were the Nazis imitating the Ottomans?

Many of the Islamic rationales and techniques used by the Ottomans to execute several genocides before and during the First World War were adopted with minor modifications two decades later by the Nazis. The Ottomans used concentration camps, death marches, and mass-murder to eliminate millions of innocent people because of their identities. The most devastating ethnic cleansing were the Armenian, the Assyrian, and the Greek genocides. In addition to exterminating the non-Muslim population of what is now Turkey, the Ottomans carried out many other genocides against Jews, Christians, Arabs, and other ethnicities and groups in Europe and the Middle East. In 1917, the Ottomans banished the whole population of Jaffa – a city of 40000 humans, as well as in-habitants of Tel Aviv and Gaza. The majority of those people were Jews, and the rest were Christian and fewer Arabs, who were considered to be beneath the ruling Muslim Turks. Thousands of the deported women and children starved and died on the roads and they were not allowed to go back to their cities by the Ottoman soldiers.

In his book "Inside the Third Reich", Adolf Hitler's senior assistant Albert Speer described how the dictator was fascinated with Islam. Hitler saw Islam as "a religion that believed in spreading the faith by the sword and subjugating all nations to their faith. The Germanic people would have become heirs to that religion. Such a creed was perfectly suited to the Germanic temperament."[356] Hitler understood that Islam could be the perfect totalitarian ideology. It has one leader, one rule, one identity, one language, and nothing is allowed to exist outside of it. Its leader is

---

356 Speer, A. (1970). Inside the Third Reich. Macmillan.

immortal. Hitler said that he wanted to exterminate the Jewish presence in Germany the same way Mohammad had done in Arabia.[357] The way the Muslim Turks obliterated the other races who were the native people of the lands they occupied is a clear example of the idea of Final Solution. They wanted to have one race which was perceived as superior to the rest.

On 1 June 1941, Iraqi Muslims attacked Jewish neighbourhoods in Baghdad, killing hundreds of Jews and wounding many more, and looting their properties. This mass attack known as Farhud was sparked by an anti-Jewish speech delivered in the famous Al-Gaylani mosque. After listening to the imam, who accused the Jewish of being the enemies of Islam based on the hadith and the Quran, the worshippers marched from the mosque to attack them. Thousands of Muslim neighbours, nomads who were living on the outskirts of the city as well as policemen joined the mob. The angry crowds killed about 180 Jews and injured many more. They looted and destroyed Jewish properties and set shops and homes on fire. This pogrom, which lasted for two days, would have continued and resulted in the annihilation of the Jewish population in Iraq, if it was not for the British forces and the Iraqi soldiers who killed a few hundred of the mob in order to stop the attack and save the Jews.[358]

To this day, many Muslims see Hitler as a hero and a perfect leader, were it not for the fact that he was not a Muslim. Several senior Muslim jurists supported him in his war against the free world. The Grand Mufti of Jerusalem, Amin al-Husseini, was a keen supporter of the Nazis and an important figure in the Palestinian war against the British and the Jews. Several Arab and Islamic movements established in the first half of the 20th century were extremely influenced by the Nazi techniques. They wanted to combine the Islamic creed with the Nazi modern practices. The most important of these organizations is the Muslim Brotherhood,

357 As above.
358 Aderet, O. (2018, Jun 4). The Jews Who Survived Baghdad's 'Kristallnacht' and Their Struggle to Be Recognized as Nazi Victims... Haaretz.; Beker, A. (2005). The forgotten narrative: Jewish refugees from Arab countries. Jewish Political Studies Review 17(3/4), pp 3-19.; Basri, C. (2002). The Jewish refugees from Arab countries: An examination of legal rights – A case study of the human rights violations of Iraqi Jews. Fordham Int'l Law Journal 26(3), pp 656-720.; Aharoni, A. (2003). The forced migration of Jews from Arab countries. Peace Review, 15(1), 53-60.; Kedourie, E. (1989). The break between Muslims and Jews in Iraq. In M. R. Cohen & A. L. Udovitch (Eds.). Jews among Arabs: Contacts and Boundaries. Darwin Press, pp 21-63.

which currently has millions of members and branches spread all over the world, supported by many regimes.

In the Nazi literature, all the out-group members (non-Aryans) were constructed as subhuman and enemies of the superior group (the German Aryans). This rationale has been an essential part of the Islamic States over the past 1400 years. Both ideologies – Islam and Nazi – attempted to conquer the world and to create a country ruled by one man, one group, and one system of thought. Islamic ideology has been more successful because it is based on a creed, thus, many can join the in-group.

12 Jihad Forever and Stealing Hagia Sophia Time and Again

Prepare for them all the force you can and the cavalry to terrorise the enemy of Allah and your enemy.[359]

Money is their God and Mahomet their prophet[360]

Invasion grew into the central principle of Islam during the reign of Mohammad and has remained so, according to Islamic original texts. The founders of Islam were warlords led by Mohammad in many battles and raids. Muslims are not encouraged to learn a trade or cultivate lands, innovate or work hard but they are required to fight and deceive others to spread their religion. All the influential figures of Islam throughout its history were fierce fighters and cunning politicians. The Prophet himself fought tens of battles. He led an army to attack the Byzantine Empire, more than 500 miles away from his hometown, without any provocation. He repeatedly declared that his revenue came from his weapon and that Allah ordered him to fight people until they surrendered and accepted Islam and paid the jizyah. People are categorized in Quran as either Muslims or criminals.[361]

Dying in battle (martyrdom) is presented as the grand prize upon which all sins are dissolved and heaven is guaranteed. It is the greatest honour and achievement for a Muslim to perish in the battlefield spreading Islam. Martyrs do not die – they remain alive after their death. They are Allah's witnesses (shohada) and Allah grants them all their wishes and pardons their relatives and beloved ones, too. As a confirmation of their loyalty to jihad, the logo of the Muslim Brothers contains a depiction of

---

359 Quran 8:60.
360 Richard O'Brien, the captain of the Dauphin who was captured by the Algerian Muslim pirates and remained in their captivity for ten years, as quoted in Brian Kilmeade & Don Yaeger. (2015). Thomas Jefferson and the Tripoli Pirates: The Forgotten War That Changed American History. Sentinel. P. 25.
361 Quran 68:35.

the Quran and two swords, Hamas's has the two swords, the Saudi flag has one sword, and Hezbollah included a Kalashnikov on theirs (despite it being made by infidels).

Offensive jihad instituted by Mohammad continued up until the 18th century with the same ideas and practices, motivated by the original Islamic texts. Every Muslim state that existed during that period took part in jihad. In 1683, Muslim invaders were attacking Vienna to add it to Greece, Bulgaria, Romania, Albania, Serbia, Macedonia, Montenegro, Bosnia, Hungary, Turkey, Syria, Iraq, Iran, Pakistan, India, North Africa, and the Arabian Peninsula, which had all been conquered through jihad.

On 2 November 2020, 337 years after the Battle of Vienna in which the Muslim invaders were defeated at the hands of the Europeans on the outskirts of the city, the Albanian Muslim Kujtim Fejzullai waged another jihadi attack. Armed with an automatic rifle, a pistol, and a machete, he killed four, wounded twenty-three, and traumatised Vienna. The attack was driven by "hatred of our way of life, our democracy," as the Austrian chancellor stated.[362] The attacker was a Muslim striving to subjugate the infidels to Islam through blood, according to the statement he recorded and which was broadcast on an ISIS's Telegram account. His family had come to Austria as refugees escaping what they described as suppression of Muslims in their native country. He had attempted to join ISIS in Syria and Iraq but was arrested and sentenced to 22 months of imprisonment in April 2019. He was released after serving less than eight months. As a result of this clemency, innocent people lost their lives and many more were wounded, and a society was psychologically devastated.[363]

Ever since the establishment of Islam and to this day, Allah's soldiers have been suffocating the Iraqi, Syrian, Egyptian, Persian, European, Indian, African, and Arab cultures and identities. The Arab invaders destroyed the old world's civilizations and replaced them with a system of belief hostile to science, art, and philosophy. The elimination of the more advanced ancient empires at the hands of the Arabs is the worst

362 BBC News. (2020, Nov 3). Vienna shooting: Austria hunts suspects after 'Islamist terror' attack.
363 Nikolic, I., Hussain, D. & Ibbetson, R. (2020, Nov 3). Pictured with his deadly arsenal: 'Lone wolf' ISIS wannabe Kujtim Fejzulai, 22, …. Daily Mail.

catastrophe humankind has ever suffered. Many medieval scholars currently described as Muslims have firmly denounced the Islamic invasions and their damaging consequences on humanity.[364] They highlighted the fact that the invaders inflicted disastrous losses on the human civilization and stalled its progress for centuries.

Muslims armies were on the offence from 622 to 1791, when they were defeated in the last Austro-Turkish war that took place inside Western Europe. This defeat was the end of the traditional Islamic invasion against Europe but not of other types of offensive jihad, such as assassinations, piracy, raids, and most recently terrorism. Before and after this battle, the Ottoman armies committed countless genocides against civilian cities and villages in Europe, Asia and Africa.[365]

Greek people who survived the Ottoman genocides and occupation succeeded in liberating themselves and a small part of their homeland by 1830. Most of the lands the Ottoman conquered from the Greek remain to this day under the Islamic rule. Many Greek cities and towns such as Constantinople and Smyrna (Izmir) were turned into ghost towns by the invaders who cleansed the native population. Ancient churches and temples had been systematically erased or converted into mosques. One of the oldest and most magnificent churches in the world, the Church of the Holy Wisdom (Hagia Sophia), is a witness to the conquerors' mentality. This cathedral was built in 537 and functioned as the seat of the orthodox patriarch of Constantinople, which was the capital of the Byzantine Empire, until 1453.

On 29 May 1453, Muslim army captured the city. Caliph Mohammad the Conqueror gave his soldiers three days to steal, rape, kill and do whatever they pleased in the city with no repercussions as a reward for their victory over the infidels (estepahat). This permission to unleash the psychopathic monsters within the soldiers on the defenceless people has been celebrated as a great triumph of Islam for more than five

---

364 See chapter 20 of this book: The Arab and Middle Eastern Intelligentsia Versus Islam.
365 See Parry, V. J., & Cook, M. (1976). A History of the Ottoman Empire to 1730. Cambridge University Press, p.104.; Shaw, S. J., & Shaw, E. K. (1976). History of the Ottoman Empire and Modern Turkey: Volume 1, Empire of the Gazis: The Rise and Decline of the Ottoman Empire 1280-1808. Cambridge University Press.

hundred years and to this day. The cathedral became the main target of the attackers as many people sought refuge in it. The Ottoman soldiers raped, tortured and enslaved masses of women and children; even the ones who took shelter inside the churches were not spared. A witness described the Muslim practices:

> After the Turks had entered the city in this manner, they set about sacking it, slaying anyone who opposed them. They swarmed about the place, and gave vent to their natural cruelty and inhumanity with every kind of cruel and lustful act, showing respect neither to sex nor to age. Some they murdered, some they debauched, they hustled the weak and aged into slavery and they chained together the young, both male and female, of every class. When they found any well-formed girl, they struggled with each other to possess her, and for the sake of the sacred treasures they fought to the death on many occasions. Their army, compounded of so many nations, customs and languages, spent three days in sacking the unfortunate city. There was no act, however wicked, that was not committed by these heathens. They laid hands even on the Church of the Holy Wisdom, that marvellous work of the Emperor Justinian, and after despoiling it of an enormous amount of gold and silver, they engaged in every kind of vileness within it, making of it a public brothel and a stable for their horses. They took the relics of the Saints from this and other churches, threw them in the middle of the streets for swine and dogs to trample on, and to be trodden underfoot by every passer-by; and the images of our Lord Jesus Christ and of His Saints were burned or hacked to pieces.[366]

The glorious cathedral was turned into a mosque. In the exact same place where the soldiers committed the most heinous crimes, they stood to pray showing their gratitude to Allah for granting them the right to kill, rape and enslave innocent humans. After the abolition of the Ottoman Caliphate in 1935, Hagia Sophia and a few other stolen grand churches which had been turned into mosques were converted into museums.

---

366 Melville, J. R. (1972). The siege of Constantinople 1453: seven contemporary accounts. A. M. Hakkert. P. 123.; See also Sphrantzes, G. (1980). The Fall of the Byzantine Empire: A Chronicle by George Sphrantzes 1401-1477. University of Massachusetts Press.

In July 2020, the Turkish president Recep Erdoğan reconverted the old church which functioned as a museum into a mosque, annulling the previous, seventy-year-old decision. His pronouncement was celebrated by the Muslim masses as a victory of their religion.[367] They were not ashamed of the crimes committed by their ancestors in this place, nor were they appalled by the fact that the grandiosity of the ancient Christian architecture dwarfs any monument erected by Muslims over the ages. They were joyful with keeping what their ancestors stole. On the first Friday mass prayer at Hagia Sophia, the imam delivered his speech while holding a sword in accordance with the Islamic tradition.[368] He praised the attending president and glorified the Islamic invaders who had defeated the infidels, killed them and captured their women, children, wealth and lands.

Many immoral propagandists justify the stealing and destruction of Christian churches, Jewish synagogues, and Zoroastrian, Hindu, Sabian and polytheistic temples which have been taking place all over the lands Muslims conquered or invaded. Some of them tend to blatantly declare that this obliteration of other people's identity was in accordance with Allah's commands and hence legitimate. Others highlight that due to the Spanish inquisition a number of mosques were converted into churches after these lands were liberated from the Arab invaders. This analogy conceals the fact that these mosques had originally been churches or lands owned by the Spanish people before the Muslims stole them and turned them into their temples. They also ignore the fact that the Muslims were present in Spain as occupiers and all the lands they possessed were the property of the locals who had been killed and displaced or treated as serfs for centuries.[369]

The Muslim way of dealing with defeated people is among the worst in history of humankind and it lasted for over a thousand years. All the – currently celebrated – caliphates regarded the defeated people as

367 Guerin, O. (2020, July 10). Hagia Sophia: Turkey turns iconic Istanbul museum into mosque. BBC News.
368 The Star. (2020, Jul 24). Emotional Friday prayers at Turkey's Hagia Sophia. [Video]. YouTube.; Al Jazeera. (2020, Jul 24). Muslim prayers in Hagia Sophia for first time in 86 years.
369 Fernández-Morera, D. (2016). The Myth of the Andalusian Paradise.

slaves and treated them and their children as such. Even after they converted to Islam, they were treated as inferior to the Arabs. The history of every country Muslims attacked in their conquest to spread Islam became a long series of massacres, pillage, suffering, and destruction.

Will Durant stated that "The Mohammedan Conquest of India is probably the bloodiest story in history. It is a discouraging tale, for its evident moral is that civilization is a precarious thing, whose delicate complex of order and liberty, culture and peace may at any time be overthrown by barbarians invading from without or multiplying within."[370]

Arab Muslims started attacking India around 664 CE, after they conquered most of Iran, Afghanistan, and parts of modern-day Pakistan. For three centuries afterward, Muslim armies would raid unprepared Indian cities, killing and kidnapping as many people as they could. They would loot whatever they could carry with them and destroy homes, businesses, and temples before going back to their strongholds. These strongholds kept getting bigger and richer due to the spoils and the slaves they seized from the raids. In contrast, Indian cities and villages kept deceasing and their lands being annexed into the Muslim domain. In 997, a Turkish Muslim warlord by the name of Mahmud became the sultan of the small state of Ghazni in Afghanistan, with the approval of the Abbasid caliph. Once he assumed power, Mahmud of Ghazni declared jihad against the heretics within his state and against the Indian people, whom he described as the enemies of Allah that must be exterminated totally. Under his command, the Muslim fighters slaughtered millions of Indians, pillaged their cities, kidnapped their children, and destroyed their civilization.[371]

> Each winter Mahmud descended into India, filled his treasure chest with spoils, and amused his men with full freedom to pillage and kill; each spring he returned to his capital richer than before. At Mathura (on the Jumna) he took from the temple its statues of gold encrusted with precious stones, and emptied its coffers of a vast quantity of gold, silver and jewelry; he expressed his admiration for the architecture of the great

---

370 Durant, W. (1954). Our Oriental Heritage: The Story of Civilization, Vol. 1. Chapter VI. The Moslem Conquest. Simon and Schuster, p 459.
371 Ibn Kathir, A. (1992). Vol 12., p 35.

shrine, judged that its duplication would cost one hundred million dinars and the labor of two hundred years, and then ordered it to be soaked with naphtha and burnt to the ground. Six years later he sacked another opulent city of northern India, Somnath, killed all its fifty thousand inhabitants, and dragged its wealth to Ghazni. In the end he became, perhaps, the richest king that history has ever known. Sometimes he spared the population of the ravaged cities, and took them home to be sold as slaves; but so great was the number of such captives that after some years no one could be found to offer more than a few shillings for a slave. Before every important engagement Mahmud knelt in prayer, and asked the blessing of God upon his arms. He reigned for a third of a century; and when he died, full of years and honors, Moslem historians ranked him as the greatest monarch of his time, and one of the greatest sovereigns of any age.[372]

Through invasions, Muslims had annexed huge swathes of land in Asia, Africa, and Europe and made them part of the Muslim domain but they have never accepted the defeated people as equals. This is because the caliphate is a theological political caste system in which the land and the subjects are ruled by one dictator who has all the political and spiritual authority. The caliph is the owner and the administrator of everything and everyone by a divine mandate in the form of the Islamic teachings. The vague and contradicting Islamic ideas scattered in the various original books of Islam are the law which the ruler is responsible for upholding. The religious institutions are subordinate to the caliph and he has the right to appoint the clergymen and make them vanish.

The caliphates of the past may appear to have been one united country but in reality, each one was divided among many warlords who were either appointed by the caliph as absolute rulers of their territories or kingpins who forced their position on him. During the Ottoman Caliphate, many areas and towns were ruled by chieftains who had forced their way into power by violence or money. In many cases, these warlords would pledge their nominal allegiance to the Ottoman caliph after they established their authority through murdering previous governors. They

372 Durant, W. (1954). Our Oriental Heritage: The Story of Civilization, Vol. 1. Chapter VI. The Moslem Conquest. Simon and Schuster, p 460.

would usually collect and send levy to the caliph in Istanbul to avoid his aggression and to stay legitimate. The various regional rulers were in a constant state of war against the non-Muslims as well as against each other. The Islamic history books are filled with stories of invasions waged by one governor of an Ottoman province against another province. The aim usually was to annex the land and take the wealth and capture slaves. The victor would ask the Ottoman caliph for his approval after the fact. The caliph, in turn, would accept the result of these civil wars as long as he got his cut. Every time an armed conflict commenced, the Islamic rhetoric that demonises and dehumanises the opponent through describing them as enemies of Allah was revived and mobilised by both sides. Every chieftain had his own jurists. These jurists were the judges and the imams, but their main mission was to warrant the ruler's acts and to mobilise people for his cause through fatwas in exchange for money.

For instance, in 1775, a local governor in Egypt, Ali Beck El-Kabir, recognized as the representative of the Ottoman caliph, mobilized an army to annex Palestinian cities which were under the control of the same caliph but had different local governors. The Egyptian army stormed the city of Jaffa, killing everyone who resisted. The Muslim soldiers captured all the inhabitants, tied them with ropes and gathered them in the city square. All the men were beheaded, including the ones who were not from the city. Their severed heads were piled up into a tall tower. The terrified women and the children were taken as slaves and divided among the soldiers after Ali Beck took the lion's share for himself. The invading army ransacked the city, then burned it to the ground before continuing its attacks against other cities. This genocide was approved by the Ottoman Caliphate retroactively and was celebrated by the Muslim masses in Egypt as a victory against infidels.[373]

From the 7th to the 19th century, Muslim warships were attacking commercial ships and European coastal towns and islands in the Mediterranean Sea. They began their raids against Cyprus, Crete, Sicily, and many other countries during the reign of Uthman. The initial attacks were orchestrated by Muawiya, who was the governor of the Levant. Muslim

---

373 Al-Jabarti, A. A. R. (1994). History of Egypt: Ajaib al-Athar fil-Trajim wal-Akhbar. (Ed. and trans. Philipp, T., & Perlman, M.). Franz Steiner.

historians report in detail how the mujahedeen would raid European cities and towns, killing and kidnapping civilians unprepared to fight. Muawiya signed a peace treaty with the Cypriots in which they agreed to pay the Muslims an annual sum of money in exchange to be spared from jihad. After Muawiya took the money, he attacked them and conquered their country, killing whoever resisted and taking women and children as slaves.[374] Crete was under attack for over a hundred years, until its people lost the will to fight, and was conquered in 824. Sicily fell to the Muslim control completely by 902, after more than 150 years of resistance.

In addition to invasions, Muslim fleets were terrorising the waters, looting commercial ships, and killing and kidnapping sailors and passengers under the guise of jihad. This form of holy war escalated between the 16th and the 19th century by four Muslim states known as the Barbary States. Morocco, which was an independent Islamic state, as well as Algeria, Tunisia and Libya, which were part of the Ottoman caliphate nominally but each had local rulers, were dedicated to piracy. The Muslim pirates abducted more than a million Europeans and Americans and sold them into slavery. Many of the captured boys were castrated to become fit to serve in Muslim houses. Women were turned into sex-slaves to pleasure the Muslim masters and bear them children.[375]

In 1786, Thomas Jefferson and John Adams, who were at the time the US ambassadors to London and Paris respectively, met with the Libyan ambassador to London to negotiate freeing Americans who had been kidnapped by Libyan pirates and to ask for suspension of such attacks against American commercial ships. He demanded that the American government pay annually a huge sum of money to his state in exchange for freeing the captives and to stop the Libyan pirates' attacks. Outraged, Jefferson asked how the Barbary States could justify attacking people who did not harm them. The Libyan ambassador replied that according to the Quran "all nations which had not acknowledged the Prophet were sinners, whom it was the right and duty of the faithful to plunder and enslave."[376]

---

374 Ibn Kathir, A. (1992). Al-Bidaya wa al-Nihaya [The Beginning and the End]. Vol. 7, p 156.
375 Davis, R.C. (2003). Christian Slaves, Muslim Masters: White Slavery in the Mediterranean, the Barbary Coast, and Italy, 1500-1800. Palgrave Macmillan.
376 Wheelan, J. (2004). Jefferson's War: America's First War on Terror 1801-1805. Carroll &

For many centuries, European countries were paying ransom to the Muslim Barbary States to avoid their aggression, and signing countless treaties, which the Muslims rarely upheld. The US also paid ransom to the Barbary after it gained its independence from Britain. In 1795, America paid a million dollars, which equalled 20 percent of the country's total annual budget, to Algeria alone in exchange for releasing kidnapped Americans and for the suspension of the Algerian pirates' attacks against the American ships for one year.[377] When Thomas Jefferson became president, he refused to pay an increased annual ransom – which was called tribute – and sent the American fleet to join Sweden's and the kingdom of Sicily's warships in fighting the Muslim states in what is known as the First Barbary War (1801-1805). In the peace agreement signed by the United States and the ruler of Libya which ended the war, America agreed to pay sixty thousand dollars to free the kidnapped Americans.

The pirates' strategy was deceitful and effective – and in more recent time it has been used by the Taliban as well as many other jihadists: they wage sudden vicious attacks against defenceless targets, then run away to hide among their people, avoiding any equal fight. Intercepting the pirates' ships or even attacking their ports was futile as for every killed man there were many new recruits willing to join the lucrative halal business. Hence, it was bombardment of the pirates' cities by the Western allies that made them realise that they could not continue harming other people's children and women while theirs were safe. This forced the Barbary States to agree to suspend their jihad against the US and its powerful allies after the First and then after the Second Barbary War (1815), but they continued storming commercial ships and coastal towns of weaker non-Muslim nations. The French conquest of Algeria in 1830 is what suspended the Islamic piracy of North Africa.

The system of the Islamic caliphate lasted until the First World War. After it was dissolved, its territories were divided into smaller states by the victorious European powers in accordance with the reality on the

Graf.; Kilmeade, B. & Yaeger, D. (2015). Thomas Jefferson and the Tripoli Pirates: The Forgotten War That Changed American History. Sentinel, p 26.

377 William L. Clements Library. (n.d.). Barbary Wars at the Clements: Early American Interactions with the Barbary States [Online Exhibit]. (Accessed June 2022).

ground. These powers administered the newly created states for some time before transferring the power into the hands of local leaders. During the time of the Western administrations, these countries experienced enormous, unprecedented development in every aspect. In every one of these countries, the life of the people improved enormously in comparison to the previous era. Societies enjoyed unprecedented freedoms; national institutions were established. Hospitals, factories and schools were built for the first time in many parts of the Muslim world. Many diseases vanished and local populations participated in the administration.

Once the Muslim-majority countries gained full independence from the Western powers after the Second World War, the ancient rules, practices, and the social hierarchy were resurrected in all these countries with no exception. One of the pivotal moments in the course of Islamic rule was the discovery of oil in Arabia in 1930s, which made the six Muslim ruling families of the Persian Gulf, in addition to Iran, Algeria, Libya, major financial and political powers. In 1973, Saudi Arabia, Kuwait, and the United Arab Emirates were rich and powerful to the degree that they imposed an oil embargo against the United States and several other countries in order to deter them from supporting Israel, which had been attacked by Syria and Egypt. This was despite the fact that the United States had been protecting these three countries for decades. Also, it was the American companies along with the British that built their oil industry. Many references use vague language saying that Arab oil producers imposed the embargo – this is not accurate as neither Iraq nor Libya participated (Iran is not an Arab state and did not take part in the embargo) and the country that did most of the oil cuts and created the panic in the market was Saudi Arabia, and to a lesser degree Kuwait and the Emirates. The United States did not retaliate against these states, who had used oil as a weapon; instead, it strengthened its relationship with them. The superpower caved in to the Arabs and its economy went into recession. As a result of the embargo, the oil price quadrupled and never went back to what it used to be, and with it surged the wealth and influence of the Gulf Islamic regimes.

This gave the old Islamic institutions the kiss of life. These regimes, armed with the mighty petrodollar fortunes, resurrected Islam as an ascending ideology seeking hegemony over the world. Their money and institutions infiltrated, influenced and subverted their nations first, and then the populations of the more secular states in the Middle East and farther. Syria, Egypt, Jordan, Lebanon, Morocco, Turkey, Malaysia, Indonesia, and Tunisia were all influenced by the Islamic ideology exported to them by the petrol-rich states.[378]

These states financed the Islamic cause all over the world, meaning to establish themselves as the decision makers and to foil the nationalistic and democratic movements that pose a threat to them. They espoused and financed the Muslim Brotherhood organization that was created in Egypt as a party dedicated to re-establishing the caliphate and making Islam rule the world. They succeeded in cleansing the whole of the Middle East from non-Muslims for the first time in history. Baghdad, Damascus, Aleppo, Homs, Basra, Mosul, Babel, Isfahan, Shiraz, Alexandria, Cairo are cities in which Christians, Jews, and other religions represented a significant portion of the populations up until the first half of the 20th century. In each and every one of these cities, non-Muslim neighbourhoods had stood for hundreds of years as a witness to the history of these regions. Currently, no one lives in these cities but Muslims divided into many fighting groups.

Currently, many Muslim countries are descending into a situation similar to the one which existed during the caliphate. Iran, for instance, is ruled by one person who is de facto caliph that in theory holds all the powers with complete disregard of the people's opinion. Within the country, there are various mafias and each one of them controls a certain area or sector. The revolutionary guard, the army, the jurists, the many security agencies, and the networks of wealthy merchants are states within the state, competing for wealth and influence at the expense of the general public. In Afghanistan, the Pashtun students of sharia toppled the elected government and declared it an Islamic emirate but most of the country remains lawless. Iraq, Libya, Pakistan, Sudan, Somalia, Syria, Yemen, and other countries are lawless societies divided between fighting Muslim groups led by warlords, with no functioning central governments.

---

378 See Arjomand, S. A. (2010). Islamic resurgence and its aftermath. In R. W. Hefner (Ed.). The New Cambridge History of Islam, IV. Cambridge University Press; Marshall, P. (Ed.) (2005). Radical Islam's Rules: The Worldwide Spread of Extreme Sharia Law. Rowman & Littlefield.

13 Sharia for the World

Whoever do not rule by what Allah revealed,
those are the disbelievers.[379]

Whoever did not rule by what Allah revealed,
those are the unfair.[380]

Rule between them by what Allah has revealed
and do not follow their desires.[381]

As an absolute ruler in Medina, Mohammad established a unifying
identity for the newly created nation. This identity was based first and
foremost on the adoration of Mohammad. He was and still is portrayed
as the embodiment of ideals that humans must follow literally, otherwise
they would burn in hell in the afterlife and suffer in this life. During
the course of ten years, he created a set of laws that governed and regulated Muslims' lives and their relationships. These laws are called sharia,
a word derived from a Jewish term which means "way" or "law." Most
of these laws were conveyed in the form of Quranic verses, sayings of
Mohammad or his acts. Rejecting any of the Islamic rules is described
in the Quran as a crime of disobedience and defection from Islam. The
first four caliphs of Mohammad, known as the "rightly guided caliphs",
expanded these laws and formalized them based on what they saw and
heard from Mohammad.

After the Arabs succeeded in creating an empire and subjugated
educated individuals who were non-Arabs, they employed writers from
among them to create official institutions responsible for formulating,
interpreting, and applying these laws, hence establishing what we know
as Islamic sharia. The last major renovation of sharia took place more

---

379 Allah in the Quran 5:45.
380 Allah in the Quran 5:44.
381 Allah in the Quran 5:49.

than a thousand years ago with the invention of Islamic jurisprudence (fiqh), which took place during the Abbasid caliphate. Since that time, these laws along with the opinions of the pioneer jurists who had been commissioned by the caliphs of their time to formulate, explain and warrant them have been governing Muslims' lives. The students of the pioneer imams created institutions dedicated to teaching these laws. Currently, there is a limited number of jurisprudence schools recognized among Muslims as legitimate. Not only in every Muslim country but also in Muslim communities in non-Muslim countries, there are jurists who live off promoting and explaining the Islamic laws, based on one of the jurisprudence schools.

Many of the ancient rules have been incorporated into modern laws of contemporary Muslim countries. Currently, no law can be drafted in any Muslim country without consulting the recognized Islamic jurists of that country. They issue their verdicts based on the original texts and the matter at hand. Many of the jurists who are appointed by the regimes are accused by their opponents of being frauds and mouthpieces for the regimes, willing to alter the Islamic rules to please their sponsors. On the contrary, intellectuals have been arguing that Islamic clergy were manipulating the regimes into applying sharia laws to create positions for themselves within the regime and hence maintain their power and income.

Islamic sharia is divided into two main spheres which overlap on many issues. The first sphere contains laws that regulate worship (ibadat), such as fasting during the month of Ramadan, pilgrimage to Mecca, dietary laws, the five daily prayers, and most importantly the tax (zakat). The second sphere contains all the laws that deal with people's interactions with each other (muamalat). The muamalat laws regulate a wide range of aspects of human life, such as "nature of the regime, transfer of power, judicial system, war, marriage, divorce, inheritance, slavery and manumission, commerce, courts, criminal system, taxation."[382] Many people become confused once they find out that such issues as food and drink or how to fast in Ramadan are part of the Islamic legal system. They

---

382 Crone, P. & Hinds, M. (2003). God's caliph: religious authority in the first centuries of Islam.

might have thought that this is a matter of the past – but this cannot be further from the truth. These laws are part of the main rationale on which Islam is based and they will always be part of its essence.

Sharia includes a penal code known as hudud that contains descriptions of what are considered crimes and the appropriate penalties, based on Allah's commands written in the Quran or stipulated by Mohammad and applied by him and or his predecessors. The definitions of crimes in Islam are vague for the most part, while the penalties are clear and harsh. Although there is a multitude of rules and in many cases, they contradict each other, nevertheless, there is a certain clear core system of laws known to most Muslims which have been enforced over the ages by both the rulers and the masses. One of the legal weapons used by Muslim regimes over the ages to crush any opposition is the following Quranic verse: "The penalty for those who wage war against Allah and his Messenger and attempt to cause corruption on the earth is none but that they be killed or crucified or that their hands and feet be cut off from opposite sides or that they be exiled from the land. That is for them a disgrace in this world; and for them in the hereafter is a great punishment."[383] In this verse, Allah instructs Muslims to kill, crucify, mutilate, or at least expel people who are deemed to be waging war against him and Mohammad. Although there is no clear definition of what "waging war against Allah" denotes, nor is there a specific classification of striving to "cause corruption on the earth," this verse legitimises the killing of anyone who is an enemy of Islam. Mohammad and his successors used this verse to justify killing, mutilating, and banishing thinkers and poets who debated or criticised them; it was used against people who disobeyed them or defected from Islam. Soldiers who fought against the invading armies as well as civilians living in the conquered regions who rejected Islam were considered to be waging war against Allah and were punished accordingly. Muslim reformers were also suppressed after being accused of waging war against Allah. Bandits and robbers were crucified.

One of the central discourses in Islam is the tale reported in all the six original Sunni books of hadith as well as in Shias' books, in which

---

383 Quran 5:33.

a group of deprived people came to Mohammad seeking help and he allowed them to stay outside the city with a herd which belonged to him, telling them to drink the camels' milk and urine as medicine. They killed the shepherd, stole the animals and fled. Mohammad sent an armed force to hunt them down. Once they were captured, he ordered his soldiers to cut off their legs and hands. Then he burned their eyes out and left them to die slowly in agony.[384] While dying, they kept begging for water to drink but were not given any and were licking the earth out of pain.

This incident, the verse, and many other similar ones have been used over the ages as a licence to annihilate any opposition. To this day, Muslim governments and terrorist organizations bring these rules against political dissidents, freethinkers, opponents, and reformists. The Iranian regime has been utilising this verse to justify the killing of tens of thousands of people, many of them on a mere suspicion of being against the regime. It has been used to call for the killing of Salman Rushdie by many Muslim jurists in addition to the Iranian Supreme Leader Khomeini. Taliban, Hezbollah, ISIS, and Boko Haram have all employed this verse to justify harming their opponents.

In the Quran as well as in Mohammad's sayings, there are many laws that include severe penalties for what is in fact normal human behaviour, such as disbelieving in an idea written in the Quran or refusing to fast or to pray. Currently, the vast majority of Muslims are illiterate or semi-literate[385]; they are unaware that sharia includes descriptions of such crimes, let alone the exact penalties for them. This makes them more willing to accept sharia as they believe it is God's law and as such, must be perfect. Furthermore, one of the most fundamental tasks of educational and religious institutions is to promote Islamic laws without explaining them. In their propaganda campaigns, Muslim organizations and jurists avoid discussing the details of sharia. They avoid any conversation about the contradictions and injustice of these commandments. Instead, they focus on simple and oftentimes misleading notions that

---

384 This incident is reported in the six trusted Sunni hadith books and in the Shia books, e.g. al-Bukhari 5685; 6802; 6803.
385 Pew Research Center. (2016, Dec 13). Religion and Education Around the World.

246

appeal to the uneducated mind. They repeat the hollow claim that if Muslim governments applied all Islamic laws accurately, people would live an ideal life. They hide the fact that many of these rules are impractical and fatal to any society.

The results of an extensive survey conducted by Pew Research Center in 2013 to examine the Muslims' perception of sharia in various countries showed that the majority considered the ancient Islamic laws the revealed word of Allah, not a man-made regulation based on God's word.[386] In another study that was conducted in 2017, 99% of the questioned Afghanis, 91% of the Iraqis, 89% of the Palestinians, 86% of the Malaysians, 86% of the Nigerians, 84% of the Pakistanis, 82% of the Bangladeshis, 83% of the Moroccans, 82% of the Djiboutians, and 42% of the Muslim Russians stated that they wanted sharia to be the law of the land. Most of them believed that the Islamic rules should apply to non-Muslims in addition to the Muslims.

Eighty-eight percent of Pakistanis, 81% of Afghanis, 76% of Palestinians, 70% of Egyptians, 43% of Russians, 43% of Albanians who supported sharia declared their support for Islamic corporal punishment. This penal law includes cutting off the hands of thieves, flogging people who drank alcohol, crucifying rioters, killing homosexuals, and other horrific physical punishments that had been enforced all over the Muslim world for centuries up until the First World War when they were limited but never ceased to exist.

When asked if they supported the death penalty as punishment for leaving Islam, 86% of the sharia supporters in Egypt, 82% in Jordan, 79% in Afghanistan, 76% in Pakistan, 66% in the Palestinian territories, 66% in Malaysia, 46% in Lebanon, 42% in Iraq, 29% in Tunisia, 15% in Bosnia, and 15% in Russia said that they did agree with the killing of apostates.

Stoning married adulterers to death was supported by 89% of the Pakistanis, 85% of the Afghanis, 84% of the Palestinians, 81% of the Egyptians, 26% among Russians, and 25% among Albanians who believed in sharia.

In France, 46% of foreign-born and 18% of French-born Muslims want sharia to be the source of law in France, according to a poll

---

386 Pew Research Center. (2013, Apr 30). The World's Muslims: Religion, Politics and Society. (Chapter 1: Beliefs About Sharia).

conducted by French Institute for Public Opinion in 2019.[387] Seventy-seven percent of the surveyed Muslims in Denmark in 2015 were in favour of following the teachings of Quran completely. In Britain, 23% of the Muslims questioned by the BBC radio in 2016 said that they supported the introduction of sharia law into the UK. Fifty-two percent said that they opposed homosexuality, and 39% said that wives should always obey their husbands.[388] One third of the Muslim sample thought that it was acceptable for a British Muslim man to have more than one wife. In Canada, Muslims almost succeeded in establishing sharia courts in 2004, was it not for the resistance of ex-Muslims.[389]

Sharia is designed to control and regulate every aspect of human life, punishing and rewarding for every act, thought, or feeling. Muslims living under sharia do not have a say in any matter concerning their lives, whether important or trivial. There is an Islamic law for everything, even the most personal issues such as choosing a name for your child or adopting a pet. Many of these laws are written in the Quran plainly, thus, no Muslim could argue against them: such is the ban on adoption and the legitimacy of polygamy. Muslims cannot choose in which laws they believe and in which they do not, especially when it comes to the ones that are contained in the Quran and have been in practice for centuries. Most of the so-called moderate Muslims tend to play in the grey area where some of the laws are not clear or can be interpreted in different ways. Nevertheless, they are aware that rejecting any rule written in Quran or agreed upon by senior Muslim jurists equals defecting from Islam as a whole.

One of the most enforced Islamic laws throughout the ages is the killing of apostates. This ruling applies to individuals who rejected Islam altogether or any of its principles. Mohammad instructed his followers to kill any person who apostatised from Islam, according to the trusted hadith books, both Shia and Sunni. Mohammad declared that "The blood

---

387 i24 News. (2019, Sep 19). Poll: 46% of French Muslims believe Sharia law should be applied in country.
388 Perraudin, F. (2016, Apr 11). Half of all British Muslims think homosexuality should be illegal, poll finds. The Guardian.
389 Sturcke, J. (2008, Feb 8). Sharia law in Canada, almost. The Guardian.; Wente, M. (2004, May 29). Life under sharia, in Canada? The Globe and Mail.

of a Muslim who attested that there is no god but Allah and I am his messenger cannot be shed except in three cases: murder, adultery while married and leaving Islam."[390] The fourth caliph Ali had burnt several people to death as punishment for apostasy.[391]

In 2015, ISIS distributed a video online that showed the execution of the Jordanian pilot Muath al-Kasasbeh. He had been captured a few days earlier, after he ejected from his military airplane which was participating in a bombing raid against ISIS in Syria. He was put in a steel cage, doused with gasoline and set on fire after being declared an apostate.

The Shia religious leader Ayatollah Ali al-Sistani ruled in an edict published in his book as well as on his website that according to Islam, if a person who was born to a Muslim father apostatised, they must be killed instantly, but if they were born into another religion and converted to Islam, then went back to their old religion, they must be given a chance to repent and reconvert to Islam, and if they did not, then they must be killed.[392] This law is endorsed by all the Muslim senior jurists, old and contemporary alike.

The most prominent imam in Qatar, the Egyptian Yousef Al-Qaradawi, said on his TV show broadcast by Al Jazeera and watched by millions of Muslims that "if it was not for the law of killing the defectors from Islam, this religion would have been dead." This senior jurist, who is one of the most influential imams worldwide due to Qatari money and his position within the Muslim Brotherhood, was honest and accurate in that statement. Muslim Brothers along with many other Sunnis worldwide regard him as their spiritual leader and he enjoys the full support of the authoritarian rulers of the rich sheikhdom. He is usually introduced as a moderate and progressive scholar when he travels to meet the leaders of other religions. In the quoted sentence, Al-Qaradawi stated what is known to all informed Muslims. Islam was spread by the sword and stayed alive by the sword, and without the sword it would vanish.

---

390 Sahih al-Bukhari 6878; Sahih Muslim 1169; al-Kafi 7:256.
391 Sahih al-Bukhari 3017.
392 Al-Sistani, Ali. (2013). Minhaj Al-Saliheen (Arabic). Chapter 3. Dar Al-Muarrakh Arabi, pp 323-324.

During his weekly program, the imam receives tens of phone calls where the callers ask him about the Islamic verdict regarding this or that matter, and he answers through reciting Quran or a saying of Mohammad. He has issued rulings on all kinds of topics, from oral sex to sanctioning the assassination of the Syrian president Bashar al-Assad. Once the imam utters the ruling, the caller has no option but to assure that he will comply and thank him for his guidance. It is unimaginable that a Muslim would disagree with any idea present in the Quran or narrated by Mohammad, regardless of its nature. The mere thought of challenging these texts is terrifying for most Muslims. Thus, the majority either somehow convince themselves that all the Islamic laws are perfect or pretend not to know that they are inhumane and contradict sound reasoning.

In 2012, the Kuwaiti parliament (which consists of 50 members) passed a law that considered blasphemy a crime punishable by death or life imprisonment. The law stated that "insulting, mocking or criticising" Allah, Mohammad or his wives by talk, painting, writing or any other form of expression is punishable by death or life in prison. Out of the forty-one Sunni MPs and ministers present in the vote, forty voted with yes and only one said no. The five Shia MPs voted "no" because they said that the law could be used against Shia and that they had been excluded from the drafting process.[393] The law was overruled by the emir of Kuwait, despite his government voting for it, due to international pressure but might be re-introduced in the future.[394]

In sharia, theft is punishable by amputating the right hand for the first time, the left for the second, and a leg for the third time, unless the thief is the ruler – then it is not applicable. Every year, impoverished people lose their hands for stealing minor things in countries like Saudi Arabia or Nigeria but never a rich man, let alone a member of a royal family.

According to sharia, a romantic relationship outside marriage is a major crime. Muslim women are not allowed to fall in love, talk to or see males except their husbands, fathers, uncles, and brothers. Men and

393 Reuters report. (2012, May 3). Kuwait close to death penalty law for blasphemy.
394 Al-Watan Newspaper. (2012, May 3). Majlis al omah yqer qanun taghliz aloqubat ala almusi' lil dhaat al-ilahyah wa al-Rasul wa Umahat al-Muminin fe almudawla althania [The Parliament approves a law that increase the punishment for apostasy]. (Arabic).

women should not interact or know each other and to this day, there is a strict segregation between males and females in Muslim communities based on the Islamic teachings. A Muslim must not experience a meaningful, passionate relationship, if he or she is not married. They must accept being sexually and emotionally suppressed. Since discussing these topics is also taboo, people's understanding of the other gender is distorted as it is based on tales, lies, and fabrications. The ban on love and the segregation between the genders are designed to create aggressive soldiers who are willing to fight in order to capture other people's women. For many regimes, this is a way of criminalising and hence controlling their population.

Hijab is compulsory in many Muslim countries, whether through written laws, such as in Iran, or through sharia principles that may not be written clearly in the criminal code but are nonetheless enforced by the system. Three Iranian women were sentenced to a total of 55 years and six months of imprisonment for disrespecting the compulsory hijab. The Islamic court in Tehran indicted the women for a video they posted in April 2019 in celebration of the International Women's Day, in which they were walking in the streets without hijabs. They were arrested and imprisoned for 4 months before being sentenced in accordance with sharia.[395] All over the Muslim world, family courts can and do strip divorced mothers of their children's custody for what is considered indecent clothing. Thus, women understand that in order to keep custody of their children after divorce, they need to cover up regardless of their feelings. In many countries, it is almost impossible for a woman who does not wear hijab to obtain a job.

The punishment for intentionally abstaining from the daily prayers or not fasting in Ramadan is death, especially if the Muslim insisted on not praying of fasting. Mohammad said that who does not pray is an infidel and he threatened to burn down the houses of people who did not attend the prayer at the mosques, with them inside.

Drinking alcohol is punishable with eighty lashes in public but if a person declared that he or she would continue drinking, then they

---

395 Amnesty International UK. (2019, Sep 13). Iran: women get 55 years in prison for promoting unveiling.

shall be killed for intentionally disobeying Allah. To this day alcohol is banned in many countries, even where non-Muslims constitute a significant proportion of the population, and the same can be said about ham. Muslims are obliged to monitor and compel each other to observe religious laws. Mohammad ordered parents to force their seven-year-old children to pray five times a day. He said that parents must beat up their children starting from the age of ten to coerce them into praying.

Listening to music is a sin, let alone composing or playing music or producing musical instruments, because in the Quran music is rejected as frivolous talk that contrasts with Allah's talk.[396] Thus, throughout the Muslim history playing music and producing and owning musical instruments was considered a major offence by Muslim jurists. Even in Andalusia during several periods music was prohibited in accordance with sharia. Musical instruments were confiscated and destroyed, and the agents of the state would search people's homes for them.[397]

Allah created all beings and he put life into them, thus, any person who depicts a living creature whether through painting or sculpture is challenging Allah. For this reason, Muslim invaders have been destroying all kinds of statues for over a thousand years.

Homosexuality is a capital offense under sharia. It carries the death penalty in the earthly life and eternal torture in the afterlife, based on the Quran and on Mohammad's sayings.[398] For centuries, Muslims have been killing homosexuals by throwing them off high places or through beheading them in public. Muslim regimes have been enforcing the Islamic laws that fit them, whether they are related to worship, relationships, or diet, with particular fierceness.

Eating, smoking or drinking in public during Ramadan is treated as a dangerous crime all over the Muslim world. In Morocco, Libya, Egypt, Saudi Arabia, Qatar, Tunisia, as well as many other countries, the police arrest many people every year and charge them with breaching the "sanctity of the holy month of Ramadan." For example, on 12 May 2019, the Kuwaiti police announced that they had arrested a teenager for

396 Quran 31:6. See Tafsir al-Ṭabarī; Tafsir ibn Kathir.
397 Fernández-Morera, D. (2016). The Myth of the Andalusian Paradise.
398 Quran 7:80-83; 25:40.; al-Bukhari 72:774.

committing a crime while two of his partners had managed to escape. The event was reported in newspapers: a police patrol noticed the three teenagers drinking water during the day in Ramadan while hiding near a road. The police immediately started chasing them and succeeded in apprehending one of the "suspects" and identified the other two. In the official announcement, the police declared that they had found a bottle of water, bread and three KitKat chocolate bars with the arrested boy. The two fugitives were picked up from their homes a few hours later and the speaker for the police held another press conference to announce that the three offenders were together charged in accordance with the criminal law of Kuwait no. 44/1968. This law prohibits all the people living in Kuwait, regardless of their religion, from eating, drinking or smoking in public during daytime in Ramadan. Violating it carries a penalty of one month in jail and/or an equivalent of US$300 fine. In Egypt, the official department responsible for issuing religious guidance, Dar al-Ifta, declared in 2016 that "the display of not fasting during the day in Ramadan is not within the personal freedoms of a person. It is a type of anarchy and an attack on the sacredness of Islam."[399] This edict and countless other similar ones issued by influential authorities have been used as a licence to harass and harm people who are not fasting in Ramadan.

Every year, hundreds of thousands of non-Muslims work in the Middle Eastern scorching heat while being banned from eating or drinking; some of them hide in toilets so they can drink some water or have some food. In the Muslim states, sharia controls the lives of all people, regardless of their religion or preference. To this day, cancer patients are not allowed to drink water inside hospitals while waiting for treatment during Ramadan. When Ramadan falls in the summer, with temperatures reaching 50 degrees Celsius (122°F), the non-Muslims workers in Kuwait, Qatar, Saudi Arabia, Bahrain, and many other countries cannot have a sip of water for more than 16 hours daily without running the risk of being arrested and sent to jail before being deported. When some

---

399 BBC News. (2016, Jun 16). 'Don't eat in public': Ramadan edict angers Egyptians.
Author's note: In the original text in Arabic, the words used were "display of not fasting", while BBC's translation refers to "eating publicly". Fasting encompasses more than just abstaining from food.

of them complain that they are not Muslims and need to eat and drink, they are told that this is a Muslim country, and they must respect the feelings of the Muslim majority or face the legal consequences. Even the American soldiers stationed in Persian Gulf would not dare to drink water in public. With every Ramadan, countless people fall sick due to the inhumane practice. Many people suffer renal failure, hypertension and diabetes complications in addition to hypoglycaemia and dehydration due to the lack of water and food for long hours.

This systematic discrimination and abuse do not concern human rights organizations or the leaders of the democratic countries who provide protection, pay for oil, and sell all kinds of equipment to the petrol rich sheikhdoms. The same dictators who enforce these laws are labelled great leaders and reliable partners by the political elite of the free world.

When Muslims say sharia covers everything, they mean it. Mohammad prescribed medications and gave explanations for illnesses, creating what has been known as prophetic medicine. He said: "healing is in three things: a gulp of honey, bloodletting cupping (hijamah), and branding with fire (cauterizing)."[400] He also said that "cumin heals all diseases except death."[401] In the Quran as well as in the hadith, honey is considered a medication for every disease. "A man came to the prophet and said, 'my brother has some Abdominal trouble.' The prophet said to him 'Let him drink honey.' The man came for the second time and the Prophet said to him, 'let him drink honey.' He came for the third time and the prophet said, 'Let him drink honey.' He returned again and said, 'I have done that.' The prophet then said, 'Allah has said the truth, but your brother's abdomen has told a lie, let him drink honey.'"[402]

For long centuries and to this moment, many people have believed in the healing powers of honey and cumin as well as burning and cutting people's skin. Countless Muslim researchers have assured that the prophetic medicine is effective and superior to science-based medicine.[403]

---

400 Sahih al-Bukhari 5683 (The book of medicine, hadith 6).
401 Sahih al-Bukhari 5688 (The book of medicine, hadith 11).
402 Sahih al-Bukhari 5684 (The book of medicine, hadith 7).
403 El Sayed, S., and others. (2014). Therapeutic Benefits of Al-hijamah: In Light of Modern Medicine and Prophetic Medicine. American Journal of Medical and Biological Research 2(2), pp 46-71.

A simple search on Google Scholar for "prophetic medicine" yields 114,000 results. One of these studies is a "scientific" paper published by the American Journal of Medical and Biological Research in 2014, entitled: "Therapeutic Benefits of Al-hijamah: in Light of Modern Medicine and Prophetic Medicine." In this paper, the eight Egyptian professors of medicine maintained that cutting people's skin and making them bleed is therapeutic because it was recommended by Mohammad. Similarly, the International Journal of Molecular Biology published a paper in 2018 entitled: "Prophetic medicine is the cheapest, safest and the best remedy in the prevention and treatment of hypertension (high blood pressure)–a mini review." The two "scientists" started from the point of view that "The Prophet did not speak a single lie in his lifetime. He made specific statements on 37 ailments and 61 medicinal plants, herbs and shrubs while making prescriptions for the sick people."[404] He must be right, not science.

No human can live rationally without constantly breaching several Islamic laws, since all the human instincts and needs are censored, controlled and in many cases prohibited. Music, alcoholic drinks, dancing, romantic relationships, painting, sculpting[405], and most importantly free-thinking cannot be purged from any society without inflicting permanent damage on the society's psyche.

No state has ever applied all the Islamic laws for a long time. No society did or could live under such conditions for a significant period of time. Hence, all the Islamic caliphates and states that were established to apply sharia had breached it on many occasions in order to survive. Even the most fundamental current organizations such as Al-Qaida, the Taliban, and ISIS have broken many of the Islamic laws and were condemned for that by their followers and opponents.

---

404 Musharraf, H. M., & Arman, M. S. I. (2018). Prophetic medicine is the cheapest, safest and the best remedy in the prevention and treatment of hypertension (high blood pressure) – a mini review. International Journal of Molecular Biology 3(6), pp 245-250.
405 Based on several hadith of Mohammad; see al-Bukhari 3:428; 4:47.

14 Allah Handing Out Girls; Halal Rape: Harem, Slavery, and the Parasitic Economy

O prophet, we have made lawful for you all your wives
whom you have given their bride price (mahr) and what
your right hand owns of what Allah has given to you
of the captives as spoils of war.[406]

How dreadful is the word sabay (captives) and how ugly
the ones who said it, invented it, taught it, implemented it
and transformed it into history and religion.[407]

Women are raped, daily [408]

One of the ideas commonly used to ridicule Muslims and Islam is the
notion of Allah giving out virgins as sex-slaves to mujahedeen who die
while fighting for him. Many Muslims and non-Muslims tend to deny the
whole notion out of ignorance or dishonesty, or both. The idea of houri is
one of the fundamental principles in Islam. It is written in Quran many
times and with many synonyms, in clear language. In one verse, Allah
promised the martyrs that: "We shall marry them to houris"[409], and in
another one he stated that: "Houris (fair women with wide beautiful eyes)
who look like pearls"[410] would be given to Muslims in heaven. Houris are
described repeatedly in Quran and in Mohammad's sayings as beautiful,
submissive sexual girls created as a reward for Muslim males. There are no
sexual rewards for women in heaven, although the married ones may get

---

406 Quran 33:50.
407 Abdullah al-Qasemi, a renowned Saudi scholar who renounced Islam and wrote several
books against it.
408 Aby Bakhat Selim, a captured Jihadi from Mozambique. Quoted in France 24. (2022, Feb
9). Captured jihadists in Mozambique say insurgency 'weakening'.
409 Quran 44:54.
410 Quran 56:22; see Sahih, Pickthall, and Al-Hilali translations.

their earthly husbands – who would also have many additional girls. The unmarried ones need to stay celibate. Al-Qasemi stated that "the tale of this paradise was nothing but an obscene wet dream of a sexually deprived mind."

Alluring new recruits with promises of sex has been a common Islamic practice which started in Mohammad's time and continues to this day: Allah pledged many sex-slaves, named as hand-possession from the captives, to his soldiers if they won a war or a battle and stayed alive – and delivered on this promise by allowing soldiers to make sex-slaves out of captive women and girls. The only problem was, what happened if the soldiers died? To solve this puzzle, Allah promised to compensate fighters after death with houris. Houris will satisfy the martyr's sexual needs. In the Quran as well as in Mohammad's sayings, these girls are portrayed in a way that is appealing specifically to nomad teenagers of the Arabian desert. They are virgins, thus pure in the eyes of the nomads. They are confined to their homes or tents – no one can see them, which is an appealing feature for self-doubting, possessive youths. They are submissive and most importantly, there are plenty of them, in contrast to the desert milieu where everything is scarce.

Apprehending people and turning them into slaves has been an essential part of Islam from its onset and cannot be banned, according to Muslim jurists. It has been the backbone of the Islamic economy since the beginning and to this day. Every Muslim city had slave markets, where kidnapped girls and castrated boys were the goods.[411] Notable Muslims owned many slaves, who worked in their lands and served at their houses for free. The hard labour in Muslim countries was done by the slaves along with non-Muslims who had to pay the Islamic levy (jizyah) to save their lives and their loved ones. Muslims were dedicated to continuing their role as soldiers of the offensive war to capture more slaves and annex more land and wealth. This practice is what allowed Islamic states to acquire vast wealth and expand.

From 2014 to 2018, Islamic State mujahedeen in Iraq and Syria posted countless videos to gain new recruits. The main message of many

---

411 Hoyland, R. G. (2019). Seeing Islam as Others Saw It: A Survey and Evaluation of Christian, Jewish and Zoroastrian Writings on Early Islam. Gorgias Press.; The History of al-Ṭabarī, Vol. 8-33.; Sahas, D. J. (1972). John of Damascus on Islam: the 'Heresy of the Ishmaelites.' Brill.

of these videos was: if you fought for the Islamic State, you would gain slave-girls in this life and houris in the afterlife.[412] In a famous video available on YouTube, the influential Saudi imam Abdullah al-Muhaysini, who was a known preacher before he joined jihad in Iraq and became a senior leader of ISIS, is seen with a young Saudi teenager who is about to blow himself up amid Shias. The boy was recording this video to say goodbye to his mother in Saudi Arabia and to encourage other Muslims to follow suit. The imam pontificated happily that the mother of this child should remember that he was going to the houris as a groom. When in heaven, he will find the beautiful girls waiting for him – you must be happy for your son, he said while staring into the camera. The boy was smiling nervously as if he was under the influence of a psychoactive substance, not realizing that he was about to kill innocent people and would die in agony. It appears that all what was on his mind was the idea of stunning virgins waiting for him. Interestingly, the imam who was preaching about the importance of suicide missions had been keeping himself and his children away from them.

In an article published in the New York Times entitled "ISIS Enshrines a Theology of Rape", the reporter interviewed several teenage girls who had been captured by the Islamic State fighters. They all described how the Muslims considered raping non-Muslims a virtuous act sanctioned in Islam.

> In the moments before he raped the 12-year-old girl, the Muslim took the time to explain that what he was about to do was not a sin. Because the girl practiced a religion other than Islam, the Quran not only gave to Muslims the right to rape her – it condoned and encouraged it, he insisted. He bound her hands and gagged her. Then he knelt beside the bed and prostrated himself in prayer before getting on top of her and raped. When it was over, he knelt to pray again, bookending the rape with acts of religious devotion. "I kept telling him it hurts – please stop," said the girl, whose body is so small, an adult could circle her waist with two hands. "He told me that according to Islam he is allowed to rape an

412 See Murad, N., & Krajeski, J. (2017). The Last Girl: My Story of Captivity and My Fight against the Islamic State.

unbeliever. He said that by raping me, he is drawing closer to God." Then "he said that raping me is his prayer to God. I said to him, 'What you're doing to me is wrong, and it will not bring you closer to God.' And he said, 'No, it's allowed. It's halal,'" said the teenager, who escaped in April with the help of smugglers after being enslaved for nearly nine months.[413]

Thousands of girls and women who had been exploited as sex-slaves by ISIS in Iraq were brought to Germany for treatment and to be protected. A German psychologist who has been working with more than 1,400 of these victims stated that "The youngest girl I examined was 8 years old. And she was about eight months in the hands of ISIS. She was sold 10 times. That means in the period of eight months she was raped hundreds of times, every day." He explained further that "About a third of the women and girls are on medical psychological treatment, but about 300 are not ready. They need time. Their trauma is far from over". He also indicated that many of the former captives were suicidal and at least twenty of them had taken their lives.[414] In Germany, these victims were placed in secret locations to protect them from ISIS sympathisers who live in that country.

ISIS burned nineteen Yazidi girls in Mosul, Iraq for refusing to be sex-slaves. The brave girls were put in a metal cage, doused with petrol and set on fire to die in agony before hundreds of spectators as a punishment for disobeying Islamic law.[415] The carrying of the burning in public was designed to terrorise other captives and make them surrender.

The fighters of the Islamic State in West Africa known as Boko Haram kidnapped thousands of girls from their public secondary school in the town of Chibok in Nigeria in 2014. The majority of the kidnapped were Christians. Abubaker Shekau, the leader of Boko Haram, declared in a recorded statement that he was instructed by Allah to enslave these

---

413 Callimachi, R. (2015, Aug 13). ISIS Enshrines a Theology of Rape. New York Times.

414 Tachibana, Y. & Cobiella, K. (2017, Sep 24). Once Used as Sex Slaves by ISIS, These Yazidi Women Are Rebuilding Their Lives. NBC News.

415 Independent. (2016, Jun 6). ISIS burns 19 Yazidi women to death in Mosul for 'refusing to have sex with fighters.'; Fox News. (2016, Jun 7). Yazidi girls burned alive for refusing to have sex with ISIS captors. New York Post.

girls. He stated that "slavery is allowed in my religion, and I shall capture people and make them slaves."[416]

Aby Bakhar Selim, a captured jihadi, explained that he was forced to join the Islamic State fighters known locally as Al Shabab after they raided his village in Mozambique. They beheaded his father, detained him and his brother and sister. "They raped her and now she's heavily pregnant", he said about the sister. "Women are raped, daily" and "it really hurts me. Women and children are dying for no reason", Selim told the journalists who interviewed him in prison in 2022.[417]

Another captured mujahid, this time an Iraqi ISIS soldier, stated in an interview with the BBC that he had killed more than 900 persons and raped around 50 young girls who were 15 to 16 years old in addition to 200 women.[418]

In the 21st century, Muslim fighters have kidnapped and raped tens of thousands of girls in Mozambique, Nigeria, Libya, Syria, Iraq, Afghanistan, and many other places. These crimes were carried out in accordance with original Islamic teachings that sanction and encourage the rape of non-Muslims. There are fourteen verses in Quran, in addition to many sayings attributed to Mohammad, that permit and encourage owning slave-girls and abusing them sexually with a complete disregard to their will and feelings.

In 1971, the Pakistani Army raped and enslaved between 200,000 to 400,000 women in Bangladesh – Muslim jurists sanctioned and supported this systematic mass rape through declaring the Bengali women war spoils. Hence, Muslim soldiers were killing and raping in Allah's name.[419] The victims were between 8 to 75 years old. The Pakistani Army imprisoned thousands of these women and girls in special camps established for that purpose. Thousands of the victims were killed, especially the non-Muslims, and many of the Muslims were identified as Hindu so they could be kept imprisoned for months and were forced to have "Muslim" children.

---

416 Lister, Tim (2014, May 6). Boko Haram: The essence of terror. CNN.
417 France 24. (2022, Feb 9). Captured jihadists in Mozambique say insurgency 'weakening'.
418 T-VIDEOS. (2018, Feb 10). Stacey Dooley comes face to face with an Isis commander who has raped over 200 women. BBC. [Video]. YouTube.
419 Rehman, J. L. (2012). Rape as Religious Terrorism and Genocide: The 1971 War Between East and West Pakistan. [MA Thesis]. California State University.

The Bengali government established rehabilitation centres for the victims after the war. In these centres "Girls were strapped to stretchers and taken for abortions. They were like cattle. The abortions were done in tents that were set up for the purpose."[420] Many thousands of the Bengali victims were killed by their relatives to preserve the honour of the family.

All these crimes are applications of this religion. Allah allowed Muslim men to have sexual intercourse even with married women they captured in war or owned: "it is prohibited to you married women except those your right hand possesses."[421] This verse that permits slavery declares that the slave-girls (right hand possessions) do not own their bodies and is a sufficient proof that the Quran cannot be a source of legislation or ethics for a civilized society. However, it can allure sexually oppressed psychopaths into the religion.

Mohammad's successors were all slavers and they fathered children with girls and women who had been kidnapped from their native lands by the invading Muslim armies or bought from robbers. Ali ibn Abi Talib – Mohammad's cousin, his fourth successor and the role model for Shias – owned more than eighteen concubines by the time of his death.[422] He fathered several children with these captives, who were considered inferior to their brothers whose mothers were free Arab women. In his will, he decided that the ownership of the slave-girls who had children with him would be passed to his children after his death, so they would remain slaves. This man, who has been introduced as a saint to the oblivious audience, had multiple wives in addition to the slaves.[423] He was awarded vast estates which had been confiscated from their non-Muslim owners.

Abd-Allah Ibn Abbas, one of the prominent Islamic religious authorities and the grandfather of the Abbasid caliphs, who is another cousin of Mohammad, was a famous slaver who owned countless sex-slaves. Islamic history books report in detail how this man used to spend

420 Saikia, Y. (2011). Women, War, and the Making of Bangladesh Remembering 1971. Duke University Press, p 175.
421 Quran 4:24.
422 Al-Radhi, M (Ed). (1990). The collection of Imam Ali speeches known as Nahj al-Balagha (The Path of Eloquence), Part 3., p 23. Dar Elmarefah; Ibn al-Athir, Vol. 3.; The History of al-Tabarī, Vol. 17., pp 228-229.
423 As above.; Ibn Saad, M. (1998). Al-Tabaqat al-kubra.

his time in the slave markets of Arabia examining with his hands incarcerated girls exhibited semi-naked before he would decide to procure them or not. He fathered many children with slave-girls.[424]

The Umayyad and the Abbasid Caliphates kidnapped millions of African, European, Moroccan, Indian, Kurdish, and Iranian girls and turned them into sex-slaves, in accordance with the teachings of Islam.[425] It has been reported that al-Mutawakkil, who initiated the custom of compelling Christians and Jews to wear a humiliating uniform whenever in public to distinguish them from the Arab Muslims, had more than 4000 sex slaves from the conquered Persian, Roman, Indian, Moroccan, African, and European nations. This Abbasid caliph, who destroyed the ancient Zoroastrian sacred places, has been glorified as a pious believer.

It was the European powers that ended Islamic slavery by force in the 20th century, when they dissolved the last caliphate and administered the Muslim world, directly banning slavery. Saudi Arabia, which was not controlled by the foreign powers, outlawed slavery in 1962, and the last slave market in Mecca was closed in that year against a fierce opposition from Muslim jurists and masses. Although the French administration banned slavery in Mauritania in 1904, it was legalised again after the country gained independence in 1960 and it was not until 1981 that the Islamic Republic of Mauritania officially banned slavery. However, it is still in practice to this day. The BBC reported that around 600,000 human beings were living in slavery in 2017 in this Islamic country.[426]

The Ottomans made the harem an official institution, regulated by laws derived from the practices of Mohammad and the Quranic texts. Thousands of women were incarcerated in countless harems spread all over the Ottoman Empire.[427] Slave-girls were systematically abused, both

---

424 Ibn Abi Shaybah (hadith): 20597; 2058; 20599.
425 See Brown, J. A. C. (2020). Slavery and Islam. Simon & Schuster.; Fay, M. A. (Ed.). (2019). Slaves in the Islamic World: Its Characteristics & Commonality. Palgrave Macmillan; Gordon, M. & Hain, K. (Eds.). (2017). Concubines and courtesans: Women and Slavery in Islamic History. Oxford University Press.
426 BBC Weekend. (2012, Aug 26). Modern slavery in Mauritania. [Radio broadcast].
427 Penzer, N. M. (1937/2012). The Harem: An Account of the Institution as it Existed in the Palace of the Turkish Sultans, with a History of the Grand Seraglio from Its foundation to the Present Time. HardPress.; Peirce, L. P. (1993). The imperial harem: Women and sovereignty in the Ottoman Empire. Oxford University Press.

physically and psychologically. They were subjected to sharia-approved rape and torture. Countless girls were drowned in the Bosporus after being put in sacks for attempting to escape their misery in the caliph's palace.[428] The ones that remained alive were broken psychologically. They lived the worst type of torture, permitted by the religion that introduces itself as the most merciful.[429]

After the fall of the Ottoman Empire, the inhumane practice of harem was disclosed and condemned by Turkish intellectuals. They highlighted the suffering endured by millions of people under pathological Islamic laws which ruled for long, dark centuries. This ethical movement was reversed with the ascent to power of the theocratic state in the 21st century. The Turkish first lady defended the harem in a public speech in 2016, calling it a school for women.[430] Emine Erdoğan, the wife of the president of Turkey who has been in power since 2003, was simply being loyal to her belief and was defending her source of power. Her husband became the ruler of Turkey and her family has amassed huge fortunes through propagating the idea that Islam is the only system that would create perfect life in this world and in the afterlife. Thus, she must defend all the Islamic practices, including the enslaving of women. The same religion that brought her to power and made her wealthy accepts slavery and genocide and thus, these practices must be constructed as noble. Her husband has been striving to re-establish the Islamic Caliphate so that he could become the caliph.

Many people living in Arabia are the children and grandchildren of girls who were brought from slave markets or kidnapped at sea or from their homelands in the first half of the 20th century. The infamous ex-ambassador of Saudi Arabia, Bandar bin Sultan, is one of the known children of African slave-girls. His mother was sixteen years old when his

---

428 In one of the most known incidents, Sultan Ibrahim had 278 of his concubines drowned in the Bosporus at the same time because he suspected that they had relationships with men other than him.

429 Penzer, N. M. (1937/2012). The Harem: An Account of the Institution as it Existed in the Palace of the Turkish Sultans, with a History of the Grand Seraglio from Its foundation to the Present Time.; Peirce, L. P. (1993). The imperial harem: Women and sovereignty in the Ottoman Empire.

430 Euronews. (2016, Mar 10). Turkish First Lady: harem was 'school' for women.

father got her pregnant while she was serving in his palace.[431] It is said that he refused to recognize Bandar as his son for a long time and made him live as a slave. The grandson of that African woman was appointed the Saudi ambassador to the UK in 2019, and her granddaughter – the ambassador to Washington, DC in 2021.

The Saudi prince Saif Al-Islam Al-Saud wrote a novel entitled "A Heart from Bengalan" to describe the suffering of his mother Maryam, a slave-girl from Bengalan, Iran. She and her friend were kidnapped by Baluchi bandits near her hometown in 1944. She was a twelve-year-old on her way to her aunt's house in a nearby village when the tribesmen abducted her. They took her first to a cave where hundreds of kidnapped girls and boys were held – they were between 12 and 14 years old, tied with rope and given very little food and water. The terrified and anxious children could not understand that they would never see their loved ones or their homeland again. Most of them fell sick from the dirty food, the polluted water, and the fear of the unknown.

The prince's mother describes how the criminals who had captured these innocent children were fasting and praying regularly while abusing helpless children. They did not feel guilty or ashamed for abducting young girls and boys who belonged to their ethnicity and selling them to the Arabs as slaves.[432] On the contrary, they felt righteous because slavery is permitted in Islam and prophet Mohammad himself owned slaves. The robbers, who were devoted Muslims, whipped an eleven-year-old boy and a girl because they overheard them flirting, which constitutes a sin in Islam.[433] Although it is not usually permitted to enslave Muslims, the bandits found a justification to categorise their victims as infidels, thus enslaveable.

Four days after she was captured, Maryam was shipped with hundreds of other abducted girls and boys to Oman. Oman had been economically dependent on the slave trade for centuries. There were all kinds

431 Walsh, E. (2003, Mar 24). Profiles: How the Saudi Ambassador became Washington's indispensable operator. The New Yorker.
432 Al-Saud, Saif Al-Islam. (2004). Qalba min Banaqlan [Heart from Bangalan]. (Arabic).; Al-Farabi, p 54.
433 As above.

of businesses that thrived on trading with children abducted from Iran, Pakistan, India, and Africa. Before disembarking, the captain of the ship told the kidnapped to be good Muslims and surrender to Allah's will. If they thanked Allah and asked Him sincerely, He would answer their prayers and grant them their wishes and who knows, maybe their lives in slavery would turn out to be better than their lives with their parents in their hometown as free people, the pirate said.[434] Maryam describes how the pirates were afraid of the English navy which was trying to stop the slave trade, but they were never afraid of Allah or other Muslims. Once the ship reached an Omani port, the children were bought by local slave traders.

Maryam portrays how she and other girls were imprisoned for months in a slave-house in Muscat where they were being fed and groomed to increase their price. She remained in that house until one of the wives of the Sultan of Oman turned up. She was looking to pick new girls for her husband but she did not take Maryam to her husband's bed. She rather bought her so she would use her as a gift to a member of the house of Al-Saud who had gifted kidnapped Georgian girls to the Omani Sultan the year before. The Saudi sheikh didn't keep her for long in his possession; he passed her to one of the Saudi king's many sons, named Saud, who succeeded his father as a king later on.

In the end, Maryam became one of King Saud's countless concubines and lived all her life caged in one of his many palaces among his hand-possessions. She was never elevated to the position of a wife. Her children were considered below their half-brothers whose mothers were free Arabs. Thus, they could never be monarchs nor hold any senior positions. The novel written by her son to document the severe injustice and anguish she suffered is an illustration of one example of the consequences of the Islamic texts that were the law of the land for centuries. Although these events took place in 1940s, similar calamities happened to Iraqi and Syrian girls in 2010s.

Throughout the history of Islam, humans have been subjected to the most gruesome suffering to satisfy pathological desires of the few, which have been justified by the original texts and praised and defended by the

---

434 As above.

jurists. Throughout the past 1400 years, boys were abducted from their parents to become servants or soldiers in Muslim armies.[435] Millions of European, Iranian, Turk, and African children were kidnapped, castrated and abused physically and psychologically to serve as eunuchs. In the 10th century, the court of the caliph in Baghdad had more than four thousand white eunuchs and seven thousand black eunuchs. From the 15th century until the beginning of the 19th century, many of the slaves in the Muslim world were European children kidnapped from ships in the Mediterranean Sea and coastal villages and towns. It is reported that more than a million Europeans were kidnapped by Muslim pirates and sold into slavery in what is known as the Barbary slave trade.[436] It is estimated that at least 11 million Africans were enslaved by the Arabs over the ages and many more millions died on the slavery routes.[437]

Slavery is still common and legitimate in many Muslim countries but in new forms and with new names. It can be seen in the treatment of women (wives, daughters) by the laws. A man can divorce his wife at any time and without any obstacle. In contrast, a woman must file a law case and wait for years to be granted a divorce after she has proven that she was abused beyond the accepted discipline. If a husband hit his wife several times, it could be seen as acceptable discipline by sharia courts. Moreover, according to the law in all the Muslim countries, the father has the right to discipline his children and his wife by violence. A woman cannot live independently from her guardian's house. In most Muslim countries, it is illegal for a single woman to rent a hotel room.

Furthermore, millions of expatriate workers in Muslim countries in general, and in the Persian Gulf States in particular, live in slave-like conditions due to the sponsorship system (kafala). This system is a legal cover for what is in reality a deep-rooted slavery mentality. The foreign workers, many of whom are non-Muslims, are treated as property of their

---

435 Gordon, M. (1989). Slavery in the Arab world. Rowman & Littlefield.
436 Davis, R. C. (2003). Christian Slaves, Muslim Masters: White Slavery in the Mediterranean, the Barbary Coast, and Italy, 1500-1800. Palgrave Macmillan.
437 Gordon, M. (1989). Slavery in the Arab world. Rowman & Littlefield.; Sowell, T. (1999). Conquests and cultures: An international history. Basic Books.
See also New African Magazine. (2018, Mar 27). Recalling Africa's harrowing tale of its first slavers – The Arabs – as UK Slave Trade Abolition is commemorated.

sponsors, who are usually sheikhs or rich local businessmen. They are stripped of their basic rights by law and subjected to all kinds of abuse without being able to defend themselves. They are the ones who carry out hard labour while getting very little in return. For the duration of their contract, they do not have the right to leave the country without the permission of their sponsors. They are not allowed to change their work, and they need their sponsor's signature for every bureaucratic matter. The sponsors have the right to cancel their residency at any time, in which case they must leave the country within 15 days, even if they lived there for decades, otherwise they would be arrested and deported by the police. If they were charged of committing any crime or offence, they could be deported without a court hearing. Even when working for the government, they are not allowed to become permanent residents, let alone citizens, and they would not get a retirement pension.

The economy of every Muslim state, starting with the first ones and to this day, has been a parasitic and rentier economy. Up until the 20th century, they based their economy on slavery, jizyah, piracy, and invasions. Manufacturing and agriculture played a minor role and were done by non-Muslims for the most part.

Contemporary Muslim writers have attempted to downplay slavery in Islam after realising the ethical deficiency of the original Islamic narratives which detail how Mohammad promoted, practiced, and benefited from slavery. They have been fabricating stories to whitewash Mohammad's biography and obscure the Quranic texts. In these tall tales, they claim that the Prophet did marry this or that slave after he freed her, or that he proposed to free some of his slaves but they preferred to remain captives. These lies cannot be found in the original books of Islam; they also contradict the Quran. Another notion usually brought up by propagandists to deceive credulous audience is the instruction in Quran and hadith to the Muslim slavers to free slaves who are Muslims. In several texts, Allah/Mohammad instructed the slavers to free one of their slaves as a punishment for the owner once he committed a major sin such as killing another Muslim. What they fail to highlight is that these texts sanction and normalize slavery of humans, including Muslims.

15 Killing and Raping Other Muslims

Throughout its history, Islam's followers have been divided into various fighting sects, with each sect divided into several sub-sects. Each sect and sub-sect considers itself the embodiment of Islam while casting the members of other divisions as infidels, hypocrites, or heretics, who therefore must be eradicated. Although they all share the belief in the main principles of Islam that comes from the same book (the Quran) and the teachings of the same Prophet, each one of the many sects has its own spiritual/political leadership and ideas or practices that differentiate the in-group members from other Muslims. Moreover, usually the members of each one of the small sects share a tribal or ethnic identity coupled with their religious one. Hence, the infighting between Muslims has been the norm for over 13 hundred years, with the issue of who is Muslim and who is not as a powerful weapon used by the various parties to warrant aggression. This internal war between Muslims that started right after the death of the founder of Islam is still ongoing. Currently, Muslim communities are in a state of war against one another, with every group claiming that they are the true believers and their enemies are infidels who must be eliminated.

A major survey which included 38,000 face-to-face interviews was conducted by Pew Research Center in 2012 to examine the unity among Muslims. The participants were asked if they considered Shias as fellow Muslims. Fifty-three percent of the Egyptians, 50 percent of the Moroccans, 43 percent of the Jordanians, 41 percent of the Tunisians, and 40 percent of the Palestinians stated that Shias were not Muslims.[438] This is even though the Shia population is estimated to be between 150 to 200 million and that they believe in Allah, Mohammad, and the Quran. When asked if they considered Sufis as Muslims, 50 percent of the participants

---

438 Pew Research Center. (2012, Aug 9). The World's Muslims: Unity and Diversity. [Report].

from the Middle East and North Africa, 32 percent from Southern and Eastern Europe, 24 percent from Southeast Asia and just 18 percent from Central Asia said "yes". Let's not forget that a percentage of the respondents were Shias or Sufis themselves.

On 12 June 2014, Sunni Muslim fighters of the Islamic State (ISIS) captured thousands of unarmed cadets who were originally stationed in Camp Speicher in Tikrit, Iraq. These cadets deserted their base after the area surrounding their camp had fallen to ISIS supported by the local population. The cadets did not want to fight ISIS and were trying to get to their homes in the different Iraqi provinces and towns, when they were stopped at checkpoints set up by the Islamic fighters and their Sunni tribal allies around the base and on all major roads that connect the predominantly Sunni area with the rest of the country. ISIS fighters separated Sunni from Shia and non-Muslim cadets. Sunnis were allowed to continue their journey to their homes while Shias and non-Muslims, who were mainly Christians and Yazidis, were handcuffed and taken to the Presidential Palace's compound in Tikrit. The Sunni slaughtered all the Shia and the non-Muslim cadets. The young men were executed in cold blood before being thrown into the river which turned dark-blood-red.[439] The perpetrators filmed and broadcast the carnage live online to garner support from their fellow Sunnis worldwide and to terrorise Shia and non-Muslims. More than 1700 human beings, who were mostly under the age of twenty, were killed within a few hours by joyful Sunnis shouting "Allah Akbar". The victims' crime was being infidels.[440]

On 28 February 2005, the Jordanian Sunni Raed Al-Banna committed one of the worst massacres in Iraq's modern history when he detonated a fuel truck filled with explosives and petrol among poor Shias seeking seasonal work in a market in Hillah. He killed more than 166 and injured more than 146, many of whom became permanently disabled. The suicide bomber was a law graduate who had lived in California during the 9/11 attacks. He was inspired by Al-Qaeda's attacks

---

439 UNAMI. (2019, Jun 12). Statement from UNITAD Special Adviser on the fifth anniversary of Camp Speicher massacre. [Press release].
440 Nordland, R., & Rubin, A. J. (2014, Jun 15). Massacre Claim Shakes Iraq. The New York Times.; BBC News. (2016, Feb 18). IS Camp Speicher massacre: Iraq sentences 40 to death.

which had claimed the lives of thousands of innocent people in NYC and Washington, DC to join the jihad. He went back to Jordan and joined a jihadi cell that sent him to Iraq to exterminate non-Muslims. In Iraq, his chosen jihadi mission was to kill Shias in their homeland because they were infidels and hence, they must be annihilated.

Upon receiving the news of their son's death, his family in Amman celebrated his heroic sacrifice. They threw what they thought to be a lavish martyr's wedding to show their pride and support for the suicide bombing of innocent Iraqis. Crowds of people flocked to that reception to congratulate and celebrate with Al-Banna family the martyrdom of their son. The suicide bomber was praised as a champion of the one right religion by the many guests who attended; many of them later gave interviews to newspapers and news websites.

The name "wedding" came from the notion that the dead terrorist who was considered a martyr had become a groom in heaven and his bride would be the many virgin girls (houris) created by Allah to reward Muslims who die in jihad. From 2003 to 2012, more than a hundred Palestinians, 700 Saudis, 300 Kuwaitis, and 100 Syrians carried out suicide bombings in Iraq. They killed over a hundred thousand persons and wounded many more, some of whom became disabled. The majority of the victims were Iraqi civilians.[441]

Sunnis carried out numerous suicide attacks in Syria, Lebanon, and Iran, killing masses of Shias, Alawites, Druze, Ismailis, and Sufis, who they considered heretics and thus, enemies of Islam rather than fellow Muslims. They also attacked Shias in Kuwait and Saudi Arabia with suicide bombings.

In Egypt, a Sunni mob assaulted a gathering of around two dozen Shias on 23 June 2013 in a village near Cairo. The mob of over a thousand angry people was mobilised by two Sunni imams outraged by the Shias congregating in a private house. They used stones and Molotov cocktails to kill everyone inside the house. The main target was a Shia preacher deemed anti-Sunni, Hassan Shehata, who had been a prominent Sunni imam before converting to Shia creed. He came out of the house along

---

441 NBC News. (2005, Jun 30). Most suicide bombers in Iraq are foreigners.

with three other men to protect the children and women held in the house. The mob beat, stabbed and lynched the four men in front of a hysterical crowd of children, women, and elders who gathered to celebrate. The victims were Shias practicing their beliefs inside their house, which is a crime in the eyes of devoted Sunnis. Videos taken by some of the attackers and posted online showed the killings and the four dead bodies being dragged in dusty streets while being beaten and spat at by the euphoric crowd.[442]

In Iraq, the Shia-Sunni sectarian war which peaked between 2006 and 2009 claimed the lives of tens of thousands of innocent people. Many of the victims were targeted because of their supposed sectarian identity. Sunnis have killed tens of thousands of Shias through suicide bombings, indiscriminate shootings and other forms of terrorist attacks. Shia militias kidnapped thousands of Sunnis, executed them and dumped their corpses in deserted areas.

One of the crimes that stands out as an extreme consequence of the religious animosity between Iraqi Shia and Sunnis is the Dujail wedding massacre. In November 2006, a caravan that was carrying celebrating members of two families and their friends on their way to the wedding venue was stopped by Sunni militants. The armed Sunni, who had set up a fake checkpoint, kidnapped around 70 passengers. They separated the captives into four groups: males, females, children, and the groom and the bride who were kept together. They lined up the handcuffed males and shot them in the back of the head while their children and wives were watching. Afterward, they chained fifteen children aged between 2 and 12 and attached concrete blocks to their legs before they threw them in the Tigris River to die before the eyes of their mothers and sisters. The women were handcuffed, raped, then executed.

The bride and the groom were taken to Bilal Mosque, to the Egyptian imam who had issued the fatwa that permitted the rape and the killing of these people in the first place. He interrogated the couple to confirm their sectarian identity, then told his followers that they could continue with raping the bride and kill her with the groom afterwards. They kept the girl in the basement of the mosque, where eight men raped

442 Human Rights watch. (2013, Jun 27). Egypt: Lynching of Shia Follows Months of Hate Speech: Police Fail to Protect Muslim Minority.

271

and tortured her over the course of eight days. Afterward, they cut-off her nipples, slashed her chest open, and shot the groom before her eyes. They tied the two dying people and threw them in the river to perish.[443]

The assassins recorded their crime on their mobile phones and these recordings were used as evidence against them after they were captured by the police. The fifteen killers confessed to their crime and each one of them explained his role in detail in recorded admissions that were aired by the Iraqi TV along with pictures and videos taken from their cell phones.[444] They stated in the confessions that the bride was a Sunni and the groom was a Shia, thus, such a marriage was a major sin and a defection from Islam on the part of the Sunni bride and her family, punishable by death and slavery. As for the groom and his family, the killers affirmed that they were Shia and hence enemies of Islam that must be cleansed from the face of the earth, according to their belief and to the edict issued by the Egyptian imam.[445]

The number of sectarian attacks has declined in the past few years but the war continues to this day and can flare-up at any moment. Tens of thousands of people remain unaccounted for.

Shias and Sunnis have been massacring and suppressing each other in Afghanistan, Pakistan, Iran, Iraq, Turkey, Syria, Lebanon, Saudi Arabia, Kuwait, Bahrain, Yemen, Egypt, Tunisia, and Nigeria for centuries. Each and every form of aggression has been used in that perpetual feud, including mass-rape. Countless women and children have been raped in Syria, Iraq, Iran, Pakistan, Bangladesh and many other countries as a result of this war.

Millions of Afghanis, Pakistanis, Iranians, Iraqis, Lebanese, Syrians, and Algerians have been expelled from their homes at the hands of other Muslims because of their sectarian or ethnic identities. Iranian Sunnis are treated as a fifth column in their country and the opposite is true for Shias in most of the Sunni-majority countries.

---

443 Elaph News. (2011, Jun 16). Alhukam biaedam munafidhi jarima "eurs alDijil" fi Baghdad [Death sentence for the perpetrators of the 'Dujail wedding' crime in Baghdad]. (Arabic).

444 DaysPain. (2011, Jun 5). Documentary: A visit to the Dujail wedding crime site. A dialogue with criminals. (Arabic). Al Iraqiya TV. [Video]. YouTube.

445 CBC News. (2011, Jun 16). Iraq sentences 15 to death for party massacre.

The first major genocide of the 21st century was committed by the Sudanese Army and its allies of the Arab Muslim Janjaweed militiamen against African farmers in Darfur. This ongoing massacre started in 2003, when the Sudanese soldiers and their allies began carrying out an ethnic cleansing campaign against the Africans. The Arab attackers would kill every adult male, rape females and young males, ransack everything and burn the buildings to the ground. Babies were bludgeoned to death by the Arab fighters to spread fear and break the Africans' will to resist. Mass-rape was used systematically to destroy the Africans' sense of self. Old women and young children, both males and females, were raped in masses in front of their relatives who were forced to watch. In this ongoing genocide, the Arabs have so far murdered between 100,000 to 500,000 persons, the majority of whom were children, elderly, and females. They raped tens of thousands of girls and boys and destroyed hundreds of villages. This cleansing of the native people of that African region at the hands of the Arabs has been ignored by the international world for the most part. The way the attackers and their supporters justified this ongoing genocide and how Islamic teachings were used for that purpose has never been thoroughly discussed, let alone condemned.

The same practices of mass rape, mass killing, ransacking, and burning entire villages were used by the Iraqi Army and their Arab tribal allies against the Kurds in 1980s. The role of Islamic teachings and how they were utilized to bring about those genocides remains another taboo.

Currently, there are armed conflicts between Muslims in Libya, Sudan, Yemen, Somalia, Nigeria, Ethiopia, Syria, Iraq, Pakistan, and Afghanistan. Many other countries, such as Egypt, Turkey, Morocco, Gaza Strip, West Bank, Tunisia, and Iran, are witnessing low intensity conflicts between Islamic groups versus governmental forces and/or other Muslims. In each and every one of these conflicts, "original" Islamic texts are employed by the different fighting factions to justify their position and condemn their enemies.

NO SANCTUARY

It is not just non-Muslim places of worship that are considered legitimate targets but mosques of heretic Muslims as well. Attacking mosques, killing, and wounding worshippers while they are praying to Allah goes back to the founder of Islam, Mohammad, who received a revelation from his God instructing him to destroy a mosque that was built by a group of his followers. In that Quranic order, Allah informed Muslims that: "those who built a mosque (masjid) to cause harm and for unbelief and to cause disunion among the believers and an ambush to him who made war against Allah and His Apostle before and they will certainly swear: We did not desire aught but good; and Allah bears witness that they are most surely liars." [446] In application of this verse, Mohammad sent an armed force to burn the mosque to the ground, which they did. Muslims have been inferring from this verse and the attack which followed that any mosque built by heretics or hypocrites must be demolished.

The Kaaba, which had been considered a sanctuary by Arabs before Islam, was attacked by an army of 10,000 men led by Mohammad himself around 630 CE. After the conquest, the Muslims cleansed it from all other religions and converted the centre of Polytheism into the centre and the most sacred site of Islam. They declared it a sanctuary for Muslims only, banning non-Muslims from existing in it or in its surroundings. Allah forbade fighting in the place. But in year 692, a Muslim army attacked it. The army was sent by the Umayyad Caliphate to suppress an uprising that was led by one of Mohammad's close relatives called Ibn al-Zubayr and recapture Mecca by force. Muslim soldiers killed and wounded thousands of other Muslims inside the grand mosque after branding them apostates. They used catapults to kill the surrounded people and destroy

---

446 Quran9:107, Shakir's trans.

the fences they had put up. The Kaaba was set on fire and demolished by the attacking forces.[447] They rebuilt it later.

The practice of targeting worshippers inside mosques continues to this day. On Friday, 8 August 2021, an Islamic State fighter attacked Shias inside a mosque in the city of Kunduz in Afghanistan. The suicide bomber detonated explosives, killing and injuring 200 individuals, who were amid the noon prayer. The attacker was identified by the Islamic State's media channel as a Chinese Uygher who wanted to please Allah through exterminating its Shia enemies.[448]

On 29 August 2003, Al-Qaeda in Iraq detonated two car bombs outside the Imam Ali Mosque. This shrine is believed to be the burial place of Mohammad's cousin and caliph Imam Ali and is one of the holiest places for Shia Muslims.[449] More than 124 people, who were leaving after the Friday prayer assembly, were killed in this attack, and another 142 were injured.

The bombing of the al-Askari mosque in the city of Samarra in Iraq on 22 February 2006 triggered a Sunni-Shia war which lasted for over three years and claimed the lives of tens of thousands of civilians as well as fighters on all sides, including non-Muslims.[450]

On 20 June 1994, Sunni militants took responsibility for the bombing of the shrine of Imam Ali al-Ridha, the most sacred Shia mosque in Iran. The shrine was crowded with Shias who had come to commemorate Ashura, the holiest day in their Islamic calendar, when a bomb exploded, killing tens of people and injuring many more.

On 24 November 2017, dozens of Sunni jihadists armed with machine guns, explosives, and RPGs attacked the Al-Rawda Mosque in Sinai during the Friday prayer. The attackers opened fire and detonated

447 The History of al-Tabarī, Vol. 8.; Ibn al-Athir, Vol. 2.
448 Kullab, S. & Akhgar, T. (2021, Oct 8). IS bomber kills 46 inside Afghan mosque, challenges Taliban. AP News.
449 CNN. (2003, Aug 30). Najaf bombing kills Shiite leader, followers say.
450 Amnesty International (2007, May 23). Amnesty International Report 2007 – Iraq.; BBC News. (2014, Oct 14). Iraq: Shia militias 'killing Sunnis in reprisal attacks'.; Countervortex. (2006, Sep 25). Rape becomes weapon in Iraq sectarian war. (Iraq Freedom Congress Statement On Kidnapping And Raping Of Women In Iraq).; Human Rights Watch. World Report 2007. Iraq: Events of 2006.; Human Rights Watch. (2011, Feb 21). At a Crossroads: Human Rights in Iraq Eight Years after the US-Led Invasion. [Report].

explosives, massacring the worshippers inside the mosque, who were amid their prayer. The Muslim jihadists set cars parked around the mosque on fire to suffocate the people inside and prevent them from escaping. They attacked the fleeing people and ambulances that rushed to evacuate the casualties with explosives and machine guns. Three hundred and five humans were killed in that attack, among them 27 children, and many more were injured. The victims were targeted by the members of the Islamic State Sinai Province because they were Sufis, which makes them apostates in the eyes of many Sunnis. The same Islamic jihadi organization that took responsibility for this attack bombed a Russian airplane carrying tourists in year 2015, killing 224 people. In both attacks, the aggressors used Islamic teachings to designate the victims as enemies of Islam and consequently sanction obliterating them.

The most sacred place for all Muslims, the Grand Mosque of Mecca, was attacked time after time by Muslims killing other Muslims inside it after labelling them infidels or heretics. The last major attack took place on 20 November 1979. Hundreds of armed devoted Muslims seized the holy site of Islam. They killed the guards and took the worshippers hostage. Their aim was to establish the Islamic Caliphate after destroying the Islamic Saudi regime which they deemed non-Islamic. They were led by a young Muslim imam called Juhayman al-Otaybi and his brother-in-law, Mohammad al-Qahtani, who was declared as the guided redeemer (Mahdi) sent by Allah before the judgment day to establish a pure Islamic state. They held on inside the mosque and repelled several attacks waged by Saudi forces, killing more than 700 Muslim soldiers and policemen. After two weeks of fierce fighting, the Saudi forces with the support of French commandos, who were required to phonily convert to Islam to be able to participate in the attack, managed to recapture the Grand Mosque. They killed, wounded and captured hundreds of the rebels. Many of the captives were then beheaded by the Saudi government in public squares of different Saudi cities to deter their sympathizers.

16 Females in Islam

LET THE GIRLS DIE FOR THE HIJAB

On 11 March 2002, a massive fire broke out in a middle school for girls in Mecca. Hundreds of girls and fifty-five female teachers were stranded inside the school. Upon the arrival of the fire fighters and the paramedics to the scene, they found several members of the Islamic Police (officially known as the Committee for Promotion of Virtue and the Prevention of Vice) blocking the gate of the school. Members of the Islamic Police were barring the girls and their teachers from leaving the school by force because some of them were not fully covered. They also prevented the fire fighters, the paramedics, and the parents from getting inside to rescue the stranded girls and women. They reasoned that there might be girls who are not wearing full hijab and thus, it is forbidden in Islam (haram) for any stranger to see them. They wanted to prevent any contact that might happen between the rescuers and the girls, even the covered ones, as it is also strictly prohibited in Islam.

A report by Mecca's Civil Defence Department stated that "the Islamic Police were at the main gate of the school" and "intentionally obstructed the efforts to evacuate the girls. This resulted in increasing the number of casualties, we told them that the situation was dangerous and it was not the time to discuss religious issues, but they refused and started shouting at us. Whenever the girls got out through the main gate these people forced them to return through another gate. Instead of extending a helping hand to the rescue workers, they were using their hands to beat us up."[451] In a report published by Al Riyadh newspaper, students described how the Islamic policemen prevented the locals from helping the traumatised girls and their teachers.[452] They did not

---

451 Human Rights Watch. (2002, Mar 15). Saudi Arabia: Religious Police Role in School Fire Criticized.

allow the people who came to help to enter the school despite them carrying fire extinguishers. [453]

Fifteen girls burned to death, another fifty suffered severe burns and many more were badly injured. Most of them could have been saved, was it not for the Islamic teachings that compel females to cover up and segregate males from females, enforced by those bureaucrats. This incident is one of many that sheds light on the Islamic mindset regarding females. Many Muslims consider hijab more important than the lives of their daughters. Thus, countless girls have been killed by their relatives for rejecting hijab.

It was not until 2016 that the power of the Islamic Police was finally restricted, and the people were partially freed from their suppression. The restraint of the Islamic Police's power, although welcomed by many people in Saudi Arabia, was fiercely opposed by many Muslims inside the country and abroad. They condemned what they considered the abolition of the organization that was enforcing Islamic laws. Since that decision, the Saudi king and the crown prince have been the target of constant vicious attacks by international Islamic movements, especially the Muslim Brothers, who are using all means to defame the current rulers.

Millions of women worldwide wear hijab. Many of them do not know why they are doing so. The idea of hijab is mentioned in the Quran: "O Prophet tell your wives and your daughters and the women of the believers to draw their cloaks (veils) all over their bodies (i.e. screen themselves completely except the eyes or one eye to see the way[454]). That will be better, that they should be known (as free respectable women) so as not to be abused."[455] In another verse, Allah instructed Mohammad to "tell the believing women to lower their gaze and guard their

452 Al-Lihibi, W. & Al-Nifai, S. (2002, Mar 14). Albaed akad.. wa alkhir nafa: Riwayat mutanaqida an mane rijal hayyat al'amr bialmaeruf 'frad aldifae almadanii min mubasharat 'iinqadh talibat almadrasa [Some affirmed, while others denied: Contrasting stories about religious police preventing civil defence personnel from rescuing schoolgirls]. Al-Riyadah Newspaper.
453 Middle East Online. Akaz Newspaper. (2002, Mar 14). Maqtal altalibat fi Hariq Mecca: Itham Almutawaah be Anhom wara Alkarethah [The killing of female students in a fire in Mecca: the accusation of the 'mutawwa'ah' of being behind the disaster]. (Arabic).
454 This is the interpretation of Marmaduke Pickthall.
455 Quran 33:59, Pickthall's trans.

genitals[456] and not show their beauty except what is visible from it and to wrap their covers over their chests and not show their beauty except to their husbands or their fathers or their husbands' fathers…"[457]

Hence, it was Allah who instructed Muslim women to cover up. The reason behind this order was to distinguish the free Muslim women from slaves and non-Muslims. Through wearing hijab, free Muslim women obey Allah and supposedly protect themselves from being harassed by men. Caliph Omar banned non-Muslims from wearing hijab and would beat them up if he caught them covered. Thus, the hijab was and will always be a uniform created to differentiate obedient free Muslim women from their inferiors. Slaves and non-Muslims are seen as filth with no rights. They do not deserve to be protected from harassment. The hijab is also a clear mark that a female has surrendered utterly to Islamic teachings which regulate every aspect of her life, including her clothes. Most importantly, it shows the validation of the notion that she is a sexual object that must be covered so it won't attract men. Muslims believe based on the Quran that covering the whole body including the hair is a must for all women but disagree on whether veiling the face is part of the hijab or not. Many of the jurists contend that women are allowed to show their faces as long as they do not intend to seduce males. In contrast, influential imams have declared over the ages that according to their understanding of the Quran females must cover their faces including their eyes (burqa) so they won't seduce men. They explain that the face and the eyes are part of the female's beauty, thus, must be disguised. Others have agreed that the woman's face must be veiled but not her eyes (niqab).

The Iranian Islamic regime considers forcing women to wear hijab regardless of their religion or preference and enforcing strict segregation between the two genders one of its most glorious accomplishments. The rulers have been using hijab as a means to assure their dominance. They are the ones who decide what women can and cannot wear. Ann Linda, the Swedish Trade Minister, wore hijab during her official trip to Iran in 2017.[458]

---

456 The literal translation of this phrase is "guard their vaginas". This Quranic verse shows the author's obsession with female genitals.
457 Quran 24:31, see Sahih International, Sarwar, and the literal trans.
458 BBC. (2017, Feb 13). Sweden defends officials wearing headscarves in Iran.

For more than forty years, Iranian police and the religious militias have been arresting and harassing females for not wearing the Islamic hijab. Women in Iran must cover their entire hair and their whole figure properly, in accordance with Islamic teachings that regulate female dress. Strict segregation between males and females is enforced all over the country. In 2014, girls were attacked with acid in the heart of Isfahan for wearing an inappropriate hijab. Several young girls lost their eyesight, and their faces were scarred permanently as a result of the attacks.[459] The Iranian regime did not arrest or charge anyone and, as usual, blamed the girls and the Americans and foreign powers. In 2020, the most senior Iranian political and religious leader of Isfahan encouraged harming females who do not wear the proper hijab, stating that "we must make the social environment unsafe for these people."[460] He also reminded the Iranians of the acid attacks and of the fact that they have no say when it comes to hijab.

In October 2021, videos and photos that showed a pharmacist being beaten by several of her colleagues inside the clinic where she worked became a trend on Egyptian social media. The bruised girl posted a video on her Facebook page after the attack, stating in it that she had been bullied and harassed for a long time by her colleagues for not wearing the hijab and for taking care of dogs, which are considered filthy animals by Muslims. On the day of the attack, several of her co-workers ambushed her in the stairs while she was exiting her work and started beating her while others were filming with joy, she said.[461] Many accounts came to defend the attackers and insult the girl who was defying Allah's orders and seducing men by not covering her hair, as they said.

Coercing females to commit to hijab at an early age is a mandatory religious practice currently enforced all over the world, and if a female chose to remove it when she is mature enough to decide, she most likely

459 Lipin, M. (2018, Jul 20). Iranian Acid Attack Victim Pursues Legal Fight Despite Claim 'Case Closed'. Voice of America News.

460 Al-Monitor. (2020, Oct 13). Cleric reopens scars of acid attacks after threatening Iranian women.

461 Al-Arabiya. (2021, Oct 11). Vidyu 'athar ghadaban fi Masara: Darb wasahal saydalaniatan bisabab alhijab [A video sparks outrage in Egypt: Pharmacist beaten and dragged in Egypt as punishment for not wearing hijab]. (Arabic).

would suffer for it. Families who do not compel their females to wear hijab are defamed and ostracised by the society and could be attacked by organized mobs. Criticizing the hijab is a crime in Muslim countries and can be categorised as blasphemy, which most often carries severe penalties. Muslim females in Western countries who reject hijab are stigmatized, harassed and in many cases abused physically and psychologically. Social media platforms abound with stories of girls who were disowned, killed or tortured at the hands of their relatives as punishment for refusing hijab. Thousands of women and girls have shared their traumatic experiences with hijab online using the hashtag #LetUsTalk, hoping to make people aware of women and girls' suffering caused by this mandatory Islamic uniform. They posted their pictures with and without hijab, describing how they had been shamed, threatened, beaten, and disowned by their parents and their relatives to force them to embrace the Islamic dress code for females. Many girls from different Muslim countries detailed how they had been arrested by the police and thrown in jail for showing their hair or parts of their figures. Some talked about how they had lost custody of their children and others described how they had been expelled from their colleges or fired from their jobs. Athletes, actors, academics, young and old, have described how they were compelled by society, the state as well as foreigners to wear the hijab, in most cases starting from when they were toddlers, against their will. While these victims were hoping for sympathy and solidarity, the US special envoy for women in Afghanistan, Rina Amiri, put on hijab while meeting the Taliban in Oslo in January 2022.[462] Surrender is victory.

The different perceptions of the hijab, personal freedoms, and women's rights are a clear example of the conflict between Islamic principles on the one hand and the values of the modern civilization on the other hand. Many Muslims who left their countries have brought the mandatory hijab as well as the contempt for human rights with them to the non-Muslim lands.

The issue of banning hijab in public came up in the debate between the two candidates for the 2022 French presidential elections. Although

---

462 Kabul Press. (2022, Jan 26). Wearing Hijab in Oslo: Rina Amiri Was Influenced by the Taliban.

both President Emanuel Macron and his challenger Marine Le Pen seemed to agree that many Muslim women in France were forced to wear hijab including burqa or niqab, they disagreed on banning the Islamic uniform in public spaces. Macron stated that "banning hijab in the suburbs would create a civil war."[463]

In Austria, the highest court overturned a ban on hijab for elementary school children. This took place in December 2020, days after a Muslim waged a jihadi attack killing and wounding dozens of innocent people in the heart of Vienna. The ban, which was deemed unconstitutional and discriminatory by the supreme court, had been introduced to protect the children from being forced to wear religious uniform at the early age of 6 to 10 years. Through this sentence, the judges decided that it is legal for Muslim parents to put their daughters in religious dress at any age. The judges also confirmed that Austrian schools must accept that Muslim girls can be different from the rest of the society. They must have known very well that these children who are put into hijab are not mature enough to decide on such a matter. They also should have known that once put into hijab, the female is compelled to cover all her body and to wear loose thick clothes so she would not arouse sexual desires in males. Once a girl is put into hijab, she would not be able to take it off without serious consequences, unlike any symbol of other religions that can be put on and taken off, the judges must have known.[464]

In the ruling, the judges explained that from the material in support of the ban submitted by the government it was clear that the ban targeted the Islamic headscarf, and this was against the principle of equality and the state's obligation to neutrality in relation to religion. This ruling ignores the fact that there is only one religious group which forces its females to wear a mandatory uniform starting in their childhood and penalises them if they reject it. The judges were too timid to rule that it is unethical to force any human to wear specific religious clothes, let alone impose them on children who are not mature enough to decide. They did not declare that children must be protected and that in a democratic

463 The 2022 Presidential Debate, available on YouTube: France 24 English. (2022, Apr 11). The Debate: Le Pen confirms plan to ban Muslim headscarf in public.
464 DW. (2020, Dec 11). Top Austrian court lifts headscarf ban in elementary schools.

society, parents who ban their children from education over clothes are not fit to be parents and must not be trusted with raising children. This ruling is a clear example of cowardice and dishonesty being veiled as decency and tolerance. It is a win for the hijab at the expense of children's rights and their future.

WOMEN AS PROPERTY AND CHILD BRIDES

> I have not seen anyone more deficient in intelligence
> and religion than you women.[465]
>
> Mohammad

Throughout the history of Islam, women have been subjected to un-paralleled dehumanising, systematic abuse and suppression.[466] Their feelings, personalities, and identities have been repressed by the unalterable laws that constructed them as sinful and subordinate to men. Allah has declared:

> Men are in charge of women by what Allah has favoured some over the other and by what they spend from their money. So righteous women are devoutly obedient, guarding in [the husband's] absence what Allah would have them guard. But those [wives] from whom you fear disobedience advise them, abandon them in bed, and beat them. But if they obey you, seek no means against them. Indeed, Allah is ever Exalted and Grand.[467]

This passage summarises how Islam views females. They are inferior to males because Allah has created them as such. A good woman is an obedient woman. Husbands have the right to discipline their wives through advice, abandonment, and beating. There are numerous other passages in Mohammad's sayings and in the Quran that highlight the same idea. The teachings of Islam present females as evil and irrational in comparison to males. This appraisal has been influencing all types of laws for more than a thousand years. Because of it, women suffer normalised systematic abuse and discrimination. They are conditioned to accept inferiority.

---

465 Sahih al-Bukhari 304.
466 Brown, J. A. C. (2020). Slavery and Islam. Simon & Schuster.; Fay, M. A. (Ed.). (2019). Slaves in the Islamic World: Its Characteristics & Commonality.; Gordon, M. & Hain, K. (Eds.). (2017). Concubines and courtesans: Women and Slavery in Islamic History.
467 Quran 4:34.

Laws and practices which discriminate against females, suppress them and treat them as inferior to males in every Muslim country and community, whether it is Saudi Arabia, Iran, the Taliban or ISIS, are in most cases exact implementations of the orders of Allah. These laws and practices are written in the Quran, explained and reinforced in Mohammad's narratives, and have been formalised and publicised by Muslim jurists over the ages. Women shall not hold positions of judges and their testimony is half that of males in some regards, and in other regards – invalid. Allah has decided that women must be given half that of their brothers: "Allah commands you in regard to your children's to the male, a portion equal to that of two females."[468]

Mohammad taught that women are "deficient in intelligence and religion."[469] He married numerous women and owned several slave-girls. Aisha was 6 years old when the Prophet married her, and he consummated the marriage when she was 9 years old; he was 55. A father has the right to marry off his child daughter at any age, according to countless edicts issued by the senior Muslim jurists over the ages, based on the Quran, the hadith, and the biography of Mohammad. Such marriage is still in practice in many Muslim countries. In one of the reported incidents, a 9-year-old Afghani girl was married by her aging father to a 55-year-old man in November 2021.[470] Some theologians rule that consummating the marriage must not take place before the wife has had her first period, while others rule that it can take place if the girl is fit for sexual relationship even if she did not reach puberty. The latter ones base their ruling on the same Quranic verse that sets the legal duration for which women must wait before remarrying, as it also mentions the females who "have not menstruated."[471] Thus, for hundreds of years and to this day, Muslims have considered it halal to consummate marriage with young girls who have not menstruated.

---

468 Quran 4:11.
469 Sahih al-Bukhari 304.
470 Coren, A., Yeung. J. & Bina, A. B. (2021, Nov 1). She was sold to a stranger so her family could eat as Afghanistan crumbles. CNN.
471 Quran 65:4.

The Grand Ayatollah Khomeini ruled in an infamous edict that it is halal for the husband to use his wife sexually even if she is a toddler, without intercourse. He used the Arabic word "radeaah" meaning a female baby that is still breastfed, which is less than two years old according to sharia. He went further, explaining that a husband has the right to sexually enjoy the child wife through rubbing his sexual organ against the toddler wife's body. This edict is something a Sunni would likely bring up in a conversation when he is upset with his Shia interlocutor. The edict was included in Khomeini's book of jurisprudence printed and distributed all over the world in various languages to be used as a guide for Muslims. Many copies were bought by Sunnis just to have a proof of this Shia law in order to mock them, without realising that many of their jurists share the same belief since it comes from the Quran and the hadith. This practice is not being condemned as paedophilia because it is religiously based. Muslims worldwide defend this criminal behaviour as legitimate and an ethical tradition.

In the past few years, many adult Muslim men crossed into Europe, illegally, with their child brides. In 2016, there were at least 1152 under-aged married girls among the refugees in Germany. Three hundred and sixty one of them were under 14 years old.[472] In 2010, Norway allowed ten girls younger than 16 years to remain with their older husbands while their asylum application was being processed.[473] The child wives were treated as adults in a complete disregard of the Norwegian law. They were granted asylum as families rather than being rescued from this abuse.

Muslim women are compelled to perceive polygamy as both normal and moral because it has been legitimated by Allah in the Quran and was practised by Mohammad and all the founders of Islam. Every now and then, a Muslim woman appears on a TV talk show to say with pride that she has arranged for her husband to marry another woman and that she is fine with that because it is halal. This mentality is the product of intergenerational indoctrination by violence and economic suppression.

---

472 Harris, C. (2017, Jan 25). Refugee brides: what should Germany do about its child marriage problem. Euronews.
473 Doyle, A. (2016, Apr 21). Child brides sometimes tolerated in Nordic asylum centers despite bans. Reuters.; BBC News. (2016, Sep 30). Migrant child brides put Europe in a spin.

Females are being persuaded that their entire body as well as the hair is considered "awrah" – a term that comes from aar (shame) – thus, must be fully covered, similarly to the sensitive parts of the male body. One of the most influential contemporary Islamic preachers, Abu-Ishak, said in a public lecture that the woman's face is similar to her genitalia. Other jurists exempt the face and the hands from covering.

Allah ordered females to be confined to their homes: "stay (waqarn) in your houses, and do not display yourselves like that of the times of ignorance and perform prayers and give zakat and obey Allah and his Messenger." The verb stay (waqarn) in this passage designates the feminine gender only, hence Allah is ordering females to be restrained to their homes. This decree had governed the lives of Muslim women until Western powers dismantled the last Islamic Caliphate and empowered them against the opposition of the Islamic clergy. For instance, in Southern Yemen and due to Western influence in the second half of the 20th century, women were allowed to study and work but since the national regimes took full power, they reversed that movement and females were brought back to the dark ages. Currently, Muslim jurists, organizations, and regimes are striving to re-establish the home incarceration of women as the norm. In March 2022, the Taliban shut down girls' high schools and banned them from traveling without a male guardian. A few days later, the Kuwaiti Ministry of Islamic Affairs declared that wearing hijab, not interacting with males, the approval of the guardian are the conditions women need to respect if they want to work. Staying at home is better, the official department affirmed in the same published statement. Divorced Muslim mothers suffer in many countries because of the sharia laws that give the custody to the father. According to sharia, children are the property of the father; the mother has no significant rights, and no rights at all if she was not a good Muslim.

In Germany in July 2021, two Afghani brothers killed their 34-year-old sister Maryam for deserting hijab and assimilating into Western life. The rejected asylum seekers Sayed H., 26, and Seyed H., 22, lured their older sister to meet them in Berlin; they choked her and cut her throat. According to the German prosecutors, the two Muslims, who were living off taxpayer money, dismembered the mother-of-two's body, stuffed the severed parts in a suitcase, took it in a taxi and on a train and buried it in woods away from where they lived. After they were arrested, they told the investigators that "we treat women differently than you do. A woman is like a servant who does the housework, cooks and looks after the children." Another Afghani woman who lived in the same building as Maryam said that she was afraid that she would also get killed by her relatives as she did not wear hijab.[474]

474 Bunyan, R. (2021, Dec 28). Two Afghan brothers are charged in Germany with Murdering their sister 'because of her Western way of life'. Daily Mail.

HONOUR KILLING

Every year, many thousands of Muslims across the world murder their daughters, wives or sisters in what they describe as honour killings. In 2010 alone, 33 females were killed in North America and 67 in Europe; 96% of the killers in Europe were Muslims and the rest were Sikhs, while in North America, 84% were Muslims and the rest were Sikhs and a few Hindus. In the same year, 800 Muslim females were killed in the Islamic Republic of Pakistan, and around 1000 killings were reported in India, mainly among Muslims.[475] In Iran, at least 8000 girls were killed between 2010 to 2014 by their relatives.[476] Killing females for the purpose of preserving the family's honour is an epidemic in almost all the Muslim countries. Most of these crimes go unreported; the disclosed number is nothing but a fraction of the reality.[477]

The Parliamentary Assembly of the Council of Europe stated in 2003: "The Assembly notes that whilst so-called 'honour crimes' emanate from cultural and not religious roots and are perpetrated worldwide (mainly in patriarchal societies or communities), the majority of reported cases in Europe have been amongst Muslim or migrant Muslim communities (although Islam itself does not support the death penalty for honour-related misconduct)."[478] This false and self-contradicting dishonest statement ignores the fact that honour killing is warranted by Islamic teachings recognized as authentic by Muslims worldwide regardless of their ethnicity, sect or culture. The justification of the honour murder comes directly from Islamic laws that regulate the guardianship of females and the guardianship of the blood. In Islam, the father is the

---

475 Chesler, P. (2018, Apr 16). Honor Killing Is Not Just a Muslim Problem. Tablet Magazine. Excerpted from Chesler, P. (2018). A Family Conspiracy: Honor Killing. New English Review Press.
476 Parsa, F. (2021, Aug 26). Iranian women campaign to stop the rise in "honor killings". MEI.
477 Chesler, P. (2010). Worldwide Trends in Honor Killings. Middle East Qtly 17(2), pp 3–11.
478 Parliamentary Assembly. (2003, Apr 4). So-called "honour crimes". Resolution 1327.

legitimate guardian of his daughter, and thus she cannot marry, work, or travel without his permission; in the case of the father's death, the guardianship is transferred to the paternal grandfather or the eldest brother. When a woman is murdered, the guardian has the right to pardon the killer. A father must not receive capital punishment if he murdered his child, even without valid justification, and his penalty is to pay the blood-money to the Muslim ruler or to the mother of the victim as compensation.

The case of the Saudi preacher Fayhan al-Ghamdi, who raped and tortured to death his five-year-old daughter Lama, is a clear example of how sharia views the parental relationship. This imam, who used to deliver speeches in mosques and on TV channels to advise people on how to live their lives and on what is halal and what is haram, was indicted by the Saudi criminal court for raping, torturing, and killing his daughter. He was sentenced in 2013 to eight years in prison and 600 lashes. The court of appeal dropped the rape charges and altered the manslaughter charge to excessive discipline. The imam was released from jail after less than two years and was ordered to pay blood money to the daughter's mother in accordance with the sharia.[479] In Iran, the maximum penalty for honour killing is ten years in prison, and most fathers convicted of killing their daughters are either acquitted or jailed for a few years.[480]

Moreover, according to sharia, killing an adulterer female is a reasonable reaction on the side of the husband, brother or father. There are several hadith that warrant the killing of a wife, if she is caught cheating. Mohammad himself oversaw the stoning of several persons to death after they had confessed to committing adultery.[481] Over the ages, both Shia and Sunni jurists have ruled that the fair punishment for adultery is stoning to death if the person was married, based on hadith. These notions, although concealed from foreigners' eyes, are being taught in

479 Toumi, H. (2015, Aug 26). Saudi preacher who killed his daughter released. Gulf News.
480 Radio Free Europe. (2020, Aug 29). Iranian Father Jailed For Nine Years For Beheading Teenage Daughter In 'Honor' Killing. RFE/RL.; BBC. (2020, May 27). Romina Ashrafi: Outrage in Iran after girl murdered 'for eloping'.
481 Sahih al-Bukhari 7, 43, 63, 86; Sahih Muslim 4191, 4196.

the educational systems all over the world. They justify honour killing and the degrading of humans.

Reading on the topic in Wikipedia, we find a claim that honour killing goes across cultures and religions and is not at all Islamic. On the same website, a passage blames a French law that was adopted in Lebanon during the French administration for encouraging honour killing, claiming that it inspired the legal systems of Islamic countries to impose light sentences for such a crime. This twisted rationale proves that the writers are defending the practice by distracting the attention away from Islamic teachings which warrant it and from the fact that Muslims are the vast majority of the perpetrators worldwide. It attempts to conceal the fact that Muslim communities and countries had been practicing honour killing for centuries before the French occupation of Lebanon, which lasted for a few years and sought to stop this practice. Muslims had their sharia laws which considered killing an adulterous wife, sister, or daughter a legitimate and moral act ages before France was an imperial power. Statistics attest that the vast majority of the killers and the victims are Muslims, despite being a minority within humanity. The fact that some people who are either Sikhs or Hindus committed this crime in a lesser number does not revise its connotation with Islamic teachings.

Some Muslims in the diaspora are facing a predicament, as they want to live in a prosperous liberal modern society that respects human rights but at the same time want to keep their sharia, which reduces women to property of men and sanctions killing them in order to protect the family's honour.

In Sweden, Fadime Sahindel was murdered at the hands of her father in 2002 for dating a Swedish man. This is a vivid example of how Muslim immigrants tend to bring their mentality and practices with them to non-Muslim societies. The 27-year-old Kurdish girl was threatened and harassed by her brother, father, and other members of the community for dating a Swedish boy; then, the Swede was killed in a suspicious car accident in 1998, a month before the couple's planned date to move in together. In 2002, Fadime was shot by her dad in front of her other two sisters for dating a Swede four years earlier. How did the father obtain a firearm? Why did the police not protect her? And who else took part in the crime? These are questions that have never been answered – not by the Swedish justice system nor anyone else.

The murder of Banaz Mahmod in London in 2006 and the traumas she and her sisters suffered throughout their lives are a clear proof of the prevalence of psychopathy among Muslim communities manifested in the normalisation of women's suppression. Banaz, who was born in Iraq in 1985 and moved with her family to the UK in 1995, was subjected to female genital mutilation along with her four sisters when they were children. Her older and younger sister were forced to marry much older men when they were 16 and 17 years old. Similarly, when Banaz was 17, she was forced to marry an illiterate, cruel man who was ten years her senior. She was raped and beaten by her husband, and when she complained to her parents, they did not help her. Her husband's behaviour was seen as acceptable: men have the right to discipline their wives according to Islam and there is no such thing as marital rape in sharia. When she left the man after two years, she had to move back in with her parents, since women in Muslim societies are not allowed to live on their own.

Banaz disappeared in January 2006, shortly after her family found out that she had been seeing a man from their community. No one reported her missing but the boyfriend, who feared that she might have been killed by her relatives. The initial investigation was unsuccessful; the parents and other family members tried to deceive the police and many individuals from the Kurdish community collaborated with them, attempting to uphold their traditions rather than the law of the land. The Mahmods told the police that they were a liberal family who would not force their daughters to do anything against their will. Finally, an investigation led by Detective Caroline Goode discovered what had happened to Banaz and found her dismembered body buried more than a hundred miles away from her home in South London. The girl had been tortured, gang-raped, and murdered in a premeditated attack organised by her father and uncle to protect the family's honour. Her

---

482 Goode, C. (2020). Honour: Achieving Justice for Banaz Mahmod. Oneworld Publications.; Julios, C. (2016). Forced Marriage and 'Honour' Killings in Britain: Private Lives, Community Crimes and Public Policy Perspectives. Routledge.
483 Friscolanti, M. (2016, Mar 3). Inside the Shafia killings that shocked a nation. Maclean's.

father, uncle, three cousins as well as three other Kurdish people were convicted in the murder.[482] Her family would not hold a funeral for her and buried her in an unmarked grave.

This case highlights how irrational, immoral thinking and practices are being accepted and normalised by a society even in countries in which the laws do not support them.

In Florida on 1 January 2008, an American Muslim taxi driver Yaser Abdel Said killed his two daughters: Sarah, 17 years old, and Amina, 18 years old, because he suspected that they were seeing boys. After the event, his family were hiding him for more than 12 years in a clear indication of their support for what he had done.

A year later and this time in Canada, Afghani parents and their son were convicted of killing their three daughters as well as the father's first wife (with whom he didn't have children but remained married to her). Mohammad Shafia settled in Canada with his second wife Tooba Yahya, their seven children, and his first wife Rona Ahmad, who was registered as a live-in maid on the visa, in 2007. Mohammad, who had taken the seventeen-year-old Tooba as a second wife when he was thirty-six, killed his two daughters Zainab, 19 and Sahar 17 because he suspected that they were having relationships with boys and killed the third daughter Geeti, who was 13 years old, for covering up for her sisters. He also killed his first wife because she was disobedient. Both his other wife – the mother of the slain girls and their brother took part in the killing and the planning of the crime. The three killers convinced the unsuspecting victims to go on a family road trip. On a secluded lake, they killed the three girls and the first wife by holding them under water, one after another. Then they put the corpses in a car which they had bought before the trip and rammed it with their car, so it fell into the water. After reporting them missing, the father and the mother were passionately calling for the police and the general public to help them find their beloved daughters and the maid. In a phone call intercepted by the police, the mother said that her slain children deserved to die since they "betrayed Islam, they betrayed our religion and creed." After the police confronted them with the undeniable evidence, they kept lying and were defiant and arrogant even after the guilty verdict was delivered.[483]

In Iraq, Shia women who had been abducted and raped by ISIS were rejected by their families after they were freed. They were told by their own parents to kill themselves or to at least stay away from their homes because they brought shame. The same happened to Sunni girls who had been kidnapped by Shia militias.

This collective pathological definition of honour and women is part of the way Islam views females. It is a clear symptom of the mass moral insanity afflicting Muslim societies.

FEMALE GENITAL MUTILATION

It is estimated that more than 200 million living females have been victims of genital mutilation.[484] The vast majority of these girls and women
are Muslims living in the Middle East and Africa. According to UNICEF
reports, 98% of females aged between 15 to 49 in Somalia, 91% in Egypt,
88% in Sudan, 89% in Mali, 69% in Mauritania, and 23% in Yemen have
been subjected to FGM.[485] In these countries, female genital mutilation has been practised to this day because it is sanctioned in Islam.[486]
Several sayings attributed to Mohammad and conveyed in the trusted
books of hadith approve the cutting of the female genitals.[487] Thus, it is
impossible to persuade devoted Muslims who believe in these books and
consider them divine guidance that FGM is a crime and a violation of
women's rights. In many countries, the pressure from the international
community has been compelling the governments to put an end to it
but the struggle is far from over as millions of girls still suffer from this
inhumane harmful practice every year.

Egypt has the largest number of females who have been subjected to
genital mutilation. Although there are millions of non-Muslim Egyptians,
who are mainly Christians, the victims are exclusively Muslims. Despite
being criminalised since 2008, most of the procedures are done to this
day by professional medical personnel. Most girls who live in the cities
undergo this mutilation shortly before they reach puberty but in rural
areas new-born girls as young as five days old are subjected to it. Since
2016, the Egyptian parliament, due to the international pressure, has set
penalties for individuals who carry out FGM to between five to seven

---

484 UNICEF. (2016). Female Genital Mutilation/Cutting: A global concern. [Fact sheet].
485 UNICEF. (2020, Feb). Female Genital Mutilation in Egypt: Recent Trends and Projections.
486 See Fernández-Morera, D. (2016). Chapter 5. Women in Islamic Spain: Female Circumci-
sion, Stoning, Veils, and Sexual Slavery. In: The Myth of the Andalusian Paradise.
487 Sahih Muslim 349, 257; Sahih al-Bukhari 5891.

years imprisonment, and up to fifteen years if they caused permanent disability or death. These laws remained ink on paper for the most part, as the number of prosecuted cases is negligible. In 2017, the general attorney investigated three cases, and only one case resulted in a conviction. Half the participants in a study which investigated the perception of this custom said that FGM could prevent adultery.[488]

Muslims brought this practice with them to the West. In the United States, a network of Muslim medical doctors has been conducting FGM on young Muslim girls with the approval of their parents in different American cities.[489] Currently, this practice is common across Europe and in most cases swept under the rug while the victims who dare to speak are told to accept what happened to them since it is their culture.

In an attempt to absolve Islamic teachings from the responsibility for this practice, many commentators argue that FGM existed before Islam or is not limited to Muslims. They forget to mention that it was approved and sanctioned by Islamic teachings. Hence, it is still rife among Muslims, unlike a very long list of traditional practices which had been opposed by Islam – such as adoption or consuming pork – and hence disappeared.

---

488 El-Mouelhy, M. T., Johansen, E., Ragab, A., & Fahmy, A. (2013). Men's perspectives on the relationship between sexuality and female genital mutilation in Egypt. Sociology Study 3(2), pp 104-113.
489 Baldas, T. (2021, Sep 16). Feds: Doctor in female genital mutilation case part of secret network who cut girls. Detroit Free Press.

THERE IS NO RAPE IN SHARIA

In 2022, a 42-minute-long recording of a conversation between a girl named Nida Tahir and the Supreme Leader of the Ahmadi Muslims (fifth caliph) Mirza Masroor was posted online and created an uproar on social media. Nida, who turned out to be the granddaughter of the previous Ahmadi religious leader, said in that conversation that she had been raped by Mahmood Shah – Masroor's brother-in-law of and an influential imam who was expected to become the next supreme leader. She said that the rape took place at the grand religious centre of the Ahmadis (Khilafat House) and that she demanded justice. In his reply, the spiritual and political leader of millions of Muslims explained that in sharia a woman cannot prove being raped without four Muslim male witnesses who would testify to seeing the rape. He told the protesting girl that according to the Quran, hadith, and Mohammad's biography, if a woman accused a man of raping her without witnesses and the man said that the sexual relationship was consensual, the two parties would be punished for committing adultery. If he denied the occurrence of a sexual intercourse, she alone would be punished for adultery.

The girl tried to explain that she had proof that she was raped but the imam explained that in sharia the only reliable proof are Muslim male witnesses. He kept referring to Mohammad – the Prophet said this and the Prophet said that. He told her to keep what had happened to herself and not to damage the reputation of Muslims.

Mirza Masroor leads millions of people all over the world and controls a huge budget. He oversees several mosques and centres, among them the biggest mosque in the UK. Western decision makers compete to receive his support and blessing and praise him passionately. For instance, the Canadian Prime Minister Justin Trudeau received him in 2016 at the Prime Minister's office in Ottawa. Trudeau addressed Masroor saying: "Your Holiness, your friendship and leadership is very important to Canada and we appreciate the way the Ahmadiyya Muslim Community condemns all forms of extremism."[490] Among Masroor's followers are several elected politicians in the West, such as Baron Ahmad of Wimbledon.

The Ahmadiyya spiritual leader's argument with Nida Tahir was based on the original Islamic teachings accepted by all the other Muslim jurists. Sexuality is regulated clearly in Islam and rape is impossible to prove: who would rape a woman before four witnesses willing to testify against him and who would admit committing rape which is punishable by stoning to death? The famous Egyptian jurist Saharawi, who served as Minister of Islamic Endowment in his country and was considered one of the most important Muslim theologians all over the world for many decades, defended this notion through stating in his TV programme broadcast by many national TV channels in the Middle East that it is impossible for a man to penetrate a woman against her will.

Moreover, marital rape is permissible in Islam. Mohammad said that whenever a woman refused to answer her husband's demand, she committed a sin and would be cursed by the angels.[491]

490 Ahmadiyya Muslim Community Press & Media office. (2016, Oct 19). Prime Minister of Canada receives Head of Ahmadiyya Muslim Community in Ottawa. [Press release].
491 Sahih al-Bukhari 3237.

CONDONING COMPULSORY PROSTITUTION

One of the central ideas in Islam is women's chastity. Sexual relationships are closely monitored and regulated in Quran and hadith, especially for females. But there are different laws for different people. A passage in the Quran deals with the issue of forced prostitution of slave-girls: "do not compel your slave-girls to prostitution, when they desire to stay chaste, in order to seek the frail goods of this world's life and whoever compels them, then surely after their compulsion Allah is forgiving and merciful."[492] In this passage, Allah instructed believers not to force the slaves they captured in wars or bought from slave markets to prostitution. At the same time, he assured that if the masters nevertheless did that, he will pardon them. Hence, this passage permits Muslims to force their captives to practice prostitution as there is no penalty for this act. It also sanctions prostitution of slave girls, if they agreed to it.

Jurists tend to defend this verse by arguing that it came in reply to certain individuals who were forcing their slave-girls to practice prostitution against the girls' will. Thus, God sent this divine order to discourage them and other Muslim slavers from continuing this practice and to promise forgiveness for the slaves. Nevertheless, they cannot deny that none of the Quranic passages indicate that there are any specific penalties for the masters. All what they could say is explain that Allah will forgive just the victims, without a proof for this claim. They hide that Allah does not punish the wicked masters. Most importantly, there is no mention in this passage or any other one that people are equal and that no man shall rape a woman or force her to do anything against her will, let alone sexually exploit her. There is no denouncement of slavery, no condemnation of sexual slavery, no punishment set for slavers.

---

492 Quran 24:33.

TEMPORARY AND TRAVEL MARRIAGES:
GIVE THE GIRLS "THEIR WAGES"

Marriage in Islam is a transaction in which the groom or his family pays a sum of money known as mahr (bride price) to the guardian of the bride in exchange for marriage in front of two Muslim male witnesses. Once the guardian takes the money and accepts the marriage in front of the witnesses, the groom becomes the guardian of the bride in place of her father. When Mohammad's cousin Ali proposed to marry his daughter Fatima, the Prophet asked if he had money to pay the bride price.

Shias believe that the teachings of Islam allow a male and a female – if she is not virgin – or her guardian – if she is a virgin – to engage in a specific type of marriage that is valid for a timed period. In this transaction, an amount of money is paid by a male to a female's guardian in exchange for sex under the disguise of marriage. This marriage is not intended to establish a family or to produce children and the two persons do not need to move in together. There are no rights for the wife whatsoever except the money she or her guardian receive at the beginning. This exchange is called the "enjoyment marriage" and "temporary marriage" and it is currently practiced unofficially among the Shia worldwide. The Shia argue that it is sanctioned in Quran: "It is prohibited to you your mothers and daughters and sisters… and married women except your hand possession… and it is lawful for you to seek with your money desiring chastity not adultery thus pay them their wages for what you have enjoyed from them."[493] The verse is describing the money paid to females in exchange for sex as wage (ujur), not dower (mahr) which is a requirement in traditional Islamic marriages.

There are also several sayings attributed to Mohammad's grand-children that warrant and encourage this form of marriage. Many of

---

493 Quran 4:23-24.

the senior companions of Mohammad as well as influential jurists have practiced this type of marriage over the ages, according to various hadith. After the Iranians were pushed into illiteracy and poverty, this practice became rampant in that devastated country. The ayatollahs' regime has been encouraging enjoyment marriage, and many of its senior leaders are accused of sexually exploiting impoverished underage girls via this practice. After the fall of Saddam and the ascension of ayatollahs and their militias to power in Iraq, they encouraged this practice among Iraqis. The BBC did an eye-opening investigation disclosing this malignant practice; they aired it in a TV programme entitled: Undercover With The Clerics: Iraq's Secret Sex Trade. This documentary shows how the imams are playing the role of the procurer, encouraging and benefiting from this halal sex trade.[494] As this type of marriage is not registered officially, women who get pregnant as its result as well as their children find themselves in a real crisis. Thus, many of the women abort the children or desert them right after birth. Vulnerable Syrian, Lebanese, Iranian, Pakistani, and other females have been exploited under this practice for ages while imams have made fortunes from facilitating it.

Sunnis in general refuse this form of marriage, describing it as veiled prostitution. Some of them claim that the Quranic passage which warrants such marriage has been abrogated. Others contend without any explanation that the verse does not denote temporary marriage, and the wages mentioned in the verse are the normally required bride price. In summary, they agree that this form of marriage is not currently halal and has not been halal for many centuries. Thus, in Sunni countries the enjoyment marriage is illegal. However, they accept another similar form of marriage, which they name "travelling marriage". This marriage consists of a contract in which a male and a female's guardian – if she is a virgin – or the female herself – where she is not – agree that the male has the right to have a sexual relationship with the female in exchange for an agreed-upon bride price. The two parties do not live together, and the so-called husband does not have to support the wife. No children are expected to be born and no family to be established. The entire thing is

---

494 BBC News Arabic. (2019, Oct 9). Undercover With The Clerics: Iraq's Secret Sex Trade. [Video]. YouTube.

kept a secret. The main difference between Shia's temporary and Sunni's travel marriage is that the latter has no prearranged expiry date. In both cases, the man can terminate the relationship whenever he feels so, with no consequences – but not the woman. Many Muslims studying in the West engage in such types of marriages. Currently, thousands of children have been left behind by their Muslim fathers who run away back to their homelands after they get an infidel woman pregnant.[495]

495 See Hague, B. (2022, May 18). The forgotten children of Saudi Arabia. ABC News.; Website: Saudi Children Left Behind.

ISLAM HAS HONOURED WOMEN!

Prior to Islam, women enjoyed more rights and freedoms almost all over the world, including Arabia and other parts of the Middle East, in comparison to the Islamic ages. Arabs had female deities and several queens ruled over the capitals of Arabia. Many females were independent rich merchants, and many were renowned poets and priests. Women had the right to inherit their husbands' wealth in most of the Arab societies. Khadijah herself was a wealthy woman and an independent merchant before she married Mohammad – who was working for her. She was 15 years older than him and had had two previous husbands whose wealth she inherited. Mohammad did not marry another woman or owned a slave while she was alive. Polygamy was prohibited among the Christian Arabs as well as many other nations such as the Egyptians and the Iraqis. More than that, there were several types of marriages practiced in pre-Islamic Arabia that allocated different rights and duties for the two parties. In the "agreement marriage", both sides stipulated their conditions and had to abide by their words. Another form of marriage was called "benna" which allowed the woman to retain full independence from her husband as she was the owner of the house. In the combined marriage, a woman married a group of men and if she had a child, she had the power of choosing the father from among them and the chosen man could not object to her decision, and he was responsible for supporting the child. There is not one report of an Arab man who married an underage girl let alone a six-year-old in any of the history books which talk about Arabs before Islam. Muslims tend to say that Islam has honoured women, claiming that prior to Islam Arabs used to bury their new-born daughters. This notion mentioned in the Quran contradicts logic as well as the Islamic records. How could a society that worshipped females and allowed them to be queens, merchants, and poets consider them shame that must be killed? How did these people survive if they were killing their females – who was doing the childbearing?

Finally, it is enough to compare the ancient Egyptian, Persian, Greek, and Roman females' traditional clothing with the modern Muslims' hijab to realize the gap.

17 Psychological Analysis of Mohammad's and Muslims' Mental Health

ALLAH, HUMANITY, AND THE MEANING OF LIFE

In Dostoevsky's fascinating novel "The Brothers Karamazov", one of the brothers asks what would prevent people from committing all sorts of crimes if there was no religion. If there was no God and hence no ethical code derived from heaven, and most importantly, if there was no super-power that enforced it, why would people restrain their evil desires? He argues that if there was no God, then everything is permissible. People won't restrain themselves – and why would they?

Every system of belief, whether it is earthly or religious, provides a story that explains human suffering and offers solutions. The main story of humanity in Islam revolves around the tale that the whole world was created by one and only God. This God is a schizophrenic omnipotent all-knowing and all-seeing dictator. He is described as being kind and ruthless. He created the world in seven days and all the creatures in it for the sole purpose of them worshipping him. Among Allah's creatures are angels who have been created from light. The angles are obedient, non-thinking serfs. They spend all their time praising Allah and praying to him to satisfy his never-ending need for adoration. Some of them have a very specific purpose in addition to worshipping, such as Gabriel, who was entrusted with delivering Allah's messages to the selected prophets over the ages, hence he has been without a job for more than 14 hundred years now. Azrael is the angel of death: he takes human souls out of the body when the predetermined time comes. Next, Allah created Adam and Eve from mud. Allah ordered all the angels to bow to Adam. One of the angels who was a jinni disobeyed Allah. He was created from fire unlike the rest of the angels. He argued that he was superior to Adam because he was made from fire while Adam was made from mud. He also pointed out that he had been worshipping Allah for a long time before the creation of Adam and thus, it was not fair that he was made inferior to the newly created serf. Allah did not provide a valid reply to that opinion but rather he was outraged and expelled the devil from paradise and cursed him and his offspring, who were not born yet.

Allah awarded heaven to Adam and his wife. They were instructed to eat from all the trees except one. Adam disobeyed Allah's order by eating from the forbidden tree because he listened to the devil who had sneaked into heaven. Allah expelled Adam and Eve from heaven to earth and ordered them to worship him constantly; he also gave them rules that all humans must follow so they could go to heaven after death and avoid being eternally tortured by fire. The main purpose of the devil and his offspring, who belong to jinn, is to incite humans to disobey Allah's rules. Allah sent several messengers to guide humanity to worship him, among them Noah, Abraham, Moses, and Jesus. The people refused the guidance of all these messengers, and Allah destroyed many cities and villages as a punishment. The followers of the last two messengers – the Christians and the Jews – had spoiled Allah's words and their religions became invalid. The rest of humanity worshipped fake deities; thus, Allah sent the Seal of Messengers, Mohammad, to the whole of humanity with a sword. Every human worldwide must accept Mohammad as their leader and their guide in this life in order to be saved from Allah's revenge.

Therefore, the purpose of all humanity's earthly life is to worship Allah and to force every other person to do it by all possible means, including deceit and violence. Humans must endure this miserable life in order to live the eternal one. The current life is a temporary struggle in which humans are subjected to constant painful exams by Allah with no purpose but to satisfy his narcissistic ego. If Muslims follow the teachings of Islam and Islam only, not logic or passion, they might be rewarded with an eternal life of idleness and sex, they are told.

Allah has assured repeatedly in the Quran that he is the one who leads people to believe or misleads them to become disbelievers: "Then Allah misleads whom He wills and guides whom He wills. And He is the All-Mighty, the All-Wise."[496] Allah declared that he could have made all people believers, but he didn't want to: "And if Allah had willed, He could have made you [of] one religion, but He causes to stray whom He wills and guides whom He wills. And you will surely be questioned about what you used to do."[497] Allah affirmed that his wish is to torture humans and jinn eternally: "And if We had willed, We could have given every soul its guidance, but the word from Me will come into effect [that] I will surely fill Hell with jinn and people all together."[498]

People in general are described in many verses of Quran as evil, disobedient and intellectually defective. The majority are dishonest and unwilling to surrender to Allah unless forced by the few violent devotees and even then, they may stay hypocrites. Thus, the majority of mankind will be eternally tortured in hell. Even people who believed in Mohammad and fought for him but committed what is considered a major sin will be treated like infidels and thrown into the raging inferno. The list of the major sins in Islam is endless. It starts with not believing in Islam or any of its countless teachings, abstaining from any of the duties such as jihad, praying, haj, and many others. Sins also include eating prohibited food, having a romantic relationship without marriage, homosexuality, composing music, painting, and a myriad of other acts and thoughts. Due to the number and nature of the things Muslims are obliged to do and the things they cannot do, very few humans will be saved from the anguish and be granted heaven. They are a small minority by default, according to the Quran.

Thus, throughout its long history, the devoted followers of this religion have been in a constant state of unrest. War, suppression, conquest, invasion, slavery, fear, and deception were the means of survival for the Muslim states, masses, and rulers. Islam is a mythical authoritarian apocalyptic ideology that cannot live without many enemies, injustice, and conflict. Every terrorist attack and oppression that takes place in the present day has its roots and justification in the discourse

---

496 Quran 14:4, see Al-Hilali & Khan trans.
497 Quran 16:93, Sahih International trans.
498 Quran 32:13, Sahih International trans. (Some translators add the word 'evildoers', which is not in the original Arabic text, to alter the meaning of the verse and make it less appalling.)

that reports the practice of Mohammad and his associates and in the Quran. The same texts that depict Mohammad and his companions as divine role models motivate terrorism, invading other people's countries, authoritarian reign, oppressing women, and slavery. Explicit verses in the Quran and orders of Mohammad encourage and sanction every type of aggression against non-Muslims and against non-conformist Muslims. The teachings of Islam support violence against the members of any group of people that violate its strict laws. Thus, terrorism and the condoning of terrorism result from the teachings of Islam and are based on a well-established tradition.[499] Terrorists are obedient soldiers of an apocalyptic ideology which seeks the annihilation of all humans, including its few true disciples.

---

499 For further discussion, see Kurzban, R., & Christner, J. (2011). Are supernatural beliefs commitment devices for intergroup conflict? In J. P. Forgas, A. W. Kruglanski & K. D. Williams (Eds.). The psychology of social conflict and aggression. Psychology Press, pp 285–299.

POST-MORTEM PSYCHOLOGICAL ANALYSIS OF MOHAMMAD

When applying theories of clinical psychology to analyse Mohammad's personality as constructed by the different narrators in the books of sayings, biographies and the Quran, we find ourselves dealing with an incoherent tale of an abnormal person.[500] Many parts and pieces are missing, and many details seem to have been added after the events. Consequently, there are numerous contradicting aspects and characteristics of this historical persona that could not possibly have existed in one person. In contrast, certain tales seem realistic and lucid; no one could have made them up completely or from scratch. The fact of the matter is that there is a character which has been built and propagated through influential discourse for political ends. This character has been the role model for millions of people from beyond the grave for centuries and to this day. Thus, it is important to examine this persona as constructed in his followers' psyche by the main narrative.

Let us begin by considering Mohammad's abnormal childhood. He lacked a male role model and a mother figure as he had never met his father and was rejected by his mother. He did not have siblings and spent his childhood in foster care. Throughout his youth, he failed in distinguishing himself in any significant way. He travelled to the centres of civilizations, interacted with different cultures and customs but could not benefit from this knowledge. He was a student of ancient myths and religions, but nothing came out of that devotion. Mohammad had failed in becoming a political leader, a successful merchant or a famous poet despite his interest in these three careers. This can be attributed to his lack of critical thinking, a clear deficit in creativity, and the way his people

---

500 See Patrick, C. J. (Ed.). (2018). Handbook of psychopathy. Guilford Publications.; Fox, D. (2015). Antisocial, Borderline, Narcissistic and Histrionic Workbook: Treatment Strategies for Cluster B Personality Disorders. PESI Publishing & Media.

perceived him. Mohammad was an underachiever who worked for an old widow, married her and was dependent on her for most of his life. He did not marry another woman or have any romantic relationships while the old, rich woman was alive.

By the time he was 40 years old, he had no substantial accomplishments, hence, he was escaping to caves to avoid people, his wife, and most importantly – his feelings of disappointment. He was spending long nights in meditation. He wanted to show the people who looked down on him that they made a big mistake. Mohammad yearned to prove himself, and the only way that this was available to him was through a miracle.

In the Quran as well as in Mohammad's sayings, we notice several symptoms of mental disorders. Stories like the ones detailing ascending to heaven on a winged beast and speaking to invisible creatures and dead people can be categorized as hallucinations or lies produced by a disturbed mind. Several Quranic passages can be categorized as delusions, especially the ones concerning evil jinn or countless conspiracies against him by almost everyone, including his wives. The way he distrusted all people around him, including his relatives, is typical of paranoid persons. The Greek historian Theophanes (d. 818) and many other intellectuals after and before him suggested that Mohammad was epileptic, based on the descriptions of the fits he experienced while receiving the revelations. He used to sweat profusely, lose consciousness, shake and hear voices. It is also reported that he would relate seeing people whom others with him did not see. These symptoms are extremely similar to those of the temporal lobe epilepsy fits.

Psychopathy, or antisocial personality disorder, is another illness from which Mohammad could have suffered. It is the medical classification of the abnormal lack of conscience and the feelings and behaviour related to it.[501] The main symptoms are lack of empathy, emotional shallowness, disregard of others' feelings and rights, deceitfulness, impulsivity, irresponsibility, pathological lying, lack of remorse,

---

501 See Hare, R.D. (1999). Without conscience: The disturbing world of the psychopaths among us. Guilford Press.; Fox, D.J. (2020). Antisocial, Narcissistic, and Borderline Personality Disorders: A New Conceptualization of Development, Reinforcement, Expression, and Treatment. Routledge.

aggressiveness, and pathological need for constant attention and adoration. Most people diagnosed as psychopaths have a number of these symptoms but rarely all of them.

In his book "Mask of Sanity", Hervey Cleckley describes in detail how psychopaths mask their abnormal psyche. They strive to present themselves as social, reasonable, attractive and intelligent individuals. They justify and disguise their pathological thoughts, desires and behaviours. They lead a parasitic lifestyle based on taking advantage of people around them. They enjoy hurting others and playing with their emotions. Psychopaths are capable of planning and executing complex plots to achieve their dishonest goals. One of the main features of this personality disorder is the mental capacity to justify any committed wrongdoing. They can also create a vivid discourse which incriminates any act of others they perceive to be against their interests. The way they warrant their crimes is based on a number of specific steps: constructing their crimes as necessary and legitimate acts, dehumanising and demonising their victims, portraying themselves as the victims rather than the aggressors, denying any wrongdoing. They build the story of their acts in a biased way that absolves them from culpability and places it on their victims. They use historical accounts in a biased way which fits their desired ends. They are habitual liars, who lie for the sake of lying and with confidence.

Psychopaths[502], or individuals diagnosed with antisocial personality disorder[503], are responsible for their acts; they are fit to stand trial. They are considered rational in the sense that they are aware of their behaviour and its consequences. They do have the ability to understand, explain and justify their behaviour. Although they know what they are doing and comprehend the consequences of their acts for other people, that does not make them stop or sincerely regret what they have done. Their rationale is built around themselves and their perceived benefits. They lack the ability to sympathise with other people. They do not want to put themselves in the place of those who are affected by their acts. Deception,

---

502 As above.
503 American Psychiatric Association. (2013). Diagnostic and statistical manual of mental disorders: DSM-5 (5th ed.).

aggression, and manipulation are their usual means of achieving their goals and feeling satisfied with themselves. They enjoy the suffering of others while leading a parasitic lifestyle. They have a pathologically grandiose sense of self-worth and a neurotic need for admiration and stimulation.[504] Most importantly, psychotherapy as well as medications are ineffective in producing positive effects. Studies show that psychopaths cannot be treated or cured. Many of the people who assumed that there was good in psychopaths and attempted to help them ended up among their victims.

Mohammad's character, as portrayed in various original Islamic books as well as contemporary media productions, bears many characteristics of a psychopath. He led a parasitic life: he was dependent on his wife's money until the age of fifty, and after that he lived off the spoils seized by his soldiers after invading defenceless villages and caravans. The Islamic tradition attests that he had the most grandiose sense of self-worth known of any human who walked on this planet. His life shows that he had a pathological need for stimulation and adoration. This need may explain his countless invasions as well as his numerous marriages and intimate relationships. Pathological lying is one of the main characteristics of psychopaths, and although Muslims believe that Muhammad was a candid man, the Quran reports numerous times that Meccans called him a liar repeatedly. Meccans describe Mohammad's behaviour, especially in dealing with his enemies, as being cunning and manipulative, which are important traits of psychopathy. Psychopaths are shallow in their emotions as they are incapable of experiencing deep emotions. They display, however, dramatic short-lived sham emotions designed to influence their audience. This symptom explains the inability of Mohammad to show deep, lasting emotions toward anyone throughout his life. Although he expressed extreme anguish due to the death of his first wife, it took him a few days after her death to marry two women at once. He had several close associates but never decided to appoint a second in command. He married his stepson's wife after forcing him to divorce her. He attacked people who had supported him when he was an orphan. He

---

504 Patrick, C. J. (Ed.). (2018). Handbook of psychopathy. Guilford Publications.

captured and sold women and children with complete disregard of their pleas. He ordered the beheading of prisoners and assassinated unarmed people. All that with an obvious lack of remorse or guilt.

Mohammad's persona, as constructed by Muslim historians and hadith narrators, is incapable of feeling guilt as he does not err. Muslims cannot imagine Mohammad being remorseful: he is above humans and above mistakes. Mohammad proclaimed several times that he was the one and only perfect human and all people must follow his example. He promised his soldiers the treasures of Persian and Byzantine Empires when he was an insignificant chieftain of a small group. This is an example of the lack of realistic long-term goals, which is a trait of psychopathy. It is true that Muslims toppled the two ailing empires decades – in the case of the Persian – and centuries – in the case of the Byzantine – after the death of Mohammad but that does not mean that Mohammad had a long-term plan or vision. The fact that he had not organised his succession or the hierarchy of power within his establishment is one of the main causes of the never-ending bloody schisms and civil wars between Muslims which started right after his death and still go on.

The way Muslims are instructed to view themselves, the world, and others, and the way God and his prophet were constructed as terrifying omnipotent figures have with no doubt contributed to the prevalence of psychopathy among adherents. Discourses that promote suppressing women, non-Muslims, and dissidents are a licence for psychopaths to fulfil their pathological desires while being shielded from punishment. Over the ages, countless warlords have used the discourses that promote jihad, slavery, suppressing women, and discrediting the opponents for their personal interests.

An analysis of the speeches and acts of Saddam Hussein, Muammar Gaddafi, Omar al-Bashir, and Khamenei as recent examples of the countless Muslim dictators who used Islam to get into power would reveal several common psychopathic reasonings.[505] They were all superficially charming and pathological liars with a grandiose self-worth based on presenting themselves as the representatives of the only valid religion.

---

505 See Wiggins, S., & Potter, J. (2008). Discursive psychology. In C. Willig & W. Stainton-Rogers (Eds.). The SAGE Handbook of Qualitative Research in Psychology. Sage, pp 72 - 89.

All of them led parasitic lives before and after getting into power. They were destroying their countries and killing their people without showing any remorse or guilt. Every one of them constructed himself as Allah's representative on earth. They all accused their opponents of being an enemy of Allah, arguing that they must be exterminated. They all claimed to be guided grand leaders who did not err. They all blamed the disastrous consequences of their corruption, incompetence, and crimes on others, refusing to accept responsibility for their failures as well as their wrongdoings. They all said loud and clear that the other Muslim leaders were traitors and cowards, but they nevertheless were willing to collaborate with them. Each one of them claimed to be the great, beloved Muslim leader while killing and incarcerating his citizens and forging elections. They all used rhetorical techniques typical of psychopaths to justify their corruption and aggression. In their talk, they distorted the reality to present themselves as noble and ethical, failing to accept the fact that they were nothing but selfish dictators who destroyed their countries and killed millions of innocent people to satisfy their sick desires. They wiped out the local intelligentsia, whom they perceived as a threat to their narcissistic ego. All of them turned their countries into corrupt, lawless, religious, feudal fiefdoms with the use of the Islamic discourse.

Saddam and Khamenei claimed to be descendants of Mohammad and devoted followers of his teachings; Gaddafi and al-Bashir were satisfied with presenting themselves as dedicated Muslims. Saddam commissioned calligraphers to write a copy of the Quran with his blood to show his devotion to the book. He built thousands of mosques and penned 'Allah Akbar' on the Iraqi flag. He presented the war he waged against Iran as a continuation of the Islamic invasion of Persia. Khomeini, on the other hand, stated that he would not stop the war until he cleansed the holy lands of Karbala and Najaf from the Baathists, whom he declared infidels.

The four dictators strived to turn their countries into Islamic states through introducing Islamic laws, building grand mosques, and showing animosity toward non-Muslims. These dictators justified their psychopathic crimes through constructing Mohammad as their role-model. Through claiming to be devoted disciples of the eternal moral leader of humanity who waged countless wars, exterminated his opponents, and conquered the whole of Arabia in less than ten years, they justified and defended their crimes.

It is important to stress that Saddam Hussain – who has been presented by Western media as secular – established Saddam Islamic University in 1989 to advance sharia and Islamic studies. Moreover, following the example of Mao Zedong's cultural revolution, the Iraqi dictator launched a religion-based movement which he named the "faith campaign" (Hamla Imaniyya), to Islamise Iraqi society in accordance with the Sunni doctrine. As a consequence of this movement, tens of thousands of Sunni mosques were built across Iraq, and the public educational system was altered to become dedicated to teaching Islam in accordance with the Sunni understanding. Laws were redrafted to become more compatible with sharia. One of these laws decriminalizes the killing of adulterer women by their male guardians. The suppression of Shia, who were the majority of the Iraqis, as well as other non-Muslim minorities – who made together more than 65% of the Iraqi population – amplified to unprecedented levels.

PARANOID SOCIETY

The dictatorial hereditary regimes which amassed huge fortunes from exporting oil had decided to turn their states into religious dictatorships. The adoration of Allah, the Quran, Mohammad, and the dictators in power constitutes the ideology governing Islamic states from Afghanistan to Mauritania. Through embracing Islam as the source of laws, the dogmatic regimes created paranoid societies and at the same time unintentionally destabilised their states.[506]

In these societies, people suffer from an inferiority complex resulting from their traumatising fear of Allah and the state, as well as low self-esteem, which is inserted into them by the religious institutions which control the media and education. As a defence mechanism, such people present themselves as superior to all other people and nations. Individuals who are constantly reminded that they are worthless sinners who deserve to end up in hell along with their loved ones, while at the same time they are assured that they are following the one and only valid religion through which they can be saved, are living through a constant psychological roller-coaster. On the one hand, they are guilt-ridden and in constant need of guidance and guardianship to assure them that they are on the right path and to ease their distress. On the other hand, they are the chosen people to rule the world and guide humanity through the teachings of the last divine revelations. They are told by the clergy that their governments are not Islamic because they do not implement all the Islamic laws. At the same time, they are compelled to observe rules that cannot be endured by humans without severely disturbing their quality of life and their psychological balance. These paradoxical stressors include thought police, five-time-a-day obligatory prayer, dietary laws like abstaining from water and food during daylight in Ramadan, spreading

---

506 See for comparison Rozic, P. S. (2015). The paranoid state. Demokratizatsiya, 23(1), p 77.

Islam, rejecting any non-Islamic practice whether done by other people or the state, and the duty to pay a significant percentage of their income toward religious causes.

Faithful Muslims remind each other continuously that Allah is watching them and thus they must be careful to avoid his capricious retribution. They strive to prevent fellow Muslims from committing any sins to protect themselves from being considered accomplices by Allah. The belief that Allah is constantly watching and judging every thought, every move, and every desire can and does cause severe psychological trauma.

To aggravate the psychological distress, Muslims are told in the Quran that there are two angels accompanying every person non-stop to record all their deeds, words, and thoughts. These ideas are ingrained in the Muslim subconscious through the original discourse introduced to them at an early age. Muslims live in fear of losing the membership in their group and finding themselves cast as infidels rather than believers. They are incapable of resisting the fear inserted into them by the Quranic verses which they cannot comprehend but as Allah's rules.[507]

The boundaries of Muslim identity are highly sensitive to divergence and independent thinking. A person can become an infidel because of one idea or a simple, natural behaviour that is incompatible with the teachings of Islam. Being cast as an infidel entails losing everyone and everything. In many countries, if a person was found guilty of being an infidel, her (or his) marriage would be annulled, she would lose her job, her own family would disown her, and she could be thrown in jail for a long time; she could be executed either by the law or at the hands of devoted Muslims acting with the support of the society and authority.

The mental images of these severe consequences make believers terrified, nervous, self-doubting and self-hating. Regardless of how devoted and faithful a person is, there is always a chance that he or she has made a major sin and consequently offended Allah and other Muslims. Muslims pray in the streets, in parks, and in airport corridors to show off their submission to Allah and their disregard of non-Muslims. They constantly scream into the megaphones attached to the countless

507 Al-Najjar, Kamel. (2010, Nov 15). Alkhawf waljahl huma hajar al'asas [Fear and ignorance are the foundation]. (Arabic). Modern Discussion, Vol. 3186. Available at www.ahewar.org.

mosques, distressing themselves and everyone around to ease their and other Muslims' fear of Allah and his gruesome inferno. They blow themselves up, killing themselves and innocent people, to avoid Allah's eternal torture. They are constantly seeking confirmation that Allah is satisfied with them – but he will never reassure them. He does not speak in public, Mohammad is long gone, and other Muslims are equally horrified.

Muslims' aggression and their emotional revulsions are symptoms of the psychological distress caused by their belief and the circumstances created by this belief. The fear of Allah, his prophet, and other Muslims controls and spoils every moment of life of for many people. Many of them long to kill themselves in the name of Allah to be relieved of the numerous psychological anxieties they are living in. To justify the endless psychological traumas Muslims are exposed to, jurists construct life as a mere passage to the afterlife. The goal of every human is to satisfy Allah in the way Allah has chosen: by enduring inhumane, unnecessary suffering. While thinking that they are securing their passage to heaven, Muslims are inadvertently spoiling their lives.

18 Reforming Islam from Within: Moulding Water

POST-MORTEM DERADICALIZATION OF MOHAMMAD AND AXING THE IMAMS' POWER

Many of the so-called moderate Muslims have been trying to rewrite the history of Mohammad in order to alter some of Muslims' beliefs and consequently behaviour. They want to create a new version of Islam that could coexist with current international civilization and the universal humanistic values, without touching on the foundations of the religion. Islam Bihari and Tom Holland are among the famous current writers trying to portray Mohammad as a gracious leader. The Prophet is the role example of Islam, hence if he is presented as a man of peace, this would affect the attitude and behaviour of millions of people. Their strategy is simple and straightforward: they try to cherry-pick from the original books to reconstruct Mohammad's character in a specific way which fits their agenda. Their goal is to solve the problems of jihad and misogyny which are abhorred by many educated Muslims.

It is a similar case with deradicalisation programmes intended to rehabilitate convicted terrorists in prisons: their main goal is to remove the idea of jihad from the philosophy of Islam while they praise and glorify the religion as a whole.

It is a well-intentioned idea and it shows a genuine interest in ending some of the issues. But it is neither right nor fruitful. That is because it entails deleting half the Quran as well as the hadith and discrediting the history, historical heroes, and intellectual authorities while accepting the rest. Mohammad is portrayed in the Quran and all the Islamic biographies and hadith as a warlord who has commanded numerous genocides, participated in raids and orchestrated assassinations in the name of Allah. He ordered the torture of his critics; he enslaved thousands of people and was merciless in his treatment of them. Ransacking and kidnapping vulnerable towns and caravans was the main source of income of his state throughout his reign that lasted for ten years.[508] Islam was spread by indiscriminate violence, as the Quran itself attests numerous times.

More importantly, throughout the ages, Muslim imams made their living, gained fortunes, had multiple wives, owned sex-slaves, and amassed fame and power mainly through their monopoly on jurisprudence. They have been controlling Muslims' lives for centuries through propagating the idea that Islam is the one and only valid source of law. The Quran and the other original texts are their assets and means. These discourses are the only source of their revenue and influence. Thus, for them defending every principle written in these ancient passages is defending their existence. If Muslims were to freely critique the original Islamic texts, tens of thousands of imams would become jobless. These people's only skill is memorising and repeating the ancient narratives, deducing edicts from them which function as laws, and being a mouthpiece for the authority. For centuries, they have been promoting and using violence against anyone who questions their belief in order to sustain their livelihood. Unlike clergy in some of the other religions, who could function independently from the state, Islamic clergy has always been either part of the regime or the ruling class.

Most of the current Muslim regimes in the Middle East and North Africa are corrupt, hereditary, kleptocratic mafias led by uneducated people who are either devoted Muslims or opportunists convinced that they attain part of their legitimacy from the ancient books of Islam and hence, they finance imams that sway the masses into obedience. In contrast, Islamic institutions and the influential imams have always maintained a double-sided position, even if the ruler himself was a jurist: they praise the regime to sustain their income while highlighting its mistakes to preserve their popularity and credibility among the dissatisfied public. They discourage the population from demanding its basic rights but at the same time they implicitly attribute the injustice and suffering to the

---

508 Al-Wakidy [alt. Al-Waqidi], M. (1856). History of Muhammad's Campaigns [Kitab al-Maghazi].; Ibn Kathir, A. (1992). Al-Bidaya wa al-Nihaya [The Beginning and the End].; The History of al-Tabarī, Vol. 1-40.

regime's failure to apply the Islamic laws. To remain relevant, Islamic institutions have aimed at keeping the mistrust and the deep hatred between the authority and the people alive. They always keep a distance between themselves and the regimes which fund them.

Ali Sistani, the most influential Shia cleric, is a clear example of the power and influence of Islamic clergy as well as their hypocrisy. This man immigrated from his native country Iran to Iraq in 1951 to enrol in a seminary in the Shia religious capital Najaf. He lived for decades on the allowance paid to students by the senior jurists, until he himself became one of the senior theologians (ayatollah) and started running his own seminary and collecting charity from the public. When his mentor, the previous grand ayatollah died, the senior associates declared Sistani as their new leader. They transferred the network of schools and mosques to Sistani's supervision and began transmitting his edicts to the public. This made him the most influential Shia jurist alive. It is estimated that he is the spiritual leader for more than 50 million humans (followers).

He has been living in Iraq for more than seventy years but still rejects its citizenship. Every government which has been formed in Iraq since 2003 was supported by him and his vast religious institution. Every president, prime minister and other important politician has visited his modest house in Najaf. They usually held press conferences outside his home to boast about how they were honoured to meet the grand ayatollah and listen to his instructions.

The ayatollah has been kept away from the public eye to preserve his status as above humans. He does not pray in public or give speeches. Through his representatives, Sistani has endorsed and brought to power the consecutive Shia-led governments in Iraq since the fall of Saddam. These Islamist politicians have proven to be among the most corrupt and incompetent in the history of Iraq to the degree that the population reminisces with sentiment about Saddam's era. Many of those who got into power have been involved in crimes against humanity, terrorism, and sectarian cleansing. The country that sells more than 3 million barrel of oil every day, suffers from shortages of electricity, water, and medications while the education, health, and judiciary systems are non-existent in many parts of Iraq and dysfunctional wherever they exist.

The many imams who represent Sistani and deliver his guidance to the people have been constantly criticizing the corruption and the incompetence of the politicians they had previously endorsed. Despite the constant harsh verbal criticism, they have never failed to remind their audience that toppling a Shia-led government would lead to chaos, which is worse than the status quo. They also warn against the return of the old Sunni regime to power. The imams' main message is that Sistani is the grand leader in charge of guiding all believers and the imams are his associates.

Sistani issues edicts on all kinds of matters and transmits them through his numerous agents, his website, as well as published books, and millions of his followers worldwide abide by them. According to him and his followers, he has the exclusive right to decide what is halal and what is haram based on his understanding of the original texts. In his main book, "Minhaj Al-Saliheen", he declares that apostates must be killed and that there is no minimum age for girls to marry. He also rules that if the wife was less than 9 years old, the husband can use her sexually in any way he pleases without intercourse.[509] Throughout Saddam's reign, he did not issue one edict condemning the genocides and the mass-crimes committed by that regime against the Shia or any other group of people. He did not show any opposition against Saddam and thus, he was allowed to become the leader of the Shia, recruit deputies, collect charity money, establish and control mosques and schools all over Iraq and abroad. He appoints as well as removes imams and judges not just in Iraq but in many other countries with the approval of the governments.

He has always been portrayed as the selfless ascetic jurist who lives in a modest rented home and does not take much from the money collected from his millions of followers. The funds collected under his supervision are dedicated to helping destitute Shias as well as to spreading Islam, his representatives assure the public. In 2007, Sistani spent a fortune on a trip to the best hospitals in London for a medical check-up. He charted a Boeing 747 airplane from Kuwait for his private use. Dozens

---

509 Al-Sistani, Ali. (2013). Minhaj Al-Saliheen (Arabic). Dar Al-Muarrakh Arabi.

of his servants and assistants accompanied him on that trip. Although he distances himself from overt financial issues, Iraqis accuse several members of his family, especially his son and son-in-law, who have been his assistants all their lives and are also imams, of holding huge fortunes and owning several wealthy businesses which were established with the money he and his associates embezzled.

In Iraq, there are several other grand ayatollahs who influence the lives of millions of people worldwide through their monopoly on distinguishing right from wrong, based on their understanding of the Islamic texts and their affiliations with states and organizations. They control seminaries and mosques and hence receive substantial income from donations and levy, in addition to governmental subsidies and handouts. Every Shia, male and female alike, has to give up one fifth of his or her assets annually to the Shia jurist he or she follows. This is considered the share of Mohammad and it must be paid to the senior jurist since he is the current representative of Mohammad's legitimate successor – the hidden Imam. This money is supposed to be divided among Mohammad's descendants, Islamic students, the impoverished, and to spread Islam. Tens of millions of Shias comply and each year they send one fifth of their gains to the ayatollah they follow because they think he is the most knowledgeable in sharia.

In Iran, Shia imams have been the rulers of the country since 1979. Most of them joined the opposition to the monarchy after it started to lose its control. They instigated Iranians against their old master and ally, accusing the Shia king of being an apostate and a veiled enemy of Islam. Before they changed sides, many of the jurists who are now in power had been staunch servants of the Iranian dictator, justifying his crimes and defending him through claiming that he was not aware of his men's corruption. But once they saw the ill king was on his way out, they joined the opposition, showing their willingness to cooperate with all the other factions, including communists and anti-religion groups. Once the last Iranian king left his country, the imams stole the revolution and declared themselves the authority. They brought to power the first supreme leader Khomeini, who appointed himself the head of the state and the source of authority controlling all the branches of the regime through the students of the religious schools, claiming to be the representative of Islam and the deputy of Mahdi – the Hidden Shia Imam.

The ayatollahs staged a coup against all the other factions that participated in the revolution. They also purged all the supporters of the old regime and the Iranian intelligentsia and technocrats. They were all cast as enemies of Allah that must be exterminated in order for the country to prosper. Khomeini and his ayatollahs promised the masses that they would create a heaven on earth if the people conceded their rights and obeyed them while they re-established the state of Mohammad: the true Islamic state. They gradually took control of every aspect of public and private life. They infiltrated and subverted the educational, judiciary, security and the media institutions, purging anyone who dared to be independent, let alone opposing the new rulers. They kept attributing every problem and failure to the old godless regime and its sinful followers while assuring people that through implementing Islam they were building the perfect state.[510] They kept telling people to be patient and wait, and their version of Islam would conquer the world. Animalistic violence was the essential means of the Islamic regime in dealing with the people. In one of his early speeches, Imam Khomeini said that "the executions in Islam are the executions of mercy, it is like a doctor ridding our society of corrupting influences with his knife, when we follow Allah's orders, an entire society is reformed/cleansed. If we chop off the hands of four thieves in public squares, theft will be finished in the society. If we were to publicly flog those engaging in sins, there will be no sins left in society." This Orwellian mentality has been an essential hallmark of the Islamic regime right from its start to this moment.

As a consequence of following Allah's orders, the jurists threw Iranians into a bloody eight-year-long conflict with Iraq, in which millions of Muslims were killed or injured. They have been supporting terrorism around the globe. They have been destroying the Iranian economy, the judicial system, the educational system. They established a brutal police state ruled by a supreme leader – a tsar and an imam in one. The students of the religion have taken over the whole country, treating

---

510 Bakhash, S. (1985). The reign of the Ayatollahs: Iran and the Islamic Revolution. Tauris.; Seliktar, O., & Rezaei, F. (2020). Iran, Revolution, and Proxy Wars. Springer International.

the rest of the Iranians as enemies. Iran's wealth has been a booty for the senior imams and their students. They drove millions of educated people out of the country and stole their properties in the name of Allah. They killed and tortured millions of citizens after labelling them infidels or hypocrites.

Over the four decades, Iranian jurists transformed themselves and their families into a wealthy ruthless mafia with official armed militias and dodgy financial organizations. Iran slid from a relatively prosperous, fairly functioning country into a lawless failed theological kleptocratic narco-state run by religious militias.

The first supreme leader Khomeini, who was born in a small village in Iran to an Indian family, was intoxicated with power to a degree that made him delusional.[511] He behaved like a ruthless god. In 1989, he sent an official delegation with a formal written letter from him to Mikhail Gorbachev. Their mission was to convince the General Secretary of the Communist Party to become a Shia and turn the Soviet Union into a Shia state. The Iranian supreme leader, who was semi-literate and had never studied anything but the obsolete ancient books of Islam, sent his assistants to lecture the Soviet leadership on how to save their country. He stated in his letter that the only way for the USSR to survive its crisis was through following the ancient teachings of the Arabs who invaded Iran and subjugated its people by violence. The Russians needed to give up their ideology, religion, and identity and become followers of Mohammad, his cousin Ali, the descendants of Ali recognized as the true imams by the Shia. They must consequently follow Khomeini since he was the grand jurist who had the right to issue commands. Gorbachev described this event as one of the most bizarre things he had ever experienced. But Iranian propaganda has been claiming that the Russians regretted not complying with the Iranian supreme leader's guidance. The official website of Khomeini falsely states that: "Gorbachev regretted his ignorance to Imam's warnings three years before the collapse of the Soviet Union and said: 'I think Imam Khomeini's message was addressed to all the ages through the history.' He also added: 'When I received this message, I felt

511 Fallaci, O. (1979, Oct 7). An Interview with Khomeini. New York Times Archive.

the person who had written this letter was thoughtful and caring for the world's destination. By studying that message, I understood that he is a person who is worried for the world and is willing for me to understand the Islamic revolution more."[512]

To this day, millions of Shias adore Khomeini and consider him their leader despite him being dead for decades. Pictures of his stern face are still hanging in the official institutions and the streets of Syria, Lebanon, Iraq, and Iran in addition to private homes and mosques. His followers see him as the greatest mind of his time, and perhaps to this day, as he knew sharia better than anyone else, as they claim, and this is what matters – not science or literature, or progress, or compassion. The fact that he killed hundreds of thousands of people, led his country to destruction and contributed to the demise of neighbouring Iraq are irrelevant to his enthusiasts. The fact that he was a dictator who used the state to satisfy his pathological personal needs is not an issue, either. He was an Islamic imam who deceived the West and enforced sharia, and this is enough for millions of people to have followed him blindly while he was alive and to still adore him decades after his demise.

The current supreme leader, Ali Khamenei, is one of the richest, most autocratic and most corrupt men on Earth.[513] He has made his affluence and influence through being a loyal member of the jurist mafia before becoming its head. In every speech and every interview, he repeats passages from the Quran and from Mohammad's sayings, claiming that these old talks are the solutions to what is going on. He introduces Islam as the one and only virtuous religion that is in war with every other – evil – ideology and religion. He portrays the suffering and injustice in which Iranians are living, which in fact result from his regime's corruption, as a great blessing. He describes non-Muslims as immoral, destitute, wretched people. He presents himself as the one and only person who represents Allah. He warns against all non-Muslims as well as these Muslims who according to him are hypocrites, apostates, or infidels.

---

512 The Institute For Compilation And Publication Of Imam Khomeini's Works. (2012, Jul 25). Gorbachev's response to Imam Khomeini.
513 Stecklow, S., Dehghanpisheh, B., & Torbati Y. (2013, Nov 11). Khamenei controls massive financial empire built on property seizures. Reuters.

In Afghanistan, the Taliban leaders – who are Sunni imams – took over the country after toppling the elected government, once the US troops withdrew in August 2021. Similar to the Iranian imams, they see themselves as virtuous and superior because they studied Quran and the hadith, and hence they must rule the rest. In both countries, there is no freedom or personal life as the theologians control every aspect of human existence.

In 1969, the Saudi crown prince Faisal ousted his brother king Saud through an edict issued by 34 senior imams. The theologians lead by the grand mufti of Saudi Arabia and the dean of the Islamic University of Medina legitimised the coup d'état through presenting the Muslim king as unfit to continue as a ruler from the Islamic point of view, which they represented.

THE FALLEN REFORMISTS

> Obey Allah and obey the Messenger and those in authority
> (owlo alamar) among you[514]
>
> Allah

In Islam, politics, religion and business are inseparable. The head of the state is the guardian of the nation (wali alamr). He is the head of religion, the chief of legislative and judicial authorities, the master of the army, and the keeper of the wealth. These theologians have been and always will be politicians, judges, part of the administration, as well as merchants.

Thus, Islam is not likely to change from within because it is intolerant of change. In fact, it is in the habit of executing anyone who dares to challenge it or attempts to transform it into an ideology compatible with human nature and a progressive society. Throughout the ages many have attempted, and they lost to the traditional powers.

Mahmoud Taha, one of the most important Muslim reformists of the 20th century, was convicted by the Sudanese courts of the crime of campaigning for abolishing sharia. The general prosecutor accused him of rejecting one of the fundamental principles of Islam that is the eternal validity of sharia as the one and only source of laws. The most influential Islamic institutions: Saudi Alma council and Al-Azhar issued edicts declaring the reformist an apostate and an enemy of Islam, since he attempted to alter a divine Islamic law. They called upon the Sudanese authority to execute him along with his followers and to ban his ideas. Mahmoud Taha was found guilty of apostasy and was sentenced to death by both the criminal court and the court of appeal on 8 January 1985, three days after his arrest. The court sentence stated that Mahmoud Taha must be hanged to death, must not be buried in a Muslim cemetery and all his properties must be confiscated. There were four other defendants in that case, who were also sentenced to death but were given a month to repent and renounce their ideas, which they did to save their lives.

---

514 Quran 4:59.

The ruling also declared all Taha's sympathisers as apostates who must hence face the same fate. The Sudanese president ratified the sentence on the same day it was issued. Muslims worldwide received this sentence with an overwhelming joy. The books and pamphlets that contained the reformist's ideas were banned all over the Muslim world.[515]

This old theologian, who sought to reform specific principles of Islam and make the religion harmonious with modern civilization, was hanged in public on 18 January 1985, thirteen days after his arrest. The crowd that attended his execution was cheering and waving copies of the Quran in ecstasy. He suffered this fate despite the fact that he was a devoted Muslim; all what he was trying to do was to offer a different interpretation of some of the Islamic principles. He wanted his people to live "here and now" rather than in the jails of ancient texts. He did not realize that he was challenging the official version of Islam and the powerful institutions dependent on it.

In Egypt, the renowned university professor Farag Foda was gunned down by Muslim assassins with machine guns while leaving his office, in 1992. The Islamic Group that took responsibility for the assassination declared in a published statement that the academic was an apostate and an enemy of Islam, thus, he had to be killed. He was an influential thinker who wrote several books calling for an Islamic reform. Through the use of logic, sarcasm, and evidence, he argued that concepts such as slavery and corporal punishment do not fit with modern values and must be suspended. He called for a free, democratic society ruled by manmade laws susceptible to change while he continuously affirmed his adoration of Islam and Mohammad. This call was declared as an act of war against Allah not just by radical movements but also by many influential jurists of Al-Azhar and the council of Islamic jurists of Saudi Arabia. In the trial of Foda's killers, several prominent imams gave testimonies as expert witnesses on Islamic teachings. They all defended the killers' action, declaring that according to Islam the victim deserved to be killed, although it should have been done by the authority, not individuals. The head of Muslim Brothers praised the assassination of Farag Foda, and

---

515 Miller, J. (1997). God has ninety-nine names: reporting from a militant Middle East. Simon & Schuster.

a prominent Islamic professor at Al-Azhar wrote a book arguing that Farag Foda killed himself by waging a war against Islam.[516] The killers were pardoned by the elected Muslim Brother president Mohammed Morsi once he got into power in 2012. After his release from prison, one of the assassins defended what he had done, stating in a TV interview that "the punishment of an apostate is death."

In November 2021, the famous lawyer Ahmad Abdu Maher was sentenced in absentia to five years in prison for blasphemy by the State Security Court. The sentence indicated that the book Maher wrote to defend Islam, as he claimed, contained defamation of Islam and represented a threat to the national security. In that book, Maher argued that Islam was a moral religion that did not compel its followers to hate or hurt Christians and Jews. It did not allow husbands to hit their wives, and Mohammad had not attempted to commit suicide. He also stated that it was not legal to have sex with babies and the Islamic invasions were not an application of the religion. In a famous interview, he called for reforming the Islamic textbooks taught in Al-Azhar. He showed that these books sanctioned the killing of non-Muslim prisoners of war and eating their dead bodies. He criticized the literal following of the hadith books by Muslims, highlighting that the composers of these books were born after the events. These ideas were seen as blasphemy by an Egyptian lawyer who filed a legal complaint against Maher accusing him of insulting Islam. The Egyptian general attorney accepted the complaint and classified the book as a crime that threatened national security. Hence, he submitted the case to State Security Court, which is designated to hear matters involving terrorism, treason, espionage, and similar major offences.[517] This court's sentences cannot be appealed, except on procedural grounds, and for decades have been accused of lacking independence and impartiality and of being used against freethinkers, reformists, and political dissidents.

Over the ages, countless thinkers across the world have been suppressed or killed for attempting to reform Islam. Despite being one of

---

516 Soage, A. B. (2007). Faraj Fawda, or the Cost of Freedom of Expression. Middle East Review of International Affairs 11(2), pp 26-33.
517 ARB – News. (2008, Aug 26). Egypt's State Security Courts to be Abolished. Carnegie Endowment for International Peace.

the most important Muslim mystics, Al-Hallaj (d. 922 CE) was accused of blasphemy by other imams who convinced the ruler to execute him. He was lashed in public before they cut off his hands and decapitated him. His dead body was scorched, and the ashes thrown into water.

Even the five senior Muslim scholars who founded the main Islamic jurisprudence schools (madahib) did not escape the Islamic inquisition. They were all persecuted after being labelled sinners, heretics or infidels by their opponents. Abu Hanifa, a Persian known as the greatest jurist, who founded the first school of Sunni jurisprudence which still carries his name Hanfi and currently has millions of followers all over the world, was persecuted by the Muslim caliph of his day after being accused by other jurists of being heretic and a threat to the unity of Muslims. He was flogged in public, jailed, tortured, and starved inside a prison cell to his death. The founders of the other three Sunni schools of fiqh were all accused of being heretics by their opponents and were imprisoned and tortured by the caliphs of their times. The founder of Shia jurisprudence, Jafar al-Sadiq, was also jailed and tortured, and many of his children and grandchildren were beheaded after being branded heretics.

THE ISLAMIC HYDRA AND STABILITY: OXYMORON

Kamel Al-Najjar describes Islam as Hydra – a monster with many heads. The main philosophy of every one of these heads (which are the sects of Islam and organizations which belong to each sect) is to stay in bed with the ruling regime and at the same time cooperate with the devil to change the regime so that the one head would hold all the power and treasure solely. Every time one of the heads, such as a branch of the Muslim Brothers, a Salafi movement, a group of Shia theologians, a tribal alliance, or a military junta gets into power, the other heads attempt to form an alliance with it and strive to replace it, simultaneously. Deception and violence are the main means, and both considered moral.[518]

Almost every Islamic organization in every Muslim country has taken a stand against the administration of the country and cooperated with it at the exact same time. Accusing the government and the population of suppressing good Muslims and of not adhering to the correct rules of Islam has been the theoretical cornerstone of almost every movement that got into power in the Muslim world.[519] In Afghanistan, the Taliban with the support of many Muslim countries waged a 20-year war against the elected Afghani governments after accusing them of being infidels and puppets of the non-Muslim Americans. Once it took over Afghanistan, the Khorasan Islamic state started its warfare to topple the Taliban after accusing them of being infidels and a puppet of the non-Muslim Chinese.

The biggest Islamic organization: the Muslim Brotherhood has been claiming that its members were suppressed in almost all Muslim countries because they were the good Muslims while the rulers are apostates and the masses are heretics or ignorant at best. In Egypt, the

---

518 Al-Najjar, Kamel. (2011, Mar 16). Althoeban Alislami Mutaeaded Alroaas [The Islamic Hydra]. (Arabic). Modern Discussion Vol. 3307.
519 See Miller, J. (1997). God has ninety-nine names: reporting from a militant Middle East.

birthplace of this international organization, it has been instigating the masses against every regime and every leader, accusing them of being the enemies of Islam. For over eighty years, its members have been claiming that if they got into power, they would create the religious state where people would live the Islamic utopia.

The two books that are considered the constitution of this movement were written by Sayyid Qutb. "In the Shadow of Quran" and "Milestones on the Road" have a simple ideology: Islam is the one and only valid system of ideas, it must control every aspect of the personal and social life, and people who deviate from its teachings are infidels. Qutb has declared clearly in his books that all Muslim societies are no longer Muslims since they do not apply many of the Islamic laws such as cutting off thieves' hands, stoning adulterers to death or collecting jizya from Christians and Jews. He constructed all non-Muslims as evil, unethical enemies and called for confronting them.

This organization was set up in 1928 by a group of uneducated workers employed by Suez Canal Company as a religious and political movement. It was supported by the Egyptian monarch in the 1930s and 40s to undermine the liberal and national parties and extend the Egyptian influence to other Muslim countries, until it assassinated an ex-prime minister in 1948. It played an important role in the 1952 military coup which ended the monarchy. Several persons of the ruling junta were members of the organization. The 1952 revolutionary regime dissolved all the political parties and persecuted their members, with the exception of the Muslims Brothers who were allowed to work as both a political party and a religious organization. Nonetheless, in 1954 the Brotherhood attempted to kill Gamal Abdel Nasser, the prime minister and the de facto head of state, who was one of their supporters, and it is said that he had taken the oath of allegiance as a member of the organization. Their aim was to concentrate the power in the hands of the traditional hierarchy within the organization. Afterward, the Egyptian regime banned the Brotherhood and started persecuting its members. Many of them escaped to the Gulf States which welcomed them and allowed them to establish branches of the organisation. Starting from the fifties until this day, Gulf States have sponsored the Muslim Brothers and shared power with them to counter internal opposition.[520] They also used this organization to beset the Egyptian, Syrian, Iraqi, Yemeni regimes and to influence these societies. They allowed it to control many of the important governmental and private institutions, especially in the financial, educational and judicial sectors inside the Persian Gulf States. Moreover, these regimes used this organization as a political tool against the West. With the money they received from the Gulf States, the Muslim Brothers established many financial institutions as well as Islamic centres and mosques all over the world. In Kuwait, members of the Muslim Brothers have been appointed to serve as ministers in every government formed in the past six decades. Several of their members were appointed as ministers of oil, overseeing the wealth of the country. In Saudi Arabia as well as Bahrain and the Emirates, Muslims Brothers were part of the government and enjoyed unparalleled support from the ruling families for decades. Qatar has been their main headquarters for over 25 years and Al Jazeera is one of their many media platforms. It seems that recently the Saudis and the Emiratis realized the danger Muslim Brothers pose to them and started to curb their influence.

In 2011, the Muslim Brothers took over the Egyptian parliament, and the following year, when their candidate Mohammed Morsi was elected president of Egypt with less than 52 percent of the votes in an election that witnessed rampant violations by their supporters, they became the ruling party. Once in power, they sought to purge the government, the judicial system, the media, and the educational system of the non-members of the organizations. None of the independent people were appointed into the government they formed. They justified putting tens of thousands of their unqualified followers in key positions by claiming that their members were more pious than the rest of the society.

Nonetheless, they continued many of the policies they had considered non-Islamic beforehand. The same laws that the Muslim Brothers denounced as against Islam when they were not in power, such as maintaining diplomatic relations with Israel, collecting tax from people, allowing banks to charge interest, and many others, continued during

---

520 Freer, C. J. (2018). Rentier Islamism: The influence of the muslim brotherhood in Gulf monarchies. Oxford University Press.

their reign. They tried to justify these practices through a rhetoric that contradicted their old mantras. Hence, they were described as un-Islamic by many of their Islamic allies, specifically the Salafis, who complained that the Muslim Brothers' regime was suppressing true Muslims. In April of 2013, millions of Muslim Brothers and their supporters took to the streets of Egypt, vowing to fight to death for the Muslim Brother president, as a reaction to the much larger mass protests demanding his removal. They warned the Egyptian army against listening to the demonstrating crowds. Nevertheless, Morsi was deposed, arrested by the army in his palace along with his bodyguards and many of his assistants and they were thrown in jail without resistance. The jihadists carried out several terrorist attacks but were faced with sweeping violence. The Muslim Brothers staged sit-ins in the middle of Cairo to assemble their supporters and show their power. The speakers in the main sit-in declared jihad to reinstate the Islamic regime and promised to stand their ground until Morsi was freed and the military coup foiled. The Egyptian army attacked the Rabaa sit-in; a number of the protesters were killed or injured but the vast majority of the Muslim Brothers run away. Many of the angry screamers from Rabaa left the country altogether and moved to the West, where they have been living off social security handouts while spreading Islam and pledging to topple the regime through the use of Twitter and Facebook. The Muslim Brothers were removed from power through a military coup supported by millions of Egyptians who had been protesting the suffocating control of the Islamists, their corruption and incompetence.

In Morocco, Algeria, Libya, Tunisia, Sudan, Syria, Lebanon, Iraq, Saudi Arabia, Yemen and several other countries, the Muslim Brothers as well as all other Islamic movements have been undermining the legitimacy and the authority of the regimes by accusing them of being traitors and enemies of Islam. This systematic attack and the propagation of this divisive ideology have contributed immensely to the state of instability and regression these countries have been in for decades.

If we were to review the history of the Muslim world in the past thousand years, we would find that it has been in a constant turmoil. International wars, civil conflicts, military coups, dictatorial regimes, uprisings, and bloody revolutions have been the norm in that part of the world.

19 Islam and Regression

> Seeing individuals dedicate themselves to tyrannical death cults
> led by suicidal maniacs is bad enough. Knowing that I may have
> contributed to their choices is terrible.[521]

If a society is to progress, it needs to embrace an adaptive system of ideas
and rational laws which unite its people and allow them to actualize
themselves as individuals. To progress, the state must separate religion
from public life. It must grant equal rights to its members regardless
of their race, gender, or any other collective affiliation. Protecting the
freedom of conscience, expression, and belief and enforcing the rule of
law are prerequisite for the existence of a progressive society. Advancing science as an objective method of examining and understanding
the world is the only way to bring about real sustainable development
on a societal level.

In an Islamic state, there is no place for independent or critical
thinking, dissent, or self-expression. It creates an environment toxic to
creativity and progress. In the broadest definition, human civilizations
and progress are built on the past and previous lessons learned. The wheel
paved the way for the wagon, which paved the way for the car – with a
multitude of developments in between. Progress demands creativity and
discontent with what exists. Someone sees a problem, defines it, and solves
it, often through a tedious process of trial and error. Of course, this is a
simplification but the point is, Islam is threatened by anything that does
not reflect back on its teachings with praise and adoration. There can be no
problems except the problem of not recognizing the perfection and wonder of Islam, Mohammad, and the sharia. Islam is the ultimate catch-22.

---

521 Musa Cerantonio, the most famous Australian jihadi preacher. Born to an Italian-Austra-
lian family outside of Melbourne, he converted to Islam as a teenager and later became an imam.
He hosted an Islamic show on the Saudi Islamic channel Iqraa. He was sentenced to 7 years in
prison in 2019 for planning to flee the country and join ISIS. In prison, he left Islam. Quoted by
Wood, G. (2022, Mar 31). Why an ISIS Propagandist Abandoned Islam. The Atlantic.

Islam glorifies itself while at the same time it has no capacity to self-reflect. Music, art, and other forms of cultural expression thrive in environments where individuals can explore different forms, break barriers, and come up with original ideas. But in Islam there are no original ideas because the only worthy ideas are the ones that came from Allah via Mohammad 1400 years ago. As far as Islam is concerned, there was nothing of value before and nothing of value outside of its teachings.

The perfect Islamic state is a despotic police state, which cultivates obedience through animalistic fear. It is based on sheer adoration of the authority and on the suspension of creative thinking. There is no need to study the world empirically, as Allah has stated that "we have left out nothing in this book."[522] Thus, Muslim imams have outlawed almost every significant human invention. They outlawed printing to protect the Quran from being tampered with; they banned cars, trains and airplanes because Allah stated that he created animals to transport us. They fought against the modern education. They outlawed coffee because it had an effect similar to alcohol. Organ transplantation was outlawed by the vast majority of Muslim theologians for several decades because they deemed it an interference with Allah's design. In the 1980s, the influential imam Muhammad al-Sharawi stated that the human body is the property of Allah and thus, no one had the right to donate any part of it. If Allah decided to take his slave's life, who are we to impede that, he stated. He also said repeatedly that he had not read any book but the Quran in more than 30 years.

Arabs had been using a lunisolar calendar that contained an intercalary (leap) month for centuries pre-Islam. Shamans of a specific tribe oversaw the interlocution, which was called "nasi" and aimed to make the lunar calendar consistent with the solar one and hence, with the seasons. Nasi was prohibited by Allah in the Quran[523], and this made the Islamic calendar futile as it could not be used for farming, sailing, travelling or any other activity related to or affected by the sun's position. Since the abolishing of nasi, Islamic months keep shifting in relation to the weather cycles. For instance, the month of Ramadan could come at

522 Quran 6:38.
523 Quran 9:37.

any time of the solar year. People cannot organize many of their daily activities based on this inconstant calendar but at the same time, they need to adhere to it as religious events are based on it. This is but one of the many destructive effects of this religion.

Boris Johnson wrote in 2007, before becoming Britain's Prime Minister, that "There must be something about Islam that indeed helps to explain why there was no rise of the bourgeoisie, no liberal capitalism and therefore no spread of democracy in the Muslim world. It is extraordinary to think that under the Roman/Byzantine empire, the city of Constantinople kept the candle of learning alight for a thousand years, and that under Ottoman rule, the first printing press was not seen in Istanbul until the middle of the 19th century. Something caused them to be literally centuries behind."[524]

In a nutshell, Islam is a militarised ideology that needs to wage jihad against all non-Muslims, cuts off thieves' hands, kills homosexuals, prohibits music, forbids sculpting and painting, sanctions slavery, rejects democracy, separates men from women, bans interest on loans, bans alcohol and kills its producers, enforces a strict dress code on females, stones people to death for adultery if they were married, kills apostates, kills rebels or severs their arms and legs, bars freedom of expression, outlaws personal rights in order to survive.

The perfect Islamic state requires every person to pray five times a day, fast during Ramadan, obey the caliph, have many kids and several wives, and monitor everyone around him all the time. If the caliph defected from Islam by doing or saying something which is considered prohibited, then it is the duty of Muslims to kill him. In that sense, Islam is like a virus – when there are no more enemies to hate or infidels to kill, no more communities to raid, it will ultimately turn on itself and be forced to either mutate or die.

---

524 Quoted by Perraudin, F. (2019, Jul 15). Boris Johnson claimed Islam put Muslim world 'centuries behind. The Guardian.

DEMOLISHING CULTURE, HERITAGE AND ART

Blowing up the 1400-year-old Bamiyan Buddhas in March 2001 was an episode in the long history of Islam's continuous eradication of human heritage, culture and progress. One of the people who was forced to carry out the destruction of the ancient monuments described in an interview with the BBC how the Sunni fighters kidnapped twenty-five Shias and forced them to implant the explosives inside the gigantic ancient statues by drilling deep holes in them. The Shias were treated as disposable tools by their abductors. They were forced to work continuously for 25 days, and when one of the prisoners could not carry the heavy loads because he had broken his leg, the mujahedeen slew him on the spot.[525]

Believers worldwide joined the Taliban in celebrating the destruction of the ancient Buddhas, which had been in that site for centuries before Islam. This was not the first attempt – over the past thousand years, several Muslim leaders attempted to abolish these cultural monuments, and they did manage to destroy parts of them. They obliterated various other similar sites. The Muslim demolishers of cultural heritage were following the example of the founders of Islam and its role models, as they asserted. Muslims worldwide believe that when Mohammad captured Mecca, the centre of polytheism in Arabia, he destroyed all the symbols and artefacts of other religions. He ruined the idols, the statues, and the paintings, including the ones depicting Jesus and Mary. He rejected all statues, paintings, and scriptures as anti-monotheistic sinful idols which thus had to be destroyed. This story of Mohammad is reported in what the vast majority of Muslims consider the authentic sources of Islam. It is taught in the public schools, glorified in various films and sermons.

In the Heliopolis Museum, vandalized ancient statues stand witness to the early Muslims' animosity toward human heritage, history, culture,

---

525 Behzad, N. & Qarizadah, D. (2015, Mar 12). The man who helped blow up the Bamiyan Buddhas. BBC Afghan. [Archived].

and art.[526] In the seventh century, the invaders destroyed the heads of numerous marvellous statues, in accordance with their religion's teachings, which ban sculptures and drawing of live beings and consider them idols that must be demolished. The perpetrators of that mass vandalism are role models for contemporary Muslims worldwide who are following the written teachings of Islam. In addition to more than fifteen sayings of Mohammad that ban such practices, among them this one: "The people who will receive the severest punishment from Allah will be the picture makers."[527] There are several Quranic passages which ban idols: "Wine, gambling, idols and divining arrows [a fortune-telling device] are filth, made by Satan, therefore, refrain from it."[528]

The practice of destroying heritage has continued over the ages as an application of Islam. In the 12th century, Saladin's son and his heir commanded the destruction of the Giza Pyramids in Egypt. He considered these monuments symbols of paganism, and thus anti-Islamic, which must be razed. Unlike his predecessors, who knew that they could not afford to execute such an expensive and difficult project, he commissioned a huge workforce to obliterate this human treasure. After eight months of forced labour, the mission turned out to be extremely challenging and much more expensive than expected, thus the Muslim governor decided to let the pyramids be for the time being.[529]

In the past few decades, Islamic movements and governments have destroyed some of the most valuable ancient artefacts, archaeological sites, and monuments in Syria, Afghanistan, Libya, Kuwait, Saudi Arabia, and Iraq in an attempt to remove every pre-Islamic symbol from the face of the earth. Turkish troops which invaded and occupied North Cyprus in 1974 oversaw the ruining and looting of over 500 churches in one of the most vicious organized destructions of heritage and art.[530]

During the Syrian civil war, Islamists destroyed more than 120 ancient churches[531] and countless Yazidi and Jewish places of worship and

---

526 Photographs of statues from Baalbek are available at Livius.org.
527 Sahih al-Bukhari 5950; 5951; 3224.; Sahih Muslim 2107.
528 Quran 5:90.
529 Lehner, M. (2008). The Complete Pyramids. Thames & Hudson.
530 Morris, C. (2002, Jan 18). Shame of Cyprus's looted churches. BBC News.
531 The National. (2019, Sep 11). More than 120 churches in Syria damaged or destroyed by war.

monuments.[532] The sixth century glorious Saint Elijah monastery which had stood for hundreds of years in Mosul was destroyed in 2014. In 2012, Muslims torched the Saint Mary Church of the Holy Belt (Um Al Zennar) in Homs which stood on site that had been a Christian place of worship since the first century CE.

In the 21st century, Muslims ruined countless ancient archaeological sites, including Nimrud, Nineveh, Hatra, and Palmyra, which had persisted for thousands of years as a mark of the greatness of ancient human civilizations. The fighters of ISIS burned more than 8000 original manuscripts just from the Mosul Museum – some of them were thousands of years old.

The Islamic State of Iraq and the Levant circulated numerous pictures and videos which show its fighters destroying ancient artefacts and burning original manuscripts while shouting 'Allah Akbar'.[533] Engaging in this practice was designed to win support for jihad. A Catholic priest from Mosul cried that Christian history was "being barbarically levelled."[534] Statues thousands of years old were bulldozed at the hands of the illiterate believers[535], who were following the teaching of Islam, as they claimed. They looted many artefacts and sold them on the black market to finance their holy war.[536]

The mujahedeen captured the renowned Syrian scholar Khaled Al-Asaad and savagely tortured him for over a month to force him into cooperation.[537] Despite the sadistic torture, he refused to reveal where valuable artefacts were hidden. After realizing that there was nothing which could break the will of the scholar, the mujahedeen brought the wounded old man to the main square of Palmyra, whipped him, then

---

532 Curry, A. (2015, Sep 1). Here Are the Ancient Sites ISIS Has Damaged and Destroyed. National Geographic.
533 BBC News. (2015, Jul 2). Islamic State militants 'destroy Palmyra statues'.
534 BBC News. (2016, Jan 20). Iraq's oldest Christian monastery destroyed by Islamic State. [Archived]; Gander, K. (2015, Jul 9). Isis 'kills four children' as it reportedly destroys ancient church in Iraqi city of Mosul. Independent.
535 UNESCO. (n.d.) Lion statues destroyed.
536 Swann, S. (2019, May 2). Antiquities looted in Syria and Iraq are sold on Facebook. BBC News.; Greenland, F. (2016, May 31). Inside ISIS' looted antiquities trade. The Conversation.
537 Hubbard, B. (2015, Aug 20). Syrian Expert Who Shielded Palmyra Antiquities Meets a Grisly Death at ISIS' Hands. The New York Times.

beheaded him in front of a celebrating crowd. They put his mutilated body on a cross as punishment for apostasy and fighting against sharia. In their pamphlets, they declared that the distinguished archaeologist was an apostate serving idolatry and symbols of sinful cultures in an act of direct disobedience to Allah, thus he deserved to be tortured and killed in accordance with sharia.

The mujahedeen in Africa destroyed the ancient sites in the city of Timbuktu in 2012. They declared these old cultural locations non-Islamic, thus they had to be razed entirely. One of the criminals who led the attacks on Timbuktu, Ahmad al-Faqi al-Mahdi, was prosecuted by the International Criminal Court in Hague.[538] In the trial, the prosecutor Fatou Bensouda said: "This crime affects the soul and spirit of the people"; he compared the attacks on the ancient African sites to the destruction wrought by Islamic State militants on Palmyra in Syria and the Taliban's destruction of the Bamiyan Buddha statues in Afghanistan. Al-Mahdi pleaded guilty and was sentenced to just nine years in prison for the destruction of that part of the world's heritage and history.

The war on heritage is not limited to jihadis, since many Muslim regimes which are signatories of the United Nations' treaties protecting world culture and heritage have been destroying and neglecting archaeological sites and artefacts because they saw them as un-Islamic. Countless numbers of ancient sites, temples and churches, some of them more than a thousand years old, have been destroyed all over the Muslim World.

Invaluable and irreplaceable ancient human heritage has been ruined at the hands of devoted Muslims[539] because it constitutes a proof that people did live and nourish without Islam, and great civilizations existed in spite of it. It attests that the old civilizations were more advanced than the Islamic one in almost all aspects and left great marks which dwarf anything Muslims have created.

---

538 Escritt, T. (2016, Mar 1). Mali rebel destroyed ancient Timbuktu shrines, ICC told. Reuters.
539 BBC News. (2015, Mar 7). Islamic State 'demolishes' ancient Hatra site in Iraq.

SLAYING THE SPIRIT OF CIVILIZATION:
FREEDOM FOR THE ENEMIES OF FREEDOM

The most crucial front of the war being waged by adamant believers is the systematic assault against the essence of civilization. The freedom of expression, the freedom of conscience, as well as simply art, music, science, rule of law, and personal rights are all under constant, systematic attack by people and states who consider all these products of civilization sins. These fundamental principles intrinsic to progress are eroding swiftly worldwide. The regimes of Muslim petrodollar states, their religious institutions and their oppressed masses are imposing a tribal anti-civilization agenda on almost every society of this world. Human rights are shrinking, and democracy is being systematically devoid of its essence by people who firmly believe that they were entrusted with the ultimate truth and that it is their duty to silence any disagreeing voice. People worldwide are scared to express their opinions regarding Islam and Muslims. It is as if mujahedeen with the support of the illiterate masses and the hereditary regimes have been monitoring the rest of humanity. Academics are frightened to discuss any topic that could offend Muslims, and universities are no longer capable of holding a debate or invite a speaker of which the Muslim students do not approve. Yale University refused to print the cartoons of Muhammad – or any other illustration of him – in a book that was dedicated to discussing them, "The Cartoons That Shook the World".[540]

The publication of the novel "Satanic Verses" by Salman Rushdie resulted in several jurists issuing edicts calling on Muslims to assassinate the writer as retribution for insulting the prophet Mohammad. Angry protests against the book and its author were held across the world, including Europe and the United States. Ayatollah Khomeini declared

---

540 Cohen, P. (2009, Aug 12). Yale Press Bans Images of Muhammad in New Book. The New York Times.

in his fatwa that it was a duty of every Muslim to kill Rushdie; he also offered millions of dollars as a reward. After living for 33 years under the death threat, Salman Rushdie was stabbed more than ten times on the stage of an educational centre in Western New York on 12 August 2022. He was about to give a lecture about places and communities that protect persecuted writers. After the attack, thousands of Muslims took to social media to celebrate. They stated ardently that there is no freedom of speech when it comes to criticizing Islam and words are crime if they felt offended. None of the Muslim states condemned the attack.

The assassination of Samuel Patty by Abdoullakh Anzorov on 16 October 2020 was yet another episode in the war against freedom of speech. The killer stabbed the history teacher several times before beheading him in the middle of the street as punishment for discussing the cartoons of Mohammad in the classroom. The attacker was shouting "Allah Akbar" while beheading the defenceless teacher; he posted a video of his crime online. Several people had helped the killer carry out his murder.

The killer was given a hero's funeral in his native Chechenia. A massive crowd of Muslims who considered him a hero and a martyr attended his celebratory funeral, which started at a grand mosque. Many Muslims all over the world praised the murderer and condemned the French nation for allowing the cartoons of Mohammad to be displayed. The Kurdish New Statesman writer Dana Nawazar, who lives in the UK, condemned the French police for shooting Anzorov.

Muslims initiated boycotting campaigns of French goods to intimidate France. In Kuwait, Turkey, Qatar, and Iran, governmental and non-governmental organizations led hatred campaigns against France and the French people. The main message was clear: beheading people in the streets is not a crime but showing a cartoon that mocks Islam is. The Islamic president of Turkey Erdoğan and the Pakistani prime minister Imran Khan were among the first to campaign against France. The former prime mister of Malaysia declared that Muslims "have the right to kill millions of French people for the massacres of the past" in his response to the killing of the French teacher and the cartoons of Mohammad.[541] This killing was an extension of the massacre at Charlie Hebdo which itself is an episode in a long war that has aimed to censor people through terror.

On 19 February 2015, hundreds of Muslims attended the burial of the Palestinian Muslim Omar El-Hussein killed by Danish police and thousands attended the mosque ceremony held for him in Copenhagen. Many of the mourners shouted 'Allah Akbar' and others laid flowers at his grave. One of them stated: "There were a lot of young people that you don't normally see there... because they knew Omar. Some of them were gang members. They are my brothers too because they believe in Allah and the Prophet Mohammed." [542]

Armed with a machine gun and pistol, El-Hussein attempted to sneak into a cultural centre where an event organized by the Lars Vilks committee to discuss blasphemy, freedom of expression, and the attack against Charlie Hebdo was held on 14 February.[543] His aim was to kill Lars Vilks and the attendants. He shot and killed Finn Nørgaard, a 55-year-old film director, who attempted to prevent him from entering the centre. After that, he fired dozens of bullets through the windows, wounding several people. When police officers who were securing the event returned fire, he fled. The following day, he attacked a synagogue which had a bat mitzvah event. Omar shot and killed a 37-year-old Jewish man who was on security duty by the gate of the synagogue and wounded two Danish security officers; he fled the scene unharmed. He was shot in an exchange of fire with Danish police which took place in a flat where he was hiding, on 15 February 2015. Four Arab Muslims, who had extensive criminal history, helped and supported Omar. They provided him with the guns, clothes, and internet access. In court, they were extremely defiant and one of them, Mahmoud Rabea, insulted the judges several times. Another one stated in court that Lars Vilks deserved to die for criticising Mohammad.[544]

The slaying of the Japanese professor of comparative culture Hitoshi Igarashi is another episode of this war to silence everyone who dared to discuss Islam. He was a well-respected scholar who had translated

---

541 Duncan. C. (2020, Oct 29). Muslims have a right to 'kill millions of French people' over past actions, former Malaysian PM suggests. Independent.
542 The Guardian. (2015, Feb 20). Copenhagen shootings: hundreds attend funeral of gunman.
543 Eleftheriou-Smith, L.-M. (2015, Feb 15). Copenhagen shootings: Police say suspect shot dead by officers was a 22-year-old with a history in criminal gangs. Independent.
544 The Local. (2015, Feb 16). As it happened: Denmark mourns terror victims.

many important works to Japanese, among them the novel "The Satanic Verses", which criticizes some Islamic ideas. He was stabbed in his neck, face and hands just outside of his office at the University of Tsukuba in Northeast Tokyo. His dead body was found on 12 July 1991.[545] Professor Koji Kamioka maintained that what happened was "a very Islamic way of killing."[546] The killer was never apprehended, the investigation was closed, and many Japanese bookstores refused to sell the novel out of fear. No significant post-mortem acknowledgment for the brave scholar was held and he is all but forgotten. Terror prevailed.

Another Muslim attacked with a knife the Italian translator of "The Satanic Verses" Ettore Capriolo in his house in Milan on 3 July 1991.[547] He stabbed him several times in the neck, hand and chest. The attacker was not captured, either, and he may well be living happily in Europe, preaching about tolerance and multiculturalism and denouncing European Islamophobia.

To this day and despite all the sacrifices, criticising polygamy, slavery, genital mutilation, child marriage, honour killing, obligatory hijab, corporal punishment or discussing the Islamic conquests is treated as a crime almost all over the world. Many non-Muslim governments and institutions are in alliance with the regressive petrodollar states in their battle against the spirit of civilization: against critical thinking and freedom of speech. Many other states and organizations have either given in or are oblivious to the long-term consequences of this struggle.

In many parts of this world, non-Muslims living in their native non-Muslim countries are forced to alter their way of life to comply with the teachings of Islam enforced by immigrants, petrodollar-funded organizations and their allies. Muslim refugees and asylum seekers are deciding for Europeans, Americans, Canadians, and Australian what they should wear, what they should eat and what they should say and not say in their homelands. Tolerance, multiculturalism, cultural differences, and

---

545 Weisman, S. R. (1991, Jul 13). Japanese Translator of Rushdie Book Found Slain. The New York Times Archive.
546 Helm, L. (1991, Jul 13). Translator of 'Satanic Verses' Slain: Japan: The stabbing of a scholar at a campus near Tokyo may be related to Salman Rushdie's controversial novel. Los Angeles Times.
547 Reid. T. R. (1991, Jul 13). 'Satanic Verses' Translator Found Slain. The Washington Post.

equality are terms used to censor and suppress any criticism of Islam or Muslims but never for challenging the Islamic teachings that dehumanise non-Muslims. They are also disguising the cowardice and immorality of numerous Western decision makers, scholars, and journalists.

The justice secretary of Scotland, Humza Yousaf, a devoted Muslim proud of his Pakistani origin, sponsored a legal bill that would have made the Scottish legal system similar to his country of origin in regard to the freedom of speech, had it passed in its original form. Humza said that "Conversations over the dinner table that incite hatred must be prosecuted under Scotland's hate crime law."[548] This law, introduced to intimidate and punish people for what is considered prejudice and to protect minorities from hate talk, could have turned the Scottish society into a paranoid sadomasochistic fragmented totalitarian community. Journalists, artists, and academics would be held accountable for what they say, write and produce. Critics argued that "the bill could lead to author J. K. Rowling facing a seven-year prison sentence for expressing her concerns about the impact of trans rights on women."[549] The initial draft of the Hate Crime Bill was written in a vague language designed to sow fear and intimidate people into not speaking their mind or not discussing any controversial topic. Although it went through an extensive modification, the bill that was approved by the Scottish Parliament made the state a part in private conversations – which is a hallmark of failed autocratic states.[550] This law, passed in the motherland of David Hume and Adam Smith, is similar to the ones used in backward countries to suppress intellectuals and terrorise the general public. It is clear evidence of the deterioration of freedoms in a place that was once a beacon of science, philosophy, and freethinking. It is also a good example of the issues that are deemed vital in the 21st-century Scotland.

Over the ages, jihadists have used the freedoms in the Western societies as a weapon against these societies' values and people. Ayatollah

548 McLaughlin, M. (2020, Oct 28). Hate crime bill: Hate talk in homes 'must be prosecuted'. The Times.
549 BBC News. (2020, Dec 15). Why is Scotland's Hate Crime Bill so controversial?
550 Hate Crime and Public Order (Scotland) Act 2021. See also Hate Crime and Public Order (Scotland) Bill: Explanatory Notes, available on the Scottish Parliament Website. (SP Bill 67 introduced in the Scottish Parliament on 23 April 2020).

Khomeini was a political refugee in France in 1979. He took advantage of the laws that protect freedom of speech, liberties, minorities, and human rights, and the tolerance of the French society, to disseminate his malignant ideology. He preached his dangerous ideas which call for the killing of apostates and the rejection of freedoms and equality in that liberal country. Once in power, he ended the freedom of speech, human rights and liberties for the Iranians. He sponsored terrorism worldwide. He issued edicts sanctioning the killing of writers, political dissidents, and intellectuals. He ordered the execution of tens of thousands of innocent people. His mafia regime carried out terrorist attacks all over the world, in which many innocent people lost their lives. He assassinated several people inside France as well as across the world. In 1983, less than four years after the return of Khomeini from France, his followers carried out the Beirut barracks bombings, killing 241 American military personnel, 58 French soldiers and 6 civilians, and wounding more than 150 other individuals. These people were part of a United Nations peace-keeping force aimed to end the civil war.

The same applies to many of the current Iraqi politicians who had been living in Europe and the USA while Saddam was in power. They were allowed to freely propagate their jihadi ideas and create organizations based on exclusive sectarian identities. These organizations are currently in power suppressing Iraqis, banning all sorts of liberties.

It is not just politicians but also the masses who are stifling the freedom of expression. In Indonesia on 8 August 2020, a mob attacked a seventy-year-old Catholic man for criticizing Islam on his twitter account. The victim, Apollinaris Darmawan, was an ex-Muslim who had been freed from prison in March 2020 after serving four years for criticising Islam. The raging huge mob stormed the old man's house, viciously assaulted him, dragged him into the street, stripped him of his clothes completely and kept beating him. The police intervened afterward, arrested the old man, not his attackers, and put him in jail. They issued a statement assuring the public that they started collecting evidence to charge the man with blasphemy which is punishable by law in Indonesia. The man's crime was that he said: "Islam is not a religion but a heretical teaching that silences and uncivilizes [sic] its people."[551]

Thus, hundreds of Muslims went to his home to demonstrate that he was wrong and that Islam in fact makes its followers civilized.

In Nigeria, the predominantly Muslim regions were allowed to establish sharia as the rule of the land. This resulted in many Muslims being put on trial for offending Islam. In 2015, one of the Islamic courts sentenced nine people to death for blasphemy.[552] On 10 August 2020, a Nigerian Muslim singer named Yahaya Sharif-Aminu was sentenced to death for insulting Mohammad. He was found guilty of blasphemy by the Islamic court for writing and circulating a song via WhatsApp that praised a Muslim imam in a way which elevated him above Muhammad, according to the court's sentence. An angry mob attacked Yahaya Sharif-Aminu's family home, burning it down. In September 2020, another Islamic court sentenced a 13-year-old boy to ten years in jail and forced him to carry out menial work while imprisoned for using "disparaging language against Allah" in a private conversation with a friend who then reported him.[553]

Many non-Muslim governments are censoring their citizens' rights to express their thoughts, if these are not acceptable by Muslims. On 12 August 2020, Indian police arrested an Indian man in Bangalore for writing a post on his personal Facebook page that contained what could be seen as an insult to Mohammad. A Muslim mob took to the streets, attacking the police and non-Muslims and setting properties on fire. The police intervened and arrested the man, not the violent mobsters.

In 2021, the United Kingdom submitted to a Muslim mob, again. A British teacher was suspended, left his home and went into hiding because he showed the Charlie Hebdo cartoons of Mohammad in a classroom in Batley Grammar School. Dozens of angry Muslims gathered outside the school to intimidate British society. One of the protesters, who was neither a student nor a parent of a student in the school, stated to the media: "This is a time when we can't stay quiet,

---

551 Epa, K. (2020, Aug 13). Police arrest elderly Indonesian Catholic for blasphemy. UCA News.
552 BBC News. (2015, Jun 26). Nigeria court in Kano sentences nine people to death for blasphemy.
553 van Eyssen, B. (2020, Sep 17). Nigeria: UNICEF criticizes boy's 10-year jailing for blasphemy. DW.

we need to stand up and let them know, the head teacher, the school and the governing body, that this is not something light. There is a line you can't cross."[554]

None of the protesters was arrested or questioned despite the fact that they closed the road and breached the peace. To the contrary, the head teacher Gary Kibble apologised "unequivocally", adding that the teacher had "given their most sincere apologies" and had been suspended pending an investigation. The teacher was cleared later of any wrongdoing as he was carrying out his duty, introducing students to different ideas and allowing them to debate and form their opinions.[555] He along with two other staff members who had been suspended refused to return to work over fears for their lives.

In 2018, Europe's Highest Human Rights Court upheld a verdict from 2011 by an Austrian court which convicted an Austrian woman of the crime of disparaging religious doctrine. According to the sentence, the woman committed an offence by describing the marriage between Mohammad and Aisha as "paedophilia".[556] As previously discussed, Mohammad was fifty-two and Aisha was six years old when he married her, and he consummated the marriage when she was nine years old, according to the original Islamic sources.[557] Muslims worldwide acknowledge this account as factual and hence, a source of legislation. They also acknowledge that the prophet had several other wives when he married Aisha. The person convicted in the trial had also said that Mohammad was a warlord, which is another accepted view of Mohammad by Muslim jurists, historians, and masses but not by the European court, apparently.

In April 2022 (during Ramadan), Muslims rioted in India, Sweden, Israel and Spain. In Sweden, they attacked the police and civilians, set police cars and a school on fire and vandalised public property in many cities. These organized riots were an objection to the burning of a copy

554 BBC News. (2021, Mar 25). Prophet Muhammad cartoon sparks Batley Grammar School protest.

555 Sky News. (2021, May 27). Batley Grammar School: Teacher suspended over Prophet Mohammed image row can return to classroom.

556 Global Freedom of Expression. (2018, Oct 25). E.S. v. Austria. Case number: App. No. 38450/12. Columbia University website.

557 Sahih al-Bukhari 3894, 3896, 5133, 5134, 5158.; Sahih Muslim 1422.

of the Quran by a group led by Rasmus Paludan, a Danish-Swedish politician who claims that Muslim immigrants are violent and that they have turned parts of Sweden into no-go zones. The rioters overwhelmed the police and forced them to flee from the centres of several cities. Sweden's National Police Commander Jonas Hysing said that 26 policemen and 14 civilians had been injured. He also highlighted that many criminals known to the police participated in the riots. The main target for the rioters was the Swedish police and society, and some of the rioters attempted to murder police officers, Hysing confirmed in a press conference.[558] The same people who had been welcomed into Sweden as refugees a few years before and given homes and generous handouts were shouting "Allah Akbar" while spreading mayhem across the country. In news reports, the Muslim rioters were presented as "people", "protesters", "counter-protesters". Their Islamic identity and their motives were completely obscured.

Muslim countries condemned Sweden for allowing the burning of the Quran but they did not utter a word of criticism against the aggressors. For instance, Turkey's foreign ministry denounced Sweden for "hesitation to prevent provocative and Islamophobic acts… under the cover of freedom of expression". Iran's foreign ministry's spokesperson stated that: "Iran strongly condemns the burning of a copy of the holy Quran in the Swedish city of Linköping by a Danish racist extremist element which was done under the protection of the Swedish police under the pretext of freedom of speech." Iraq's foreign ministry announced that it summoned the Swedish ambassador to warn that allowing the burning of the Quran had "serious repercussions" for "relations between Sweden and Muslims in general, Muslim and Arab countries, and Muslim communities in Europe".[559] Through allocating the blame to the Swedes, these countries condoned the Muslims' attacks.

In the same week and this time in Israel, mobs of Muslims started a riot in Jerusalem during the Jewish holiday of Passover. On 21 April,

---

558 Voice of America News. (2022, Apr 18). Sweden Links Riots to Criminal Gangs That Target Police.
559 Al Jazeera. (2022, Apr 19). Sweden riots over Quran burning: What is happening?; BBC News. (2022, Apr 19). Dozens arrested at Sweden riots sparked by planned Quran burnings.

they attacked the police and Jewish civilians in order to prevent the Jews from celebrating. Clashes erupted when crowds of Muslims stationed in Al-Aqsa used fireworks, stones, sticks and other objects to attack the policemen who were near the site. The Arab league convened an urgent meeting and issued a statement supporting the Palestinian rioters and condemning Israel. They warned that allowing non-Muslims to pray in east Jerusalem "threaten[s] to ignite a cycle of violence and pose[s] a menacing threat to security and stability in the region and the world."[560]

In Spain, Muslim immigrants attacked a Holy Week procession, pelting Christians with rocks and projectiles to prevent them from practicing their religion in public.[561] Similarly in India, thousands of Muslims, many of them armed with swords, took to the streets assailing non-Muslims and vandalising public and private property to prevent the Hindus from celebrating Shubha Yatra. It first started when Muslims stationed in a mosque in Delhi attacked a Hindu procession. One of the Hindu eyewitnesses described what happened to the BBC: "We were unarmed and not in a mood to fight. It felt like a shower of stones and glass shards hit us." Another witness said that "the attack was planned. We were surrounded and attacked with stones, swords and knives."[562] Several Muslim states condemned India for what they described as Hindu aggression against Muslims. The Islamic motives of the attackers were never highlighted by the media, neither was the reaction of the Muslim countries. The mobs in the four countries were following the teachings of Islam.

Whether it is suppressing all other religions as they are offensive to Allah or donning the hijab, if a person accepts one Islamic rule, he or she needs to be ready to accept them all.

560 Al Jazeera. (2022, Apr 21). Arab League urges Israel to stop Jewish prayers at Al-Aqsa Mosque Arab League: 'Al-Aqsa and Haram al Sharif in all its area is a sole place of worship for Muslims.'
561 Miami Standard News. (2022, Apr 18). Muslim Youths Attack Easter Week Processions in Spain – Pelt Christians with Rocks and Projectiles – Police Called In (Video).
562 BBC News. (2022, Apr 18). Jahangirpuri: Shock and anger in Delhi after religious violence.

VICTIMHOOD

Ideologies which seek to dominate the world tend to cast their followers as superior people and victims simultaneously. In the Nazi ideology, the Aryan race was presented as superior, yet oppressed by inferior immoral groups. The enemies were constructed as subhuman and evil by nature. Hence, violence was warranted by being introduced as a necessary means to protect the good from the evil. It could be perceived as a benevolent act, as its ends are justified.[563]

In Islam, Muslims are constructed as the victims of the evil, ungrateful disbelievers who intentionally rejected their creator. Jews, Polytheists, Christians, Buddhists, Hindus, Atheists, and heretics were presented as evil enemies harming Muslims by their sheer existence. This portraying of Muslims as victims has been a hallmark of Islamic mindset throughout its long history. It has been employed to justify terrorism, slavery, corruption, Islamic conquests, and all other wrongdoings committed by Muslims over the ages. Muslims were suppressed in Mecca, that is why Allah allowed them to attack caravans and all the cities and towns of Arabia, according to the Islamic rationale. Muslims wanted to spread Islam, that is why it was their duty to invade other countries, kill the men and enslave women and children. Muslims are the only virtuous humans; this is why they must dominate the rest of humanity.

Nowadays, Muslims accuse the Chinese of suppressing the Muslim Uyghurs and occupying Muslim lands. They denounce the Israelis and accuse them of suppressing Muslims and stealing their territories. The Europeans are accused of mistreating Muslim minorities and being enemies of Islam, and of taking over Spain, Greece, Hungary and Bulgaria which used to be part of the Muslim world. The Americans have

---

563 See for comparison Zur, O. (2005). The psychology of victimhood. In R. H. Wright & N. A. Cummings (Eds.). Destructive trends in mental health. Routledge, pp 45-64.; Vollhardt, J. (2020). The social psychology of collective victimhood. Oxford University Press.

been pronounced enemies for attacking and killing Muslims, Indians for illegally occupying the Muslim lands in Kashmir and suppressing Indian Muslims, Africans for rejecting Islam and oppressing Muslim minorities, and Russians for killing Muslims and occupying their lands. At the exact same time, Muslims are convinced that they are superior to all these nations and their beliefs. All the problems of Muslims come from the non-Muslims, they assure.

In the past 50 years, Islamic organisations and media outlets financed by oil-rich regimes with the accomplice of their Western allies have succeeded in creating the dominant discourse that constructs Muslims as the innocent victims who contributed to science and philosophy, and the rest of humanity as criminals. The vast majority of Muslims have been brainwashed to believe that there was no Jewish presence in Palestine before the 20th century. The fact that Arabs and Muslims banished more than a million Jews from their homelands and seized their properties in the 20th century is never mentioned. The suppression and cleansing of millions of Iraqi, Egyptian, Syrian, Lebanese Christians from their motherlands and the ransacking of their homes at the hands of Muslims is never brought up. Many people do not know or are unwilling to recognize that Baghdad, Damascus, Casablanca, Basra, Cairo, Alexandria, Jerusalem, and many more cities and towns had ancient significant Jewish and Christian populations and that these people represented the successful manufacturers and merchants of these cities up until the second half of the 20th century. The atrocities committed against them as well as all other non-Muslim communities are kept out of the public discussion by a warped narrative propagated by paid thinkers.

Recently, Western countries have been vilified as imperial powers who toppled national regimes in the Muslim world; they have been accused of occupying Muslim lands and interfering in their internal affairs. For instance, the United States has been condemned for invading Iraq by both the devoted Muslims as well as many liberals calling it falsely an attack on a sovereign country. They conceal the fact that the Iraqis had been begging the USA to liberate them from Saddam and his criminal regime for decades beforehand. In fact, in March of 1991 both the Shia and the Kurds, who represented more than 85% of the Iraqis, revolted against the Sunni-led regime and took over 15 out of the 18 provinces of Iraq. The Arab Sunni regimes pressured the USA not to help the revolting people out of fear that toppling Saddam's Sunni regime would install Shias and Kurds in power. Saddam was allowed to use his heavy artillery and helicopters against the Iraqis. After he crushed the uprising, thousands of civilians were picked up from the streets and their homes; many were executed in public without a trial. Tens of thousands of people disappeared. Their bodies were found after 2003 in over two hundred mass graves that covered Iraq from north to south. The international community stood idly by, watching this crime against humanity unfold.

People who claim to be ethical denounce the American invasion of Iraq which ended Saddam's atrocities against defenceless humans who were calling for help, but they never utter a word against him or his allies. In Syria, the West is denounced by Muslims and their liberal allies for not intervening militarily on the side of the Sunni Islamists who sought to topple the Syrian regime. Had they interfered, they would have been denounced as invaders. Bombarding ISIS in Syria and Iraq is also considered a crime by many Muslims, among them the killer of the British MP David Amess, Ali Harbi Ali.

In contrast, the American invasion of Kuwait has not been a subject for debate or a cause to denounce the United States; Kuwaitis celebrate their liberation at the hands of the Americans from their fellow Muslims and approve of the American army stationing in their land. Loud liberals and their Muslim allies would never dare to offend the Kuwaitis.

Muslims calling upon non-Muslim powers to help them against other Muslims is not a new phenomenon. Before the First World War, the Arab masses and their senior leaders agreed with the British and the French that they join them against the Ottoman Caliphate. Thousands of Arab soldiers fought with the Allies against the Ottomans in Arabia, Kuwait, Syria, and Jordan. They celebrated the arrival of the Allies to end the Islamic caliphate. These facts are concealed to construct the non-Muslims as the villains and Muslim tyrants as victims.

Islamic terrorist organizations and regimes which have conducted numerous genocides, promising to rule the whole world by violence and to destroy every non-Muslim country, still complain that they are the victims. Muslims who illegally cross the borders into non-Muslim countries complain loudly about Islamophobia, prejudice, discrimination and suppression they suffer because of their religion. Better yet, the Muslim refugees who are asking for free shelter and hand-outs claim to be superior to the people helping them and demand to be treated as such. A Syrian refugee who illegally crossed into Germany said in a filmed interview that he thought Allah had sent him and the other Muslim refugees to guide the Germans to the true religion.

20 The Arab and Middle Eastern Intelligentsia versus Islam

THE MYTH OF ISLAMIC GOLDEN AGE AND THE GREAT "MUSLIM" SCHOLARS

The great philosophers and scientists who dedicated their lives to science, who stood up to Islam and paid a dear price for rejecting its teachings and discrediting its founders are currently introduced as Muslim scholars. The BBC's "Science and Islam" documentary presented by Jim Al-Khalili, "The Story of God with Morgan Freeman," Sigrid Hunke's "Allah's Sun over the Occident" and numerous other documentaries, articles, books about 'Islamic philosophy', 'Islamic civilization', and 'Islamic science' are a blatant betrayal of these medieval intellectuals. The same individuals who were declared heads of infidelity, apostates and enemies of Islam by the Islamic authorities and the most senior Islamic jurists of their times and considered as such to this day, have been converted to Islam hundreds of years after their death by people who either did not read their works or attempted to use them as means to deceive us through fabricating history.

In the widely available film "Science and Islam," the British professor of physics, who works at Sussex University stated shamelessly that Islam encouraged science. He said that Mohammad had encouraged his followers to "seek knowledge (ulem) even in China." He failed to highlight that this saying attributed to Mohammad is considered a forgery by the senior Muslim jurists and masses. The British/Iraqi professor, who claims to be a descendant of Mohammad, also failed to mention that knowledge – ulem – in Islam denotes exclusively the Islamic narratives, not the empirical science nor philosophy. Most importantly, if Mohammad had indeed encouraged his followers to seek knowledge, where is the tangible evidence for that?

Mohammad had never been interested in science, math, literature, art, or philosophy according to the original Islamic books. He did not establish a school or encourage his followers to study anything but his sayings and the revelations he dictated to them. Mohammad was illiterate or semi-literate at best, according to Islamic tradition. Allah told Mohammad: "Neither did you read any book before it, nor did you write any book with your right hand."[564] Furthermore, Mohammad told his followers: "We are an illiterate nation; we neither write nor know accounts."[565]

The prophet of Islam did not leave one written manuscript; he left no library, no school, no monument, no invention, no painting, no music, and definitely no science. He did not even write down the revelations he received in one volume. This despite being an absolute ruler for ten years in a region that had had libraries, schools, art, and monuments for ages before his birth.

He killed the most prominent scholars of his time and destroyed their work; his soldiers destroyed the schools and libraries of the Old World's great civilizations. Hardly any Arabic, Aramaic or Persian literature has survived the Islamic conquest. According to Muslim historians, Mohammad's father-in-law and second successor Omar ordered the burning of the great library of Alexandria, saying "if it contains what is compatible with the Quran, then it is superfluous, and if it contains what differs, then we do not need it. The word of God is sufficient." Muslim scholars perpetuate the destruction of the library at the hands of Muslims as a fact. This saying has been propagated over the centuries to highlight the superiority of the Quran to man-made science, literature and philosophy. This story belongs to the canon I vividly remember having been taught at school.

Islam cleansed the Arabian Peninsula of science, music, literature to rule unchallenged.[566] The Arab scholar Ibn Khaldun lamented that the Arab invaders were never involved in creating knowledge and did not contribute to it in any significant matter. He assured that they

---

564 Quran 29:48.
565 al-Bukhari 1913.
566 See Hoyland, R. G. (2019). Seeing Islam as others saw it. Gorgias Press.; The history of Al-Tabarī, Vol. 1-40.; Fernández-Morera, D. (2016). The Myth of the Andalusian Paradise.

savagely destroyed the existent civilizations. He also highlighted that the philosophers and scientists who emerged within the Muslim world were not Arabs.[567]

Scholars currently introduced as Arab Muslims were, indeed, not Arab nor Muslims. They were the descendants of the conquered nations who attempted to preserve their heritage. The great independent thinkers were definitely following in their ancestors' footsteps in pursuing science, music, art, and philosophy in spite of Islam, not because of it.[568] The caliph who embraced science and philosophy was Al-Mamun, a son of a Persian slave-girl, and he was not a Muslim by any standard. He was in conflict with Muslims and Islam throughout his reign and used his authority to suppress them. He was considered an infidel and an enemy of Islam by the senior Islamic jurists of his time and has been called so up to this day. He was the one who established the Wisdom House and hired non-Muslim thinkers, most of whom were Christians and Jews, to translate and disseminate the Greek and Roman scholarly work. This took place 200 years after the death of Mohammad. This project, which was fiercely opposed by the jurists and masses, is what paved the way for a limited number of thinkers to contribute to philosophy and science. Al-Mamun had never concealed his animosity toward Islam and Muslim scholars. He jailed and tortured the most important Islamic jurist of all times, Ahmad ibn Hanbal, whose ideas are currently followed by many millions of Muslims. He also suppressed all the other jurists who followed the Quran and the hadith. Another rarely mentioned fact is that the entire project was destroyed after the deaths of this infidel caliph and his brother who had continued the endeavour, as the successors went back to the Islamic rule.

Dr Amira Bennison, a professor at the University of Cambridge, said in the same BBC documentary that "the dramatic successes of the Arabs as they poured out of Arabia were such that a lot of people did sort of observe and say, they must have God on their side, this must be the true God. Some people did convert, or if they didn't convert, they did

567 Khaldun, I. (2012). The Muqaddimah. Lebanon.
568 See Crone, P. (2016). Islam, the Ancient Near East and Varieties of Godlessness: Collected Studies in Three Volumes, Volume 3. Brill.

submit to Arab Muslim political control for that reason." This baseless idea that contradicts both historical accounts and logic propagated by a Cambridge University professor and broadcast on a national British TV, without objection whatsoever, is a clear sign of the crisis of Western societies. This is similar to saying that due to the victories of ISIS or Taliban many victims thought that God was on the invaders' side and they converted to Islam. In reality, some people did convert to Islam in the areas conquered by ISIS in Syria and Iraq in 2016 for different reasons: some to save their lives, and some to steal and rape with impunity, but not because they thought God was with the Muslim mass-murderers and rapists. No sane let alone moral human can explain a victory of merciless fighters as a sign that their God is the true God. Otherwise, God would have been on the side of Hitler, Stalin, Genghis Khan, and the countless ruthless dictators who all claimed to be right, and the masses of victims would have joined their ideologies willingly.

In fact, Muslim historians have shown in detail that the conquered people detested Islam and its cruel followers; the majority preferred paying the heavy ransom called jizyah and being treated as second-class citizens rather than converting. It is reported that an old woman in Samarkand asked the Muslim soldiers who had just conquered her town, who sent them to her land. 'Allah', the soldiers replied. 'I did not know that Allah has thieves', the woman responded.[569] Significant portions of the populations of Baghdad, Damascus, Jerusalem, Alexandria, Cairo, Isfahan, Shiraz, and many more ancient cities remained non-Muslim up until the 20th century when many of the non-Muslims were killed or displaced. The French, the Spanish, the Italian, the Greek, the Serbs, the Indian, and other nations resisted Muslims' rule for centuries and liberated their lands through bloody conflicts. More are yet to follow.

When it comes to discussing the medieval scholars, the so-called radical Muslims have proven to be far more honest, knowledgeable, accurate and rational than the self-styled liberal intellectuals and moderate scholars. To this day, senior imams consider, and rightly so, all the important philosophers and scientists who lived in the Muslim-dominated

---

569 Jabran, A. (2012). Lusus Allah: Inqdh alyutbya al-Islamiyah. [The Thieves of Allah, rescue of the Islamic utopia]. (Arabic). Dar Al-Jawahri.

countries during the Middle Ages infidels or apostates who rejected Islam and fought against it. They show the original writings of these philosophers, highlighting the explicit rejection of Allah, his messenger, and the tenets of Islam that they contain, to prove their views. They emphasise the fact that there is not a single endorsement for the Quran, hadith, Mohammad, or sharia in any of their writings.[570]

Influential Muslim jurists have declared over the ages that philosophy, literature, music, art, and science were never part of Islam and they would never be. In fact, they are the antidote.

570 See Al-Ghazzali, S. A. (1963). Tahafut Al-Falasifah [The Incoherence of the Philosophers]. Pakistan Philosophical Congress.; al-Jawziyya, Ibn al-Qayyim. (1985). Al-Sawa'iq al-Mursalah 'alal Jahmiyyah-wal-Mu'attilah [The thunderbolts sent on Jahmiyah and Muatelah]. (Arabic). Riyadh: Dar Al-Asimah.

The greatest medieval physician and one of the most influential Middle Eastern philosophers of all times is without doubt Abu-Baker Al-Razi (854-925). The biography of this thinker is a clear proof of the boundless animosity between Islam and science on the one hand, and the hypocrisy of many modern academics on the other hand. This independent scholar was a Persian, not an Arab, and was born and lived most of his life in his native Iran, which had fallen to the Arab invading armies and had been liberated by its people several times before his birth. By the time of his death and for centuries afterward, most of his people were still non-Muslims and they continued revolting against the Muslim rule.[571]

One of the greatest minds that walked this Earth, he contributed to the advancement of medicine, chemistry, and philosophy. He revitalised the Greek tradition and considered himself a pupil of the great philosophers. He was a musician and an independent thinker distancing himself from the authority. The feebleness of Islamic authority, raging armed civil conflicts, and the people's admiration for his philanthropic work as a physician as well as the fact that his homeland was not fully Arabized at his time is what saved him from the sharia's sword. He was a kind and caring physician, treating the impoverished for free, teaching medicine and philosophy while freely speaking his mind. Al-Razi rejected the whole idea of prophetic mission – the foundation of Islam. He discarded Mohammad, contending that he was a "charlatan" and a "mentally sick" person. He stated that Mohammad had not performed any miracle to support his grand claims. He found the idea of the Quran being a divine miracle irrational. When challenged to present something similar to the Quran, he said:

---

571 Houtsma, M. Th., and others. (Eds.). (1913–1936). First Encyclopaedia of Islam (9 vols). E. J. Brill, p 100.

If you meant something like it according to the aspects by which one discourse is superior to another, we should produce for you from the words of the eloquent, the literary, and those skilled in rhyme and poetry, a thousand like it, more articulate than it in terms of phrasing, more succinct, elaborate in rhyme. If these do not meet your approval, then we would demand of you an example of what you want.[572]

Al-Razi wrote three books dedicated to discrediting Islam and to contesting its canons: The Prophets' Fraudulent Tricks, The Stratagems of Those Who Claim to Be Prophets, and On the Refutation of Revealed Religions. They were all destroyed by the Islamic authorities. All what has survived are segments from these books quoted in books of his opponents contemporary to him. In the surviving extracts, Al-Razi rejects the idea that God would single out an individual to be his messenger to the rest of mankind (i.e. Mohammad). He argues that God must have created people equal and should treat them equally, if he is just. He should communicate with all humans in the same manner rather than choosing one person and ignoring the rest of humanity. The Persian thinker describes the Quran as a book that "does not reveal anything concealed." He ridicules Muslims' defence of Quran through comparing their arguments to sounds of goats, loud and devoid of substance. He assures that if a book can be an eternal miracle, that could be "books of geometry… or books on logic and the books on medicine in which there is science of the care of the bodies." He argues that since God has endowed people with minds, there is no need to send someone to guide us, the brain is sufficient. He also contends that many of the teachings of Islam contradict both nature and science. Thus, they are unfit to be followed. He states that religious students are brainwashed by the authority figures who themselves are mere charlatans:

> As a result of their being long accustomed to their religious denomination, as days passed and it became a habit. Because they were deluded

572 As quoted in Butterworth, C. (Ed.). (1992). The Political Aspects of Islamic Philosophy: Essays in Honor of Muhsin S. Mahdi. Harvard University Press, p.87. See also Hecht, J. M. (2004). Doubt: A History: The Great Doubters and Their Legacy of Innovation from Socrates and Jesus to Thomas Jefferson and Emily Dickinson.

by the beards of the goats, who sit in ranks in their councils, straining their throats in recounting lies, senseless myths and 'so-and-so told us in the name of so-and-so...'[573]

This philosopher suffered terribly for his intellectual integrity. His books were destroyed; he was persecuted and to this day he is deeply despised by devoted Muslims.

Avicenna or Ibn Sina (980-1037) is another great philosopher like Al-Razi fraudulently portrayed as an Arab Muslim scientist while he was neither Arab nor Muslim.[574] His ancestors were Persians who converted to Ismailism, a sect considered heretical by the vast majority of Muslims to this day. Avicenna is the "imam of Atheists" and a "role model for the renouncers and disbelievers", according to Ibn Qayyim (d. 1350), one of the most influential Islamic jurists of all times.[575] The former head of Saudi Arabia's Supreme Court of Justice and the senior jurist Saleh Al-Fawzan affirmed that Avicenna is an atheist philosopher who rejected Islam. Al-Fawzan, who is also a member in the Council of Senior Scholars, Saudi Arabia's supreme Islamic institution, ruled that any Muslim who praises Avicenna is either an ignorant who does not know that the physician was an infidel and hence must not discuss such matters, or an infidel himself.[576]

Avicenna explicitly refused all the principles of Islam. He rebuffed the idea of a personal God and rejected Mohammad as the messenger of Allah to humanity. Although it seems that he might have been a deist, or that he was not as fearless as Al-Razi or his situation was more restrictive than Al-Razi's, nevertheless, he did not condone any of the fundamental Islamic beliefs. He considered the revelations mere hallucinations. He favoured philosophy and science to Islam. He believed that the world was ancient and not created by a deity. He was persecuted and incarcerated

---

573 Hecht, J. M. (2004). Doubt: A History: The Great Doubters and Their Legacy of Innovation from Socrates and Jesus to Thomas Jefferson and Emily Dickinson.
574 As above.
575 al-Jawziyya, Ibn al-Qayyim (d. 1350). (1975). Ighathatu lahfaan min masaa'id ash-shaytan [The Aid of the Yearning from the Devil's Traps]. (Arabic). Dar Al Maaref.
576 Al-Fawzan, Saleh. (2003/1424 AH). The abrogated commentary on the Noneyah poem. Part 3, p.1328. Dar Alfurqan.

repeatedly for being a freethinker and for his animosity toward Islam. The prominent Islamic jurist ibn Taymiyyah assured that Avicenna, like Al-Razi, was an atheist who at best would accept some heretical Islamic ideas. He affirmed, correctly so, that the great philosopher had categorically rejected Mohammad and Islam.

The third giant of the Middle Ages who adamantly opposed Islam throughout his life and currently is being introduced as a Muslim is Al-Farabi (872-950). This Turkish or Persian student of logic who translated and disseminated Greek philosophy stated in the clearest language that he favoured philosophy to the teachings of Islam. He argued against all the fundamental Islamic beliefs, stating that Allah did not know everything, he had not created the world, and religions were manmade ideologies by rulers to control their subjects.[577] Throughout his prolific writings, he had never mentioned the Quran, Mohammad, or the Islamic teachings in any flattering way, despite living under Islamic regime. He was deemed a disbeliever and an enemy of Allah by the senior Muslim jurists of his time and endured much suffering for his ideas.

When discussing Averroes (Ibn Rushd, 1126-1198), many contemporary scholars fail to highlight the Islamic inquisition he had been subjected to. They do not inform their audience that he was indicted for heresy by an Islamic court and was banished from his hometown, and his books were burnt. Like all the other scholars, he was a student of Greek philosophy and was not an Arab.

Al-Khwarizimi (Algorithmi), who contributed to mathematics and is considered one of the founders of algebra as well as astronomy, was a Zoroastrian Persian scientist, not an Arab nor a Muslim. This man, who coined the term algebra and who studied the Greek, Roman, and Indian ideas and added to them, is being introduced as an Arab and Muslim in complete disregard to the facts and ethics. He lived in his home country as well as Baghdad and both places were inhabited by Christians, Zoroastrians, and Jews; his teachers were non-Muslims, and it was the Europeans who appreciated his ideas. Ibn Taymiyyah confirmed that Al-Khwarizimi was not a Muslim and not needed by Muslims.

---

577 Al-Farabi, Abu Nasr. (1991). Kitab Almilat wa Nousos Ukhrah [The religion and other texts]. (Arabic). Ed. Mohsen Mahdi. Dar Al-Mushreq.

Al-Kindi, who was a devoted student and an avid translator of Greek philosophy, is also falsely presented as a Muslim scholar. He flourished during the reign of al-Mamun and was suppressed once religious caliphs took power and reinstated sharia. This intellectual, who contributed to music, physics, and science, was tortured and died alone after being convicted of striving against the last revelation. He had never sponsored any of the main Islamic ideas. Ibn Qayyim wrote that Al-Farabi, Avicenna, Nasir al-din al-Tusi, and the other philosophers had all rejected Islam and they were all infidels.[578]

---

578 al-Jawziyya, Ibn al-Qayyim (1975). Ighathatu lahfaan min masaa'id ash-shaytan [The Aid of the Yearning from the Devil's Traps]. (Arabic).

A POET,
A NOVELIST,
AND THE SATIRIST IMAM OF DISBELIEVERS

It is unjust to speak about Middle Eastern medieval scholars without discussing Ibn al-Rawandi, Ibn-Almuqaffa, and al-Ma'arri, as they are among the greatest Middle Eastern thinkers of all times.

Ibn al-Rawandi is the bravest intellectual critic of Islam throughout the ages, as many argue. He was a Persian whose parents were Jewish. It is reported that when some Jews learned that he had become a Muslim, they were delighted because they predicted that he was going to confront Islam the same way his father had done with Judaism. There is a dispute regarding the exact dates of his birth and death. Most resources indicate that he lived in the ninth century. He studied Islam thoroughly, moving between the different Islamic schools of thought and studying under the prominent scholars of his time. He was constantly searching for the true Islam. Every time he joined a sect, he would meticulously examine its ideas before rejecting it, showing its shortcomings. He was commissioned by members of one of the Islamic sects to write a book that would support their sect's main positions and debunk the arguments of another sect, with which they were in conflict. He did write the book and took 400 dirhams as his fees. Later on, he told the ones who commissioned him that they needed to pay him another 400 dirhams if they did not want him to write a book debunking his own earlier book which he had written for them. They did, and he kept his promise.[579]

After years of studying Islam and being a prominent thinker of different sects and schools, Ibn al-Rawandi refused this religion as a whole and became a fierce critic of its foundation and of its followers' mentality. He wrote several books that disclosed and contested Islam's underpinning

---

579 Ibn al-Khayyat, A. (1925/1992). Al-Intisar, Wa Alrad Ala Ibn-Alrawandi Almulhid [The Victory and the reply to Ibn-Alrawandi the atheist]. Al-Dar Al-Arabiya llkitab/ Awraq Sharqis.

ideas, highlighting its deficiencies with logic and satire. He has been considered the imam of disbelievers.

All of the many books he had written were destroyed. The only segments and quotes that have survived are those written in the books of his contemporaries who were his opponents. His most important manuscript was The Book of Emerald, which was written in the form of a dialogue between him and his mentor Al-Warraq. It survived the Muslim inferno only in some detailed descriptions and quotes in his rivals' volumes.[580] He named the book Emerald, hinting at an ancient myth that snakes are afraid of the precious stone – snakes being the Muslim theologians, and his book a talisman against their poison. In it, the two scholars argued that people did not need a divine revelation to know right from wrong. They did not need revelations to live their lives, to build the necessary instruments and to observe and understand nature.[581] Al-Warraq argued that people had learned how to create lutes and to play them through observing that a stretched, dried sheep's intestine attached to a piece of wood produced beautiful sounds when pounded upon. People created science that immensely improved their lives, without any divine guidance. Thus, people could understand themselves and the world through observation, study, and through trial and error, not through illogical tales that had no substance.[582]

Ibn al-Rawandi criticised Quranic passages in a sarcastic style. He pointed out that the angels sent by Allah to support Muslims in Badr were feeble, as they along with the Muslims could not kill more than seventy men, most of whom were old. He questioned where the angels and Allah were during the battle of Uhud, in which the believers were defeated at the hands of Polytheists. He also said that Allah had no means of accomplishing anything but murder, as if he was a vengeful nemesis of the humankind.[583] A god who inflicts illness upon his subjects cannot be counted as one who treats them wisely, "nor can he

---

580 As above.
581 Hecht, J. M. (2004). Doubt: A History: The Great Doubters and Their Legacy of Innovation from Socrates and Jesus to Thomas Jefferson and Emily Dickinson.
582 As above.
583 Ibn al-Khayyat, A. (1925/1992). Al-Intisar, Wa Alrad Ala Ibn-Alrawandi Almulhid [The Victory and the reply to Ibn-Alrawandi the atheist]. Al-Dar Al-Arabiya llkitab/ Awraq Sharqia.

be said to be looking after them or to be compassionate toward them. The same is true concerning he who inflicts upon them poverty and misery. Also, who punishes the disobedient by eternal fire is a fool." He thought that the afterlife described in the Quran as the reward for the believers was appalling rather than appealing. The idea of many virgin slave-girls does not interest any self-respecting rational person, neither do the notions of numerous white young boys, he reasoned. He explained that the idea of food and drink in abundance described in Quran as an incentive for the believers was the product of a poor, primitive nomads' imagination.

He exposed many discrepancies in the Quran, concluding that this book was poorly written and lacked substance. "The Quran is the speech of an unwise being, and that it contains contradictions, errors and absurdities." How would Allah say in a verse that he knows everything and say in another that the whole life is a constant test for people so that he could know who is good and who is evil? Does he know or he does not? If he does know, why bother with all this nonsense – if he does not, why would he describe himself as all-knowing?

Ibn Al-Rawandi ridiculed the Quranic notion of rivers of honey, milk and alcohol being heavenly rewards, as he said that no one fancied honey or milk except famished people, and he asked why people needed a river of alcohol. He ridiculed the idea that in heaven men would wear bracelets made of gold, saying this would make them look like gypsies' brides. He concluded that all the ideas and descriptions of heaven and hell were the creation of a simple, uncultured, primitive mind. Ibn al-Rawandi "disputed the reality of the miracles of Abraham, Moses, Jesus and Muhammad and claimed that they were fraudulent tricks and that the people who performed them were magicians and liars." He mocked the rituals of the hajj, assuring that no good would ever come from walking in circles around a bunch of stones. He also wondered why Kaaba was more important than any other building. In his part, Al-Warraq described Allah as a fool, saying: "He who orders his slave to do things that he knows him to be incapable of doing, then punishes him, is a fool."[584]

---

584 As above.

Muslim mobs, after learning what Ibn Al-Rawandi and his friend Al-Warraq had written, went in pursuit of them, but the two fled and stayed in hiding for some time. Al-Warraq was captured and thrown in jail until his death. It is reported that Al-Rawandi managed to hide in a Jewish man's house where he died at the age of 36 or 40.[585] He might have been killed by an angry mob or executed by the authorities – we would never know, but his legacy is still alive.

The creator of the first known Arabic literary masterpiece, Ibn-Al-muqaffa, is currently introduced as a Muslim intellectual, despite the fact that he lost his life in the most gruesome of ways at the hands of Muslims for being an infidel. He was indicted for heresy and the Islamic authority burned him alive in 759. They had his flesh cut off slowly and burned it in front of his eyes before they sat him on fire in public. This Persian Zoroastrian man who converted to Islam at an old age was the translator of the beautiful Indian animal fables "Panchatantra" from Persian to Arabic. He also wrote several important manuscripts that encouraged critical thinking and logic.[586] He argued that the old civilizations were superior to the Islamic systems. Through his writings, he highlighted various philosophical questions and attempted to answer them based on logic and evidence while rejecting Quran and hadith implicitly.

The last but by no means least of the great independent thinkers of the Middle Ages who confronted the Islamic ideology I wish to discuss is Abu'l-Ala Al-Ma'arri.

Abu'l-Ala is a poet many centuries ahead of his time
Abu'l-Ala is Lucretius of Islam and Voltaire of the East[587]

This great poet and philosopher had shown immense integrity in disseminating sound reasoning against the religious mentality. He objected to the idea that Allah is fair, saying:

---

585 Ibn al-Khayyat, A. Al-Intisar.
586 Latham, J. D. (1990). Ibn al-Muqaffa' and Early 'Abbasid Prose. In J. Ashtiany and others. (Eds.). Abbasid Belles Lettres (The Cambridge History of Arabic Literature), pp 48-77.; Guidi, M. (Ed. & trans.). (1927). La Lotta tra l'Islam e il manicheismo: Un libro di Ibn al-Muqaffa' contro il Corano confutato da al-Qasim b. Ibrahim. (Italian). R. Accademia Nazionale dei Lincei.
587 Von Kremer quoted in Amen Rihani's translation of selected works of Abu'l-Ala Al-Ma'arri, (1920). The Luzumiyat of Abu'l-Ala. James T. White & Co.

If your fortunes are not given to the wise and you give insane and fool
Then it is not a fault of who sees what he doesn't like and disbelieve[588]

In another poem, he discussed how Islamic traditions were created:

O fools, awake the rites you hold as holy
Are cheat contrived by men of old
Who lusted after wealth and gained their lust
And died in baseness – and their law is dust.
'We have been told the truth';
And if they refused,
The sword was drenched in their blood[589]

He highlighted the stark discrepancies in sharia. In one example, he asked how hand amputation was the fair punishment for stealing half a dinar while the compensation for damaging a human's hand was 500 dinars. He repeatedly stated that the mind is the real prophet and that people are either wise and nonreligious or religious with no brain:

Hanifs[590] are erroneous, Christians are not guided
Jews are confused and Zoroastrians are misled
The people of the earth are one of two
An intellectual with no religion
And religious who has no brain[591]

Al-Ma'arri lived most of his life in solitude. He rejected Islam after gaining a thorough understanding of its ideas and became a student of philosophy and ancient Eastern schools of thought. He argued that the ideas of this religion were lies propagated initially through violence until they became a tradition. He even wrote a book in a style similar to the Quran as a challenge to the claim that the Quran was a miracle and superior to humans' talk, thus could not be replicated. He contended

588 Ibn Kathir, A. (1992). Vol 12., p 73.
589 Quoted in Hecht, J. M. (2004). Doubt: A History: The Great Doubters and Their Legacy of Innovation from Socrates and Jesus to Thomas Jefferson and Emily Dickinson.
590 This title denotes pure monotheism and is still used to describe Muslims.
591 Ibn Kathir, A. (1992). Vol 12., p 73. (Author's translation.)

that many people followed Islam due to the fact that Mohammad had spread his teachings through violence:

> Lo! There are many ways and many traps
> And many guides, which of them is lord?
> For verily Mohammad has the Sword,
> And may have the truth – perhaps! perhaps![592]

He ended his life when he was summoned to the governor to be questioned about his ideas. He did not want to be tortured or forced to give up his beliefs in exchange for his life.

I wish to highlight again that throughout the history of Islam intellectuals have stood up to its wrath, risking their own and their loved ones' lives. Many criticized the Quran and pointed out its illogical ideas while being aware that the authorities and the illiterate mob would use every means to silence them and hurt their families and friends. Several thinkers rejected the Shahada (testimony), which is the first pillar and a requirement of Islam, stating that it is an illogical and dishonest act. Forcing people to testify that "there is no god but Allah and Mohammad is the Messenger of Allah" to become Muslims contradicts ethics and reason. People should not attest to what they have not seen and cannot prove. Ingraining this testimony in children's minds is not logical nor ethical, they argued.

In conclusion, the philosophers and scholars currently being introduced as medieval Muslim thinkers had shown forceful antagonism toward Islam and a clear disregard of Mohammad and his teachings. None of them considered the Quran as a valid source of knowledge or ethics. They were all loyal students of ancient Greek philosophers, freethinking, and logic. They excelled in and advanced philosophy, music, literature, and science despite the fierce opposition of Muslims and Islamic teachings.

What is currently being promoted as the Islamic Golden Age is in fact a short era within the Abbasid Caliphate during which one of the caliphs limited the influence of Islam and Islamic jurisprudence on the

---

592 Al-Ma'arri, Abu'l-Ala. (2019). The Diwan of Abu'l-Ala. The Good Press.

public life. This allowed freethinking, music, art, and translations from the Greek and Roman philosophy, astronomy, mathematics, science and literature to flourish at the expense of religion. The figures who led and contributed to the progressive movements during that short era and afterward were non-Muslims and non-Arab. The renowned medieval philosophers, musicians, astronomers, and scientists who are currently introduced as Arab Muslims were – rightly – considered infidels and students of Polytheists, Christians and Jews by the Islamic jurists of their times and are seen as such to this day. All the great medieval scholars were persecuted by the Islamic authorities, jurists and masses for following logic and refusing to surrender to Islam. The Golden Age was secular, not Islamic.

ENDLESS INQUISITION:
FOURTEEN CENTURIES OF PERSECUTION

The contribution of Muslims to science, philosophy, art, and literature throughout the past 1400 years is insignificant in general and more so in comparison to their numbers, natural resources, and grandiose claims. The invading Arabs annexed the centres of the old world and exterminated numerous cultures and civilizations without substituting their intellectual products. No scholarly alternative arose in Muslim countries as freethinking was stifled. Science and scientists have been shunned, as the only true form of knowledge is the verses of the Quran and the sayings of Mohammad. Music is considered a major sin by the influential Islamic authorities, based on Quranic texts. Paintings and sculptures have been prohibited, based on original Islamic teachings. Nonetheless, many writers to this day refuse to acknowledge the fact that Mohammad and Islam's opposition to critical thinking, science, and philosophy have caused irreversible damage to civilization and stalled human progress for centuries.

Mohammad instructed his followers to believe that diseases come from Allah rather than to empirically search for their earthly causes. He deemed the idea of infection – known and valued in the Arabian Peninsula at his time – as false. His famous saying "there is no infection"[593] was the core idea of how devoted Muslims must understand illnesses. When he was challenged by a shepherd who told him that if one camel with scabies mixed with healthy ones, he would infect them all, Mohammad objected replying: "who infected the first one?"

Up until the 21st century, devoted Muslims would not accept that there are contagious diseases and thus they must avoid the areas affected by pandemics and isolate the infected people. In the Quran, Allah ordered

---

593 Sahih al-Bukhari 5776, 5316.; Sahih Muslim 2224.

Muslims to believe that: "Nothing shall ever happen to us except what Allah has ordained for us."[594] One of the incidents taught to Muslims to emphasise this notion is the story about a number of Mohammad's companions who refused to escape from the Plague of Amwas that inflicted Syria in 638-639. Thousands of the invading soldiers died in that plague because they refused to leave, believing that everything was predetermined.

The systematic destruction of schools and libraries in Northern Africa, Egypt, Levant, Mesopotamia, Persia, India, Andalusia, Greece, Anatolia, Bulgaria and all other Islamised countries was in most part the application of the idea that the Quran is the perfect book which contained all what humans needed and Mohammad was the perfect person who solved all the important questions.

The practice of hunting down and killing freethinkers, critics and scientists which started with the establishment of the first Islamic state by Mohammad and continued during the reign of his guided caliphs evolved into an authoritative official institution. During the Umayyad Caliphate, countless notable thinkers and reformists were killed, had their arms severed or were imprisoned after being charged with heresy. The influential thinker Ma'bad al-Juhani, who argued against predestination, supporting the notion of free will, was crucified by the orders of the caliph less than 70 years after the death of Mohammad. A few years after that, another caliph cut off the arms and legs of the renowned thinker Ghaylan al-Dimashqi before crucifying him for disseminating the same idea.

The Abbasid caliphs killed tens of thousands of people on the mere suspicion of them being heretics, freethinkers or apostates. They created an institution called "department of heresy/heretics" (Diwan al-Zanadiqa) to exterminate the theoretical opponents of Islam. This apparatus's responsibility was to hunt down every thinker who criticised Islam, rejected its teachings, attempted to reform its practice, or propagated a different ideology. Since most of the scholars were Persians, they were usually accused of hiding the beliefs of old Persian religions. For centuries, this organization was the Islamic thought police, court of law, and executioner all in one. Its main goal was to protect Islam from any

---

594 Quran 9:51, see Al-Hilali & Khan trans.

challenge through eliminating any person whose rationale differed from what was written in the Quran and Mohammad's talk. Thousands of poets, writers and intellectuals were killed, imprisoned and tortured after being classified as "zindiq".[595] The victims were never allowed to defend themselves; once this institution, the caliph, local governor or a jurist declared a person a zindiq, he would be beheaded, burned or crucified in public. After this institution ceased to exist, the Islamic judiciary, as well as the Muslim masses, took over its duties. To this day, Muslims do not tolerate any reasoning that is independent from Islam, let alone in opposition to it. Therefore, it is not a coincidence that Muslim countries are the least free and the most corrupt countries on Earth.

The number of "Muslim" Nobel laureates in science is three: one from Pakistan, an Egyptian, and a Turk. Abdus Salam, the one and only Pakistani who was awarded the Nobel Prize in any of the branches of science, belongs to the persecuted Ahmadi sect. This sect has been declared as heretics by the state of Pakistan – Abdus's country of birth, and by every other Muslim country. It is not just the governments – the vast majority of Sunni and Shia Muslims consider Ahmadis infidels, too. Hence, they are treated as criminals all over the Muslim world and are legally prosecuted under the laws of blasphemy, if they disclosed their beliefs. The man introduced as Pakistani Muslim Nobel Prize laureate lived and studied in Britain and married a British woman. In Britain, he was treated fairly and was allowed to be an important scientist – not in his native country. The other two individuals who are considered Muslim Nobel laureates are both American citizens, living in the USA, where they were educated, and married to Western women. Had they been living in their countries of origin, they would have been forced to alter their ways of living, and perhaps thinking, or face the wrath of the society. No Muslim have ever been awarded the Nobel Prize in economics, physiology or medicine.

The one and only Arab Nobel laureate in literature, Naguib Mahfouz, was stabbed with a knife in his neck several times in broad daylight in Cairo at the age of 82. The attack on his life was an implementation of several Islamic edicts (fatwas) that declared the old man an apostate and

---

595 The History of al-Ṭabarī, Vol. 29.

an enemy of Allah. The imams who issued these fatwas ruled based on the Quran and the hadith, and after reading his work, that every Muslim is obliged to kill Mahfouz. The thirteen attackers, who were members of the Islamic Group, stated in court that they carried out the assassination attempt against Mahfouz because he was a disbeliever (kafir). When the judge asked the man who stabbed the old writer how he knew that Mahfouz was an infidel, he replied: 'from his books.' 'Which one of his books?', the judge asked. 'I do not know, I did not read them, I do not know how to read or write, but several jurists have declared him an infidel based on his writings', the assassin stated.

Decades before the assassination attempt, the most influential Egyptian Sunni institution Al-Azhar persecuted him, banned several of his novels and declared him an apostate. Many Muslim countries have been banning his writings to date; they are considered blasphemous. When reading his novels, it is obvious that the man was against Islam.

His predecessors alike, the most important contemporary Arab poet, Nizar Qabbany, rejected and repeatedly ridiculed Islamic principles in his poems. He was considered an apostate by the Islamic institutions as well as the general public. Hence, when he died in his exile in London in 1998, Muslims abstained from attending his funeral. The most influential Kuwaiti poet of all times, Fahad Alaskar (died 1952), was also unyielding in his rejection of Islam, both in his poetry and his life. He led a solitary, short life in poverty and was persecuted by the authorities and the masses for his adamant anti-Islamic views. His family and the society excommunicated him and no one attended his funeral except for three expatriates, who most likely did not know him or his ideas.

The figurehead of what is called the Egyptian Renaissance, Taha Hussein, was persecuted by Al-Azhar and the masses over more than twenty years. He was prosecuted by the Egyptian general attorney for his writing and was dismissed from his job as a university professor. His books were banned and confiscated in Egypt as well as many other countries. He did subtly criticize the principles of Islam and attempted to question the factuality of the Quran: he said that we should not believe what is written in the Quran. This was enough to make him an enemy in the eyes of the Islamic institutions and the masses.

The one and only Turkish Noble Prize laureate in literature, Orhan Pamuk, has been prosecuted and indicted by the court of law, harassed by government and the Islamic authorities, and his books were burned in rallies for acknowledging the Armenian genocides.

Turan Dursun was a prominent imam who for years held the position of the Mufti of Siva. After gaining a deep understanding of Islam and reading about other religions and schools of thought, he renounced his religion and resigned from his lucrative public post. He chose to suffer financially, socially, and put his life at risk to remain loyal to his beliefs. He preferred to work as a garbage collector than to remain an influential mufti and preach what he saw as an unethical ideology. He stated that he did not want to be a hypocrite. After struggling for years, he worked for the Turkish radio and television corporation, first on an administrative post, then as a producer. He wrote several books and many articles with the focus on examining Islam and morality. He argued that Mohammad has ruined many people's lives, made them accept wrong as right and the other way around, and stalled the progress of humanity.[596] On 4 September 1990, the unarmed, unaware 56-year-old man was on his way from his home to work in Istanbul, when assassins shot him seven times. They were professional killers linked to the Iranian regime. The mastermind of the murder was arrested in 1996 and sentenced to life imprisonment but the gunman who carried out the killing is still at large.

In his youth, Abdullah al-Qasemi was one of the most notable Muslim scholars in Arabia. He studied Islam in different countries before settling in Al-Azhar to continue his religious education. There, he proved to have a deeper understanding of the religion than the renowned teachers and thus, he got into several theoretical battles with them and ended up writing books to disclose their shortcomings. He was expelled from Al-Azhar. Subsequently, he dedicated his life to studying and defending "the right Islam" as an independent scholar. He published several important books that discuss the pure teachings of Islam. After becoming a renowned religious authority, he rejected Islam altogether and wrote several shocking books that portrayed this religion as an evil regressive

---

596 Dursun, T. (1992). Hayatını anlatıyor. (Turkish). Kaynak Yayınları.

manmade ideology which is causing terrible suffering to humanity. He contended that the Islamic god is evil and mentally disturbed. He said that the notion of young boys (ghilman) as a reward in paradise is an insult to the Arabs because it suggests that they are attracted to boys. He described heaven as a ghastly place devoid of noble causes and centred on the fulfilment of animalistic instincts. He wondered how the prophets would enjoy lying in houris' beds while their parents are being tortured in hell. He was rejected by his society, banished from his country, suffered three assassination attempts and lived in poverty and solitude all his life. His books are still banned; printing or possessing them is punishable by heavy jail sentences in many countries.

21 Muslims in the Footsteps of Mohammad, from the Caves of Mecca to the Caves of Afghanistan

Slay the infidels wherever you find them[597]

For more than 1400 years, followers have been walking in the footsteps of their leader, repeating what he did with the Arabs, the Jewish, and other nations. One of the recent major recreations of the early Islamic genocides took place in Iraq and Syria a few years ago. When the fighters of ISIS stormed the towns of Yazidis and Christians in August of 2014, "men and women were separated immediately. Adolescent boys were told to lift up their shirts, and if they had armpit hair, they were directed to join their fathers and older brothers. In village after village, the men and older boys were driven or marched to nearby fields, where they were forced to lie down in the dirt and sprayed with automatic fire."[598] Younger boys and females were enslaved and given to the fighters as a reward, in accordance with Islam's teachings. This enactment of Mohammad's treatment of non-Muslims was and always will be legitimate for people who believe that the Quran and the hadith are divine revelations and hence the eternally valid source of guidance.

In Libya, thousands of Muslims formed a branch of the Islamic State in Syria and Iraq and pledged allegiance to al-Baghdadi as the caliph. They captured several cities and towns and enforced sharia with the approval of many of the residents. They killed countless non-Muslims; among the victims were dozens of Christian Egyptians who had been living in Libya for years – they were beheaded on camera for being disbelievers of Islam.[599] They also targeted judges and officials because they considered them disbelievers. Thousands of foreigners as well as locals joined the Libyan branch of ISIS, participating in the halal looting,

597 Quran 9:5.
598 Callimachi, R. (2015, Aug 13). ISIS Enshrines a Theology of Rape. New York Times.
599 BBC News. (2015, Feb 15). Islamic State: Egyptian Christians held in Libya 'killed'.

380

destruction, and slaughter.[600] The mujahedeen kidnapped and enslaved thousands of women. Girls were exhibited as sexual slaves for sale in accordance with sharia. These practices were never sincerely denounced by the influential jurists in Libya or another country. They ended by war.

600 Faucon, B. & Bradley, M. (2015, Feb 17). Islamic State Gained Strength in Libya by Co-Opting Local Jihadists. The Wall Street Journal.; Human Rights Watch. (2014, Nov 27). Libya: Extremists Terrorizing Derna Residents.

TARGETING CHILDREN

In November 2021, on the Remembrance Day, a Muslim suicide bomber attempted to kill new mothers and their newly born babies in Liverpool Women's Hospital. Emad al Swealmeen, who had been planning the attack for more than seven months, had entered the UK illegally in 2013. His asylum application was rejected several times starting from 2014 but he was allowed to remain in the country and was being given an allowance in addition to free accommodation, free medical care and free dental care for all these years (that's more than seven years). He pretended to have converted to Christianity but kept worshipping in mosques. In Ramadan (April) of 2021, he spent every day of the month in a mosque while preparing his bomb. His initial target was the Anglican Cathedral where the Service of Remembrance was held. He changed his mind and decided to go to the maternity hospital, once he realised that he would not make it to the cathedral on time due to traffic. The one who foiled the attack and saved the lives of innocent people was a brave taxi driver, David Perry, who noticed that al Swealmeen had something suspicious on him, so he jumped out of the car locking the terrorist inside it near the entrance to the hospital. The explosives went off killing Swealmeen and turning the taxi into a fireball. The incident did not put Islam or the corrupt system which for years had allowed such a criminal to live off taxpayers' money, on trial.

On the first day of September 2004, more than thirty armed Muslims, some of them Arabs with British citizenships, stormed school No. 1 in Beslan, Russia.[601] It was the first day of school and many parents were in the school with their children. The Muslim mujahedeen, armed with machine guns, RPGs, explosives, and suicide vests seized the school and took more than 1100 persons hostages. These were students, parents, and

---

601 Al Jazeera. (2005, Jan 1). Rusia tuhadid huiat 17 min munafidhi eamaliat madrasat Bislan [Russia Identifies 17 of The Beslan Attackers]. (Arabic).

school staff in the midst of their normal life, unaware that a group of people considered them an enemy that should be killed.

The Muslim militant leader, Shamil Basayev, issued a statement taking responsibility for this Islamic attack – as he claimed. He said that he had wanted to attack a school in Moscow or Saint Petersburg but had not had enough money to carry out such costly operations, he had therefore settled for the Beslan School. The Muslim mujahedeen executed around twenty people in cold blood immediately after taking control of the scene, to break the people's will to resist and to terrorise the outside world. The hostages were held for 52 hours.

While the fighters were holding these people hostage, the Muslim world seemed divided into those who supported the attack and others who seemed to have fallen into a deep coma and chosen not to show solidarity with either side. No protest was organized, no condemnation, no Islamic decrees, no denunciation and no calls of any value to release the children and their parents. Muslim communities in the Western world along with their usual liberal allies did not take to the streets to condemn the ongoing crime. A thorough review of the reports covering this crime in Arabic media networks is sufficient to show that it was justified and even promoted by the vast majority of them.

The standoff ended when an explosion took place inside the school and then a battle erupted between Russian special forces and the mujahedeen. Three hundred and thirty-three innocent people were killed, among them 186 children, and 753 people were injured, including 221 children. Shamil Basayev blamed the Russians while promising to continue the jihad. Many Muslim news networks also accused the Russian forces of being responsible for the death of the victims, not the criminals who attacked a school or the belief that warrants such an act.[602]

On 16 December 2014, a group of seven Muslims re-enacted Beslan's massacre, this time in Pakistan. A Chechen, two Afghans, an Egyptian, a Moroccan, and a Saudi armed with machine guns, grenades, and explosive belts, affiliated with Tehrik-i-Taliban Pakistan organization sneaked into a Pakistani school in the city of Peshawar. This school

---

602 Al Jazeera (2004, Oct 4). Basayif yatabana eamaliat madrasat Bislan [Basayev takes responsibility for Beslan school attack]. (Arabic).

belongs to the Pakistani Army and most of its students are relatives of army personnel, whom the movement categorizes as enemies of Allah. The Muslim terrorists killed 149 people, among them 134 children and school staff members, and injured another 121, mainly students. The students killed or injured in the attack, who were between 8 and 18 years old, were considered infidels, thus killing them was legitimate according to the jihadi organization which fights for implementing sharia and creating a caliphate in Pakistan.

In April 2015, another group of mujahedeen – this time members of the Somali Islamic movement Al-Shabab – attacked Garissa University College in Kenya. The spokesperson for the movement stated that the attackers released Muslim students and seized the Christians. He also stated that the mujahedeen's "mission was to kill those who are against the Shabab." One hundred and forty-two students were slain and another 79 were injured in this attack, in addition to a number of soldiers and policemen.

On 9 August 2001, Hamas and the Islamic Jihad Movement carried out a suicide bombing targeting Jewish children and mothers who were inside Sbarro Pizza restaurant in Jerusalem. The place was filled with children, babies, and women, when the Muslim suicide bomber detonated his explosive killing 15 and injuring more than 130 human beings.[603] Almost half of the casualties were babies and children; most of the other victims were women. The accomplice of the suicide bomber, Ahlam al-Tamimi, who played a part in the planning and transported the suicide bomber to the restaurant, was detained, prosecuted and sentenced to life in jail but was released in a prisoner swap in 2011.[604] She moved to Jordan, where she was received as a hero and currently hosts a TV talk-show promoting Islam and jihad. In many interviews, she has described how the Palestinian people received her attack with joy. They were congratulating each other for the "martyrdom attack" that claimed the lives of children and women, she said repeatedly. When she first learned from a journalist who was interviewing her in prison that she had killed eight children, she smiled and continued the interview.

603 Roth, F. (2010, Aug 9). Nine years after the Sbarro massacre. Jerusalem Post.
604 Roth, F. (2014, May 4). Who cares about justice? About the victims? About truth? Jewish Press.

In a TV interview she made right after her arrival to Amman, she said: "I do not regret what happened. Absolutely not. This is the path. I dedicated myself to jihad for the sake of Allah, and Allah granted me success. You know how many casualties there were [in the 2001 attack on the Sbarro pizzeria]. This was made possible by Allah. Do you want me to denounce what I did? That's out of the question. I would do it again today, and in the same manner."[605] Two American citizens were killed in the attack and FBI placed al-Tamimi on their most wanted terrorist list but Jordanian authorities did not agree to extradite her. The child murderer is still living freely in Jordan, a country which is considered an American ally and receives billions of dollars as gifts from the American as well as the European taxpayer.

In April 2002, the Saudi ambassador to the UK, Ghazi Algosaibi, published a poem entitled "The Martyrs" glorifying the suicide bomber Ayat al-Akhras, who died while carrying out an attack against Israeli civilians a few days beforehand. The poem was published in a London-based Arabic newspaper. In it, Algosaibi said that suicide bombers "died to honour God's word". He described the murderer Ayat as the gorgeous girl who "embraced death with a smile while the leaders are running away from death. Doors of heaven are opened for her."[606] Ayat's target was to kill people in a supermarket. She was stopped at the entrance by a 55-year-old security guard who wanted to search her bag. She detonated her bomb, killing a 17-year-old Israeli girl, the guard and herself. Her crime was celebrated all over the Muslim world, and many people pledged to contribute significant amounts of money to her family.

The Palestinian Authority has a department called the Martyr Fund, which pays monthly salaries to the families of dead terrorists. It also pays salaries for the imprisoned and wounded ones. In 2017, $345 million of the $693 million that the PA received as foreign aid (mainly from the European Union and the United States) went to this fund. Palestinian

---

605 A clip from an interview with Ahlam al-Tamimi on Memri. (2011, Oct 19). Released Terrorist Ahlam Tamimi, Sentenced to 16 Life Terms in Prison, Takes Pride...; Horovitz, D. (2020, May 5). Failed by Israel, Malki Roth's parents hope US can extradite her gloating killer. The Times of Israel.
606 Harris, P. (2002, Apr 14). Saudi diplomat's poem for killers. The Guardian.

authority also pays a lump sum to fallen terrorists' families right after every attack. For instance, in June 2021 the family of the terrorist who killed two Israelis received $42,000 as a gift. The former Israeli prime minister explained why many families encourage their children to carry out suicide bombings. It is because the Palestinian Authority, represented in its president Mahmoud Abbas, finances terrorists and looks after their families financially: "President Abbas should stop paying terrorists to murder Jews. You know how much he pays? He pays about 350 million a year to terrorists and their families. Each year. That's about a little less than 10% of the total Palestinian budget. That's an incredible number, he pays Hakim Awad, the terrorist who murdered this beautiful family of Ehud and Ruth Fogel and their three children and a 3-month-old baby girl, he pays Hakim Awad this murderer. Over the lifetime of this killer he will be receiving 2 million dollars. I have a message for president Abbas. Stop paying terrorists! Because what message does this send to Palestinian children? It says murder Jews and get rich!"[607] In short, American and European taxpayers' money is sponsoring terrorism.

The Palestinians carried out 40 suicide bombings in 2002 and 47 in 2003. After each one of these terrorist attacks, the family of the murderer would organize a celebration and money would pour from the rich Muslim regimes in addition to the Palestinian Authority.

Saddam used to pay $25,000 for every suicide bomber's family, $10,000 for the ones killed in confrontations. He also used to pay $5000 for the ones whose homes were destroyed by the Israelis and $1000 for the ones who were wounded.[608] Hence, the number of suicide bombings declined significantly after his removal. In 2015 and 2016, the Palestinians carried out one suicide attack each year. Since then, they have been randomly stabbing and shooting Israeli civilians instead.

On 19 December of the same year, another Tunisian carried out a vehicle-ramming attack in Berlin. He drove a stolen truck through a Christmas market, killing 11 people and injuring 56 others. The killer,

607 Haaretz. (2018, Mar 6). Full Text and Video: Benjamin Netanyahu Addresses 2018 AIPAC Confab.
608 ABC News. (2006, Jan 7). Saddam Rewards Suicide Bombers' Families.; The White House Archives: President George W. Bush. (n.d.). Saddam Hussein's Support for International Terrorism.

Anis Amri, had crossed the border into Italy illegally in 2011 to escape a four-year prison sentence for robbery in his home country. He had lied about his age, claiming to be a minor to remain in the European Union. He participated in setting the migration reception centre on fire, injuring several people; he later committed a robbery, and spent four years in a jail in Italy for the two crimes. After serving his sentence, he was released into the streets of Europe as a clear indication of the misjudgement and incompetency of some of the people who were in charge of enforcing law in that country. According to his rap sheet in Tunisia, he was a drug dealer, an addict, a robber, and a devoted Muslim at the same time. He resurfaced in Germany, where he applied for asylum under various fake aliases and committed several crimes while trying to recruit terrorists. He attempted to buy weapons from an undercover police officer and was heard planning to carry out a suicide attack, nevertheless, he had still not been arrested. He also established connections with some Arab Muslims who had German citizenships and were active in supporting jihad in Germany. The German criminal investigation agency warned in March 2016 that he was planning a suicide attack and recommended immediate deportation, but the local government refused to deport him, despite him being in Germany illegally and having been involved in drug dealing and knife fights. To this day, the rationale behind this crime, the accomplices, the incompetent and corrupt German officials who facilitated this crime have not been held accountable.

In Nigeria, jihadists have been targeting non-Muslim children for decades if not for centuries.[609] In February 2014, Islamic fighters attacked a college, killing 59 boys. In April 2014, the rebels of the Islamic State in West Africa commonly known as Boko Haram kidnapped more than 270 Christian schoolgirls; over a hundred of them were still missing in 2021. On 11 December 2020, Boko Haram attacked a secondary school in North-Western Nigeria, kidnapping more than 400 students.[610] These attacks against non-Muslim African children were neglected by the

---

609 UNICEF. (2018, Apr 13). More than 1,000 children in Northeastern Nigeria abducted by Boko Haram since 2013. [Press Release].
610 Arora, A. (2020, Dec 17). Nigerian Authorities Aware Of 330 Kidnapped Schoolboys' Location, Says Governor. Republic World News.

Muslim-owned media networks as well as by the Western media which claim to care about black people.

At 10 a.m. on 12 May 2020, Sunni Muslim fighters stormed the maternity ward of a public hospital in Kabul. The mujahedeen were shooting at everyone. They killed several newborns, 12 new mothers, and several nurses. Many more children, mothers and medical workers were wounded. This ward was targeted because it was run by the international medical charity Médecins Sans Frontiers (MSF) and some of the workers there were foreigners (non-Muslims); also, the hospital was situated in a predominantly Shia area. Hence, the Afghani workers and the patients were considered infidels by the Sunni fighters.

The residents of the same neighbourhood were targeted again on 8 May 2021 by three explosive devices.[611] The first was a car bomb placed in front of the gate of a high school which teaches boys and girls in separate shifts. It was detonated when female students were leaving the school. As the students were fleeing the scene in panic after the first explosion, the other two bombs were detonated to kill and maim as many as possible. At least eighty-five people, most of whom were schoolgirls, lost their lives and hundreds more were severely injured. The Taliban stated that the Islamic State fighters had carried out this massacre, which they did not deny.

Neither the mass killing of the schoolgirls, nor the murdering of new-borns, new mothers and medical workers was sufficient to motivate Muslims to hold one protest anywhere. Neither were these crimes sufficient for the vast majority of Muslim intellectuals to point at what inspired the criminals. Unlike the Danish cartoons, all the killing of children at the hands of Muslims did not outrage the masses or their traditional "liberal" allies. It did not become headline news and no significant action was taken by the international community.

611 Reuters. (2021, May 8). Car bombing at Afghan school in Kabul kills 55, injures over 150.

22 Halal Narcotics

On 1st July 2020, Italian police announced the seizure of over one billion US dollars' worth of narcotics produced by the Islamic State of Iraq and the Levant. The 14 metric tons of amphetamine was the product of the mujahedeen in Syria to be sold to non-Muslims. In the past few years, these militants have stood among the world's leading producers of synthetic drugs. The goal is to destroy non-Muslim youths and make money to finance the holy war, as they claim.

Various reports and testimonies have affirmed that many of the mujahedeen worldwide are drug addicts and that suicide bombers take high doses of drugs to numb their feelings before killing themselves and others. This is not a novel phenomenon, nor is it limited to a specific terrorist organization; the relationship between jihad and narcotics is ancient and vital. It goes back many centuries, and the current jihadis being among the leading producer and consumers of narcotics are walking in the footsteps of their ancestors.

Right after the Taliban took over Afghanistan on 15 August 2021, the production of opium skyrocketed. New markets sprung up all over the country and more farmers ditched their old crops for opium. In Kandahar, the stronghold of Taliban, opium has become the main business, as most of the farmers turned to grow the poisonous plant. Taliban fighters protect the production and the open trade of the drug, and their guards keep the media away.[612]

Afghanistan has been a major international exporter of opium and radical Islamic movements for more than a 100 year. The Afghani mujahedeen's main source of income has been the narcotic trade and foreign aid. Many journalists falsely claimed that the production of opium in Afghanistan started with the Soviet invasion and that it was the CIA

---

612 Trofimov, Y. (2021, Nov 21). Afghanistan's Opium Business Cranks Up as the Taliban Look the Other Way. The Wall Street Journal.

who taught the Afghani how to cultivate opium. This lie shows deep ignorance of both the history of Afghanistan as well as the relationship between opium and Islam in general, and jihad in particular. Centuries before the establishment of the United States of America, psychoactive substances had been cultivated in Afghanistan, Iran, Turkey, Egypt, and Morocco as well as many other Muslim countries.

The Assassins movement established around 1090 in Iran was a jihadi order known for using drugs, especially hashish, to motivate its soldiers. This Islamic order adopted both suicidal attacks and narcotics to achieve its religious goals. It established a powerful Islamic state which lasted for around three hundred years and controlled swathes of land and cities across the Middle East.[613]

Another lie that has been propagated worldwide is the notion that the Taliban succeeded in halting the production of opium during their first reign. The fact is that Taliban warlords are opium dealers and they have been producing opium, smuggling and selling it for decades before and after they introduced a superficial ban which lasted for less than one year. This ban was a means to establish themselves as a legitimate regime before the international community.[614] In the year they reduced the production of opium, they claimed it was forbidden in Islam, forgetting the fact that they as well as other Muslims had been producing and using it for centuries. Currently, the Muslims of Afghanistan are the largest producer of opiates. "The Taliban have counted on the Afghan opium trade as one of their main sources of income", according to Cesar Gudes, the head of the Kabul office of the UN Office of Drugs and Crime (UNODC).[615]

Releasing the drug dealer Bashar Noorzai from American prison has been one of the main priorities of the Taliban for many years. This devoted Muslim who was indicted for smuggling 50-million-dollars' worth of heroin into the US had fought the Soviets and was one of the key leaders and financers of the Taliban with the use of his drug money.

613 Bradford, J. T. (2019). Poppies, Politics, and Power: Afghanistan and the Global History of Drugs and Diplomacy. Cornell University Press; United Nations Office on Drugs and Crime. (Created 1949, Jan 1). Opium Production Throughout The World. In: Bulletin on Narcotics, p 6.
614 Rice, G. (2019, Apr 11). Afghanistan's transformation into a narco-state. ASPI The Strategist.
615 Landy, J. (2021, Aug 21). Profits and poppy: Afghanistan's illegal drug trade a boon for Taliban. Reuters.

The Algerian civil war between Islamists and the Muslim regime, which lasted from 1991 to 2002, is another illustration of the ancient marriage between jihad and narcotic. The mujahedeen, who killed tens of thousands of Algerians after accusing them of apostasy for supporting the government or rejecting the Islamists' reign, were involved in all kinds of criminal activities. They were financing their jihad through narcotics, extortion, racketeering, kidnapping, and other forms of organized crime.[616] They justified the production and distribution of drugs, kidnapping people, robbery, extortion, mass rape, and assassinations through constructing their crimes as legitimate Islamic practices or as necessary means to establish Islamic caliphate – the most noble of all causes.

The Islamic Republic of Iran is another country where opioids go hand in hand with the upsurge of religious rule.[617] After the toppling of the last Muslim king, who had some secular views, the clergymen became the absolute rulers of Iran. Under them, the vast rich country descended into a lawless state, devastated in every aspect, including drug addiction. The draconian laws, the suppression of the people, the dismantling of the institutions, and the ruling jurists' corruption and direct involvement in narcotics increased the addiction. According to official Iranian estimates, 2.8 million Iranians are addicts, with two thirds of them on opium. Addiction, production, and smuggling of drugs have been on the rise since the inception of the Islamic regime. Official Iranian military units have been running global narcotics networks. The revenue of the drug trade is used by the theological regime to fund terrorism, buy loyalty, and suppress the Iranians.[618] At the same time as the rulers have been overseeing the production, smuggling and selling of all types of drugs, they have publicly hanged thousands of Iranians on the charges of possession, trafficking, or using illicit drugs; many more thousands were jailed. Despite the public hanging and long jail sentences for the users and small traders, Iranian society has lost the war on drugs.

616 Martinez, L. (2000). The Algerian Civil War, 1990-1998. C. Hurst & Co.
617 United States Department of State, Bureau for International Narcotics and Law Enforcement Affairs (DOS INL). (2019). International Narcotics Control Strategy Report, Vol. I: Drug and Chemical Control.; DOS INL. (2015). International Narcotics Control Strategy Report.
618 WikiLeaks. (E-mail sent 2011, Nov 18. Released 2013, Feb 13). The Global Intelligence Files: Re: [CT] [OS] US/IRAN/CT Iranian drug ring funding terror?

Currently millions of Iranians declare that they are addicts.[619] It is needless to stress that the precise dimension of the addiction crisis in Iran is far from being fully known as many people would not risk stating that they are breaking the law in a country with no freedom of speech, rule of law or independent judiciary. In their public speeches, Iranian rulers lay the blame for their own crimes which resulted in the narcotics crisis on everyone else – as with all other failures.[620]

In Lebanon, the Islamic Shia militia that controls the southern region is yet another clear example of how the ends justify the means in the jihadi psyche. The Party of Allah (Hezbollah) has one of the most sophisticated international criminal networks which deals with narcotics, money laundry, extortion, and other forms of organized crimes. The Drug Enforcement Administration of the United States, which has worked for years to crack down on Hezbollah's activities, stated:

> The DEA's targeting of Hezbollah began about thirteen years ago with Operation Titan, which intercepted the sale of multi-ton cocaine shipments by Hezbollah associates in cooperation with the Colombian drug cartel La Oficina de Envigado. Notable cases since then have included Lebanese Colombian drug kingpin Ayman Joumaa and the Lebanese Canadian Bank.
>
> In the past six years, the DEA provided assistance that led to the arrests of a number of prominent actors in Hezbollah's global criminal support network, including Ali Fayyad (2014), Ali Koleilat (2014), Altaf Khanani (2015), Hassan Mansour (2015), and Ibrahim Ahmadoun (2015). In 2016, Operation Cedar targeted an international money laundering scheme, leading to the arrests of Hezbollah operative Mohamad Noureddine and others via concurrent raids in Belgium, France, Germany, and Italy. CNTOC financial investigators also played a central role in the arrest and indictment of Kassim Tajideen, a Hezbollah financier sentenced to five years in prison and ordered to forfeit $50 million in August 2019.[621]

619 Moradinazar, M., Najafi, F., Jalilian, F., and others. (2020). Prevalence of drug use, alcohol consumption, cigarette smoking and measure of socioeconomic-related inequalities of drug use among Iranian people: findings from a national survey. Subst Abuse Treat Prev Policy 15, 39.
620 Calabrese, J. (2007, Dec 1). Iran's War on Drugs: Holding the Line? MEI.
621 Fernandez, J. (2020, Jan 10). The DEA's Targeting of Hezbollah's Global Criminal Support

The Party of Allah is the protector of the Shia drug kingpins and their narcotic plants in southern Lebanon. It also provides protection to all kinds of organized criminal activities in its strongholds, while at the same time it is part of the Lebanese government and has many members in the Lebanese parliament.

In the BBC's documentary "Meeting a Lebanese drug lord", the Shia drug kingpin spoke brazenly on camera about his illegal business and about fighting ISIS. He was showing off his arsenal of weapons, his drug production facilities, and his cannabis farms. He and his armed militias repeatedly mocked the corrupt Lebanese government. He stated that the drug lords bribed Lebanese politicians and officials and controlled them. He also said that the Lebanese armed forces would not dare to stand up to the drug lords. He claimed that the drugs were for export to non-Muslims only. Ali Shamas said that "the United States and Europe are exporting terrorism to us and we sell them drugs in retaliation." He spoke from Hezbollah's heartland, where the Lebanese government is not allowed. He claimed that he had used his weapons to fight the radical Sunnis and boasted that he had killed several Syrian soldiers and had no regrets about it.[622] The Shia fighters who control the region do not see anything wrong in producing and smuggling narcotics which have been ruining the lives of millions of people. The founder and spiritual leader of Hamas, Ahmed Yasin, said in an interview with Al Jazeera that Palestinian mujahedeen obtained weapons from Israelis in exchange for hashish.

It is common for Muslim drug lords to defend their criminal activity by stating that it is intended for infidels and hence, it is halal in Islam.[623] Selling the infidels drugs which destroy their nervous system is a good way to penalize them for rejecting the true religion: Islam. A Bangladeshi Muslim drug kingpin took it a step further when he argued publicly that it was the Muslims' "noble responsibility to spoil the Western society with drugs."[624]

Network. The Washington Institute for Near East Policy.
622 Zand, Benjamin. (2017, Mar 3). Meeting a Lebanese drug lord. [Documentary]. BBC News.
623 See Bucerius, S. (2014). Unwanted: Muslim Immigrants, Dignity, and Drug Dealing (Studies in Crime and Public Policy). Oxford University Press, p 124.
624 European Foundation For South Asian Studies. (2017, Nov). 'Narco-Jihad' – Haram money for a Halal cause? [Report].

Immigrant Muslim criminal networks are among the main smugglers and distributors of drugs into the Netherlands and Belgium and from there, to the rest of Europe. Through drug trafficking, money laundry, tax evasion, extortion, racketeering, assassination, and political corruption, the Moroccan mafia have been transforming the Netherlands and Belgium into failed states. The chairman of the biggest Dutch police union stated that the Netherlands "have the characteristics of a narco-state" resulting from the activity of Islamic organized crimes networks.[625] Since they moved to Europe, the Muslim criminal clans have been destroying the lives of millions of Europeans through drugs, violence, and corruption. They have created a state within the state and made European cities descend into lawlessness while making billions of Euros.[626] They have killed lawyers and journalists execution style in Amsterdam and Stockholm. Muslim drug dealers are also involved in political corruption and terrorism. For instance, the Moroccan mafia in the Netherlands that specialises in smuggling drugs and weapons has been collaborating with the Islamic Republic of Iran. Moroccan criminals have killed a number of Iranian regime's opponents and in exchange, the Islamic regime has been providing them with protection and support.[627] It is important to note that many of the European politicians, businessmen, and journalists are their accomplices and without their protection these clans would not have survived.

The notorious criminal clan boss Mahmoud Al-Zein published an autobiography entitled "The Godfather of Berlin: My Way, My Family, My Rules", in which he details how he came to Germany from Lebanon in 1982 and lived there illegally for 40 years. He also explains how he built a criminal empire in Berlin along with his clan and other Arabs and Muslims. Despite being arrested more than 80 times and being convicted of serious crimes, he was receiving 3200 Euro a month as unemployment and child benefit for him, his wife and their ten children,

625 Holligan, A. (2019, Dec 19). Is the Netherlands becoming a narco-state? BBC News.
626 Gormezano, D. (2022, Oct 2). Dutch PM under protection as the 'Mocro Mafia' drug cartel sows fear in the Netherlands. France 24..; Loudis, J. (2022, Mar 23). How the Netherlands Became a Global Cocaine Hub. The Nation.
627 Spencer, R. (2020, Apr 3). Suspected assassin for the ayatollahs found in Dubai. The Times.

in addition to free accommodation and free healthcare. In his memoir, Mahmoud described himself as a devoted Muslim, who lives according to Islam and goes to mosque at least once a week.[628] Al-Zein's clan is one of many Arab mafias which are active in Sweden, Denmark, Germany, and other European countries. They are involved in different kinds of criminal activities, from stealing to kidnapping, prostitution, smuggling and drugs.[629]

In 2008, the Al-Zein family killed (as an honour killing) their 20-year-old daughter Iptehal Al-Zein because she was adapting to the Western lifestyle. Her brother, uncle, and cousin were convicted by the German court for orchestrating and carrying out the assassination. These killers are Muslim drug dealers committed to the notion of honour rooted in Islam.

In the UK, reports published in 2021 indicate that a network of Libyan drug dealers took part in the Manchester Arena atrocity on 22 May 2017, in which a Muslim man carried out a suicide bombing attack against people leaving the arena after a concert. He killed 22 people and wounded hundreds. The gang members were in contact with the suicide bomber days before the attack. They were also guarding a car packed with explosives for weeks before the attack.[630]

In Pakistan, narcotics have been intertwined with jihad for centuries. Narcotics kill hundreds of Pakistanis every day under the gaze of the Islamic regime and its senior jurists. In that failed state, there are at least 8 million drug addicts, who are the victims of the corrupt authority, religious educational system, and Muslim drug lords.

The mujahedeen-drug dealers know very well that their product is destroying many Muslims along their non-Muslim enemies, but they do not want to give up their source of easy wealth. They simply do not have an alternative source of revenue which would allow them to continue with their absurd lifestyle. They don't want to take up regular full-time

628 Al-Zein, Mahmoud. (2020). Der Pate von Berlin: Mein Weg, meine Familie, meine Regeln [The Godfather of Berlin: My Way, My Family, My Rules]. (German). Droemer, p 213.
629 Peachey, P. & Stickings, T. (2021, Jun 8). Police target notorious Al Zein crime clan with armed raids in Germany. The National News.
630 Wright, J. (2021, May 16). The Libyan network 'linked to the Manchester Arena attack plot'. Daily Mail.

employment as it contradicts the way they see themselves as the masters of the universe. Thus, they must live an idle life with multiple wives and dozens of children. They must pray five times a day, fast throughout Ramadan, go to Mecca, socialize with their friends and extended family, and preach about sharia. This all would not leave them much time to study or work. More importantly, they do not have any skill or merit that could secure a steady income. All what they really know are the sayings of Mohammad and verses of Quran. They consider these discourses to be the science, although it has very little economic benefit except in the societies ruled by Islam.

One of the main reasons why these orders and individuals have been able to prosper from dealing in drugs and other types of organized crime is first and foremost the support they enjoy from their societies for being good Muslims. Thus, they know that they can get away with almost anything, including narcotics trade and kidnappings, as long as they present themselves as true Muslims who fight for their religion.[631]

---

631 To further understand how psychopaths maintain a positive self-image, see Patrick, C. J. (Ed.). (2018). Handbook of psychopathy. Guilford Publications.

23 Culture of Rape

In December of 2018, two Scandinavian girls went on a hiking trip to Morocco. Louisa Vesterager Jespersen, a 24-year-old Danish, and Maren Ueland, a 28-year-old Norwegian, thought that Morocco was a safe place for two non-Muslim women travelling on their own, and its people were warm and friendly. They shared pictures and videos from the trip on their social media accounts. The two girls were kidnapped a few days after their arrival by a group of men. They were tortured, raped, before being decapitated. The killers published a shocking video of the torture and the beheading of one of the girls. She was screaming hysterically in sheer agony while the Muslim men were cutting her head off under a black flag bearing the text "There is no god but Allah".

Jespersen's decapitated body had 23 injuries, and there were seven on Ueland's, according to the forensic report. Several of the killers had pledged allegiance to ISIS in a video they posted online, before attacking the girls. Twenty-three Muslim Moroccans and one European convert were indicted for taking part in this crime. The main four rapists/killers praised Allah in the court, showed no remorse and stated that they were willing to die to spread Islam.[632]

Despite a veneer of warmth and hospitality, Muslim countries are among the most dangerous places on Earth for women. In Pakistan, Afghanistan, Somalia, Saudi Arabia, Yemen, Egypt, and almost all the other ones, women are subjected to all kinds of discrimination, harassment, and systematic abuse including sexual assault and rape. It is impossible to find an objective international survey that examines the discrimination and violence against women where Muslim countries that apply sharia are not ranked among the worst in the world, despite the systematic cover up.

---

632 Maclean, R. (2019, Jul 18). Moroccan court orders death penalty for jihadists who beheaded tourists. The Guardian; BBC News. (2019, Jul 18). Morocco hikers: Three get death penalty for Scandinavian tourist murders.

In a study conducted by the United Nations, 99.3% of the questioned Egyptian women reported being victims of sexual harassment, with 96.5% saying that they have been physically assaulted. They declared that there was no safe place for women in that country.[633] Lara Logan, the CNN and CBS reporter, was savagely attacked and sexually assaulted in the middle of the packed Tahrir Square in Cairo by a huge mob of men celebrating their revolution, in 2011.[634] Mob rapes are rampant across the Muslim world and in most cases, they go unreported.

Muslim communities in the West suffer from the same problem – there, too, it results from the same ideas and practices which are dominant in their native countries. "I have the right to stab her, as well as anyone who dares to insult me," this was the Syrian refugee Abdullah's justification for attacking Vivien K., a 24-year-old German girl. The Syrian refugee brutally stabbed the girl, cutting through her liver, stomach, kidney, intestine and pancreas, and breaking her ribs in the process. Doctors had to remove her spleen and parts of the pancreas to save her life. The attack took place in a small town in Lower Saxony in March 2018. The criminal did not show any remorse or concern for his victim. He could not see his act as a crime. To the contrary, he described himself as a "model refugee" and said in his written statement that his religion Islam approved his crime: "He [the accused] explains that his behaviour was not objectionable according to religious requirements and does not understand why he has been detained."[635]

Muslim immigrants in Europe, Canada, and the United States are more likely to rape and sexually harass women than any other immigrant group.[636] In 2021, a group of Swedish researchers led by Professor Kristina Sundquist published a study about rape offenders in Sweden. The results of the study indicated that 59.2% of the convicted rapists

633 UN Women. (2013). Study on Ways and Methods to Eliminate Sexual Harassment in Egypt. [Archived].

634 Boucher, A. (2020, Apr 15). Former CBS Reporter Lara Logan Revisits Terrifying 2011 Rape by Mob in Egypt Amidst $25 Million Lawsuit. People.

635 Voltmer, M. (2018, Aug 22). Messer-Opfer geschockt von Täter-Geständnis [Knife victim shocked by perpetrator's confession]. (German). Bild.

636 Ali, A. (2021, Feb 22). Migrants and the Threat to Women's Rights in Europe: The lack of frank debate feeds Islamists and the far right, who would impose illiberal solution. Wall Street Journal.

in Sweden were immigrants; 47.7% were born outside Sweden.[637] This is despite the fact that Swedish residents with immigrant background represented less than 20% of the population at the time of the study. The researchers were investigated by the Swedish Ministry of Education in order to establish if they had "ethical license" to investigate "sensitive data" or not.[638]

Sumayya Miah, a British Muslim girl who had been raped repeatedly by her stepfather's cousin and another Muslim man beginning when she was six years old, in Britain, summarised the entire crisis: "In my culture, sexual abuse is swept under the carpet."[639]

Thus, the way Muslim communities in the West in general and the United Kingdom in particular reacted to the Aylesbury, Banbury, Bristol, Oxford, Peterborough, and Rotherham child rape and prostitution rings' scandals displayed a clear symptom of a deep psychological and moral crisis. The most important factor that tends to be overlooked when we come across inquiries into these collective crimes is the Muslim understanding of who they are in comparison to other people. Rape and sexual abuse of children are crimes that cannot be justified or condoned easily by rational people. Thus, the identity of the victims as non-Muslims and the identity of the rapists as Sunni Muslims played a key role warranting these organized crimes. The crimes have also shed a light on the way many Muslims perceive themselves in comparison to non-Muslims in the United Kingdom as well as the rest of the world. One of the victims of the Rotherham rape ring described in court what happened to her: "As a teenager, I was taken to various houses and flats above takeaways in the north of England, to be beaten, tortured and raped over 100 times. I was called a 'white slag' and 'white c…' as they beat me. They made it clear that because I was a non-Muslim, and not a virgin, and because I didn't dress 'modestly,' that they believed I deserved to be 'punished.'

637 Khoshnood, A., Ohlsson, H., Sundquist, J., & Sundquist, K. (2021). Swedish rape offenders – a latent class analysis. Forensic sciences research, 6(2), pp 124-132.
638 Winters, N. (2021, Dec 6). Professors Face Prosecution for Study Finding Migrants Commit More Rapes. The National Pulse.
639 Paget, A. (2020, Nov 13). 'In my culture, sexual abuse is swept under carpet': Brave victim, 23, tells how stepfather's cousin and lodger raped her from six-years-old – after pair are jailed for total of 36 years. Daily Mail.

They said I had to 'obey' or be beaten." [640] In that town alone, Muslim criminals have raped over 1400 girls aged 12 to 16.

The perpetrators in all these organized crimes, who had immigrated to the UK from Pakistan, Kurdistan, Kosovo, looked down on the British people. They frequented mosques and were proud of their religious identity as opposed to the natives whom they perceived as immoral disbelievers. The fact that these societies opened their country, helped them, and accepted them was perceived as weakness.

The rapists were carrying out their crimes for many years in several cities and towns and the local Muslims communities did not stop them or report them to the police. Even after the criminals in these many scandals were arrested and what was going on was disclosed, there was no sincere condemnation or apology on the part of the Muslim community. Not one protest, no flag burning, and no threats of violence. The Rotherham rapists shouted 'Allah Akbar' in court in defiance of the sentence and justice.

In June 2021, four Afghani Muslim refugees kidnapped, drugged, tortured, raped, and killed a 13-year-old Austrian girl in Vienna. The criminals dumped the naked dead body of Leonie in an empty area and went on with their lives. They were criminals and drug dealers living in the country illegally.[641] Their asylum applications were all rejected but still they were allowed to live in the country off taxpayer' money and their illicit earnings. One of them was supposed to be in prison, as he had been sentenced to two years in May of 2020 after being convicted of severe coercion and sexual coercion of a girl. The police arrested three of the criminals while the fourth one managed to leave Germany and crossed illegally to Britain, where he was immediately given free accommodation and a weekly allowance. The Afghani Rasuili Zubaidullah, 23, was arrested in Whitechapel, East London on 29 July at a taxpayer-funded hotel where he was living. His lawyer Ben Keith objected to his extradition to Germany based on a legal technicality.[642]

---

640 Hill, E. (2018, Mar 18). As a Rotherham grooming gang survivor, I want people to know about the religious extremism which inspired my abusers. Independent.
641 Cody, J. (2021, Jun 30). Vienna shocked by rape and murder of 13-year-old girl, two Afghans arrested. Remix News.

The Iranian Hussein Khavari, who choked and raped 19-year-old Maria Ledenburger, then drowned her in a nearby river in Baden-Württemberg in 2016 , had sneaked into Germany claiming to be an Afghani and a minor less than a year before he committed this crime. His father declared to the police that his son was born in 1984 which makes him 32 at the time of the crime. It was later revealed that in 2014 he had been convicted in Greece for an attempted homicide but did not serve his sentence.

In her book "Prey, Islam, and the Erosion of Women's Rights", Ayan Hirsi Ali shows clearly how illegal Muslim immigrants have brought their culture of rape into Europe. The identity of people, which influences the way they perceive themselves, others, and what is right or wrong, does not change just because they moved into a different country, she demonstrated. Ali also highlights the complacency and incompetence of the European governments.

The life story of the notable British Muslim politician Baron Nazir Ahmed, who was born in Pakistan and was created a life peer of Rotherham in the County of South Yorkshire (a member of the House of Lords for life) in 1998, is another striking indication of how widespread and complex the crisis of Muslims in the UK and other Western countries is. This man had been a prominent legislator, one of the leaders of the Labour Party, and the founder of British Muslim Councillors Forum. He led the first official British delegation to the Islamic pilgrimage. He played a major role in banning Geert Wilders from entering the UK in 2009, despite Wilders having been an elected MP in the Netherlands and having received an invitation by two members of the House of Lords. Lord Ahmed threatened to mobilize 10000 Muslims if Wilders was allowed to visit Britain's Parliament to show his movie Fitna. Gordon Brown caved in and banned Wilders from entering the UK; he was called "the biggest coward in Europe" by Wilders. Lord Ahmed also demanded the release of 'Lady Al-Qaeda' from the American jail, accusing the American administration and justice system of kidnapping and unlawful imprisonment of the Muslim woman.

---

642 Hussain, D. (2022, Jan 7). Afghan refugee who 'drugged girl, 13, with seven ecstasy pills then raped and murdered her in Austria before sneaking to Britain under a false name' tries to use legal technicality to stay in UK, court hears. Daily Mail.

The powerful and influential Muslim leader, who was a staunch defender of Muslims' rights, was accused of several crimes and misconducts starting in 1996 but was shielded from accountability. In 2019, he was finally charged along with his two brothers with attempted rape of a boy and a girl. He was also accused of using his position to have sex with vulnerable women. Despite the nature of the charges, British politicians and journalists – who had created a god out of him – kept silent. The public media networks as well as most of the newspapers, which had been hosting Ahmed and promoting him for decades, did not fulfil their duty of informing the public of his wrongdoings. On 5 January 2022, lord Ahmed was found guilty of attempting to rape a girl and of a serious sexual assault against a boy under 11 years old. He was not held accountable for all the damage he has done by spreading lies and hatred.

In August 2021, a court in Malmo awarded a convicted Muslim Syrian rapist €80000 in damages. This man along with another Syrian Muslim arrived in Sweden in 2017. They were instantly granted asylum and financial support. Immediately after they were settled, the two refugees attacked and raped several women. They kidnapped a girl and imprisoned her in a cellar. They tortured her and raped her repeatedly. The two rapists were arrested, prosecuted, and sentenced to just four years imprisonment for all their crimes. After they were sentenced, their lawyers, paid for by the taxpayers, argued that one of them was 17 years old when he committed his crimes and thus, he deserved a compensation for being tried as an adult while he had a few months left before becoming 18. The Swedish judges agreed with the lawyers' argument and ordered the Swedish state to pay the rapist more than 3 years of a university graduate's average salary, from taxpayers' money.[643]

On New Year's Eve of 2015, thousands of German girls were mobbed and sexually assaulted in the streets of their country. Countless videos and photos posted online showed massive mobs of Arab men attacking European women in Hamburg, Frankfurt am Main, Hanover, Cologne. They turned the German cities into mayhem. In some of the videos, German girls were screaming hysterically while being surrounded

---

643 Cody, J. (2021, Aug 18). Sweden pays Syrian rapist €80,000 in 'damages'. Remix News.

and abused by individuals laughing and talking in Arabic. In the city of Cologne alone, 1210 criminal complaints were made by the victims, 511 of them involving sexual assaults. In Hamburg, 195 complaints were reported, most of them for sexual crimes. Both the media and the police were afraid to state the citizenship of the looters and rapists, let alone discuss their religion and culture.[644] The German ex-chancellor Angela Merkel called for "identify[ing] the culprits as quickly and comprehensively as possible and punish[ing] them, regardless of their origin or background."[645] Six years after this mass attack which had taken place in twelve different German cities, two people were convicted for sexual assaults: a 21-year-old Iraqi and a 26-year-old Algerian; each one of them received a one-year probation sentence.

In conclusion, a mass-crime was swept under the rug, and the victims were let down by the German establishment.[646] The villains were allowed to get away with their crimes, look down on the victims, and continued living off the hand-outs taken from the German tax-payer. Many of these rapists might have successfully applied for German citizenship and can soon be eligible to become decision makers and legislators in a country that did not protect its natives.[647]

644 Scholz, K.-A. (2016, Mar 10). No change in sight for German media ethics. DW.
645 Bosen, R. (2020, Dec 31). New Year's Eve in Cologne: 5 years after the mass assaults. DW.
646 As above.
647 See Sarrazin, T. (2010). Deutschland schafft sich ab: Wie wir unser Land aufs Spiel setzen [Germany is abolishing itself: How we put our country at risk]. Deutsche Verlagsanstalt; Sarrazin, T. (2009). Klasse statt Masse [Class instead of mass]. Lettre International 86, pp 197–201.

SEXUAL ABUSE OF BOYS:
FROM GHILMAN TO BACHA BAZI

All the societies, ruled by laws derived from sharia, where imams represent intellectual authority and enjoy unparalleled powers, suffer from a multifaceted moral crisis. One of the aspects of this crisis is widespread failure to protect children from sexual abuse.

The influential Pakistani mufti Aziz ur Rehman, who led the anti-blasphemy rallies in Pakistan calling for retribution against French people for the publication of cartoons depicting Mohammad in 2020, was arrested in June 2021. The imam's troubles started after one of his students posted a video showing the prominent old jurist sexually abusing him. The male student stated via his Facebook page that he had been raped and sexually abused by the imam for many years, starting when he was a child studying in an Islamic school run by Rehman, who is forty years older than this victim. Rehman, who is a member of the board that controls the enormous religious schools' system in Pakistan, a member of a prominent religious political party and a custodian of a religious seminary, denied the accusations. He asserted that he was drugged before the filming of the abuse in which he is seen forcing himself on the student.[648] Many of his followers continued defending the rapist imam, claiming that what had happened to him was a conspiracy staged by infidels.

There are several inhumane social norms and practices enshrined in the Islamic history which have been sheltered from accountability due to the nature of the religion, the marriage between religion and politics and its historical development. Islamic teachings have failed to end them, and in many cases expanded these toxic practices. These social epidemics are usually kept hidden from outsiders' eyes to protect the image of the religion at the expense of the victims. The practice of

---

648 Reuters. (2021, Jun 21) Pakistani cleric charged with sexual abuse at religious school.

buying or kidnapping young boys and turning them into sexual objects is an ancient practice rampant throughout Muslim history. Many historians have described how the palaces of the Umayyad, the Abbasid, and the Ottoman caliphs, as well as houses of rich and powerful men during their times, were full of young (beardless) boys – ghilman. These children had mainly been kidnapped by the invading armies from their families and turned into slaves.

The word ghilman appears in the Quran several times to describe young, beautiful boys given to the believers as a reward in the afterlife. Some people understood that they are there to satisfy the sexual desires of males and hence, homosexuality with children would be accepted in heaven. Most contemporary jurists describe the boys as servants – the invention of coffee machines or robot vacuums having not been foreseen.[649] To them, stunning boys were created to hover around the believers in their afterlife while they do nothing beside having sex with the countless virgins and drinking from the alcoholic river.

In the original history books, there are numerous descriptions of how young males were used as servants and dancers throughout the ages. Some were castrated to be used as guards in harems, where kidnapped girls were imprisoned. Some were used as sexual objects. Several Umayyad and Abbasid caliphs were open about their sexual relationships with ghilman. Some of them even wrote poetry disclosing their affection toward particular young slave-boys. This practice continued throughout the era of the Ottoman Empire and up until the 20th century with a new name: kocek, which means "the small". Until the first part of the last century, boys were sold or kidnapped from their parents to be used for sexual purposes and as dancers in almost every part of the Ottoman Caliphate. In parts of Iran, Pakistan, and Afghanistan this practice is ongoing to this day under the name bacha bazi (boy play).

The American-led invasion of Afghanistan shed a light on this centuries-long institutionalized abuse of children. The Afghani victims were poor boys, usually kidnapped or sold by their families to rich, old men as sex-slaves. These children are groomed to become seductive

---

649 Quran 52:24; 56:17; 76:19.

dancers in a compensation for the strict segregation between females and males. They are victims of sexual exploitation, regular beatings, and humiliation, as their owners consider them property.

The phenomenon of bacha bazi is inextricably linked to gender discrimination. The proscription on women's attendance in male gatherings means that they are "replaced" with dancing boys. This has a negative impact on both of these vulnerable groups: women continue to be excluded from public life, remain under lock and key, and regularly face humiliation and violence, while underage boys become sex objects for men who see a woman's role as serving the family. A 2013 study by Hagar International found an extremely high rate of trafficking of boys in Afghanistan. Children over the age of 14 are more likely to be used for forced labour or as child soldiers, while boys under the age of 14 are more likely to be sexually exploited. At least 50% of trafficked children under 14 years old are victims of the bacha bazi tradition.[650]

The sexual exploitation of students in religious schools is another widespread practice which has been hidden and protected for centuries. In almost all the poor countries, schools devoted to teaching young students Quran and hadith are accused of condoning systematic abuses conducted by the powerful imams. The victims are usually students who come from impoverished backgrounds and cannot afford the official education. Thus, they are easy pray for the custodians of these schools. The religious schools are usually established and funded by donations which are given either to a specific imam who is the custodian of the school, thus, he owns the school and has absolute power over what goes on inside it, or they are given to a specific organization or a council of imams, and in this case the council members are the owners of the schools. In both cases, the need to protect the reputation of the school is the priority.

What makes things even worse is the fact that these institutions are not subjected to governmental supervision due to their nature. This pathological practice of covering up sexual abuse of children is widespread across Muslim societies.

---

650 Thorson, J. E. & Sadeq, B. (2013). Forgotten No More: Male child Trafficking in Afghanistan. Hagar International.

Even relatively wealthy and functioning countries where Islam is the official religion have not been sheltered from the epidemic of sexual abuse of children. In Kuwait, a study examining the prevalence of child abuse found that physical, emotional, and sexual abuse is rampant in that small rich country. Twenty percent of 2508 questioned university students stated that they had been sexually abused when they were children. Only 16% of the victims told their mothers and 3.4% told their fathers about abuse, while 28% told a non-parent; 68% did not talk about it to anyone. After revealing their abuse, only 20% were believed and supported while 15% were blamed. Moreover, more than one third of the survey's participants reported being physically abused. One fifth of them stated that they had been cut or stabbed with a sharp object, and 41.8% stated that they had been beaten with an object.[651]

In the UK, the court of justice found the member of the British Parliament Imran Ahmad Khan guilty of sexually assaulting a minor, on 11 April 2022. Khan, who is a Muslim of Pakistani origin and was elected to the Parliament in 2019, forced the 15-year-old boy to drink gin at a party; then he dragged him to a bedroom upstairs and made him watch pornography before sexually assaulting him. Khan initially denied the charges. He asked the court to discuss the case in secrecy, arguing that for a Muslim both homosexuality and alcohol consumption are prohibited and disclosing that he was engaged in these matters would put his life at risk inside the UK and abroad.[652] One wonders, if he was charged with supporting a terrorist organization, would he have feared for his life from his fellow Muslims?

---

651 Almazeedi H., Alkandari, S., Alrazzuqi, H., Ohaeri, J. & Alfayez, G. (2020). Prevalence of child abuse and its association with depression among first year students of Kuwait University: a cross-sectional study. Eastern Mediterranean Health Journal 26(8), pp 948-956.
652 BBC News. (2022, Apr 11). Imran Ahmad Khan: MP guilty of sex assault on 15-year-old boy.

24 Islam or the West

Many of the journalists were on our payroll, we were paying them, some of them became MPs and some became ministers in many countries, we pay them annually.[653]

Sheikh Hamad bin Jassim

It was disclosed in June 2022 that Prince Charles of Great Britain accepted millions of euros from the former Qatari Prime Minister Hamad bin Jassim. According to an article published in the Sunday Times, between 2011 and 2015 the Qatari official handed the Prince carrier bags stuffed with cash on three different occasions, totalling around 3 million euros. Charles also accepted one million pounds from Osama bin Laden's family in 2013. Winning over societies through giving money to their leaders is an ancient Islamic tradition. The Prophet himself gave tribal chiefs substantial fortunes to win their hearts for Islam.[654]

The former Spanish king Juan Carlos has been investigated for taking commissions from the Saudi royal family. The Spanish press reported that he had received 64.8 million euros in relation to a rail contract in Saudi Arabia. This type of relationship may explain why he was keen on allowing oil-rich, autocratic Muslim countries to promote their ideology in Spain without demanding equal treatment. He stepped down in 2014, and in 2020 left his country to move to Abu Dhabi in the United Arab Emirates, a country whose constitution designates Islam as the religion of the land. He was living in a $12,000-a-night hotel suite with a lover – a major sin in Islam and a crime according to Emirates' laws at that time, but as a king he is above the sharia.

For decades, sheiks have been using money to manipulate democratic countries. The funds usually come from public treasuries which

---

653 See the ex-Prime Minister of Qatar Sheikh Hamad bin Jassim in an interview with Ammar Taqi. AlQabas TV. (2022, Feb 26). Sahafiuwn wasiasiuwn earab yakhudhun rawatib min Qatar [Arab journalists and politicians take salaries from Qatar]. (Arabic). [Video]. YouTube.
654 Quran 9:60.

are under full control of the ruling families, or from various activities they are involved in, some of them illicit, which are related to their monopoly on wealth and power. Other means used by the Gulf States to infiltrate and control the advanced countries include holding major shares in big corporations and media outlets, allocating tenders to certain companies, giving donations to specific charities, employing former politicians, financing political candidates' campaigns. In addition to protecting the interests of the ruling families, spreading Islam is the main goal for these states.

The exact amount of money which the Qatari ruling family Al-Thani has spent to spread Islam all over the world and particularly to Islamise Europe and North America in the past forty years is unknown, but it is estimated to be in tens of billions of dollars. They have been turning churches into mosques and building Islamic schools and Quranic institutions across the globe. By 2014, one of their many charity organizations had built over 113 Islamic centres, mosques, and Islamic schools in Europe. Forty-five projects were completed in Italy, 22 in France, 11 in the United Kingdom, 11 in Spain, 6 in Germany, 6 in Ukraine, 2 in Hungary, 3 in Norway, 6 in Poland, 3 in Belgium, 5 in Switzerland, 2 in Iceland, 8 in Canada, one in Australia, and many in the USA.[655] Their news channel Al Jazeera is available worldwide free of charge and in different languages. It was the channel that broadcast the videos and interviews of Osama bin Laden as well as many other terrorists. One of its main programmes, "Sharia and life" presented by the Egyptian Yousef Al-Qaradawi – the religious leader of the Muslim Brothers, is designed to promote Islamic teachings as the source of all laws. In 2012, Qatar pledged to support the Muslim Brothers' regime in Egypt with 18 billion dollars.

Considered by many politicians and theorists as the most two-faced country, Qatar, or to be precise the ruling family of Qatar, has been officially backing the Americans in their war on terror while simultaneously allowing the funding of terrorist who are fighting Americans and all non-Muslims. David Cohen, the US Treasury Under Secretary for Terrorism and Financial Intelligence, stated that "There are U.S.- and UN-designated

---

655 Chesnot, C., & Malbrunot, G. (2020). Qatar Papers. How Doha finances the Muslim Brotherhood in Europe. Averroes & Cie.

terrorist financiers in Qatar that have not been acted against under Qatari law." Many of the funders of terrorism designated by the USA, UN, and the European Union have been protected by the rulers of Qatar and allowed to live and function freely. For instance, Abdulrahman al-Nuaymi, who is accused by US Treasury Department, UN, Turkey, the United Kingdom, and the European Union of funding Al-Qaeda and its affiliates in Iraq, Syria, Somalia, Yemen is a friend of the previous Amir and a link between him and radical Islamic figures, according to the Amir himself. As reported by US Treasury Department, al-Nuaymi was transferring $2 million monthly to Al-Qaeda in Iraq for an unspecified period. He also provided equipment for the terrorists in Iraq who were fighting against the Americans and the Iraqi government. Hundreds of American soldiers and many more Iraqis were killed and wounded by these terrorists.

Donald Trump described the Saudis as "the world's biggest funders of terrorism" while Hillary Clinton criticised the Saudi financing of "radical schools and mosques around the world that have set too many young people on a path toward extremism."[656] The Saudi royal family has dedicated many billions from the oil revenue to spreading Islam.[657]

> The reach of the Saudis has been stunning, touching nearly every country with a Muslim population, from the Gothenburg Mosque in Sweden to the King Faisal Mosque in Chad, from the King Fahad Mosque in Los Angeles to the Seoul Central Mosque in South Korea. Support has come from the Saudi government; the royal family; Saudi charities; and Saudi-sponsored organizations including the World Muslim League, the World Assembly of Muslim Youth and the International Islamic Relief Organization, providing the hardware of impressive edifices and the software of preaching and teaching.[658]

The Kuwaiti ruling family that prohibits non-Muslims from building places of worship and from practicing their religion on its territories has

---

656 Shane, S. (2016, Aug 26). Saudis and Extremism: Both the Arsonists and the Firefighters. The New York Times.
657 Prados, A. B. & Blanchard, C. M. (Updated 2007, Sep 14). Saudi Arabia: Terrorist Financing Issues. [Report]. Congressional Research Service.
658 Shane, S. (2016, Aug 26). Saudis and Extremism: Both the Arsonists and the Firefighters.

built thousands of mosques and Islamic schools all over the world. It is another example of the nature of the alliance between the West and the hereditary Gulf regimes. The Kuwaiti penal code punishes non-Muslims with a month in jail for drinking or eating in public during Ramadan but does not have a law to combat money laundry or financing Islamic terrorism. Over the past fifty years, Kuwaitis have spent billions of dollars on building and supporting mosques and Islamic schools across the United States and Europe, from Manhattan Islamic Centre on the 96th Street to the Islamic Centre of Kuwait in Utah to London Central Mosque Trust to hundreds of other Islamic schools and mosques. Kuwait's government directly manages many of these Islamic institutions through its embassies. The Kuwaiti permanent ambassador to the United Nations is the chairman of New York Islamic Centre, and the supervisor of that wealthy centre is the Deputy Counsel of the Kuwaiti Mission to the United Nations. The Kuwaiti ambassador to the UK is the chairman of the board of trustees for the London Central Mosque Trust & The Islamic Cultural Centre. The other two members of the board are senior diplomats from Oman and Saudi Arabia. In Italy, the Kuwaiti embassy donates millions of euros annually to the Islamic centres and distributes thousands of meals to the mosques.[659]

This investment by the undemocratic governments in spreading Islam is an application of the matrimony between money, politics, and religion in these states.[660] The rich autocratic ruling families focus on the First World rather than helping the millions of poor Muslims in their countries or other Asian and African states for political as well as economic reasons. They aim to increase their power and private wealth through propagating their religion, create followers who pose a threat to the powerful Western countries and use that as leverage to gain influence over the world with the accomplice of many politicians, academics, and journalists.

---

659 Kuwait News Agency KUNA. (2014, Oct 8). Kuwait Embassy in Rome celebrates Eid in Islamic Center.; Khan, A. (2021, Dec 19). The Islamic Center in Rome resumes its cultural activities… in the presence of the Kuwaiti Ambassador. My Kuwaits News.
660 Ehrenfeld, R. (2011). Their Oil Is Thicker Than Our Blood. In S.N. Stern (Ed.). Saudi Arabia and the Global Islamic Terrorist Network. Palgrave Macmillan.

Currently, Islam as an ideology weaponised by Iran, Turkey, Pakistan, Egypt, Qatar, Kuwait and to a lesser degree other Gulf States represents one of the most dangerous threats to the world stability. It is a genocidal, apocalyptic creed that cannot survive without conflict. Muslim fighters have carried out attacks in every corner of this planet with the support of rich regimes and devoted masses. Since the irrational increase of oil prices in 1970s, this ideology has been on the offence across the world and many of the politicians and intellectuals worldwide are either too corrupt or too frightened to face it.

Numerous individuals and organizations are working relentlessly in Europe, Asia, and America to alter the cultures of these regions to suit the Islamic principles.[661] They may not succeed in ruling the world, but they are succeeding in imposing their ideology on many countries and communities, turning them into copies of the failed Muslim states. In every city of this vast world, people are afraid to criticise Islam, to speak their minds and to mention a historical fact that could offend Muslims. Communities are losing their identities and a sense of belonging. All over the world, we see elected politicians, so-called journalists and professors caving in to Islam (and other authoritarian ideologies), hoping they would be spared from its followers' anger. Through terrorism and soft means, mujahedeen have managed to alter the way in which people of different cultures live their lives. Intellectuals have been murdered in cold blood for being loyal to freethinking.

In the last few decades, tens of millions of devoted Muslims ditched the ailing Islamic world to settle in rich and democratic European countries, Japan, Australia, New Zealand, and North America, and many more millions are expected to follow suit.[662] They are coming from lawless countries with deficient educational systems, corrupt institutions, sharia-based courts, brutal security forces, and authoritarian regimes. They believe that they have the right to live in any region they choose because the world was created by Allah and they are his beloved

---

661 See Freedman, I. (2017). Hamas, CAIR and the Muslim Brotherhood: The Plot to Destroy America. Center for Security Policy Press.
662 There are over 26 million Muslims in the European Union, 4 million in the US and over a million in Canada.

creatures.[663] After they were settled in the prosperous countries, many immigrants have decided to categorically reject the new societies' values and identity and cling to their Islamic identity.[664] They thanked their God for granting them a new future – not the people who welcomed them into their homeland.

---

663 Quran 1:128: "The earth is Allah's. He gives it as a heritage to whom He will of His slaves."
664 See Gallup & the Coexist Foundation. (2009). The Gallup Coexist Index 2009: A Global Study of Interfaith Relations (with an in-depth analysis of Muslim integration in France, Germany, and the United Kingdom).; Murray, D. (2017). The Strange Death of Europe: Immigration, Identity, Islam. Bloomsbury.

THE REFUGEE CRISIS

One of the stories that has hardly been covered by the media concerns a group of illegal immigrants travelling from Libya to Italy. During the journey, the Muslims on the boat threw 12 people overboard to their death because they were Christians. The attackers had organised themselves, intending to kill all the non-Muslims who were with them on the same boat. They did not complete their mission due to the resistance they faced. [665]

Germany is the European country receiving the highest number of asylum applications. Almost all of the seekers are from outside the European Union. In 2015, more than a million individuals, mainly Muslim males from Syria, Iraq, and Afghanistan were living off the asylum seeker welfare in Germany alone; the number went down to 384,307 by 2021, as many of them moved to rely on the unemployment welfare. In that same time, the German Army's budget was slashed to the degree that it currently lags behind countries such as Egypt or Pakistan in terms of equipment as well as manpower, leaving Germany incapable of defending itself, let alone supporting its allies and neighbouring countries.[666] In 2018 and 2019, German taxpayers spent 12.9 and 12.6 billion euros consecutively just on welfare payments for non-German immigrants, refugees and asylum seekers. Many more billions of euros were spent on their housing, education, legal fees and health care.[667] The majority of the recipients were Syrian, Iraqi, and Afghani Muslim males. Meanwhile, one out of every five German children was living in poverty at the time.[668]

As of 2021, two thirds of the Syrian refugees in Germany, 44% of the Afghani, and 37% of the Somali, who are capable of work and are

---

665 Messia, H., Borghese, L. & Hanna, J. (2015, April 19). Italian police: Muslim migrants threw Christians overboard. CNN.
666 Lt. Gen. Alfons Mais, the Chief of the German Army's comment on his LinkedIn account on 24 February 2022.
667 DW. (2019, Dec 27). Germany: Welfare payments to foreigners nearly double over 12 years.
668 DW. (2020, Jul 22). 1 in 5 children in Germany grow up in poverty.

not attending integration courses or professional language classes, are dependent on welfare money. The majority of these asylum seekers and immigrants are uneducated Muslim males, many of them with criminal records, who abandoned their country and people when they needed them and committed the crime of illegally crossing the borders of several states before arriving in Germany. Many of them have been living in Germany for more than five years without integrating into the society or working to support themselves.

Immigration laws in Western countries sanction and promote illegal immigration. In the UK, any person who intrudes into the country illegally or overstays their visa is rewarded with a weekly allowance, free housing, free education, free medical and dental care once he or she applied for asylum. If the application was rejected and the court found that the person has no ground to stay in the UK, then the government will continue giving them the weekly allowance, free housing, free medical care, free dental care, free education and other benefits at the expense of the taxpayer. This system appeals to the most dangerous and least honest people. It is an invitation for criminals and underachievers to break the law.

The case of the asylum seeker Lawangeen Abdulrahimzai is an indictment of the European establishment and their laws. The Muslim Afghani moved between several European countries, committing crimes. In Italy, he was convicted on two drug offences in July 2016. In August 2018, he killed two people in Serbia with a Kalashnikov rifle. He fled and illegally entered Norway and lived there on taxpayers' money before moving to the UK in 2019, claiming to be 14 years old while he was 19. He was given financial support and a foster home; he was enrolled in a high school where he mixed which children, all despite having been convicted in absentia for two murders by a Serbian court and despite his criminal record in Italy and Norway. British authorities failed in establishing his real biological age or checking his fingerprints against Interpol records. In 2022, he stabbed to death Thomas Roberts, 21, during an argument over an e-scooter. Many of the people who had dealt with him noticed that he was an aggressive person and could not be 14 years old but were afraid to be called islamophobes or racist if they spoke.

CONTROLLING THE MINDS AND THE LAND

In Europe, Canada, and the USA, Islamic schools designed to create devoted Muslims knowledgeable about Islam's laws and its official history
are mushrooming, bankrolled by the petrodollar and aided by some of
the democratically elected non-Muslim politicians.[669] This is despite
the fact that graduates of these schools are incapable of competing in
a free market economy. They are taught Arabic and the Quran at the
expense of science.[670]

Islamic organizations are active in prisons and among criminals all
over Europe and North America. They are converting convicts to Islam
in masses. In many cases, credulous evil felons were transformed into
bloodthirsty suicidal killers who blamed the infidels for their personal
errors.[671] The Americans Clement Hampton-El and Victor Alvarez, the
Britons Richard Reid (the Shoe Bomber) and Samantha Lewthwaite
(the White Widow), the French David and Jerome Courtailler, the German Christian Ganczarski, the Dutch Walters brothers are a few of
numerous examples.[672]

Deradicalisation programmes to rehabilitate convicted terrorists
in prisons have been created in all industrial countries. These programmes aim to persuade devoted Muslims to abandon jihad while
holding on tightly to Islam and living by all its other principles. Musa
Cerantonio, who was the most famous jihadi preacher in Australia,
described these programmes from his jail cell as "idiotic" and a failure

669 BBC News. (2010, Nov 22). Saudi school lessons in UK concern government.
670 Richardson, H. (2015, Nov 14). 'Radicalisation risk' at six Muslim private schools, says
Ofsted. BBC News.; Taher, A. (2019, May 5). Secret Government report warns over 48 British
Islamic schools are teaching intolerance and misogyny to future imams. Daily Mail.
671 Mamiya, L. H. (2005). Islam in Prison. In M. Bosworth (Ed.). Encyclopedia of Prisons
and Correctional Facilities. Sage.
672 Benjamin, D. (2007). The convert's zeal: Why are so many jihadists converts to islam. The
Brookings Institute.

from the onset as they are based on highlighting moderate texts of medieval imams as the "true Islam". [673] Any informed Muslim can easily refute the theoretical foundation of these programmes through showing that jihad and slavery are essential parts of Islam based on the Quran. Furthermore, many of these jihadists are psychopaths and as such, incapable of change. Studies show that all forms of rehabilitation including therapy are ineffective with psychopaths. [674]

An independent inquiry commissioned by the British parliament to investigate terrorism in the prison system found that Muslim terrorists control many prisons across England and Wales. They use the jail system to recruit new terrorists, radicalise Muslim inmates and separate them from the rest of the prisoners. They also attack non-Muslim prisoners for religious reasons and they established sharia courts inside British jails. [675]

Currently, naturalized citizens, illegal immigrants, and refugees in the Western countries are striving to differentiate themselves from the native populations and enforcing their way of life upon the societies they moved to. They have been reconstructing their old societies inside the non-Muslim countries. Many of them are living in neighbourhoods influenced by sharia rather than the law of the land and its values. Islamic schools, Islamic food, Islamic clothes, and Islamic media are what many Muslims in Europe and North America know and concern themselves with. This has augmented their economic difficulties and pushed many of them to live off social security payments and hand-outs distributed by the Gulf's radical Islamic charities and mosques. Consequently, the gap between these Muslim communities and the rest of the society is becoming irreconcilable.

Islamic media networks owned by the oil-producing autocratic hereditary regimes of the Gulf are the main source of information for Muslims living in America and Europe. These closely controlled outlets are dominating the minds of the immigrants in a way that increases the

---

673 Wood, G. (2022, Mar 31). Why an ISIS Propagandist Abandoned Islam. The Atlantic.
674 See Patrick, C. J. (Ed.). (2018). Handbook of psychopathy. Guilford Publications.
675 Hall, J. (2022, April). Terrorism in Prisons: Presented to Parliament pursuant to Section 36(5) of the Terrorism Act 2006. UK Government.

gap between them and the societies they are living in. A brief critical review of Al Jazeera's coverage (in Arabic) of Islamic terrorist attacks or the history of the Israeli-Arab conflict is sufficient to disclose the agenda of the Qatari ruling family who finance and control this channel.

In France, 46% of foreign-born Muslims declared that they wanted sharia to be the rule of the land, arguing that it was superior to the French laws.[676] In the UK, there are over thirty Islamic sharia councils affiliated with mosques and recognized by the British government. These councils have a substantial influence over Muslims. They are permitted to grant divorces and register marriages among other things. This creates a state within the state. In 2021, a Muslim filed a complaint with the British police against his parents. He stated that they had abused him through radicalising him. He detailed that his parents taught him to hate Britons and the West and not to befriend non-Muslims. The parents taught their son that there was a war between Islam and the West, and he needed to be ready to fight against the UK. They were creating a terrorist while living on a London council estate and receiving handouts from the infidels, the son testified.[677]

Due to their increasing numbers resulting from high birth rate combined with mass illegal immigration as well as the financial and political support they receive from the oil-rich Persian Gulf States, Muslim immigrants are gaining key positions in all the non-Muslim countries. Two Muslims who came to the United States as refugees were elected to the Congress in 2018 and then re-elected. One of them is the Somali Ilhan Omar, who described the massacre of 9/11 as "some people did something." She also refused to vote for recognizing the Armenian genocide. The other one is the Palestinian Rashida Talib, who tweeted the slogan used by Hezbollah, Hamas and other terrorist organizations which calls for the elimination of Israel: "from the river to the sea, Palestine will be free."

In the UK, nineteen Muslims were elected to the House of Commons in 2019. The current Mayor of London, Sadiq Khan, is a devoted

---

676 i24 News. (2019, Sep 19). Poll: 46% of French Muslims believe Sharia law should be applied in country.
677 Taher, A. (2021, May 29). British-born former Islamic extremist, 29, reports his parents to the police for 'radicalising him as a child'. Daily Mail.

Muslim who boasts about fasting in Ramadan. The current Justice Secretary of Scotland is another keen Pakistani Muslim who was first elected to the Scottish parliament at the age of twenty-five. The Muslim British MP of Pakistani origin, Naz Shah, addressed the House of Commons in 2021 calling for limiting freedom of speech when it comes to criticising Mohammad: "for me and millions of Muslims across this country and the quarter of the world's population that is Muslim too, with each day and each breath, there is not a single thing in the world that we commemorate and honour more than our beloved Prophet Muhammad…. When bigots and racist defame, slander or abuse our Prophet…, the emotional harm caused upon our hearts is unbearable. Because for 2 billion Muslims, he is the leader we commemorate in our hearts, honour in our lives and forms the basis of our identity and our very existence." [678]

Many of the Muslim politicians in the West, such as Sadiq Khan, Naz Shah, and Lord Ahmed in the UK, Ilhan Omar, Rashida Talib in the USA, or Omar Alghabra, Maryam Monsef in Canada, tend to state that they represent Islam and that they believe in its teachings and love Mohammad.[679] They are never pressed to explain what they think of the Islamic teachings that sanction killings of apostates, adulterers, and homosexuals. Neither do they discuss the Quranic verses that call for jihad or sanction slavery and polygamy.

In Belgium, Muslims established an Islamic political party that aims to institute sharia as the source of laws in that European country. Two of the elected members of this party stated in an interview that they wanted to separate men and women in public places and enforce corporal punishment. In Sweden, the Somali Muslim Brother Abdirizak Waberi, who was elected to the Swedish parliament as a member of the Moderate Party from 2010 to 2014, defended polygamy, stating that a man could love four women at the same time. He was charged by the Swedish prosecutors of committing several crimes, including embezzling millions of Swedish kronor, after he left the Riksdag and became

---

678 Mussa, M. (2021, Jul 06). British lawmaker takes up issue of Prophet Muhammad's sanctity in Parliament. Anadolu Agency.
679 Leftly, M. (2016, May 10). Exclusive: London Mayor Sadiq Khan on Religious Extremism, Brexit and Donald Trump. Time.

the head of an Islamic school in Goteborg. All the male students in this Islamic school graduated with full marks and were eligible to apply for college, in comparison to 71% of the female students.

In the Netherlands, Kauthar Bouchallikht, a 26-year-old Muslim of Moroccan descent, was elected to the parliament in 2021 to become the first Dutch MP wearing the Islamic hijab. She was a candidate of the Green Party, even though she had not held any position within that party before she appeared on the ninth place of its candidates list. Beforehand, she was the vice-chairman of the Islamic youth organization Femyso founded by Muslim Brothers. The head of the Green Party in the Netherlands, Jesse Feras Klaver, who himself is a son of a Muslim Moroccan immigrant, described Kauthar as the "figurehead of the green movement."[680]

The 31-year-old Muslim Syrian Tareq Alaows, who left his country and entered Germany illegally in 2015, announced his candidacy for the German Parliament (Bundestag) on the Green Party's list. He launched his campaign to become an MP in 2021, right after he had submitted his application for German citizenship. His main goals were to allow more immigrants into Germany and provide them with better housing and more benefits, from the German taxpayer's money.[681]

In 2021, Muslims in Cologne won the right to use loudspeakers to call for the Friday noon prayer from all their mosques. Henriette Reker, the mayor of Cologne, praised her own decision as "a sign of respect."[682] She previously blamed the victims of 2016 sexual assaults, suggesting that they could have prevented the mass attacks by leaving a space.[683] The same city that witnessed hundreds of sexual assaults and rapes which have gone unpunished is being steadily assimilated to the Muslim world. The call itself (azan/adhan) contains the declaration that there is "no god but Allah and that Mohammad is his messenger" which is a direct rebuff

680 NOS. (2020, Nov 17). Klaver is still supporting candidate Bouchallikht. [Klaver staat nog steeds achter kandidaat Bouchallikht]. (Dutch).
681 DW. (2021, Feb 3). Syrian refugee Tareq Alaows launches bid for German parliament.
682 Henriette Reker [@HenrietteReker]. (2021, Oct 9). (…) Den Muezzin-Ruf zu erlauben ist für mich ein Zeichen des Respekts [Permitting the muezzin call is for me a sign of respect]. (German). Twitter.
683 Al-Othman, H. (2016, Jan 6). Cologne Mayor accused of 'victim blaming' for comments after mass sex assaults. Evening Standard.

to all other beliefs. In Muslim countries, the call for prayer is transmitted over megaphones five times a day, starting at dusk and continuing into the night. The prayers, recitations of the Quran as well as imams' speeches are also broadcast over the loudspeakers with a complete disregard for people's opinions, feelings, or rights. In Kuwait, Beirut, Cairo, Alexandria, and all the other cities and towns of the Muslim world, both Muslims and non-Muslims are forced to listen to the Quran, hadith, and the imams' sermons even while they are inside their homes. They cannot complain that the dawn prayer call wakes them up or the night prayer disturbs them, nor can they protest being called infidels and filth and the evilest of beasts. When would Cologne allow all that as well?

A group of ex-Muslims staged a peaceful protest near Cologne Central Mosque against the decision. They highlighted that many of the mosques which had been granted the permission belonged to radical organizations and were affiliated with the autocratic Turkish regime. The protesters were verbally abused by the attendants of the mosque, who also attacked a reporter for a German TV station. The organizer of the protest received numerous death threats and was placed under police protection.

On the website of the New York City's Shia Islamic centre of Grand Ayatollah Al-Khoei, a section is dedicated to Islamic rules, based on his book "Minhaj al-Saliheen". These edicts are organized in the form of questions and answers or short articles. The answer to question 15. quotes the influential jurist's (now dead) rule that it is prohibited for a Muslim to defect during fighting against infidels. In reply to question 16., the quoted edict states that it is permissible to fight infidels with all available means and tools. Al-Khoei had explained this proclamation further, indicating that Muslims must take into consideration the circumstances of each era, clarifying that jihad is not limited to the use of weapons. In the answer to question 17., the quoted edict explains that elderly men, women and children should not be killed and the same applies to prisoners of war, but if the enemies used them as shields, then killing them is permitted. Al-Khoei declared that if a Muslim killed a non-Muslim woman, child, or an elderly, then the murderer should not be punished and he is not required to pay compensation. The grand ayatollah also called for the killing of apostates and anyone who verbally insults Mohammad. He declared time and again that non-Muslims are najas and hence, Muslims must wash after interacting with them. Muslims are not allowed to eat any meat slaughtered by non-Muslims, neither should they be buried in non-Muslim cemeteries. These fatwas are evident of how non-Muslims are being portrayed as subhuman enemies by Muslims even within their countries.

This ideology is being taught to Muslims in New York City by the students of Al-Khoei and despite the use of vague language, the content is clear: it is the duty of Muslims to fight against infidels with any available means. The majority of imams today are not brave enough to talk in a simple and clear English, because they believe in deception and seek to avoid the consequences of their ideas. They also do not want to provoke the unaware Muslims in addition to the international community, yet, they still succeed at delivering their message in an effective and consistent way to their targeted audience. They demonise and dehumanise non-Muslims in a systematic and institutionalized way, transforming petty criminals and helpless psychopaths into ruthless mujahedeen whom they later use as a bargaining chip. Muslims are taught throughout their lives, right from their childhood, that killing non-Muslims is an obligation. It is not a sin and produces no consequences but the satisfaction of Allah and the praise of other Muslims. In contrast, befriending non-Muslims or helping them is a major sin unless it is a way to win them over for Islam or deceive them.

Well-being and integration indexes show that many of the Muslim refugees, immigrants, their children and grandchildren have refused adamantly to be part of the countries they are settled in.[684] Over the years, many of the British- and European-naturalized Muslims have joined terrorist organizations that are in war with the countries whose

684 Adida, C. L., Laitin, D. D., & Valfort, M. A. (2016). Why Muslim integration fails in Christian-heritage societies. Harvard University Press.; Shah, S. (2019). "I Am a Muslim First..." Challenges of Muslimness and the UK State Schools. Leadership and Policy in Schools 18(3), pp 341-356.; Angenendt, S., and others. (Eds.). (2007). Muslim integration: Challenging conventional wisdom in Europe and the United States. Center for Strategic and International Studies.; Higgingbottom, J. (2020, Mar 2). 'It's a powder keg ready to explode': In Greek village tensions simmer between refugees and locals. CNBC.; Parekh, B. (2008). European Liberalism and the 'Muslim Question'. Amsterdam University Press.

citizenships they hold. Jihadi John (Mohammed Emwazi), who was born in Kuwait as a Bedoon (with no citizenship or legal right of abode), back-stabbed the British nation which had naturalized him and his family, had given them free accommodation, free health care, free education, free allowance, and a homeland. He along with other naturalized refugees and immigrants formed a group known as the Jihadi Beatles, which specialised in beheading Western hostages on camera while talking in English, a language they learned for free, to spread Islam. The second member of this group is the Sudanese El Shafee Elsheikh, known as Jihadi George, who like Emwazi came to the UK with his family as an asylum seeker, in this case from the impoverished Sudan, and for many years lived off the social security handouts. The third one is Alexanda Amon Kotey, a Ghanaian criminal and drug dealer who was born in London where he converted to Islam. The third member, Aine Lesley Davis, also comes from immigrant background and was also a criminal and a drug dealer before converting to Islam. He is married to Amal El-Wahabi, a Moroccan Muslim convicted of funding terrorism. These individuals, who have beheaded several innocent people, tortured hostages and committed other horrific crimes, had been devoted Muslims attending mosques in the UK before they joined jihad in Syria, similar to many others who immigrated to the West.

In the Fort Hood (Texas) massacre of 2009, the Muslim Palestinian/American psychiatrist Nidal Hasan, a major in the American Army, shouted 'Allah Akbar' while opening fire on his unarmed colleagues, killing 13 and injuring 32 people. He was showing his gratitude to the country that had accepted him along with his family, given them its citizenship, a future, education, and a home.

In the San Bernardino massacre of 2015, a Muslim terrorist attacked his unsuspecting colleagues, killing 14 people and injuring a further 24 with the assistance of his wife. This Pakistani man born in the United States and his Pakistani wife were planning their attack for over a year. Their aim was to kill as many vulnerable non-Muslims as they could. On the day of the attack, they left their new-born baby and went to devastate innocent people's lives; they were helped by other Muslims who saw killing non-Muslims as a noble endeavour.

In 2019, the Saudi pilot in the Royal Saudi Air Force Mohammed Alshamrani, who was on a training course at the naval air base in Pensacola, Florida, opened fire against his American classmates. He killed three navy sailors aged 19, 21, and 23 and wounded eight others. An investigation into the other Saudi trainees revealed that twenty-one of them were either involved in child pornography or jihad and anti-American rhetoric while living in the US and being trained by the Americans to become professional officers.[685] All these individuals shared one salient identity and were motivated by it.

685 Reuters. (2020, Jan 12). Saudi military trainees to be expelled from U.S. after Florida shooting: CNN.

COWARDICE AND DISHONESTY MASKED AS MORALITY

It's not just me who has lost but Danish values have lost too.[686]
Inger Støjberg

We're not at war with you, you're at war with yourselves [687]

As Muslims, we reject democracy, we reject secularism, and freedom, and human rights [688]

The same Iranian, Turkish, Kuwaiti, Saudi, Qatari undemocratic regimes which ban non-Muslims from practising their beliefs on their territories are building and financing innumerable Islamic centres and converting churches into mosques all over Europe, Canada, the United States, South America, Australia, Japan. Schools funded and run by the petrodollar-rich states are booming in countries which did not have a Muslim presence a few decades ago. These institutions are dedicated to teaching Muslims that they are the pure and superior humans, and non-Muslims are filth and evil enemies.

While devoted Muslims are forcing secular societies to change their ways of life by violence, intimidation, and bribes, some of the elite in these countries accept and facilitate these transformations in the name of multiculturalism, tolerance, and human rights.[689] These notions have been abused to systematically suffocate the modern secular identities of

---

686 Denmark's former Minister of Immigration Inger Støjberg.
687 BBC News. (2021, Oct 27). Paris attacks: UK Bataclan victim's sister addressing the terrorist in the trial.
688 The British Muslim preacher Anjem Choudary. Press TV. (2013, Apr 11). British Islamist Anjem Choudary: As Muslims We Reject Human Rights. [Video]. Memri TV.
689 To understand why many of the so-called elite are afraid to take a position, see Deneault, A. (2018). Mediocracy: The Politics of the Extreme Centre. Between the Lines.; See also Sarrazin, T. (2018). Feindliche Übernahme: Wie der Islam den Fortschritt behindert und die Gesellschaft bedroht [Hostile takeover: How Islam impedes progress and threatens society]. Finanzbuch Verlag.; Mohammed, Y. (2019). Unveiled: How Western Liberals Empower Radical Islam. Free Hearts Free Minds.

Europe, Canada, and the United States. The intimidated Westerners who are turning a blind eye to the consequences of their cowardice and apathy are accomplices in all the crimes committed by brainwashed terrorists and the autocratic states that finance them. People are held hostage by the violent devotees of one religion and their masters who aim to control every aspect of human life throughout the world.

In many countries where Muslims have carried out major terrorist attacks, the Muslim population and their political influence have boomed afterward. For instance in Britain, the Muslim population doubled between 2001 and 2011.[690] The number of Muslim MPs in the British Parliament rose from 2 in 2001 to 18 in 2019. In the United States, the number of Muslims went up from 2.35 million in 2007 to 3.45 million in 2017.[691] No Muslim had ever been elected to the Congress, until Keith Ellison became the first Muslim member of the House of Representatives in 2007. Four Muslims were elected to the Congress in 2019, all of them members of the Democratic Party.

Islam is the fastest growing religion in many industrial countries, due to a high birth rate, petrodollar influence, and fraudulent immigration policies that favour illegal to legal and dishonest people to the law-abiding ones. Muslim immigrants in the Western countries campaign relentlessly – with the help of the Gulf States' regimes – to establish the Islamic laws as the ruling ideology for their host societies as the solution to what they see as a moral decay of non-Muslims. Many Muslim leaders and organizations have been working adamantly to replace secular constitutions, civil and common law systems with Islamic laws in the secular and non-Muslim countries.[692] Worldwide, the segregation between religion and the state is under constant attack; freedom of speech and critical thinking are being curtailed on a daily basis. The eminent German thinker Thilo Sarrazin has indicated that "no other religion in Europe" makes "so many demands" as Islam: "No immigrant group other

690 Gani, A. (2015, Feb 11). Muslim population in England and Wales nearly doubles in 10 years. The Guardian.
691 Mohamed, B. (2018, Jan 3). New estimates show U.S. Muslim population continues to grow. Pew Research Center.
692 See Murray, D. (2017). The Strange Death of Europe: Immigration, Identity, Islam. Bloomsbury.

than Muslims is so strongly connected with claims on the welfare state and crime. No group emphasizes their differences so strongly in public, especially through women's clothing. In no other religion is the transition to violence, dictatorship and terrorism so fluid."[693]

"It's not just me who has lost but Danish values have lost too." This was the former Danish immigration minister Inger Støjberg's reaction to being sent to jail for separating underage girls from their alleged older husbands. The minister, while in power, introduced a restriction on housing female refugees under 18 years old with their alleged older spouses. This policy was designed to protect underage females and to combat child marriage which is illegal in Denmark. A 26-year-old Syrian refugee filed a complaint against being separated from his 17-year-old wife while their application was being reviewed. He stated that he must stay with his underage wife in the free accommodation provided by the Danish government, which was not allowed under the regulations introduced by Støjberg. The supreme court convicted Inger Støjberg of breaching human rights and sentenced her to sixty days in prison.

In December of 2021 in Toronto, freedom of speech was defeated when the largest school board in Canada cancelled a talk by the ISIS victim and Nobel Peace Prize laureate Nadia Murad.[694] She was prevented from meeting with students to discuss her upcoming book and talk about her story as a resilient woman who survived the slavery she had been subjected to and the killing of her family at the hands of ISIS. The school board superintendent, Helen Fisher, who cancelled the meeting stated that the book was offensive to Muslims and "fostered Islamophobia". Truth is evil, deceit is moral, victims are criminals.

On Friday, 24 June 2022, a Muslim attacked a bar popular among the LGBTQ community in Oslo. He killed two people and wounded more than 20 others because of their homosexual identity which is a major crime in Islam. The terrorist, who had come to Norway from Iran as a refugee and committed several crimes before this attack, had

---

693 As quoted in Bucerius, S. (2014). Unwanted: Muslim Immigrants, Dignity, and Drug Dealing (Studies in Crime and Public Policy). Oxford University Press.
694 See Murad, N., & Krajeski, J. (2017). The Last Girl: My Story of Captivity and My Fight against the Islamic State.

then been given Norwegian citizenship and allowed to move freely despite being considered dangerous by the police.

In reaction to the attack, which spread fear in Norway and caused the cancellation of Oslo Pride Parade scheduled for the following day, the Norwegian Prime Minister Jonas Gahr Støre rushed to show his support for the Muslims: "I know that many Muslims are scared and despairing. Then it is our responsibility that no one other than the person behind the attack is responsible."

Støre did not and would not highlight the perception of homosexuality among Muslims, the Islamic teachings that sanction killing homosexuals, or the failure of his government in protecting the people from terrorists.[695] The attack was celebrated, and the murderer was praised by countless Muslims all over social media platforms. At the same time, many commentators warned that this attack might be used by critics of Islam to spread Islamophobia. The President of Norwegian Parliament Masud Gharahkhani, who is an Iranian born in Tehran, did not utter a word about the motives of the Islamic terrorism.

A few months earlier, on 9 December 2021, 219 US Congress members, all from the Democratic Party, voted to pass the Combating International Islamophobia Act which was sponsored by the Muslim congresswoman Ilhan Omar. Based on this bill, the United States of America will establish an office within the Department of State dedicated to monitoring and combating Islamophobia all over the world. Commentator Mohamed Zuhdi Jasser indicated that "the freest nation on earth is now unbelievably on the verge of creating a position in our State Department charged not with protecting inalienable human rights, but with protecting a faith ideology. This will be celebrated by our theocratic Islamist enemies across the world. The US government will have a sanctioned 'American Grand Mufti' who will determine what is, and what is not, Islam. Every American Muslim, especially anti-Islamist (anti-theocratic) Muslims, will be marginalized by the new US government arbiter on Islam."[696]

---

695 Solomons, A. (2022, June 25). Revealed: Iranian refugee turned 'terrorist', 42, 'who killed two in Islamist attack' on Oslo gay bar.... Daily Mail.

696 Zuhdi, J. (2021, Dec 21). Omar's Bill will be praised by Islamic extremists all over the world. Israel National News.

THE ONES THAT SUCCEEDED IN REFORMING MUSLIM COUNTRIES

> My people are going to learn the principles of democracy,
> the dictates of truth and the teachings of science.
> Superstition must go.[697]
>
> Mustafa Kemal Ataturk

Several leaders in the 20th century succeeded in transforming their Muslim countries from poor, traditional, lawless, feudal societies into prosperous, functioning countries. They did that despite Islam, not by means of it. In every era in which a Muslim country experienced significant development, rule of law, and social freedoms, Islam was marginalised, and its institutions and ideas were rejected and kept out of the public domain by the power of the state. Kemal Ataturk in Turkey, Habib Bourguiba in Tunisia, and to a lesser degree Qasim in Iraq are among the most renowned decision makers who succeed in creating significant development in their countries over a short time. They employed the power of authority to transform their societies from Islamic to secular. They annulled Islamic laws that had been governing their peoples for centuries. They closed Islamic schools and sharia courts and empowered women by the power of law against the opposition of the masses and the religious institutions. They criminalised old Islamic practices such as slavery, polygamy, and jihad. They banned several Islamic rituals and sects. They deemed fasting during Ramadan as a counterproductive practice, harmful to the economy and a cause of poverty. They rejected the hijab as a symbol of suppression of females.

In 1957, the Tunisian president Bourguiba started a campaign against hijab. He knew the nature of the coercion females suffer to accept the hijab and how difficult and dangerous it is for them as individuals to reject it. He first removed it off one of his relatives' head during an official

---

697 Mustafa Kemal Ataturk. Quoted in Ellison, G. (1928). Turkey to-day. Hutchinson.

celebration of the Independence Day, which turned into a nation-wide programme. These scenes, aired on national Tunisian TV, created shockwaves all over the Muslim world and turned out to be a huge stride toward women's empowerment in Tunisia and the Middle East. They encouraged other women to take off hijab if they desired to, which millions of them did. The Tunisian president challenged the Islamic teachings directly, and the Tunisian jurists conceded to the state's power. Some of them went as far as ruling that hijab is not part of Islam.

To this day, all of these leaders remain sincerely admired and respected by a significant segment of their people for their decency and accomplishments, despite their adamant animosity toward Islam. In Tunisia and in Turkey, secular leaders had succeeded in freeing millions from poverty, diseases, and ignorance. They created modern secular functioning institutions in extremely short periods, and the positive effect of their policies on their societies is still evident. In Iraq, the secular state was short-lived, as the Islamic institutions managed to gain power and annulled most of the modern laws and achievements of the secular regime, taking the people back to poverty, ignorance, and religious conflicts.

The current Saudi king and his crown prince as well as the United Arab Emirates' rulers have recently realised that the Islamic clergy is a liability, not an asset. They recognised that they attain legitimacy from their powerful institutions and the fact that they control the state's revenue and budget, not from fighting groups of theologians living in the past, who praise the authority in public and undermine it in private. They could not allow the imams to remain as a state within the state and continue demolishing the regime from within. In the two countries, the power of the state has now been used to limit the Islamic institutions' influence on the public life. Religious police have been suspended, and people freed from its members' brutality and abuse. For the first time, women were granted the right to drive, travel, work, and study in Saudi Arabia. In the Emirates, a functioning secular state is being created and the religious laws are being swiftly annulled. Religious institutions have been marginalised. The overwhelming positive reaction of the general public shows that many people were fed up with the Islamic laws and the hegemony of the religious institutions but could not resist them as individuals.

THE TREACHERY OF GREAT UNIVERSITIES: ACADEMIA FOR SALE

Don't cry! Don't be sorry for what you think is happening.
Science is telling you it is not happening. Do not trust your eyes,
do not trust your hearts, do not listen to your pain[698]

The prestigious academic departments that specialise in Islamic studies, history of the Middle East, international relations, sociology as well as social psychology have for the most part proven to be strawmen when it comes to Islam and Muslims.[699] The conflict between the teachings of Islam on the one hand and the modern values and ethics on the other hand is a topic expected to have been thoroughly examined and become known at least among educated people. Also, the Islamic invasions, terrorism, homophobia, civil conflicts, and slavery should have been thoroughly investigated and explained in detail to the general public and the decision makers by the specialised academics. The truth cannot be further from these expectations.

Prominent universities that are capable of informing the general public about why terrorism has been on the rise, how it started, and highlighting its theoretical basis have been distracting attention from these issues. Lies and myths about Islamic tolerance, Islamic philosophy and Muslims' contribution to civilization have been the main message propagated by influential colleges and academics. The well-funded research institutions have failed to foresee the events of 9/11, the resurgence of the Islamic jihad, the ascent of Islamic movements before and after the Arab Spring, the identity crisis of the Muslim immigrants in the West as well as many other major events related to their specialities. At the same time, many of these institutions have forged partnerships with corrupt autocratic Islamic regimes and adopted their point of view in a blatant betrayal of the intellectual integrity and the general public's trust.

In 2020, the US Department of Education launched an investigation into the failure of Harvard and Yale Universities to report foreign

---

698 Camus, R. (2018). You Will Not replace Us! Chez l'auteur, p 26.
699 The same can be said about the failure in predicting Russia's and China's policies.

funding. The two universities concealed receiving hundreds of millions of dollars as gifts from Qatar, Saudi Arabia, China, United Arab Emirates and other regimes. The officials discovered that Yale University had not reported any gift or foreign contract in the previous four years despite having received at least $375 million from foreign countries and organizations. From 1990 to 2018, US universities and colleges reported donations from Qatar, China, Saudi Arabia, and the United Arab Emirates in the excess of US$6.6 billion.[700] The investigation of the US Department of Education trigged the retrospect reporting of another US$6.5 billion of foreign funds by some of the top American universities. This figure is expected to be an underrepresentation of the actual amount of money these universities received from abroad, especially since universities and colleges are not required to report any gift or contract below $250,000. Qatar disclosed that it donated $1,024,065,043 as gifts to American universities between 2011 and 2017. In that same period, the Saudis gave $613,608,797, and United Arab Emirates – $211,311,219.

Top American universities have accepted money from undemocratic regimes to establish Islamic and Middle Eastern departments and centres within these universities. In 2005, Kuwait donated $3.4 million to establish the Kuwait Chair for Gulf and Arabian Peninsula Affairs, which is held by Edward W. Gnehm, an Arab American and a former US ambassador to Kuwait. In 2008, the government of Kuwait gave George Washington University more than a million dollars as a gift to support the Institute for Middle East Studies (IMES). In 2011, the Amir of Kuwait Sheikh Sabah gave another $4.5 million as a gift to IMES and to the Middle East and North Africa Research Center at the Gelman Library.[701] In 2013, the same university received another $4 million from the same ruler to support the Institute for Middle East Studies and the Gelman Library's Middle East and North Africa Research Center.[702]

---

700 Neuman, S. & Turner, C. (2020, Feb 13). Harvard, Yale Accused Of Failing To Report Hundreds Of Millions In Foreign Donations. NPR.
701 The George Washington University. (2011, Feb 18). GW's Elliott School of International Affairs and the University Libraries' Global Resources Center Receive $4.5 Million. [Archived].
702 GW Today. (2013, Apr 24). University Receives $4 Million from Kuwait Government.

The exact same hereditary regimes that have been throwing their citizens in jails for expressing their ideas in a tweet or an article are sponsoring American research institutions dedicated to studying their ideology as well as the political situation of their area.

In the United Kingdom, the situation is similarly bleak as several important universities have been accepting billions of pounds as gifts from authoritarian regimes and corrupt dictators.[703] This money is given mainly to establish and support Islamic centres and departments dedicated to studying Middle Eastern politics. Oxford University's £75 million Centre for Islamic Studies has been financed by twelve Muslim states and dynasties. The same university took at least another £30 million for similar departments. The main donors have been the Saudi ruling family, the Kuwaiti ruling family, the Emirati ruling family, and bin Laden family.

A brief review of "The Journal of Islamic Studies" and "The Makers of Islamic Civilization" series which are published by the Oxford Centre for Islamic Studies is sufficient to expose the agenda of this so-called academic department as well as its insignificant impact.

The notion that there was an Islamic Civilization, which is promoted by this centre, contradicts both facts and logic. Islam is a religion that was spread by the Arab nomads through violence, not a civilization, and Muslims have always been of different sects, ethnicities, cultures, and languages. They have been divided into various states and countries throughout their history. The archaeological record of Arabia – the birthplace of Islam is the best proof that Muslims did not create any advanced form of culture. No buildings, industries, music, art produced by the founders of Islam existed in that vast area.

"The Makers of Islamic Civilization" series shows clearly how the publishing institution has been propagating the traditional Islamic point of view rather than examining it, while avoiding the pressing issues. For instance, the first book of the series was an abridged edition of a book written by Shibli Numani (1857–1914), an Indian Muslim imam, about Omar, the second caliph of Mohammad. It had first been published in

---

703 Simcox, R. (2009). A Degree of Influence: The funding of strategically important subjects in UK universities. Centre for Social Cohesion, p 86.; Cook, C. (2012, Sep 27). Saudis donate most to UK universities. Financial Times.

Urdu in 1898 and then translated into English in 1939. In the Oxford 2014 edition, the title of the book was changed from "Al-Farooq: Life of Omar the Great" to "Umar: Makers of Islamic Civilization". The book is a biased collection of accounts about Omar taken from the History of al-Tabarī and other Islamic histories. It is designed to glorify Omar and the Arab conquests through claiming that he was a fair ruler and that the Arab invaders created a civilization rather than destroyed the existing ones. Numani avoids discussing many instances which show Omar in a bad light, such as his attack against Mohammad's daughter Fatima a few days after her father's death. Also, the fact that the caliph oversaw the destruction of Egypt, the Levant, Iraq, and Iran, and orchestrated countless massacres in which tens of thousands of people were killed and many more were enslaved are not mentioned in Numani's despite the fact they are documented in the books he used as references. In that book republished by Oxford, we read that Omar, who is introduced as an ethical and great leader, had advised Mohammad to behead the captives of Badr.

Furthermore, although the Centre has published 13 books within the series, they have had almost no impact among academics. Finally, it is an irony that Ibn Khaldun, who declared repeatedly that Arabs have never contributed to civilization and that individuals of the conquered nations who had built civilizations before Islam are the ones who pursued science and philosophy, is considered one of the makers of the Islamic civilization and a book was written about him as such. Most of the other publications of this centre, whether articles or books, are mainly repetitious of what is written in the original Islamic books or superficial discussions of minor figures.

The London School of Economics' relationship with the Gaddafi regime is another example of the decay among some departments within elite schools. This prestigious university in 2008 awarded a PhD degree to Saif al-Islam (Sword of Islam) Gaddafi, the son of the Libyan dictator and one of his top assistants at the time, based on plagiarised work. It accepted money from the corrupt criminal dictatorial regime and allowed it to create an academic centre specialising in North Africa. The same Ghaddafi who killed and tortured tens of thousands of innocent people and sponsored terrorism worldwide including the Lockerbie Bombing,

Somali piracy, the IRA attacks, was praised by professors who belonged to LSE as well as other top universities. Several famous academics had visited Gaddafi in his tent, and some wrote articles claiming that the mad murderer had changed.

The University of London's School of Oriental and African Studies (SOAS) is yet another example of the damaging partnership between elite universities and Islamic regimes. It accepted £1 million from King Fahad of Saudi Arabia to set up a chair of Islamic studies. It also took money from the Iranian regime.[704]

Six British MPs signed a motion about the influence of the autocratic Islamic regimes on the prestigious School of Oriental and African Studies: "...that in the last four years the Saudi Arabian Royal Family has given more than 755,000 to the Islamic Studies Centre at SOAS and its Journal of Qur'anic Studies; notes that this journal is formally edited and advised by Yusuf al-Qaradawi, a man banned from the UK and USA for endorsing suicide bombings and the murder of pregnant women; further notes that al-Qaradawi has been condemned by over 2,500 Muslim scholars worldwide for his hate speech and intolerance; deeply regrets the fact that in 2006 SOAS co-ordinated English training for Mutassim Gaddafi."[705] David Amess was one of the sponsors of this motion.

Before being arrested on charges of corruption and embezzlement in 2017, Prince Alwaleed Bin Talal of Saudi Arabia was a major founder of Islamic institutions on a global scale. He had established several centres that bear his name in the elite British and American universities with his dubious money. In 2008, he gave £8 million to the University of Edinburgh to launch HRH Prince Alwaleed bin Talal Centre for Study of Islam in the Contemporary World. In the same year, he founded HRH Prince Alwaleed bin Talal Centre for Islamic Studies at the University of Cambridge with another £8 million.[706] He also established HRH

704 Robinson, D. (2011, Mar 9). The shame of Britain's universities: LSE is far from the only university to accept money from repugnant regimes. The New Statesman.
705 UK Parliament. Early Day Motions. (Tabled on 2011, Jun 15). EDM 1933: Saudi Arabia and the School Of Oriental and African Studies.
706 See Prince Alwaleed Bin Talal Centre of Islamic Studies at University of Cambridge website: www.cis.cam.ac.uk.

Prince Alwaleed bin Talal Centre for Muslim Christian Understanding in Georgetown University[707] and HRH Prince Alwaleed bin Talal Islamic Studies Program at Harvard University.[708]

This person was allowed to create Islamic academic centres which carry his name despite having had a reputation of being a corrupt cruel man who enjoyed humiliating people and bragged about his wealth. For decades, the Saudis were wondering why and how reputable scholars would accept funds from such a person. In 2008, he was accused by a Spanish girl of abduction and rape. The girl was 20 years old when the prince spiked her drink while she was in a nightclub in Ibiza.[709] She woke up to find herself being raped by the 53-year-old Saudi. Forensic tests found traces of semen and the sedating Nordazepam was found in her urine. The prince was never questioned, and no DNA tests were carried out to establish if he was innocent or not – the case was dropped for lack of evidence by the Spanish court of law. One of his many wives stated that he was physically and verbally abusive with her and with his other wives. She also stated that he had forced her to divorce her husband at the time and marry him in secret. She disclosed that he had had at least 42 wives.[710] Alwaleed suggested while donating $10 millions for 9/11 disaster relief that American policies were responsible for the terrorist attack. He made this comment days after the attack and while people were still searching for their loved ones under the rubble. Alwaleed has also owned significant stakes in Apple, Twitter, Citigroup, and many other American and European companies. He is but one of countless examples of how Muslim royals have been allowed to influence academia, business and politics in all the corners of the world.

An investigation by The Telegraph newspaper "has identified dozens of cases where the UK's leading universities have accepted sponsorship from regimes accused of links to terrorism or human rights violations."

707 See Prince Alwaleed Bin Talal Center for Muslim-Christian Understanding at Georgetown University website: acmcu.georgetown.edu.
708 See Prince Alwaleed bin Talal Islamic Studies Program at Harvard University 'Who we are' webpage: islamicstudies.harvard.edu/who-we-are.
709 BBC News. (2012, Mar 29). Rape case against Saudi prince dropped in Spain.
710 Parry, R. & Boswell, J. (2017, Nov 6). Exclusive: Trump's lawyer represented Saudi prince arrested in 'corruption' probe.... Daily Mail.

Professor Anthony Glees, director of the Centre for Security and Intelligence Studies at Buckingham University, said: "By donating to higher education institutions, Arab and Islamic states are able to dictate a research agenda and influence public opinion in a way which we would not allow for our political parties. Foreign donors can not only shape the debate, but they can also influence students and impressionable young minds."[711] American officials stated that "some donors are known to be hostile to the United States and may be seeking to project 'soft power,' steal sensitive and proprietary research and development data and other intellectual property, and spread propaganda benefiting foreign governments."[712] According to Andrew Percy, an MP and former British minister, "Universities have been a breeding ground for hatred in recent years and students have been radicalised on our campuses."[713] Through funding departments in all the important world-class universities, the regimes of Kuwait, Saudi Arabia, Qatar, Turkey, Iran, and the United Arab Emirates have been censoring free thinking and controlling the academic centres of the world. The same corrupt, dictatorial regimes which oppose the essence of science have been influencing the collective human consciousness. The irony is that these universities have never been in need of such money and cannot afford the consequences of consenting to this influence. This money given to the biggest and richest US and British universities did not reduce the tuition cost of their students, neither does it seem to have advanced scientific knowledge. These universities receive billions of dollars as endowments, gifts, and contracts from their governments and other democratic countries in addition to students' fees, which exceed their expenses.

The fact that influential universities of wealthy countries have been taking money from oppressive autocratic regimes and criminal dictators testifies to the severe deterioration of academia and consequently, the general public's knowledge. By accepting to make their institutions

---

711 Turner, C. & Yorke, H. (2017, Aug 13). Exclusive: MPs demand British universities stop accepting donations from dictatorships. The Telegraph.
712 U.S. Department of Education. (2020, Feb 12). U.S. Department of Education Launches Investigation into Foreign Gifts Reporting at Ivy League Universities. [Report].
713 As above.

dependent on these regimes' money and hence, accepting their influence, the administrators of these universities have been giving away the reputation, history, and future of the academic centres of the world.

These regimes and dictators would never give anything, let alone billions of dollars, without a substantial gain. The return they expect and, in many cases, have been getting from the Western academic institutions is never-ending. The universities have been restrained from any significant criticism of these regimes and their religion-based practices. On the contrary, many colleges become PR firms that strive to boost the reputation of the donors. They keep admitting unqualified students recommended by the donors. The politically motivated hiring of unqualified individuals who disseminate the points of view of these regimes has been going on for decades under the guise of diversity. This is not limited to Islamic issues as many universities and governmental institutions in the West have been fostering illogical and destructive ideas and ideologies for many decades.[714] This has affected the quality of research and teaching of these universities as well as the ideas they propagate among the public, however, with money and propaganda the degree and the nature of the damage has so far been obscured from the consciousness of the general public.

Finally, the main questions, whether regarding the principles of Islam or the practices of these regimes, have become taboos. Islam along with the Muslim regimes has become above investigation and above critical thinking. The history of the Arab conquests, the main cause of terrorism, the original teachings of Islam that clash with human rights have been treated as sensitive topics, hence researchers avoid them. This regression is relatively new – several old philosophers and writers were open in their criticism of Islam, based on its original sources. For instance, in his play "Fanaticism, or Mahomet the Prophet", Voltaire showed Islam as a violent, proselytising ideology created by a primitive warlord.

Nowadays, glorifying the Arab invaders, justifying their genocides and fabricating history have become an acceptable practice. Islamic regimes' involvement in terrorism as well as other criminal activities is

---

714 See the work of Thomas Sowell, professor of economy and an influential thinker.

kept out of the research arena and the public consciousness. Discussing the ramifications of the ongoing Islamisation of Europe and North America is treated as a crime.

It is important to stress that many reputable universities and important scholars have never accepted money or influence from the undemocratic regimes, but they remained silent for the most part. A few courageous independent thinkers have been standing alone against the high tide. Christopher Hitchens, Richard Dawkins, Douglas Murray, Ayaan Hirsi Ali, and a few others have stated time and again that Islam is the most serious threat to modern civilization. They have indicated that Islamists and their backers are stifling the freedom of speech and creating a toxic environment that impedes human flourishing. In "The Parasitic Mind", Gad Saad shows how academics in America and Europe have been twisting the facts, destroying the logical thinking and suppressing freedom of speech in general, and especially in relation to the Islamic threat. Several other researchers have demonstrated that Marxists, socialists, leftists have been enabling Islamists and supporting them in their attack against civilization.

This suicidal behaviour could be explained partially by Thomas Sowell's analyses which have shown that socialist elites are detached from reality and immune to facts. They are interested in serving themselves and promoting their totalitarian agenda at the expense of their societies and the intellectual integrity. They are willing to cooperate with the devil if they thought that it is in their interest, without consideration for the consequences.

THE RHETORIC OF THE MUSLIM BROTHERS

Allah is our objective; the Prophet is our leader;
the Quran is our law; Jihad is our way;
dying in the way of Allah is our highest hope.[715]

Muslim Brothers are the most active organization in promoting and spreading Islam worldwide. They have been creating and amending a rhetoric adopted by millions of people all over the world designed to show Islam as a peaceful and tolerant religion while at the same time embracing all the notions written in its original texts, including jihad, slavery, and the suppression of women.[716] In the past twenty years, their two most prominent thinkers were the Egyptian theologian Yousef al-Qaradawi and Tariq Ramadan.

The story of Tariq Ramadan is stark evidence of the decline of academic principles among some universities as well as the deterioration of Western media and the extent to which the Muslim Brotherhood has infiltrated Western societies. Ramadan, or 'the Doctor' as he likes to be introduced, was recognized by "Time" magazine in 2000 as one of the seven religious innovators of the 21st century. He is the grandson of the founder of Muslim Brothers organization, Hassan al-Banna. Tariq was born in Switzerland, where his family escaped to from their native Egypt after the Muslim Brothers carried out terrorist attacks in an unsuccessful attempt to topple the regime. His father, who came from a humble background, played an important role in establishing mosques and Muslim Brotherhood's branches in Europe with money from the Gulf States.[717]

---

715 The motto of the Muslim Brotherhood.
716 See Vidino, L. (2010). The new Muslim brotherhood in the West. Columbia University Press.; Lappen A. A. (2010). The Muslim Brotherhood in North America. In B. Rubin (Eds.). The Muslim Brotherhood: The Organization and Policies of a Global Islamist Movement. Palgrave Macmillan.; Gaubatz, P. D., & Sperry, P. E. (2009). Muslim mafia: Inside the secret underworld that's conspiring to Islamize America. WND Books.
717 See Johnson, I. (2010). A Mosque in Munich: Nazis, the CIA, and the Rise of the Muslim Brotherhood in the West. Houghton Mifflin Harcourt.

Tariq was supported and promoted by several Gulf States, especially Qatar. In a famous picture, he is seen standing to the right of the Qatari ruler's wife Moza while the Muslim Brothers organization's spiritual leader al-Qaradawi is posing to her left. He was introduced as the proto-type of the moderate Muslim scholar who would debate Christians and Atheists to prove that his religion was the right religion for all humans. He gave lectures at Harvard University and was employed as a professor at the University of Notre Dame.[718] In 2004, the US State Department revoked his visa for his support of terrorism but in 2010, Secretary of State Hillary Clinton changed this decision and issued an order to give him a visa. His arrival in the United States in that year was celebrated by many liberal institutions; the New York Times published an article entitled: "At Last Allowed, Muslim Scholar Visits".[719]

On the website of University of Oxford St Antony's College, we read: "Tariq Ramadan is H. H. Sheikh Hamad bin Khalifa Al Thani Profes-sor of Contemporary Islamic Studies and Senior Research Fellow at St Antony's College, teaching in the two Faculties of Oriental Studies and Theology & Religion. He is Visiting Professor at the Faculty of Islamic Studies, (Qatar); Director of the Research Centre of Islamic Legislation and Ethics (CILE) (Doha, Qatar); President of the think tank European Muslim Network (EMN) in Brussels and a member of the International Union of Muslim Scholars. He holds an MA in Philosophy and French literature and PhD in Arabic and Islamic Studies from the University of Geneva. In Cairo, Egypt, he received one-on-one intensive training in classic Islamic scholarship from Al-Azhar University scholars (ijazat teaching license in seven disciplines)."[720]

Listening to Dr Tariq's talks or reading his writings, we find a man who represents the opposite of scholarly thinking, and yet was presented as a distinguished academic and a scientific authority by prestigious universities and important media outlets. He was introduced on Oxford University's website as a professor and associate faculty member.[720]

---

718 Storin, M. V. (2004, Dec 13). Tariq Ramadan resigns from faculty. Notre Dame News.
719 Semple, K. (2010, Apr 7). At Last Allowed, Muslim Scholar Visits. New York Times.
720 See T. Ramadan's staff profile on St Antony's College, University of Oxford website. Pro-fessor Tariq Ramadan (on leave of absence). [Archived].

Not a single peer-reviewed research paper or a book written by this professor can be found on the University of Oxford's website or any other website, but we learn that his research interests are contemporary Islamic issues and Islamic revival in the world as well as Muslims in the West. Moreover, Ramadan has been presenting himself in Western newspapers, media interviews, and debates as professor of philosophy at Fribourg, while his whole relationship with this university was a one-hour lecture on Islam once a week for the duration of one course. After that course finished, five of the students filed complaints of sexual assault against the Muslim Brother.

Ramadan attempted to obtain a PhD degree through submitting a thesis that praised his grandfather and presented him as the "Muslim Gandhi." This is even though the grandfather had established the Muslim Brothers' armed militia known as the Secret Order, which was involved in criminal activities and assassinated several people, among them the prime minister of Egypt at the time. Hassan al-Banna was himself assassinated as a retribution, but the Secret Order continued its attacks against the state for decades. This intellectual treachery was prevented by Prof. Charles Genequand, the former dean of the faculty of languages at the University of Geneva. He described his former student as a "pseudo-intellectual" and a "vain opportunist."[722] Ramadan had threatened, harassed and intimidated his supervisors as well as the University of Geneva's administration to obtain his PhD degree. Despite his refusal to make the obligatory corrections to his thesis, he was awarded the scientific degree. For decades after receiving his PhD, he failed to produce any academic work. Nonetheless, he enjoyed the support of Muslim governments and masses, especially the Muslims Brothers and the Qatari patron, who flocked to his defence and threatened whomever dared to criticise him.

It is impossible to listen to his lectures without realizing that he is a propagandist who tries to defend each and every idea of Islam regardless of its nature and consequences. He was a regular guest on Al Jazeera, where his Arabic talk significantly differed from the English one,

---

721 See staff profile on University of Oxford, Faculty of Theology and Religion website [Archived].
722 Mills, S. (2018, Mar 10). Did Tariq Ramadan Lie About His University Credentials? Uncommon Ground Media.

especially when discussing jihad. He is not as straightforward as bin Laden or Zarqawi and he lacks the knowledge of Omar Abdulrahman, hence, he uses discourse designed to deceive, distract, intimidate, and disorient the listeners.

During his debate with Christopher Hitchens on the topic: "Is Islam a Religion of Peace," he showed a way of reasoning common among Islamic propagandists. Hitchens used his time to show that Islam is not a religion of peace. He supported his argument through providing examples and evidence from the original Islamic texts. In contrast, Ramadan used his time to distract the audience from the issue at hand. He used an argument popular among Muslim debaters, who would present illogical, false claims to defend every aspect of their religion. Thus, it is worth analysing it in some detail.

We join the debate from Ramadan's introductory speech:

> Let me go straight to some of the points and I'm not going to respond straight away to some of the claims on all the claims but during my talk, as it is the introductory speech, let me highlight some of the points. When I got the question of course as a Muslim and as a believer but as someone who is coming from within the realm of religions it was quite clear that to put it that way was not the right question to ask. **Is Islam a religion of peace or is Christianity or is Judaism or is Buddhism religion or spirituality of peace doesn't mean anything for me.** It's not the right question, it's not the accurate question. Not because I think that there is a good Islam and the right Islam and there are people who are acting in the name of Islam who are not representing what Islam is – this is not my point, I never said that by the way. But the point for me is really to, to try to deal with a phenomenon with religion from within and try to understand the dynamics and to understand the trends and to understand the diversity, so just to essentialize one religion by saying it's all about war, it's all about peace, and even you know, said by George W. Bush, it doesn't mean anything for me. So this is one point which is important but religions and old religions and Islam among all the other religions are dealing with human beings. And if you deal with human beings, you deal with violence and you deal with peace. You deal with

violence because human beings by definition have to do with violence, they have to deal with aggressivity with wars, and to expect from a religion not to tackle the issue is just to dream of something which is not going to happen. All the spirituality go for Buddhism, or go for the Bhagavad-Gita, you deal with violence, so this is it. Now, what is the answer coming from religions and from trends when it comes to violence and to peace – this is the right question for me. Do we have something which is coming and helping us to go towards the peace, this is for me the right question. So now, once again, when I have people speaking from outside, and this is especially the case these days when it comes to Islam, is we speak about Islam and we speak about, you know, something which is a religion that is perceived through one window or through one interpretation and we very often take what is visible through the media. But Islam is as complex as Christianity and Judaism and Buddhism and Hinduism, it's a diversity of interpretations. **Yes, you are right, the Quran is for the Muslims the very word of God, but many interpretations and many ways of dealing with the books. The problem is not the book, the problem is the reader.** Is the way [people clapping] (no, no, we have only ten minutes), so, this is why when for example you take a text and **you can do this with the Bible, with the Torah, the Gospels, it is always the same. Tell me the way you read, I will know what is in your mind** but not for sure what is in the text. And this something which is the starting point of a serious discussion in theology. Because I don't like all these intellectuals and philosophers and even journalists, they are very keen on understanding the complexity of philosophies and the simplicity of religions. That's not right. And the one to blame sometimes are the religious people themselves because the way to present their religions sometimes, which is all of dreams and hopes and not dealing with the reality, which is a complex reality (…) [723]

If we were to carry out a basic discourse analysis to better understand this talk, which is commonly used to defend Islam, we find a convoluted, self-contradicting and dangerous rhetoric. The preface of the above

---

723 92nd Street Y. (2013, Feb 4). Christopher Hitchens and Tariq Ramadan Debate: Is Islam a Religion of Peace? [Video]. (Recorded 2010, Oct 5). YouTube.

quoted talk was designed to assimilate Islam with other religions and beliefs. Through comparing Islam to other religions, the speaker deflects the question of whether Islam warrants and propagates violence. This technique is also designed to intimidate the followers of other religions from questioning Islam. It is similar to the notion: if you spoke about my faults, I will talk about yours.[724] In the same talk, Ramadan confirms that Muslims and Islam differ at the core from all the other religions, let alone spiritualities, through the belief that the Quran is the unalterable word of God. He then alludes to the idea that it could be the interpretations of the Quran that make Islam a religion of peace or not. The problem is the reader, not the book, he concludes. He avoids providing any straightforward answer to the question at hand.

If we were to believe the professor that the problem is in the interpretation of Islam rather than in Islam, can he or any Muslim state that Mohammad was wrong when he waged numerous wars and raids against people who had not interacted with him in any way, shape or form? Were the Muslims wrong throughout 1400 years for waging offensive jihad? Can any Muslim say publicly that Mohammad and his followers were not following Islam when they were kidnapping and selling women and children as spoils? Is there any written interpretation that declares killing a Buddhist, a Jew, a Christian or an Atheist as equal to killing a Muslim? Can Ramadan or any Muslim show us a religion whose God authored a book full of orders to the believers to kill, loot, and deceive others? The foundation of Islam is the belief that the Quran is Allah's literal words. It is not manmade, thus cannot be altered and must be followed accurately. Most importantly, how can anyone interpret a clear passage? Allah in the Quran says that his narrative is clear, precise, and sacred. Hence, there cannot be and there are not any major differences in all the interpretations of the Quran, especially when it comes to the main issues such as jihad, because they are repeated in many different passages within the Quran. Muslim governments and Islamic institutions use the Quran and the hadith as the source of legislation – not interpretations.

---

724 See Wiggins, S. (2016). Discursive psychology: Theory, method and applications. Sage.

Despite various complaints against him and despite repeated demands to scrutinise his credentials, Tariq Ramadan was for decades marketed as an intellectual authority by influential Western media organizations in addition to prestigious universities. He was interviewed by various TV channels to disseminate his wisdom and his "moderate" version of the one and only true religion. Various Western newspapers competed to publish his self-praising articles. He was presented as a role-model while being sheltered from any genuine challenge. He brainwashed millions of people using the halo created for him by reputable universities and powerful media outlets. For more than 20 years, Ramadan was allowed to influence people with his lies, hypocrisy, and deception regarding Islam and himself.

The legacy of Ramadan began to fall apart when two Muslim women accused him of rape in October 2017.[725] One of them was of Moroccan descent, while the other was a disabled convert to Islam of French descent known as Christelle. Ramadan's wife showed adamant support for him against the victims. This French citizen, who had converted to Islam, changed her name to an Arabic name Iman which means belief, and taken up Islamic hijab, stood by her husband's side, despite the nature of the allegations. When the complaints became public, she came to his defence with fervour.[726] In February 2018, she posted a video on her Facebook page entitled: "Liberation of Tariq Ramadan." She said in it: "He is unfortunately a victim of this media lynching and political pressure exerted against him."

For eleven months, the Islamic scholar denied having any relationship with any of the women and called them "compulsive liars". He

---

725 The Guardian. (2018, Nov 15). Tariq Ramadan: Oxford professor facing rape charges granted conditional release.
726 El Masaiti, A. (2018, Feb 15). Tariq Ramadan's Wife Speaks About Rape Accusations for First Time. Morocco World News.

defended himself vehemently, assuring his followers that he was a married Muslim man of honour. Muslims worldwide came to his defence; they, too, argued that the pious Muslim man was married and a father to four children and would never be involved in an extramarital relationship, let alone rape vulnerable Muslim women who came to him for guidance.[727] He was the President of the European Muslim Network, and this was the reason why he was being framed, his supporters contended. Thousands of social media accounts in addition to journalists and academics showed their relentless support to the "persecuted" professor.

A third woman accused Ramadan of rape in Switzerland. He remained adamant in denying any sexual contacts with any of the accusers. Numerous websites and social media accounts were portraying the victims as being part of a conspiracy to stain the Muslim Oxford professor. Christelle was accused of being an undercover spy aiming to hurt Islam through defamation of the prominent Muslim scholar. Ramadan pledged that he had met this woman once in a hotel bar for a quick chat and he kept fervently accusing her of lying.[728]

In October 2018, computer experts succeeded in extracting 399 text messages from Christelle's phone. In these messages, we see the real Ramadan: a violent, oppressive, misogynistic, opportunistic devoted Muslim rapist. At first, he denied being the author of these messages but after the computer experts provided evidence that he indeed was the author, he changed his story. The shameless man said that he had a consensual sexual relationship with Christelle. Such a relationship is a major crime in Islam, punishable by stoning to death for both parties. He justified his texts, which described beating and sodomizing the woman, through claiming that they had a submissive-dominant relationship.[729]

The professor of Islamic studies Tariq Ramadan said in a text to the disabled French woman that he wanted "to slap you, to sodomize you, to hit your buttocks, to grope, to grab your hair and to push my cock to choke you." A week after that, he sent another message: "I want to fuck

---

727 There was a strong Free Tariq Ramadan campaign. See: freetariqramadan.com [Archived].
728 Saga, A. B. (2018, Oct 25). Tariq Ramadan Admits to 'Sex Games' with 2 Rape Complainants. Morocco World News.
729 As above.

you and slap you. Piss on you and force you to lick." In a message sent from the victim to Ramadan, she says that she has medical reports that prove the trauma she suffered at his hand: "I have been waiting since the 9th for your flat and sincere apology! They hallucinated at the hospital seeing my torn anus." In another message she wrote: "I will not let any other woman get ripped like you did with me. I have nothing to lose and I would sacrifice my life, if need be, kill me."[730]

Christelle sought the help of Caroline Fourest, a French feminist and writer who debated Ramadan. Ramadan sent a message of warning to Christelle: "One day you may know the true support of Fourest to the Zionists who are killing the Palestinians. They hate me for it. Your selfishness and your fight of offended women will have to be put on a scale.... If Fourest is your friend, God will be your enemy."

This message summarises Islamic self-righteousness. God is on their side because they are Muslims and nothing else matters. For many Muslim criminals, their wrongdoings and corruption are irrelevant as long as they are believers in Allah and propagating his religion. It is evident in his texts, that Ramadan thought that he was in a place to give orders to Allah and Allah to take orders from him. This man is not just failing to accept responsibility for his crimes and show remorse; he rather sees his decent opponents as the criminals and presents himself as the victim. In this message, he is invoking the situation in Israel in a warped and biased way to distract the focus away from his crimes into a theoretical endless debate. Instead of admitting his crimes, accepting being guilty, and seeking forgiveness, he constructs the people who are trying to help his victims as Zionists, hence evil and criminal by default. It is a typical example of a psychopath's discourse that distracts and deceives people, a talk of a person with no emotions or conscience but a grandiose self-image and superficial charm. He is wearing a mask of sanity to conceal his pathological evilness which is warranted by his religion.[731]

---

730 Messages translated from French. Sauvaget, B. (2018, Sep 26). Tariq Ramadan accablé par ses SMS à "Christelle" [Tariq Ramadan overwhelmed by his SMS to "Christelle"]. (French). Libération News.
731 See Cleckley, H. (1941/2022). The Mask of Sanity: An Attempt To Clarify Some Issues About the So-Called Psychopathic Personality. Mockingbird Press.; Hare, R.D. (1999). Without conscience: The disturbing world of the psychopaths among us. Guilford Press.

In November 2018, he was granted a conditional release after constantly pleading with the judges to release him for medical reasons. On 18 March 2019, he turned up with his daughter at a conference on sexual violence. He was asked by the organizers and the attendants to leave but he ignored them while his daughter was replying to one of the offended women that this was a public meeting, and he had the right to attend.[732] This provocation is a vivid example of how a psychopath disregards the feelings and rights of others. On 11 February 2020, Ramadan was charged with two more rapes which had taken place in 2016 and 2017. He arrived at the court hearing with his Muslim, hijab-wearing wife.[733] In 2019, he published a book "Duty of truth" where he admits in a vague language that he had relationships with the women and that he was lying for months when he denied knowing them. Nevertheless, he says in it that he was charged and treated unfairly because he defended Islam.

It is not just his behaviour and rationale that should be examined but also the behaviour of his supporters as well as their motives, especially the Qatari rulers and the Muslim Brothers. The universities which recognised him as a professor along with the media networks that regularly praised him need to be thoroughly investigated and held accountable. This case should not be closed without the entire issue being exposed and examined, and all the parties who participated in it receiving their fair ends.

---

732 The National. (2019, Mar 21). Tariq Ramadan accused of "unacceptable provocation" at conference on sexual violence.
733 France 24. (2020, Feb 13). Islamic scholar Tariq Ramadan faces two new rape charges in France.

25 Conclusion

COLLECTIVE PSYCHO-ETHICAL QUESTIONS

What makes a society perceive mass killing of children, medical workers, tourists, worshippers, journalists, newborns and new mothers as a moral act? Can we diagnose the members of this society who carried out such attacks with antisocial personality disorder and deal with them as such when they were simply living by their society's norms and laws?

Is the definition of paedophilia as a psychological disorder universal or is it limited to specific societies? If we were to accept the medical guidelines and diagnostic criteria, then we would perceive the sexual desires for prepubescent children by adults as a disorder regardless of the ethnicity, culture, or religion of the perpetrator. But if there is a society that considers paedophilia a normal practice based on its heritage or religious teachings, can we call its members who engage in this practice mentally sick people and offenders? Can we describe the underage girls as victims without outlawing the religion that sanctions this practice?

In 2017, several jurists in Morocco and Egypt restarted an old controversy when they ruled that it was permissible in Islam for the husband to have sex with the corpse of his dead wife (necrophilia). They based their edicts on ancient jurisprudence books which are still taught in religious colleges across the Muslim World.[734] They also argued that it was permissible for men to have sex with an animal and that there was no penalty in sharia for such an act. In contrast, psychiatry and psychology consider both deeds as abnormal behaviours that signal psychological disorders, and laws in civilized countries criminalize such acts and punish the perpetrators.

Compelling young children to pray and fast by beating them is common among Muslims worldwide as an application of a saying attributed

---

734 Hussein, M. (2017, Sep 18). Mufaja'atun: Kutub turath tuayid fatwaa nikah almaytati… [Surprise: The Tradition Books Permit Sex With The Dead…] (Arabic). Youm7 Electronic Journal.

to Mohammad.[735] It is considered a correct practice, not child abuse, despite its harmful psychological consequences. Hence, is forcing children to pray and to abstain from drinking and eating for a month every year child abuse or an acceptable behaviour, as long as it is based on religion? What are the psychological effects of being in a society that denounces heritage, music, culture, and art? How can a society sanction mass-rape, vehicle-ramming, and beheading of defenceless people while being considered normal? How can the members of such societies maintain their psychological homeostasis? How does a collective identity develop based on such practices? How is a group of people able to harbour neurotic malevolence toward their neighbours, co-workers, and the country they live in, whose wealth they benefit from, and whose citizenship they carry? How could they disguise all these stressful feelings and sadistic beliefs? What are the consequences of this cognitive dissonance?

On the other hand, why would any country or society allow a group of people to immigrate, legally or illegally, to its territories to kill its children, rape its daughters, take its wealth, and destroy its identity? Why would a community lose the will to defend itself against others who are seeking its demise? How could a society stand idly by and watch its own offspring being slain and raped? Again, are these normal societies?

Why are many fallacies related to Islam treated as facts not just by the lay people but also by academics? Notions such as Islamic science, tolerance, or philosophy that are not just inaccurate but also extremely dangerous as they glorify harmful ideas and institutions have been propagated all over the world, in many cases by Western researchers.

Dividing Muslims into radicals versus moderates is one of the many damaging and misleading notions that have been accepted as a fact and used as a premise for discussing and understanding terrorism, suppression of women, and other similar Islamic practices. This categorization has contributed to prolonging the crisis as it acquits the religion from culpability through shifting attention from its teachings and institutions

---

735 Islamweb's reply to a question whether beating 10-year-old children to make them pray is Islamic, through citing several hadith and fatwas which call for this act: Fatwa No. 75901. (2006, Jul 16). Jawab shubhat hawl hadithi: Ealimuu 'awladakum alsalat lisabea... [The answer about doubts regarding a hadith: Teach your children to pray at the age of seven...]. (Arabic).

into unidentifiable followers. Despite such a construction being used by countless researchers, commentators as well as lay people, there is no clear definition of radical or moderate Islam. Hence, most of the discussions influenced by this idea have been fruitless if not counterproductive. Do we consider a person who has never taken part in terrorism but approves the killing of non-Muslims to spread Islam as a moderate or a radical? Can we consider people who think that it is ethical to force young girls to wear hijab as radicals and treat them as such or look at this practice as a cultural custom that should be tolerated? Having more than one wife is accepted by most Muslims and legal in Muslim countries, hence, should it be legalised within the non-Muslim countries?

In summary, the system of belief that warranted murdering children in Sudan, France, Iraq, Afghanistan, and Syria, as well as the killings of the innocent people who were working in the World Trade Centre, travelling in London's subway, Madrid's trains, or living their lives in their homelands should not be considered ethical or sane. Moreover, the society that endorses misogyny, paedophilia, homophobia, hereditary rule, and accepts tyrannical ideas and institutions while rejecting science, freedom, music, and human rights is dangerous to its members and humanity in general. Such a society should not be treated as morally and psychologically stable; it is a society with a pathological psyche and a deranged morality.

This society's norms, values, idols, collective identities must be examined and challenged vigorously. The salient collective identity that makes people murder, loot, and rape while feeling virtuous must be discussed in an objective but persistent way. The system of ideas that motivates adherents to blow themselves up in marathons, theatres, worship places, religious processions, cinemas, and commercial streets, killing random people while claiming to be the victims is a topic that needs to be analysed thoroughly in the public domain as well as in research centres. People's behaviour does not come from a void. It is the product of their ideas and identities which are influenced by their societies' norms and values. Thus, without understanding the rationale of Islam, we cannot understand or predict the behaviour of its keen followers.

PSYCHOLOGY AND ISLAM

Psychology is the branch of social sciences dedicated to examining people's cognition, feelings, and behaviour. It is the discipline that should investigate and explain the Muslims' tolerance for violence as well as the other chronic psychological problems Muslim societies are plagued with. Within psychology, there are two related branches which are the most relevant to the current question: social and clinical psychology.

Social psychology is dedicated to examining collective behaviour, social norms, group dynamics, social influence, collective identities and other related topics. It is expected that psychologists in general, and social psychologists in particular, should be working on examining the different aspects of Muslims' collective cognition and behaviour. Social psychologists are also expected to have been dedicating significant efforts to understanding the interrelations between Muslims and non-Muslims. That said, it is extremely hard to find a department or even a research unit interested in studying the collective behaviour or cognition of Muslims. The questions of how and why Muslims devoted to the teachings of Islam are willing to give up their lives in order to kill others is almost unexamined from a psychological point of view. Topics such as the religious rationale of honour killing, misogyny, child brides, and many more collectively accepted pathological behaviours are overlooked by the mainstream psychology.

The relationship between social norms and psychological disorders in general and the relationship between Islamic norms and psychopathology in particular is another field of research that has been largely disregarded by clinical psychologists. How specific beliefs are attractive to mentally disturbed individuals is an important question that needs to be investigated thoroughly. The examining of original Islamic discourses as mental constructs that affect people's psyche and consequently behaviour is also an important task to be carried out by psychologists in a comprehensive and systematic way.

Selected bibliography

Ali, A. H. (2021). Prey: Immigration, Islam, and the Erosion of Women's Rights. Harper.

Ali, J. (1993). The Detailed History of the Arabs Before Islam. Third Ed. Dar al-Alam.

American Psychiatric Association (APA). (2013). Diagnostic and statistical manual of mental disorders (5th ed.).

Antaki, C., & Widdicombe, S. (Eds.). (1998). Identities in talk. Sage.

Arjomand, S. A. (2010). Islamic resurgence and its aftermath. In R. W. Hefner (Ed.). The New Cambridge History of Islam, IV. Cambridge University Press.

al-Baladhuri, A. (1996). Ansab al-Ashraf [Genealogies of nobles]. (Arabic). Dar al-Feker.

Bradford, J. T. (2019). Poppies, Politics, and Power: Afghanistan and the Global History of Drugs and Diplomacy. Cornell University Press.

Brown, J. A. C. (2020). Slavery and Islam. Simon & Schuster.; Fay, M. A. (Ed.). (2019). Slaves in the Islamic World: Its Characteristics & Commonality.

Bucerius, S. (2014). Unwanted: Muslim Immigrants, Dignity, and Drug Dealing (Studies in Crime and Public Policy). Oxford University Press.

al-Bukhari, Muhammad ibn Ismail. (2002). Al-Jami al-Musnad al-Sahih al-Mukhtasar min Umur Rasul Allah wa Sunnanihi wa Ayamoh [Collection of Selected Authentic Reports of the Prophet, His Practices and Times] known as Sahih Bukhari. Dar Ibn Kathir.

Byman, D. (2005). Deadly connections: States that sponsor terrorism. New York: Cambridge University Press.

Chesnot, C., Malbrunot, G. (2020). Qatar Papers: How Doha finances the Muslim Brotherhood in Europe. Averroes & Cie.

Cleckley, H. (1941/2020). The Mask of Sanity: An Attempt To Clarify Some Issues About the So-Called Psychopathic Personality. Digireads.com Publishing

Conesa, P. (2018). The Saudi terror machine: The truth about radical Islam and Saudi Arabia revealed. Skyhorse.

Crone, P. (2016). Islam, the Ancient Near East and Varieties of Godlessness: Collected Studies in Three Volumes, Volume 3. Brill.

Crone, P. (2014). Medieval Islamic political thought. Edinburgh University Press.

Crone, P. & Cook, M. (1977). Hagarism: the making of the Islamic world. Cambridge University Press.

Crone, P. & Hinds, M. (2003). God's Caliph: Religious Authority in the First Centuries of Islam. Cambridge University Press.

Davis, R. C. (2003). Christian Slaves, Muslim Masters: White Slavery in the Mediterranean, the Barbary Coast, and Italy, 1500-1800. Palgrave Macmillan.

Deneault, A. (2018). Mediocracy: The Politics of the Extreme Centre. Between the Lines.

Durant, W. (1954). Our Oriental Heritage: The Story of Civilization, Vol. 1. Chapter VI. The Moslem Conquest. Simon and Schuster.

Fernández-Morera, D. (2016). The Myth of the Andalusian Paradise: Muslims, Christians, and Jews under Islamic Rule in Medieval Spain. Open Road Media.

Fox, D. J. (2020). Antisocial, Narcissistic, and Borderline Personality Disorders: A New Conceptualization of Development, Reinforcement, Expression, and Treatment. Routledge.

Freer, C. J. (2018). Rentier Islamism: The influence of the muslim brotherhood in Gulf monarchies. Oxford University Press.

Gaubatz, P. D., & Sperry, P. E. (2009). Muslim mafia: Inside the secret underworld that's conspiring to Islamize America. WND Books.

Giustozzi, A. (2018). The Islamic State in Khorasan: Afghanistan, Pakistan and the New Central Asian Jihad. Oxford University Press.

Gordon, M. & Hain, K. (Eds.). (2017). Concubines and courtesans: Women and Slavery in Islamic History.

Hare, R. D. (1999). Without conscience: The disturbing world of the psychopaths among us. Guilford Press.

Hawting, G. R. (2002). The first dynasty of Islam: the Umayyad caliphate AD 661-750. Routledge.

Hecht, J. M. (2004). Doubt: A History: The Great Doubters and Their Legacy of Innovation from Socrates and Jesus to Thomas Jefferson and Emily Dickinson.

Hegghammer, T. (2020). The Caravan: Abdallah Azzam and the Rise of Global Jihad. Cambridge, UK: University Printing House.

Hoyland, R. G. (2019). Seeing Islam as others saw it. Gorgias Press.

Ibn al-Athir, Ali. (1998). Al-Kamil fi al-Tarikh (Vol. 1-12). (Arabic). Dar al Kotob al Ilmiyah.

Ibn al-Hajjaj, Muslim. (2019). Min al-Jami' al-Sahih [Authentic collection] known as Sahih Muslim. Dar Al Kotob Al Ilmiyah.

Ibn Ishaq, M. (1998). The Life of Muhammad. Translated by Guillaume, A. Oxford University Press.

Ibn Kathir, Abu al-Fida Ismail. (1992). Al-Bidaya wa al-Nihaya [The Beginning and the End]. Vol. 1-14. Dar Al Maaref.

Al-Jabarti, A. A. R. (1994). History of Egypt: Ajaib al-Athar fil-Trajim wal-Akhbar. (Ed. and trans. Philipp, T., & Perlman, M.). Franz Steiner.

Johnson, I. (2010). A Mosque in Munich: Nazis, the CIA, and the Rise of the Muslim Brotherhood in the West. Houghton Mifflin Harcourt.

Kurzban, R., & Christner, J. (2011). Are supernatural beliefs commitment devices for intergroup conflict? In J. P. Forgas, A. W. Kruglanski & K. D. Williams (Eds.). The psychology of social conflict and aggression. Psychology Press.

Lappen A. A. (2010). The Muslim Brotherhood in North America. In B. Rubin (Eds.). The Muslim Brotherhood: The Organization and Policies of a Global Islamist Movement. Palgrave Macmillan.

Al-Ma'arri, Abu'l-Ala. (2019). The Diwan of Abu'l-Ala. The Good Press.

Marshall, P. (Ed.). (2005). Radical Islam's Rules: The Worldwide Spread of Extreme Shari'a Law. Rowman & Littlefield Publishers.

Martinez, L. (2000). The Algerian Civil War, 1990-1998. C. Hurst & Co.

Masters, B. A. & Agoston, G. (Eds.). (2009). Encyclopedia of the Ottoman Empire. Infobase Publishing.

Melville, J. R. (1972). The siege of Constantinople 1453: seven contemporary accounts. A. M. Hakkert.

Miller, J. (1997). God has ninety-nine names: reporting from a militant Middle East.

Mohammed, Y. (2019). Unveiled: How Western Liberals Empower Radical Islam. Free Hearts Free Minds.

Mohanty, N. (2018). Jihadism: Past and Present. Lexington Books.

Murad, N., & Krajeski, J. (2017). The Last Girl: My Story of Captivity and My Fight against the Islamic State.

Murphey, R. (2006). Ottoman Warfare, 1500-1700. 1st Ed. Routledge.

Murray, D. (2017). The Strange Death of Europe: Immigration, Identity, Islam. Bloomsbury.

Nöldeke, T., Schwally, F., Bergsträßer, G., & Pretzl, O. (2013). The History of the Qur'ān. Ed. and trans. Behn, W.H. Brill.

Parry, V.J., & Cook, M. (1976). A History of the Ottoman Empire to 1730. Cambridge University Press.

Patrick, C.J. (Ed.). (2018). Handbook of psychopathy. Guilford Publications.

Peirce, L.P. (1993). The imperial harem: Women and sovereignty in the Ottoman Empire. Oxford University Press.

Penzer, N.M. (1937/2012). The Harem: An Account of the Institution as it Existed in the Palace of the Turkish Sultans, with a History of the Grand Seraglio from Its foundation to the Present Time. HardPress.

Potter, J., & Wetherell, M. (1987). Discourse and social psychology: Beyond attitudes and behaviour.

Quran. (2015). King Fahad complex for Printing of the Holy Quran. Medina. Saudi Arabia.

Rehman, J.L. (2012). Rape as Religious Terrorism and Genocide: The 1971 War Between East and West Pakistan. [MA Thesis]. California State University.

Reynolds, G.S. (Ed.) (2008). The Quran in its historical context. Routledge.

Saad, G. (2020). Parasitic Mind: How Infectious Ideas Are Killing Common Sense. Regnery Publishing.

Sahas, D.J. (1972). John of Damascus on Islam: the 'Heresy of the Ishmaelites.' Brill.

Saikia, Y. (2011). Women, War, and the Making o f Bangladesh Remembering 1971. Duke University Press.

Sarrazin, T. (2018). Feindliche Übernahme: Wie der Islam den Fortschritt behindert und die Gesellschaft bedroht [Hostile takeover: How Islam impedes progress and threatens society]. Finanzbuch Verlag.

Shaw, S.J., & Shaw, E.K. (1976). History of the Ottoman Empire and Modern Turkey: Volume 1, Empire of the Gazis: The Rise and Decline of the Ottoman Empire 1280-1808. Cambridge University Press.

Sphrantzes, G. (1980). The Fall of the Byzantine Empire: A Chronicle by George Sphrantzes 1401-1477. University of Massachusetts Press.

Sprenger, A. (2018). The life of Mohammad: from original sources. Forgotten Books.

al-Tabarī, Muhammad. (1967). Tarikh al-Tabarī: Ta'rīkh al-rusl wa'l-mulūk. Vol. 1-10. Dar al-Maarf.

al-Tabarī, Muhammad. (1987-1998). The History of al-Tabarī: Ta'rīkh al-rusl wa'l-mulūk. Vol. 1-39. State University of New York Press:

—— (1989). The History of al-Tabarī Vol. 1: General Introduction and From the Creation to the Flood. (Trans. F. Rosenthal).

—— (1987). The History of al-Tabarī Vol. 2: Prophets and Patriarchs. (Trans. W. Brinner).

—— (1987). The History of al-Tabarī Vol. 4: The Ancient Kingdoms. (Trans. M. Perlmann).

—— (1987). The History of al-Tabarī Vol. 5: The Sasanids, the Byzantines, the Lakhmids, and Yemen. (Trans. C.E. Bosworth).

—— (1988). The History of al-Tabarī Vol. 6: Muhammad at Mecca. (Trans. W. Montgomery Watt & M.V. McDonald).

—— (1987). The History of al-Tabarī Vol. 7: The Foundation of the Community. (Trans. W. Montgomery Watt & M.V. McDonald).

—— (1997). The History of al-Tabarī Vol. 8: The Victory of Islam. (Trans. M. Fishbein).

—— (1990). The History of al-Tabarī Vol. 9: The Last Years of the Prophet. (Trans. I.K. Poonawala).

—— (1993). The History of al-Tabarī Vol. 10: The Conquest of Arabia. (Trans. F.M. Donner).

—— (1993). The History of al-Tabarī Vol. 11: The Challenge to the Empires. (Trans. K.Y. Blankinship).

—— (1992). The History of al-Tabarī Vol. 12: The Battle of al-Qadisiyyah and the Conquest of Syria and Palestine. (Trans. Y. Friedmann).

———(1989). The History of al-Tabarī Vol. 13: The Conquest of Iraq, Southwestern Persia, and Egypt. (Trans. G. H. A. Juynboll).

———(1994). The History of al-Tabarī Vol. 14: The Conquest of Iran. (Trans. G. Rex Smith).

———(1990). The History of al-Tabarī Vol. 15: The Crisis of the Early Caliphate. (Trans. S. Humphreys).

———(1997). The History of al-Tabarī Vol. 16: The Community Divided. (Trans. A. Brockett).

Torrey, C. C. (1967). The Jewish Foundation of Islam. Ktav Publishing House.

Vidino, L. (2010). The new Muslim brotherhood in the West. Columbia University Press.

Vollhardt, J. (2020). The social psychology of collective victimhood. Oxford University Press.

Wiggins, S. (2016). Discursive psychology: Theory, method and applications. Sage.

Zarrinkub, A. (1975). The Arab conquest of Iran and its aftermath. In R. N. Frye (Ed.). The Cambridge History of Iran, Volume 4: From the Arab Invasion to the Saljuqs. Cambridge University Press.

Index

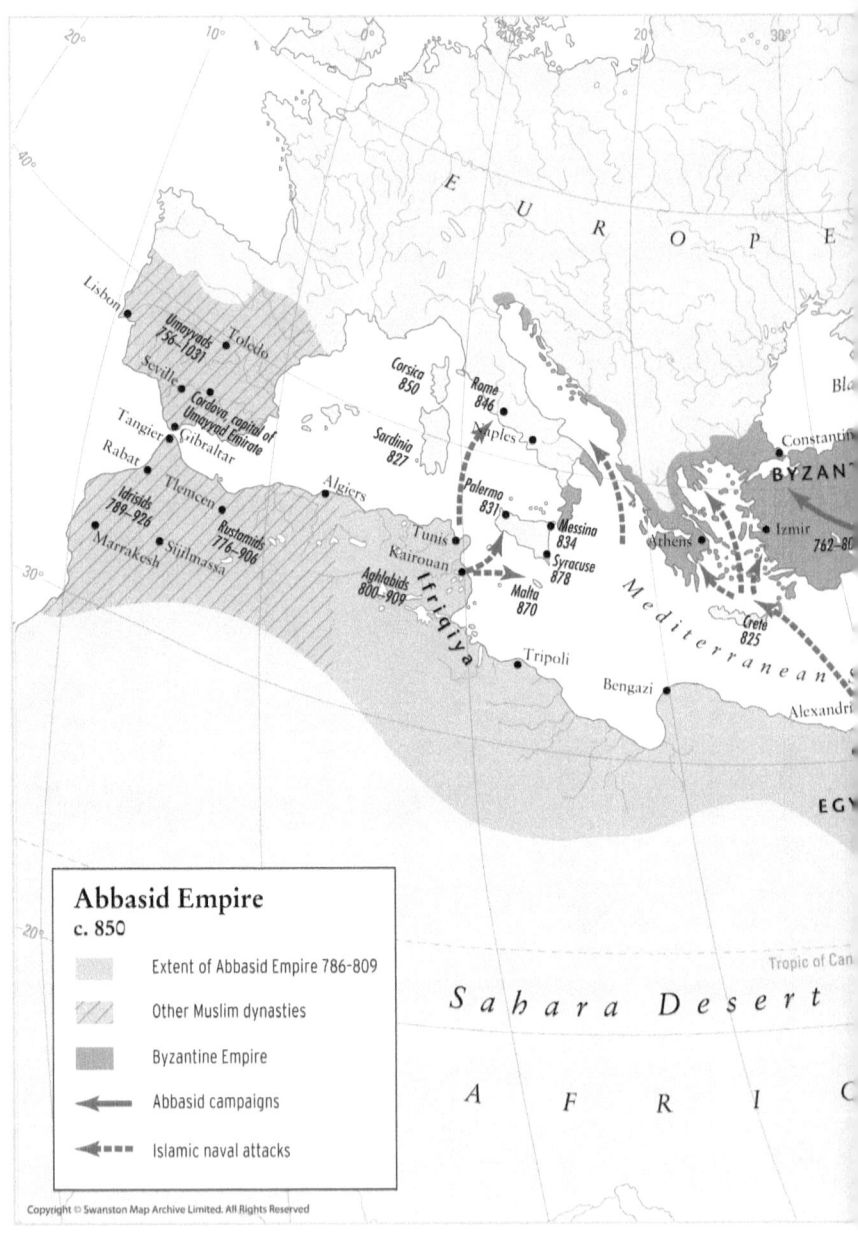

1 Abbasid Empire circa 850

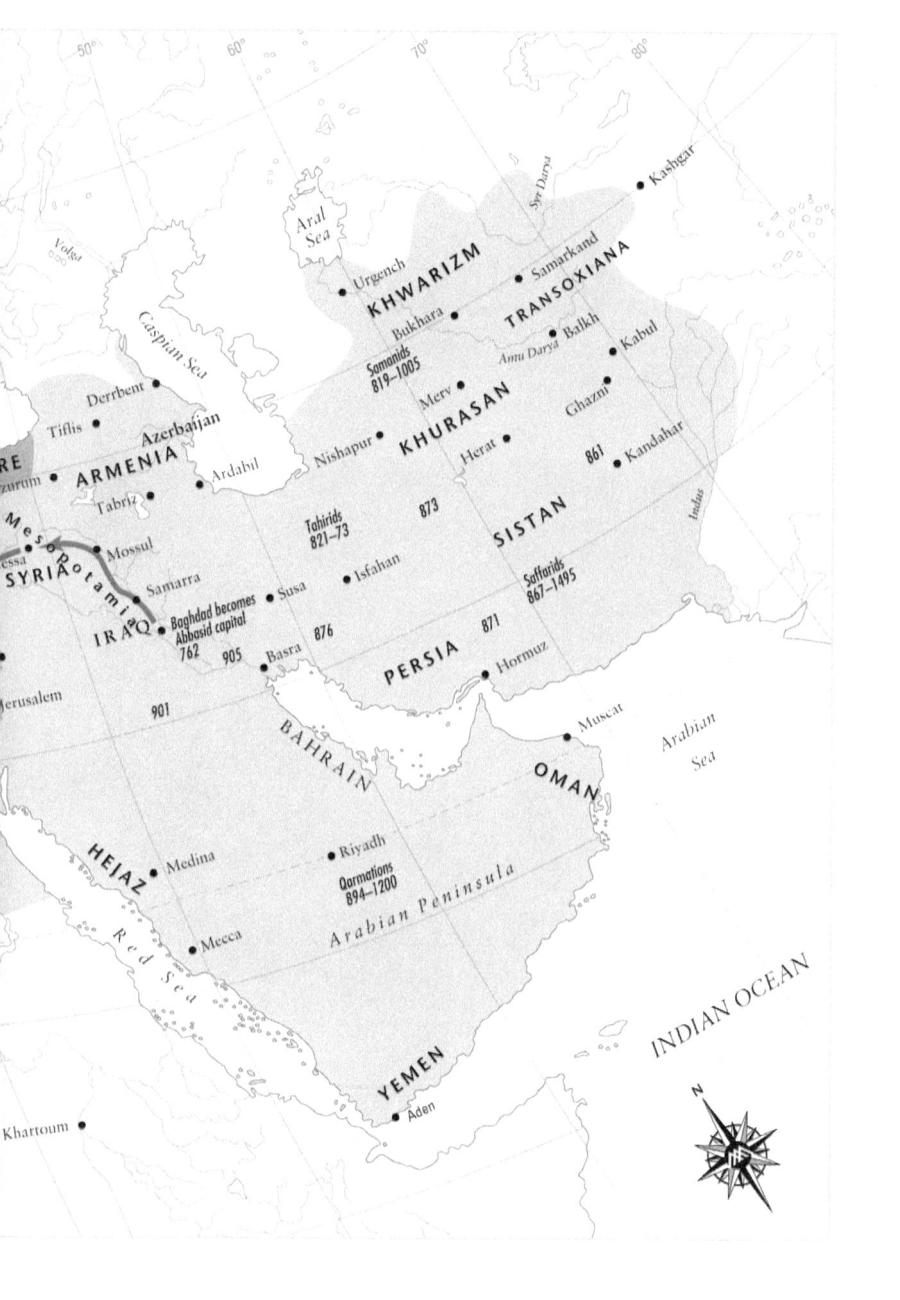

Kashgar

Aral
Sea

Urgench
KHWARIZM
Bukhara
Samarkand
TRANSOXIANA
Balkh
Samanids
819–1005
Amu Darya
Kabul
Ghazni
Kandahar
861
Merv
KHURASAN
Herat

Volga

Caspian Sea

Derbent
Tiflis
Azerbaijan
RE
zurum
ARMENIA
Ardabil
Nishapur
873
Tabriz
SISTAN

Mesopotamia
Mossul
Tahirids
821–73
Isfahan
Saffarids
867–1495

SYRIA
Samarra
Susa
IRAQ
Baghdad becomes
Abbasid capital
762
905
Basra
876
PERSIA
871
Hormuz

Jerusalem
901

BAHRAIN

OMAN
Muscat

Arabian
Sea

HEJAZ
Medina
Riyadh
Qarmations
894–1200

Red Sea
Mecca
Arabian Peninsula

INDIAN OCEAN

YEMEN
Aden

Khartoum

N

GERMANY

• Paris

FRANCE

Vienna •

AUSTRIA—HUNGARY

TRANSYLVANIA
1699

HUNGARY
1699

BANAT
1718

WALLACHIA
Bucharest • 1829

SWISS
CONFED.

Milan •

Venice •

Genoa •

Marseille •

SPAIN

Corsica

Rome •

• Barcelona

Balearic Islands

Sardinia

ITALY

Adriatic Sea

BOSNIA Belgrade
1878
Sarajevo • SERBIA
1878

RAGUSA
1718
1913

Albania

Macedonia
1913
1881

Tyrrhenian
Sea

Sicily

Ionian
Sea

MALTA

Aegean
Sea

Athens •
GREECE
1830

PODOLIA
1699

BESSARABIA
1812

JEDISAN
1792

KHANATE OF TH
1774

MOLDAVIA
1829

DOBRUJA
1878

Sevastopol • • Kaffa

Black S

Bulgaria 1878 1908
Sofia • Varna
E. Rumelia 1878

Salonica •

Constantinople • • Sinlori
• Bursa
Anatoli
• Konya
• Ankara

1878
to Brita
Cypri

Crete
1898

1912
to Italy

M e d i t e r r a n e a n   S e a

Barbary Coast

• Algiers • Bona

ALGERIA
1830 French

Tunis •

Tunisia
1881 French

• Tripoli

Tripoli

• Wargla

Fezzan

• Benghazi

Cyrenaica

1 9 1 2   t o   I t a l y

Alexandria •

• C.

Egypt
1811

1882
British
Protector

S   a   h   a   r   a

Tropic of Cancer

N

A   f   r   i   c   a

Ottoman Empire
1683–1914

Territory lost by 1718

Territory lost by 1812

Territory lost by 1881

Territory lost by 1914

Ottoman Empire, 1914

1811 Date granted autonomy

1830 Date of territory lost

0   200 km
0   200 miles

2 Ottoman Empire 1683-1914

E   M   P   I   R   E

Caucasus

Caspian Sea

DAGESTAN 1723

Baku

GEORGIA
1730

Trebizond

KARABAG
1730

OND

Erzerum

AZERBAIJAN
1730

ARMENIA

Van

Tabriz

PERSIA

Mesopotamia

Tigris

LURISTAN
1730

Aleppo

Baghdad

Euphrates

Basra

KUWAIT
1899 British protectorate

Persian
Gulf

El Hasa

Bahrain
1687 to Britain

A
r
a
b

from 1853
to Britain

Hejaz

Medina

Red Sea

Mecca

Wadi Amir

Arkato

Sana

YEMEN

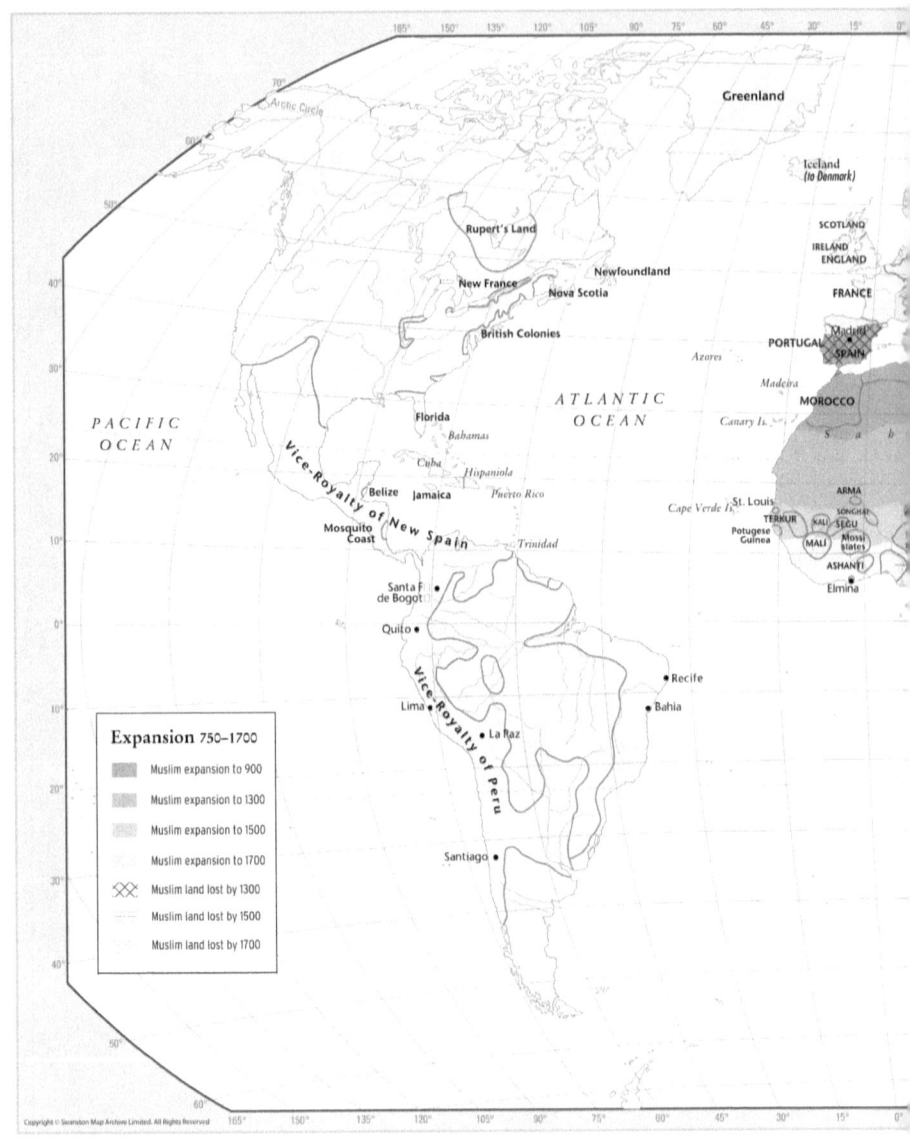

3 Expansion of Islam between 750-1700

Expansion 750–1700

- Muslim expansion to 900
- Muslim expansion to 1300
- Muslim expansion to 1500
- Muslim expansion to 1700
- Muslim land lost by 1300
- Muslim land lost by 1500
- Muslim land lost by 1700

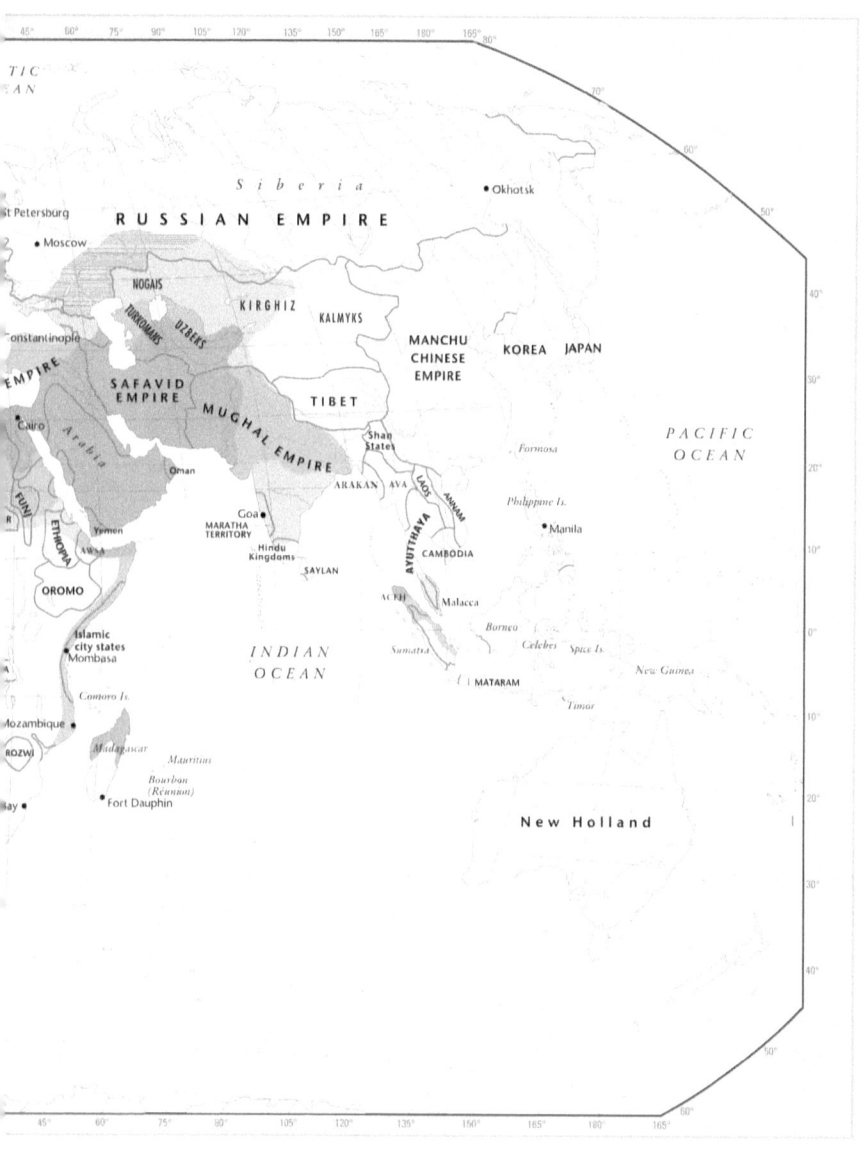

45° 60° 75° 90° 105° 120° 135° 150° 165° 180° 165° 80°

T I C
A N

70°

60°

S i b e r i a

• Okhotsk

50°

st Petersburg

RUSSIAN EMPIRE

• Moscow

40°

NOGAIS

KIRGHIZ

KALMYKS

**MANCHU
CHINESE
EMPIRE**

KOREA JAPAN

30°

TURKOMANS

UZBEKS

onstantinople

EMPIRE

**SAFAVID
EMPIRE**

MUGHAL EMPIRE

TIBET

*PACIFIC
OCEAN*

20°

• Cairo

A r a b i a

Shan
States

Formosa

Oman

ARAKAN

AVA

LAOS

ANNAM

Philippine Is.

10°

FUNJ

ETHIOPIA

Yemen

AWSA

Goa

MARATHA
TERRITORY

Hindu
Kingdoms

AYUTTHAYA

CAMBODIA

• Manila

0°

OROMO

SAYLAN

ACEH

Malacca

Islamic
city states
Mombasa

*INDIA N
OCEAN*

Sumatra

Borneo

Celebes Spice Is.

New Guinea

10°

Comoro Is.

MATARAM

Timor

ozambique •

ROZWI

Madagascar

Mauritius

20°

ay •

*Bourbon
(Réunion)*
• Fort Dauphin

New Holland

30°

40°

50°

60°

45° 60° 75° 90° 105° 120° 135° 150° 165° 180° 165°

www.ingramcontent.com/pod-product-compliance
Lightning Source LLC
Chambersburg PA
CBHW020427130626
46549CB00001B/25